PHILIP'S

STREET

Cumbria

Barrow-in-Furness, Carlisle, Kendal, Penrith, Whitehaven

www.philips-maps.co.uk

First published in 2004 by Philip's
a division of Octopus Publishing Group Ltd
www.octopusbooks.co.uk
Endeavour House 189 Shaftesbury Avenue
London WC2H 8JY
An Hachette UK Company
www.hachette.co.uk

Second edition 2008
Second impression with revisions 2011
CUMBB

ISBN 978-1-84907-180-2 (pocket)

© Philip's 2008

Ordnance Survey®

This product includes mapping data licensed from
Ordnance Survey® with the permission of the
Controller of Her Majesty's Stationery Office.
© Crown copyright 2008. All rights reserved.
Licence number 100011710.

Speed camera data provided by
PocketGPSWorld.com Ltd

Printed in China

Contents

III   **Key to map symbols**

IV   **Key to map pages**

VI   **Route planning**

X   Administrative and Postcode boundaries

1   **Street maps** at 1⅓ inches to 1 mile

172   **Street maps** at 2⅔ inches to 1 mile

214   **Street map of Carlisle city centre** at 5⅓ inches to 1 mile

215   **Index** of towns, villages, streets, hospitals, industrial estates, railway stations, schools, shopping centres, universities and places of interest

Digital Data

The exceptionally high-quality mapping found in this atlas is available as digital data in TIFF format, which is easily convertible to other bitmapped (raster) image formats.

The index is also available in digital form as a standard database table. It contains all the details found in the printed index together with the National Grid reference for the map square in which each entry is named.

For further information and to discuss your requirements, please contact philips@mapsinternational.co.uk

Key to map symbols

III

Motorway	with junction number (22a)
Primary route	– dual/single carriageway
A road	– dual/single carriageway
B road	– dual/single carriageway
Minor road	– dual/single carriageway
Other minor road	– dual/single carriageway
Road under construction	
Tunnel, covered road	
Speed cameras - single, multiple	
Rural track, private road or narrow road in urban area	
Gate or obstruction to traffic	(restrictions may not apply at all times or to all vehicles)
Path, bridleway, byway open to all traffic, road used as a public path	
Pedestrianised area	
Postcode boundaries	DY7
County and unitary authority boundaries	
Railway, tunnel, railway under construction	
Tramway, tramway under construction	
Miniature railway	
Railway station	Walsall
Private railway station	
Bus, coach station, metro station	South Shields
Tram stop, tram stop under construction	

◆	Ambulance station
◆	Coastguard station
◆	Fire station
◆	Police station
✚	Accident and Emergency entrance to hospital
H	Hospital
+	Place of worship
i	Information Centre (open all year)
🛒	Shopping Centre
P P&R	Parking, Park and Ride
PO	Post Office
⋏ 🚐	Camping site, caravan site
▶ ⊼	Golf course, picnic site
Prim Sch	Important buildings, schools, colleges, universities and hospitals
	Built up area
	Woods
River Medway	Water name
	River, weir, stream
	Canal, lock, tunnel
	Water
	Tidal water
Church	Non-Roman antiquity
ROMAN FORT	Roman antiquity
87	Adjoining page indicators and overlap bands
237	The colour of the arrow and the band indicates the scale of the adjoining or overlapping page (see scales below)

Enlarged mapping only

	Railway or bus station building
	Place of interest
	Parkland

Abbreviations					
Acad	Academy	Inst	Institute	Recn Gd	Recreation Ground
Allot Gdns	Allotments	Ct	Law Court		
Cemy	Cemetery	L Ctr	Leisure Centre	Resr	Reservoir
C Ctr	Civic Centre	LC	Level Crossing	Ret Pk	Retail Park
CH	Club House	Liby	Library	Sch	School
Coll	College	Mkt	Market	Sh Ctr	Shopping Centre
Crem	Crematorium	Meml	Memorial	TH	Town Hall/House
Ent	Enterprise	Mon	Monument	Trad Est	Trading Estate
Ex H	Exhibition Hall	Mus	Museum	Univ	University
Ind Est	Industrial Estate	Obsy	Observatory	W Twr	Water Tower
IRB Sta	Inshore Rescue Boat Station	Pal	Royal Palace	Wks	Works
		PH	Public House	YH	Youth Hostel

■ The small numbers around the edges of the maps identify the 1 kilometre National Grid lines ■ The dark grey border on the inside edge of some pages indicates that the mapping does not continue onto the adjacent page

The scale of the maps on the pages numbered in blue is 4.2 cm to 1 km • 2⅔ inches to 1 mile • 1: 23810

0 ¼ ½ ¾ 1 mile
0 250 m 500 m 750 m 1 kilometre

The scale of the maps on pages numbered in green is 1.96 cm to 1 km • 1⅓ inches to 1 mile • 1: 50688

0 ¼ ½ ¾ 1 mile
0 250m 500m 750m 1kilometre

The scale of the maps on pages numbered in red is 8.4 cm to 1 km • 5⅓ inches to 1 mile • 1: 11900

0 220 yards 440 yards 660 yards ½ mile
0 125m 250m 375m ½ kilometre

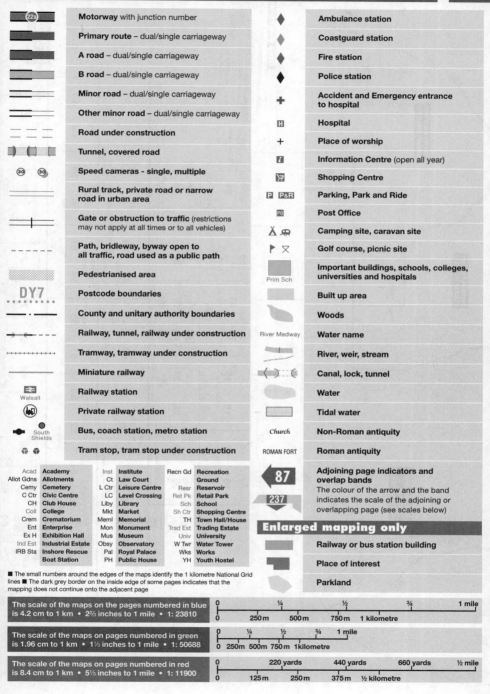

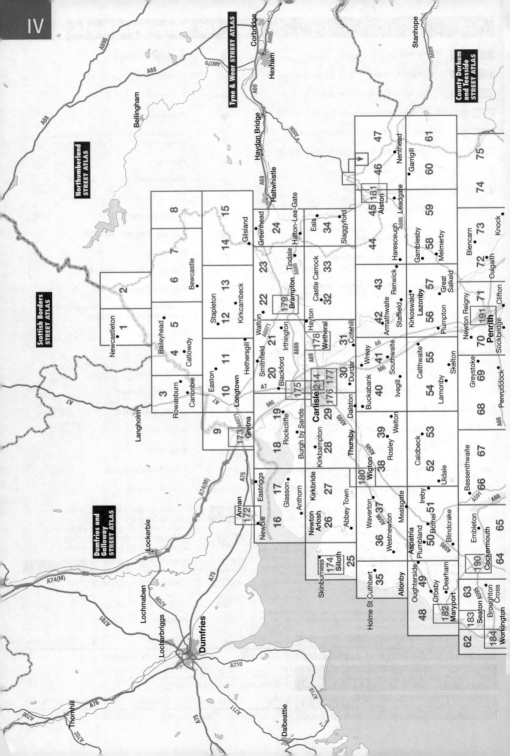

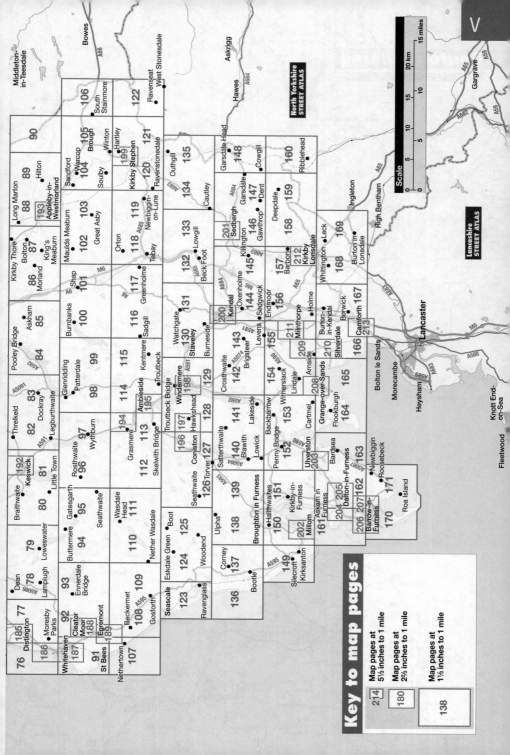

V

North Yorkshire
STREET ATLAS

Lancashire
STREET ATLAS

Scale
0   5   10   15   20 km
0   5   10   15 miles

Key to map pages

214	**Map pages at** 5½ inches to 1 mile
180	**Map pages at** 2½ inches to 1 mile
138	**Map pages at** 1½ inches to 1 mile

Bowes

Middleton-in-Teesdale

West Stonesdale
Ravenseat

Askrigg

Hawes

106
South Stainmore
122

90

Winton
Hartley
199
Kirkby Stephen
121

105
Brough
104
Warcop
Soulby
120
Ravenstonedale

Sandford
103
Great Asby
119
Newbiggin-on-Lune
135

89
Hilton
88
Long Marton
193
Appleby-in-Westmorland
87
King's Meaburn
118
Tebay
134
Cautley
148
Garsdale Head
160
Ribblehead

102
Maulds Meaburn
117
Greenholme
133
Lowgill
147
Garsdale
Dent
159

86
Morland
101
Shap
116
Sadgill
132
Beck Foot
146
Gawthrop
158
Cowgill

85
Askham
100
Burnbanks
131
Burneside
145
Killington
157
Barbon

84
Pooley Bridge
99
Kentmere
130
Staveley
144
Sedgwick
156
Endmoor
212
Kirkby Lonsdale

83
Dockray
98
Patterdale
129
198 Windermere
143
Brigsteer
155
Levens
211
Milnthorpe
169
Leck

82
Threlkeld
97
Wythburn
128
Hawkshead
142
Crosthwaite
154
Witherslack
209
Arnside
168
Whittington
167
Carnforth

81
Little Town
96
Rosthwaite
127
Torver
141
Blawith
153
Penny Bridge
208
Cartmel
166
Silverdale
213

80
Gatesgarth
95
111
Wasdale Head
126
Seathwaite
140
140 Satterthwaite
152
Ulverston
165
Flookburgh
213

79
Lamplugh
94
Buttermere
110
Nether Wasdale
139
Broughton in Furness
151
Kirkby-in-Furness
164
Bardsea
171
Roa Island

78
Dean
93
Ennerdale Bridge
109
Beckermet
125
Woodend
138
Ulpha
150
Halfhthwaites
163
Dalton-in-Furness
170
Roosebeck

77
Distington
92
Cleator Moor
108
124
Eskdale Green
137
Corney
149
Millom
162
Barrow-in-Furness
Newbiggin

76
185
187
91
St Bees
107
Netherton
123
Seascale
136
Bootle
202
204 205 207
206

186
Whitehaven
188
189
Egremont

Gosforth
Ravenglass

Ingleton
Leck
Burton in Lonsdale
High Bentham

Lancaster
Heysham
Morecambe
Bolton le Sands
Knott End-on-Sea
Fleetwood

Gargrave

Route planning

Scale

0   5   10 km
0 1 2 3 4 5 6 miles

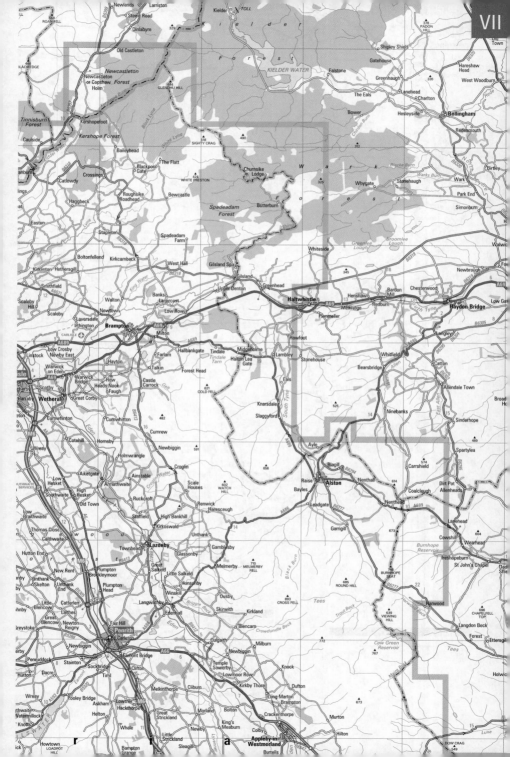

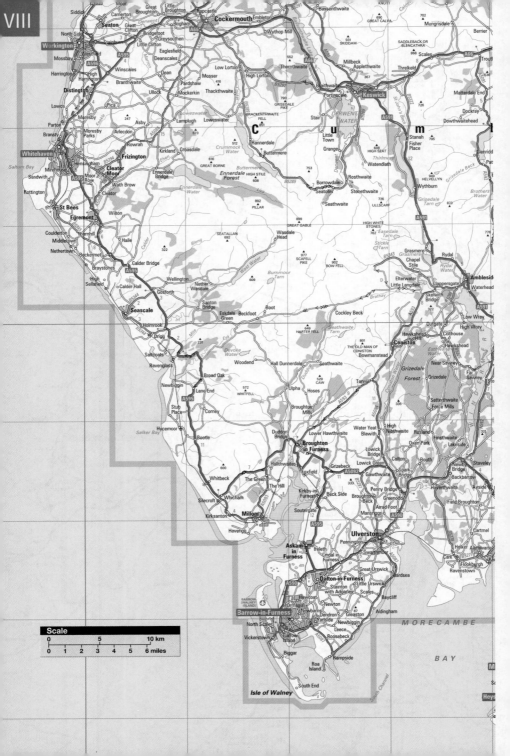

Major administrative and Postcode boundaries

- County and unitary authority boundaries
- District boundaries
- Postcode boundaries
- Area covered by this atlas

Scale

| 0 | 5 | 10 | 15 km |
| 0 | | 5 | | 10 miles |

NT
NY

Scottish Borders

Dumfries and Galloway

Northumberland

DG11
TD9
Newcastleton or Copshaw Holm
NE48

NX NY

DG14
Canonbie

DG11

DG12
Annan
Gretna
DG16
Longtown
CA6
Carlisle
CA8
Brampton
NE49

Bowness-on-Solway

Silloth
Burgh by Sands
CA3
CA2
Carlisle
Wetheral
CA5
CA1

Abbey Town
CA4
NE47

Wigton
Alston

Allonby
CA7
Renwick
CA9
DL13

Aspatria
Melmerby

Maryport
CA15
Durham

Seaton
Cockermouth
CA11
Greystoke
Penrith
Culgaith

Workington
CA13
Eden
DL12

CA14
Ullock
Keswick
CA16

Whitehaven
CA28
CA26
Frizington
CA12
Cumbria
CA10
Appleby-in-Westmorland

CA24
CA25
Cleator Moor
Rosthwaite
Glenridding
Warcop
Brough

St Bees
Egremont
CA23
Shap
CA17

CA27
CA22
CA20
Grasmere
Tebay
Kirkby Stephen

CA21
Gosforth
CA19
Ambleside
LA22

Seascale
LA23
DL11

Drigg
Windermere
LA8
NY
SD

CA18
Coniston
LA21
South Lakeland
Kendal
SC
SD

LA20
LA9
LA10
DL8

LA19
Broughton in Furness
LA12
LA7
Sedbergh
BD23

Bootle
LA11
Milnthorpe
LA6

LA18
Grange-over-Sands
Kirkby Lonsdale
BD24

Millom
LA17
Arnside
North Yorkshire

LA16
Ulverston
LA15
Flookburgh
Silverdale

Barrow-in-Furness
LA14
Dalton-in-Furness
LA5

Barrow-in-Furness
Carnforth
LA2

LA13

SC SD
Lancashire

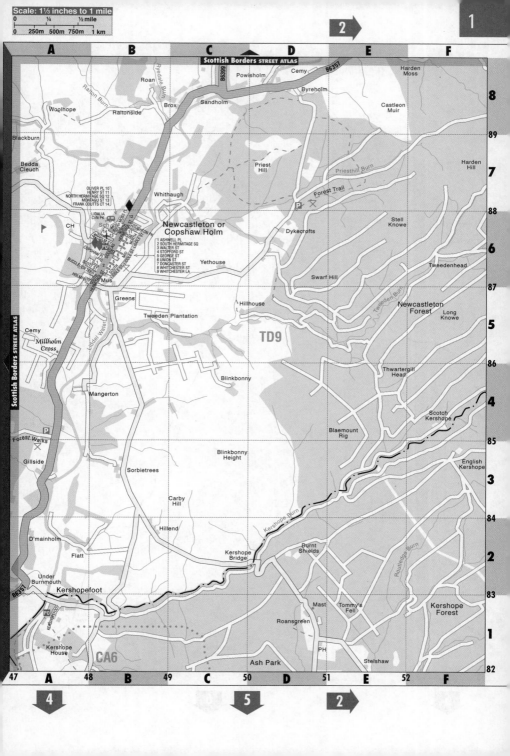

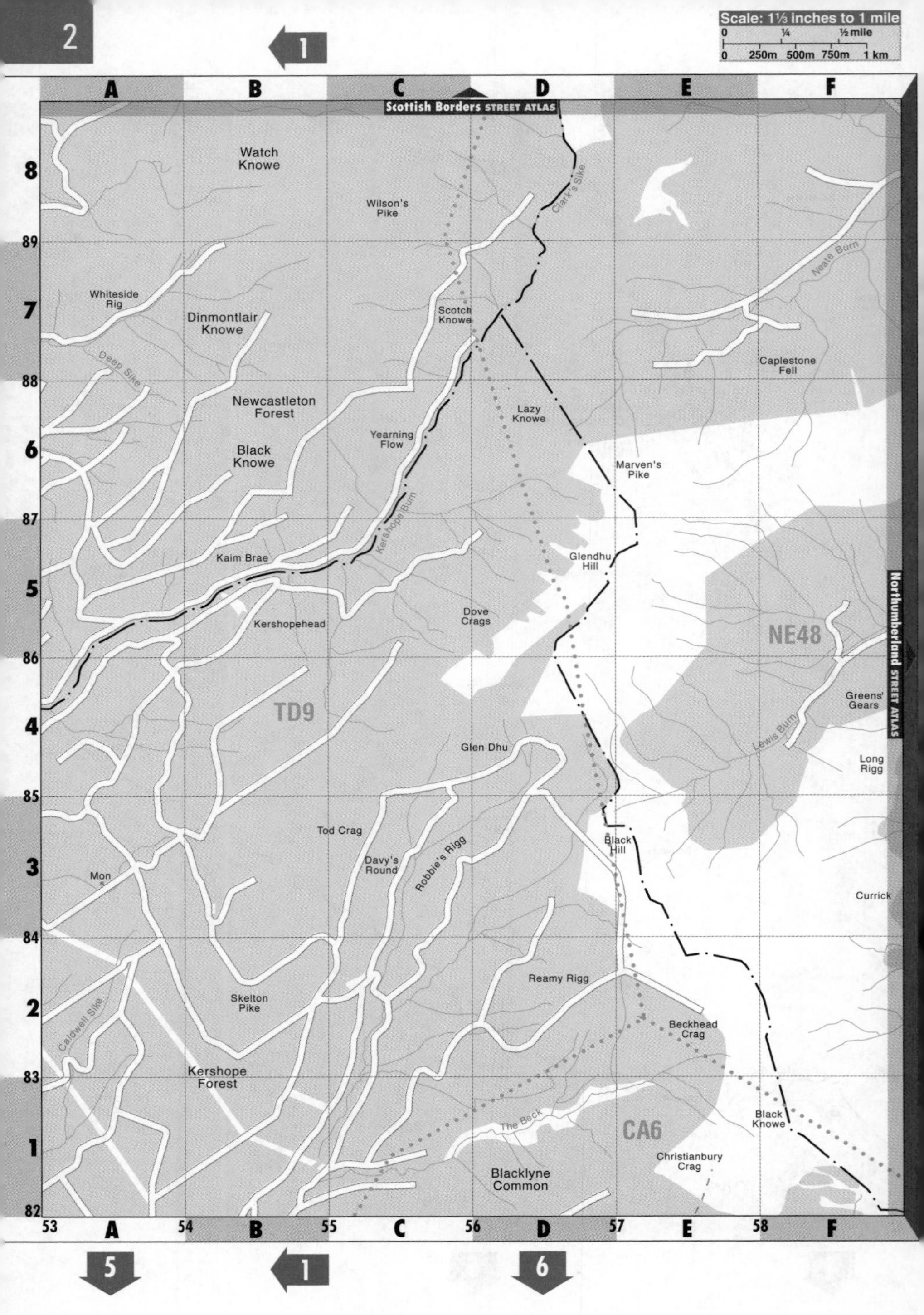

Scottish Borders STREET ATLAS

Northumberland STREET ATLAS

A   B   C   D   E   F

8

89

7

88

6

87

5

86

4

85

3

84

2

83

1

82

53   A   54   B   55   C   56   D   57   E   58   F

Watch Knowe

Wilson's Pike

Clark's Sike

Neals Burn

Whiteside Rig

Dinmontlair Knowe

Deep Sike

Scotch Knowe

Caplestone Fell

Newcastleton Forest

Lazy Knowe

Black Knowe

Yearning Flow

Marven's Pike

Kershope Burn

Kaim Brae

Glendhu Hill

NE48

Kershopehead

Dove Crags

Greens' Gears

Lewis Burn

TD9

Glen Dhu

Long Rigg

Tod Crag

Black Hill

Mon

Davy's Round

Robbie's Rigg

Currick

Skelton Pike

Reamy Rigg

Caldwell Sike

Beckhead Crag

Kershope Forest

Black Knowe

The Beck

CA6

Blacklyne Common

Christianbury Crag

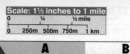

Scale: 1½ inches to 1 mile

0   ¼   ½ mile

0   250m   500m   750m   1 km

3

4

Dumfries & Galloway STREET ATLAS

Dumfries & Galloway STREET ATLAS

A7 Langholm, Hawick

Broomholm

DG13

Howgillcleuch

Hardenside

Tarrasfoot
Hill

The Hill

Albierigg

Old Irvine

Irvine
House

Auchenrivock

Tarrasfoot

Byre Burn

Irvine Burn

Mumbie
Cottages

Broomieknowe

Orchard

Upper
Mumbie

Greenburn

Outer
Woodhead

Auchenrivock
Flow

Nether
Mumbie

The Tail

Hagg

Nittyholm

Claygate

Byreburn

Barrascroft

Hagg Hill

Glencartholm

River Esk

Enthorn

Gilnockie
Tower

DG14

Thorniewhats

P

Mill

Byreburnside

Hollows

Brockwoodlees

B720

Byreburnfoot
Trail

Rowanburnhead

Archerbeck

Arbier Beck

Tarcoon

Loophill

Byreburnfoot

Sawmill

Airnlee

LIDDEL
BANK

Mossknowe

Newbie

Esk
Bank

PO

Canonbie
Sch

Prioryhill

Rowanburn

Hillhead

Greenrigg

Hawkshole

PH

Canonbie

PO

Cemy

Park
House

B720

Hughsrigg

B6357

B6357

PH

Priorslynn

B7201

Rowanburnfoot

The
Inch

Broadmeadows

Mouldyhills

Mast

Hollinhurst

Liddel Water

Fauldie

Tinnishall

Woodhouselees

Riddings
Farm

CA6

Woodhouselees
Plantation

Greenbraehead

Woodslee

Riddingshill

Riddings hill

The
Mount

Barns

Almonside

A7

B7201

Liddel Strength

D3
1 WATCHHILL PK
2 WATCHHILL RD
3 ALDERY TERR
4 THE WYND
5 ALDERY BANK
6 FORGEHOLM
7 BRIGHTON PL
8 PRIOR AVE
9 RIVERSIDE PK

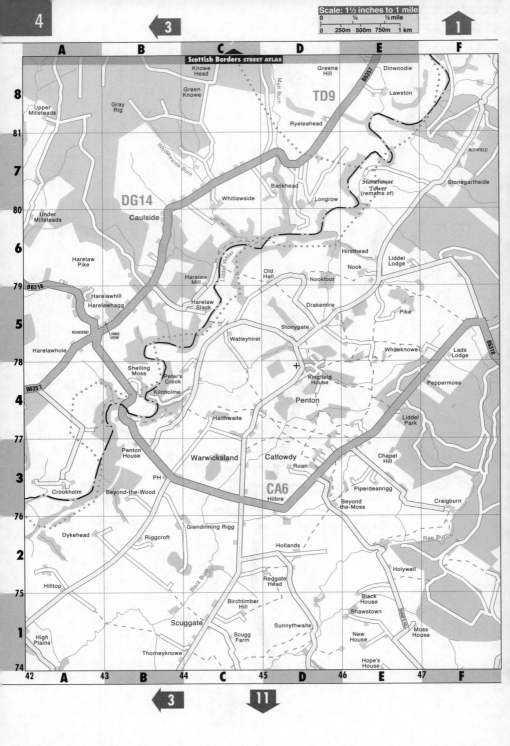

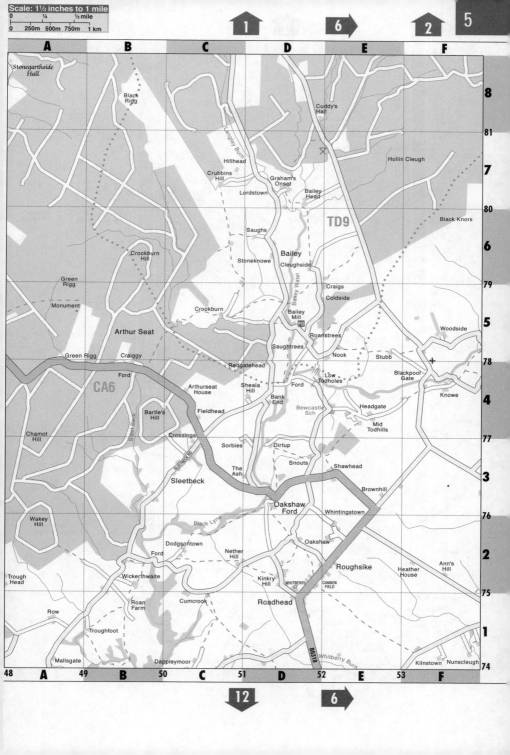

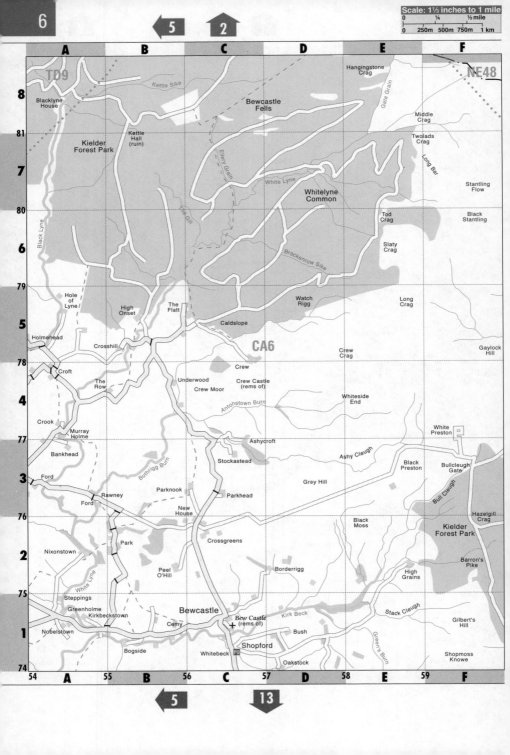

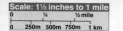
NE48

Humble
Hill

Black
Knowe

8

81

Sighty
Crag

Horse
Head

Birky Grain

7

The
Knares

Greenmeath Sike

Smuggy's
Pike

Starting Burn

Gair Burn

Long
Crags

80

Pike Burn

Stripe Sike

6

Lowe Bush

Paddaburn

Archie's
Pike

79

Greyfell Common

Tarn Beck

South Sike

Irthing
Head

Padda Burn

5

Cammock
Rigg

Red Sike

CA8

Redsike

Paddaburn

Johnny's
Crags

78

White Brae

Ford

Ford

4

CA6

Foulbog Sike

Breakshaw
Hill

Cock Play

Dry Sike

77

Highgrains
Waste

Blackrigg
Foot

Wreay
Hill

3

DANGER AREA

Hazel Gill

Potsloan

76

Birky
Shank

Leafy Rigg

Calf Sike

Hen Hill

DANGER AREA

Hart Horn

2

Little
Hen Hill

Blackshaws
Hill

75

Yellow Fawns

Greymare Hill

Blackshaws Sike

1

Jock's Hill

Whipper Slack

74

7

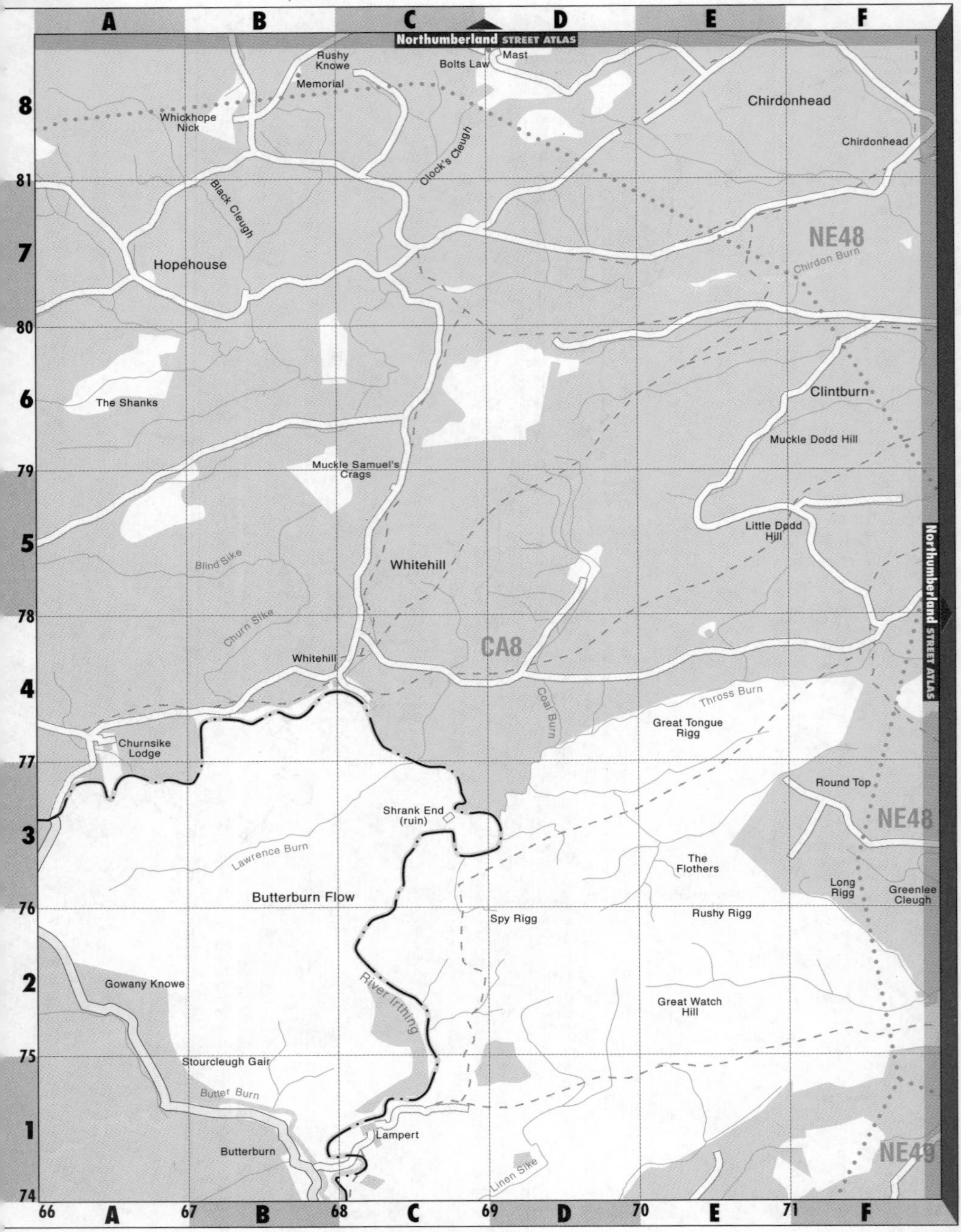

Northumberland STREET ATLAS

Mast

Bolts Law

Rushy
Knowe

Memorial

Chirdonhead

Whickhope
Nick

Chirdonhead

Clock's Cleugh

NE48

Black Cleugh

Chirdon Burn

8

81

7

Hopehouse

80

6

The Shanks

Clintburn

Muckle Dodd Hill

Muckle Samuel's
Crags

79

Little Dodd
Hill

5

Blind Sike

Whitehill

78

Churn Sike

CA8

Whitehill

Thross Burn

4

Coal Burn

Great Tongue
Rigg

77

Churnsike
Lodge

Round Top

NE48

3

Shrank End
(ruin)

The
Flothers

Lawrence Burn

Long
Rigg

Greenlee
Cleugh

76

Butterburn Flow

Spy Rigg

Rushy Rigg

River Irthing

2

Gowany Knowe

Great Watch
Hill

75

Stourcleugh Gair

Butter Burn

1

Lampert

Butterburn

Linen Sike

NE49

74

| 66 | A | 67 | B | 68 | C | 69 | D | 70 | E | 71 | F |

7

15

Northumberland STREET ATLAS

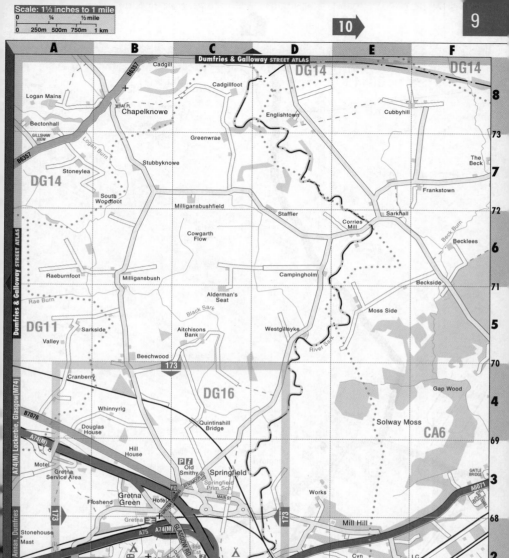

Dumfries & Galloway STREET ATLAS

Dumfries & Galloway STREET ATLAS

A   B   C   D   E   F

Cadgill
DG14
DG14

8

Cadgillfoot

Logan Mains

WRAE PL
Chapelknowe
Englishtown
Cubbyhill

73

Bectonhall

GILLSHAW VIEW

Greenwrae

The Beck

B6357

DG14

Stoneylea

Stubbyknowe

Frankstown

7

South Woodfoot

Milligansbushfield

Sarkhall

72

Staffler

Corries Mill

Cowgarth Flow

Becklees

6

Raeburnfoot

Milligansbush

Campingholm

Beckside

71

Rae Burn

Alderman's Seat

Black Sark

Moss Side

DG11

Sarkside

Aitchisons Bank

Westgillsyke

River Sark

5

Valley

Beechwood

70

173

Cranberry

DG16

Gap Wood

4

Whinnyrig

Quintinshill Bridge

Solway Moss

CA6

69

Douglas House

Hill House

Motel

Old Smithy

Springfield

GAITLE BRIDGE

A6071

3

Gretna Service Area

Springfield Prim Sch

Works

MAIR ST

173

173

Floshend

Gretna Green

Hotel

Mill Hill

68

Stonehouse Mast

Gretna

A74(M)

A75

GLASGOW RD

2

Cvn Pk

Chy

LC

Cemy

Gretna

ANNAN RD

B721

67

CH

Hotel

B7076

Kirtle Water

Old Graitney

1

Channel of River Esk

173

M6

66

30   A   31   B   32   C   33   D   34   E   35   F

For full street detail of the highlighted area see page 173.

18

10   19

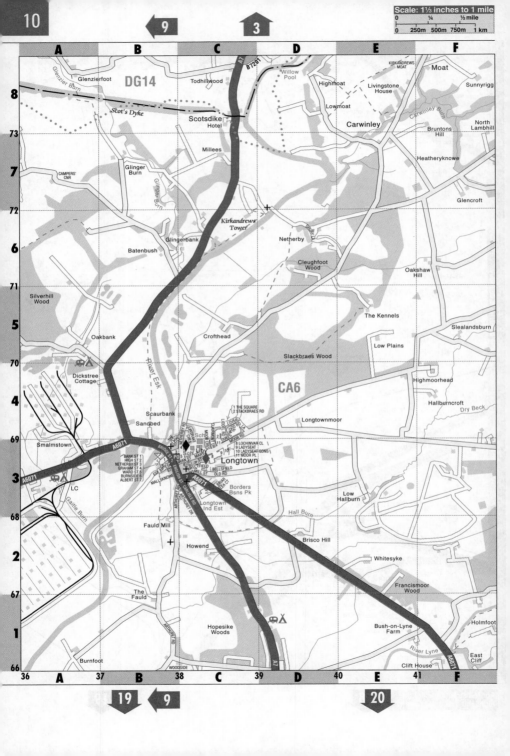

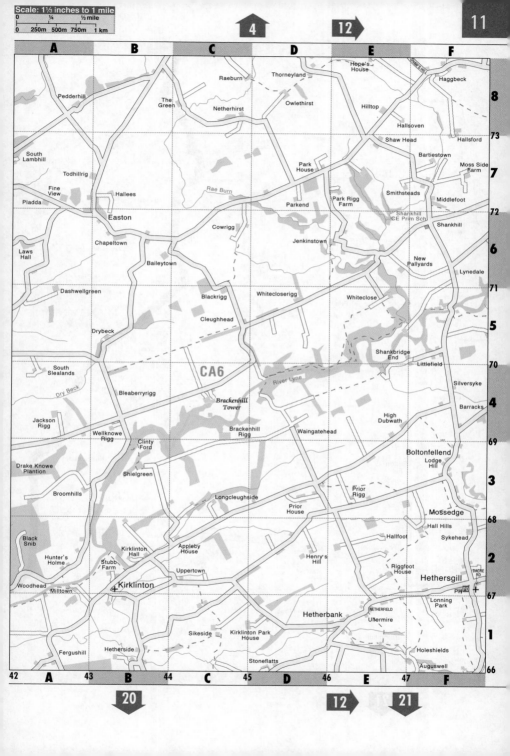

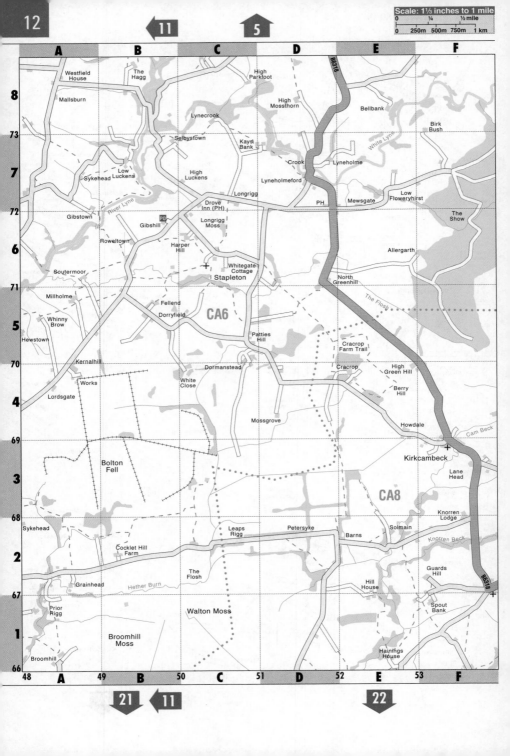

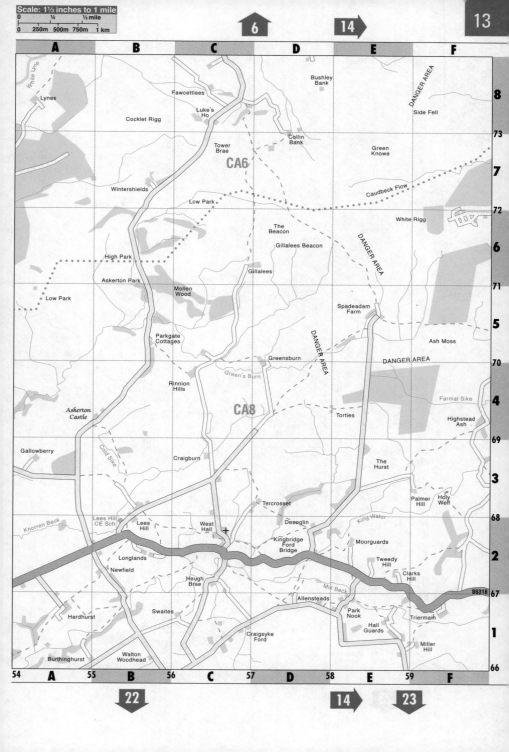

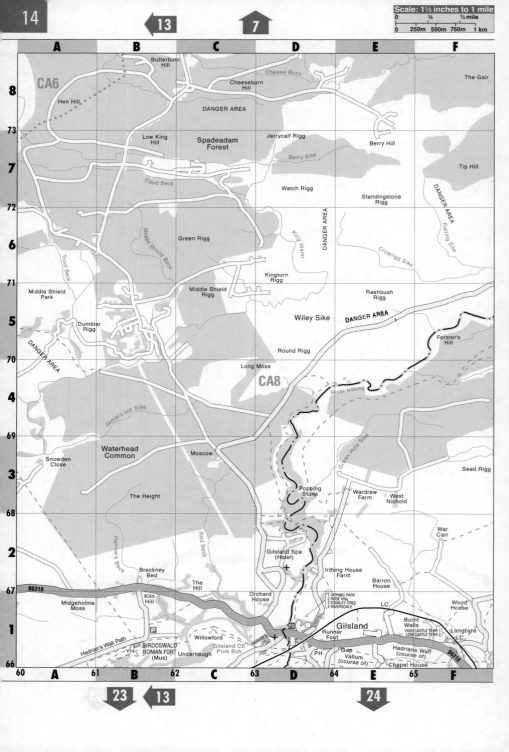

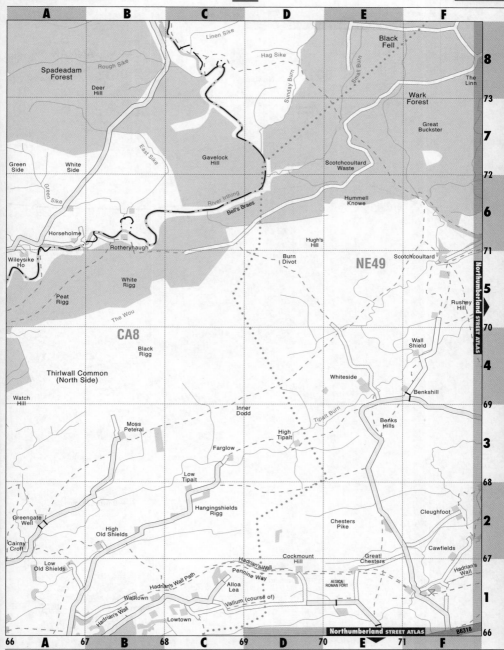

Scale: 1⅓ inches to 1 mile

0   ¼   ½ mile
0 250m 500m 750m 1 km

Dumfries & Galloway STREET ATLAS

Dumfries & Galloway STREET ATLAS

8

Hillhouse

Powfoot

Broom
Ind Est

DG12

Hayknowes

Newbie

River Annan

Annan
Hill

DG12

ANNAN

Shawhill

Plumdon
House

Sandhills

65

Newbie
Cottages

Newbie
Mains

THREE TREES RD

Works

Kenziels

Waterfoot

172

Seafield

7

Barnkirk Point

64

Channel of River Eden

6

63

5

62

Campfield Marsh
Nature Reserve

Biglands
House

4

North
Plain

Maryland
Farm

Campfield
Farm

61

Pasture
House

3

60

Herd
Hill

CA7

Bowness Common

2

59

Cardurnock

1

Masts

Anthorn

PO

1 WAVER RD
2 HADRIANS AVE
3 MORICAMBE CRES

58

15   A   16   B   17   C   18   D   19   E   20   F

For full street detail of the
highlighted area see page 172.

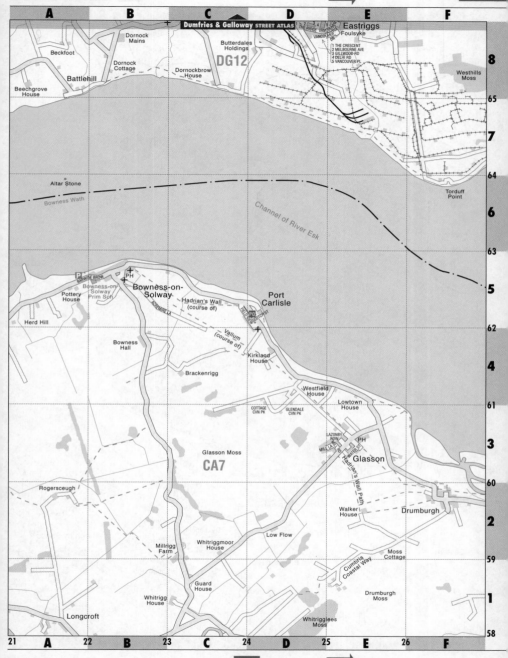

17
9

Scale: 1½ inches to 1 mile

0   ¼   ½ mile
0 250m 500m 750m 1 km

Dumfries & Galloway STREET ATLAS

Baurch

Redkirk

Lochmaben Stone

Sarkfoot Point

Clerkston

DG16

Westhills

DG12

BROWHOUSES

Redkirk Point

Channel of River Esk

Rockcliffe Marsh

CA6

Far Gulf

Near Gulf

Burghmarsh Point

King Edward 1 Mon

Burgh Marsh

CA5

North End

Hadrians Wall (course of)

Cumbria Coastal Way

Watch Hill

Burgh by Sands

MILTON

WHITE ROW

THE PACK

Hadrians Wall Path

Dykesfield

Vallum (course of)

CA7

BEECH CROFT

PH

Easton

Boustead Hill

LONGBURGH FAULD

Shield

Longburgh

WEST END GRAY

West End

Hill Farm

Burgh by Sands Sch

1 ST LAWRENCE LA
2 ORCHARD CL
3 MARSH HOUSE GDNS
4 ASH TREE SQ
5 SOUTHFIELD
6 KING EDWARDS FAULD

17

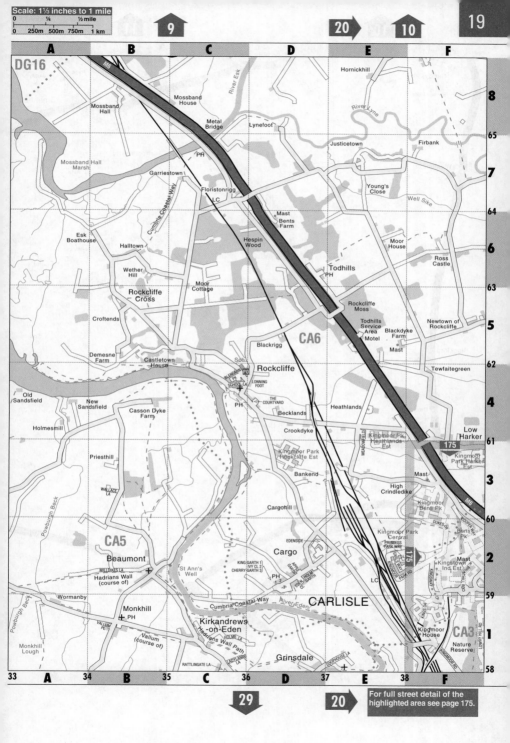

Scale: 1⅓ inches to 1 mile

0 ¼ ½ mile
0 250m 500m 750m 1 km

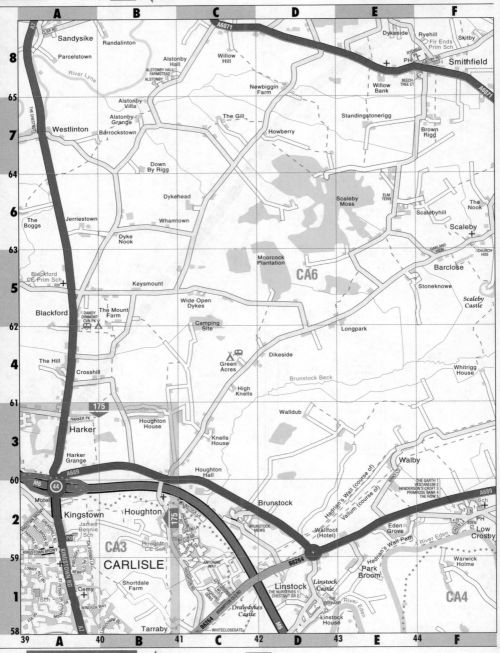

For full street detail of the highlighted area see page 175.

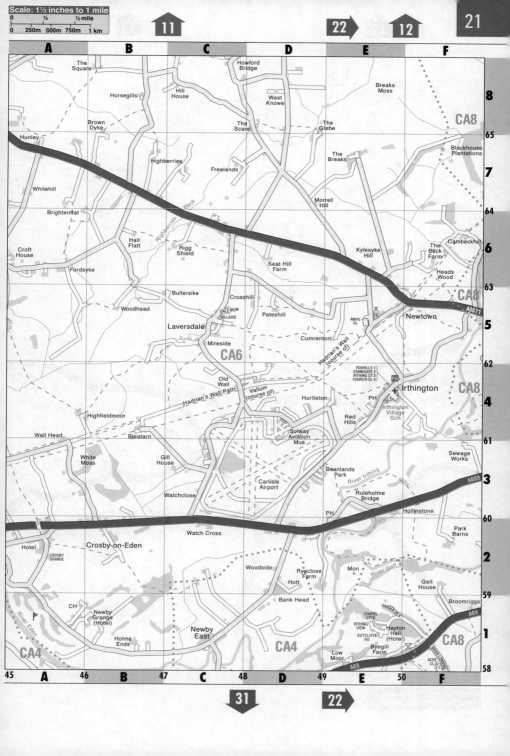

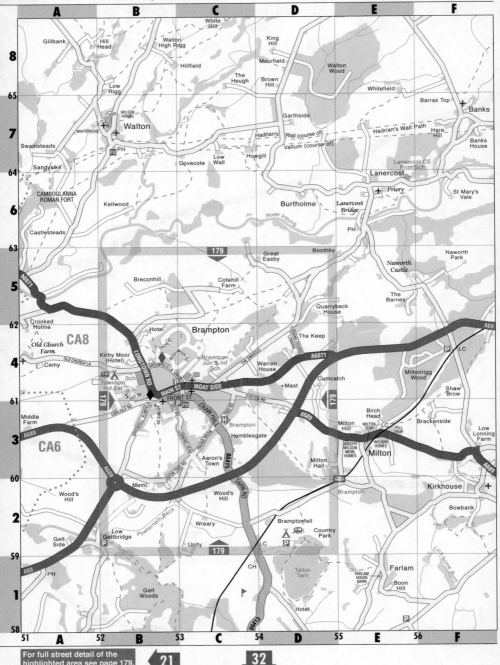

12
21

Scale: 1⅓ inches to 1 mile

0	¼	½ mile

0	250m	500m	750m	1 km

A   **B**   **C**   **D**   **E**   **F**

Gillbank
White Hill
Hill Head
Walton High Rigg
King Hill
8
Hillfield
Moorfield
Walton Wood
Low Rigg
The Heugh
Brown Hill
65
Whitefield
Barras Top
WILSON HOMES
Banks
7
Walton
Garthside
Hadrian's Wall Path
Hare Hill
WHITEHOUSE
Hadrian's
Wall (course of)
Banks House
Swainsteads
PH
Vallum (course of)
PD
Lanercost CE Prim Sch
64
Sandysike
Dovecote
Low Wall
Howgill
Lanercost
St Mary's Vale
CAMBOGLANNA ROMAN FORT
Kellwood
Burtholme
Priory
6
Lanercost Bridge
Castlesteads
River Irthing
PH
63
179
Great Easby
Boothby
Naworth Park
Breconhill
Cotehill Farm
Naworth Castle
Crooked Holme
5
Quarrybeck House
The Barnes
A6071
Old Church Farm
CA8
Hotel
Brampton
The Keep
62
Cemy
OLD CHURCH LA
Kirby Moor (Hotel)
DACRE RD
Bramton Jun & Inf Sch
The SWARTLE
A6071
P
LC
4
Sch
GREENFIELD LA
Warren House
Cumcatch
Miltonrigg Wood
Townfoot Ind Est
MAIN ST
MOAT SIDE
Mast
Shaw Brow
LONGTOWN RD
FRONT ST
STATION RD
179
Birch Head
61
PO
Milton Hill
MILTON TERR
LC
Brackenside
Middle Farm
CARLISLE RD
CRAW HALL
A689
Brampton
FELL VIEW
Low Lonning Farm
3
A689
CA6
Hemblesgate
WILSON HOMES
B6413
JOSEPH WILSON MEML HOMES
Milton
Aaron's Town
Milton Hall
TARN RD
Meml
Wood's Hill
Brampton
Kirkhouse
60
Wood's Hill
Bowbank
2
Powterneth Beck
Wreary
Bramptonfell
Gelt Side
Low Geltbridge
Country Park
FARLAM HOUSE BARN
Farlam
P
Unity
179
LC
Boon Hill
59
CH
Talkin Tarn
P
A69
PH
Gelt Woods
Hotel
1
B6413
58

51   **A**   **52**   **B**   **53**   **C**   **54**   **D**   **55**   **E**   **56**   **F**

For full street detail of the highlighted area see page 179.

21

32

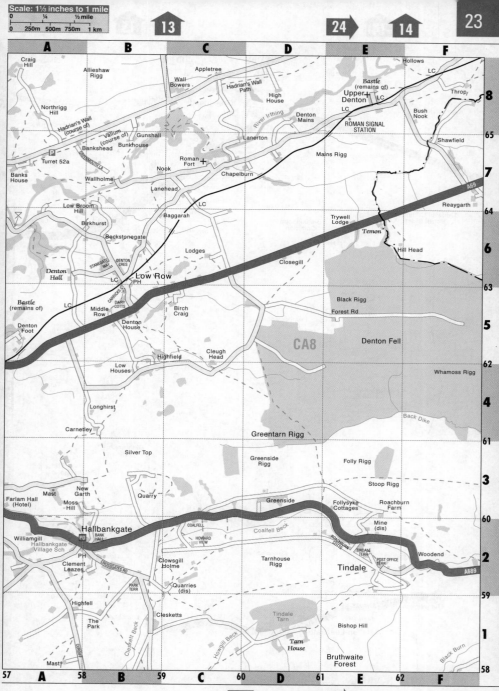

A   B   C   D   E   F

Craig Hill
Allieshaw Rigg
Appletree
Wall Bowers
Hadrian's Wall Path
High House
Hollows
LC
Bastle (remains of)
Throp
8
Northrigg Hill
Hadrian's Wall (course of)
Vallum (course of)
Gunshall
River Irthing
Denton Mains
Upper Denton
LC
Bush Nook
Shawfield
ROMAN SIGNAL STATION
65
Banks House
Turret 52a
P
Bankshead
Bunkhouse
Lanerton
Nook
Roman Fort
Chapelburn
Mains Rigg
7
A69
Wallholme
Lanehead
Baggarah
LC
Reaygarth
64
Low Broom Hill
Birkhurst
Beckstonegate
Lodges
Trywell Lodge
Temon
Hill Head
6
Denton Hall
STANEGATE WALL
DENTON CRES
LC
PH
Low Row
Closegill
63
Bastle (remains of)
LC
Middle Row
DAIRY COTTS
CARHOS CT
Birch Craig
Denton House
Black Rigg
Forest Rd
Denton Fell
5
Denton Foot
Highfield
Cleugh Head
CA8
62
Low Houses
Whamoss Rigg
4
Longhirst
Back Dike
Carnetley
Greentarn Rigg
61
Silver Top
Greenside Rigg
Folly Rigg
3
Farlam Hall (Hotel)
Mast
New Garth
Moss Hill
Quarry
Greenside
Stoop Rigg
Follysyke Cottages
Roachburn Farm
60
Williamgill
Hallbankgate
PO
BANK HALL
COALFELL
Coalfell Beck
Mine (dis)
Woodend
Hallbankgate Village Sch
PH
HOWARD VIEW
ROACHBURN COTTS
TINDALE TERR
A689
2
Clement Leazes
CROSSGATES RD
Clowsgill Holme
Tarnhouse Rigg
Tindale
POST OFFICE TERR
PARK TERR
Quarries (dis)
59
Highfell
The Park
Clesketts
Tindale Tarn
Bishop Hill
1
Clesketts Beck
Howgill Beck
Tarn House
Bruthwaite Forest
Black Burn
Mast
DIPPS

A   B   C   D   E   F

57   58   59   60   61   62   58

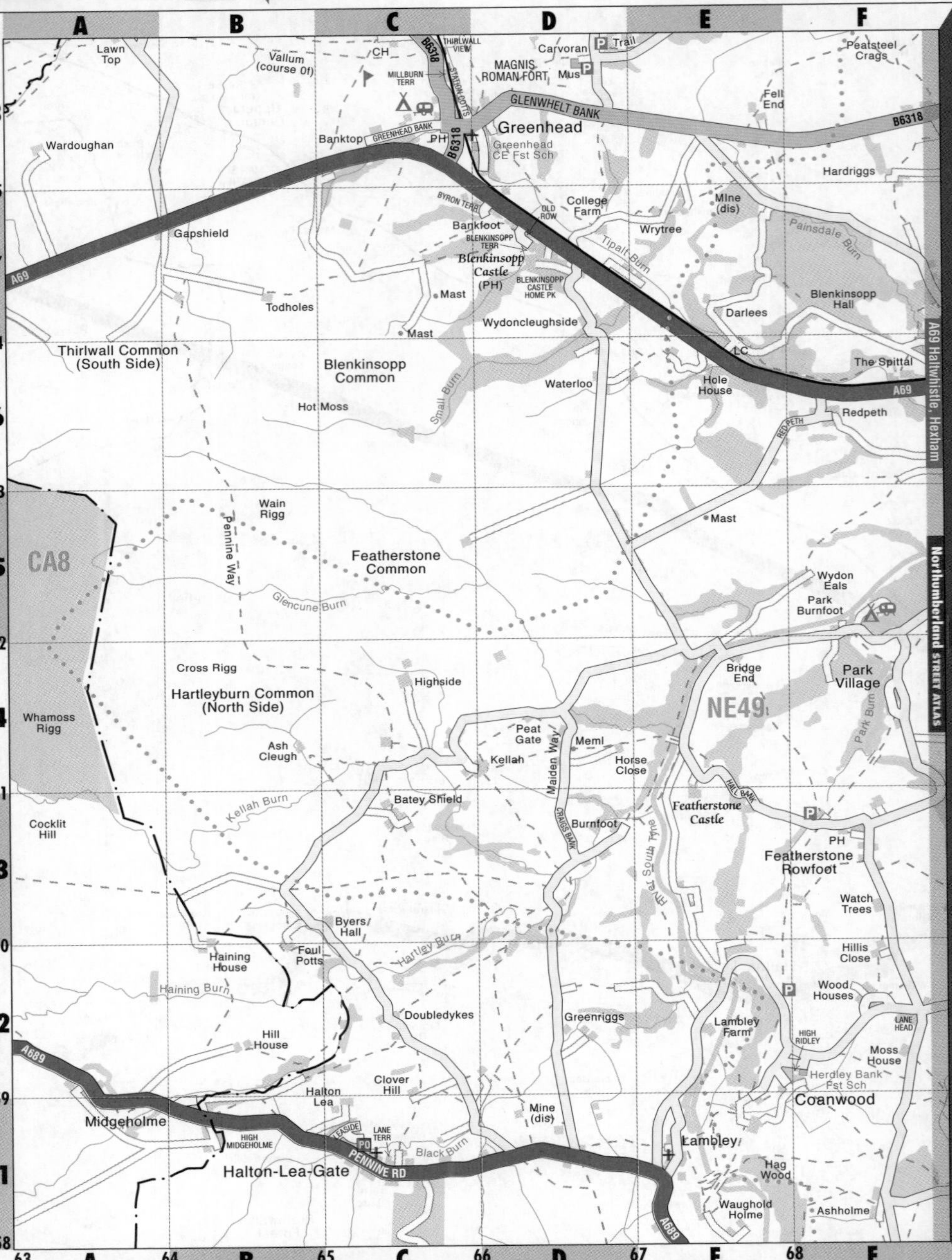

A B C D E F

Lawn Top
Vallum (course of)
CH
THIRLWALL VIEW
MILLBURN TERR
B6318
Carvoran
Trail
Peatsteel Crags

Wardoughan
MAGNIS ROMAN FORT
Mus
Greenhead
Fell End
B6318

Banktop
GREENHEAD BANK
PH
GLENWHELT BANK
Greenhead CE Fst Sch
Hardriggs

65

Gapshield
BYRON TERR
College Farm
Mine (dis)
Painsdale Burn

7
A69
Banklcot
BLENKINSOPP TERR
OLD ROW
Wrytree
Tipalt Burn

Blenkinsopp Castle (PH)
BLENKINSOPP CASTLE HOME PK
Darlees
Blenkinsopp Hall

Todholes
Mast
Wydoncleughside

64
Mast
LC
The Spittal

Thirlwall Common (South Side)
Blenkinsopp Common
Waterloo
Hole House
A69

6
Hot Moss
Small Burn
Redpeth

63
Wain Rigg
Mast

5
CA8
Pennine Way
Featherstone Common
Wydon Eals
Park Burnfoot

Glencune Burn
Park Burn

62
Cross Rigg
Highside
Bridge End
Park Village

4
Whamoss Rigg
Hartleyburn Common (North Side)
Ash Cleugh
Peat Gate
Meml
NE49
Featherstone Castle

Kellah
Maiden Way
Horse Close
PH
Featherstone Rowfoot

61
Cocklit Hill
Kellah Burn
Batey Shield
Burnfoot
Watch Trees

3
Byers Hall
Hartley Burn
Hillis Close

60
Haining House
Foul Potts
Wood Houses
LANE HEAD

2
Haining Burn
Hill House
Doubledykes
Greenriggs
Lambley Farm
HIGH RIDLEY
Moss House

A689
Halton Lea
Clover Hill
Mine (dis)
Herdley Bank Fst Sch
Coanwood

59
Midgeholme
HIGH MIDGEHOLME
LANE TERR
Black Burn
Lambley
Hag Wood

1
A689
PENNINE RD
Halton-Lea-Gate
Waughold Holme
Ashholme

58

63 **A** 64 **B** 65 **C** 66 **D** 67 **E** 68 **F**

A69 Haltwhistle, Hexham
Northumberland STREET ATLAS

A   B   C   D   E   F

8

57

7

Grune Point

Allerdale Ramble

Grune

56

Skinburnessbank

174

Hotel

Skinburness

RYGILL RD

DUNE FOOTPATH

6

Skinburness Marsh

SKINBURNESS RD

East Cote

Cumbria Coastal Way

55

Lighthouse

Sea Dike

Sea Dyke End

Silloth Bay

P
Schs
MEADOW VIEW PK.

SKINBURNESS DR.

SOLWAY HOLIDAY VILLAGE

Wath

5

54

Silloth

P
Schs
Liby

WIGTON RD

FELL VIEW

Ind Est

Airfield (disused)

174

Mast

Hartlaw

Calvo

174

IRB Sta.

CRIFFEL ST.

EDEN ST.

Docks

Mast

CH

Meadow Lodge

BS302

4

Lees Scar Lighthouse

BS300

Greenrow

CA7

Factory

Cemy

+

Parkhouse

Garth Cottage

BS302

53

BS301

Causewayhead

Blitterlees

Orchard House

Cowlyers

The Windmill

Blackdyke

3

174

52

MOORDALE CVN PK

The Close

Balladoyle

Parkhead

Flagstaff

2

Heatherbank

Dryholme

Cumbria Coastal Way
Allerdale Ramble

Wolsty Hall

COLDMIRE RD

Hayrigg

51

BS301

Pelutho Grange

Wolsty

BS300

New House

Pelutho Park

1

50

09   A   10   B   11   C   12   D   13   E   14   F

35

For full street detail of the highlighted area see page 174.

26

36

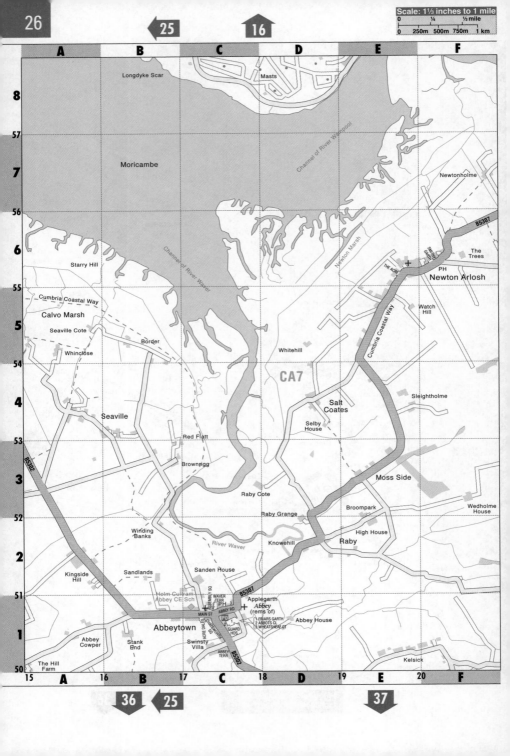

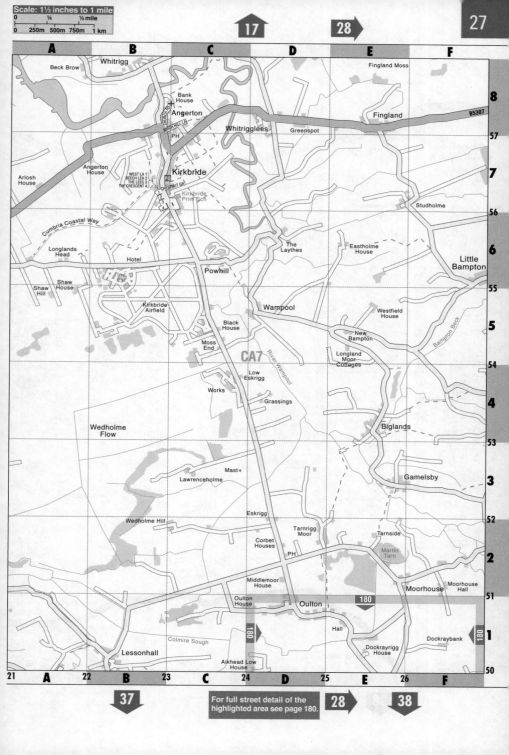

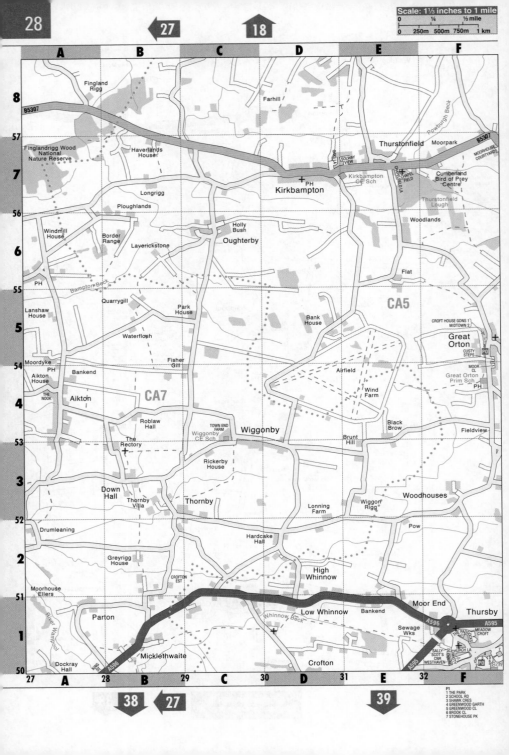

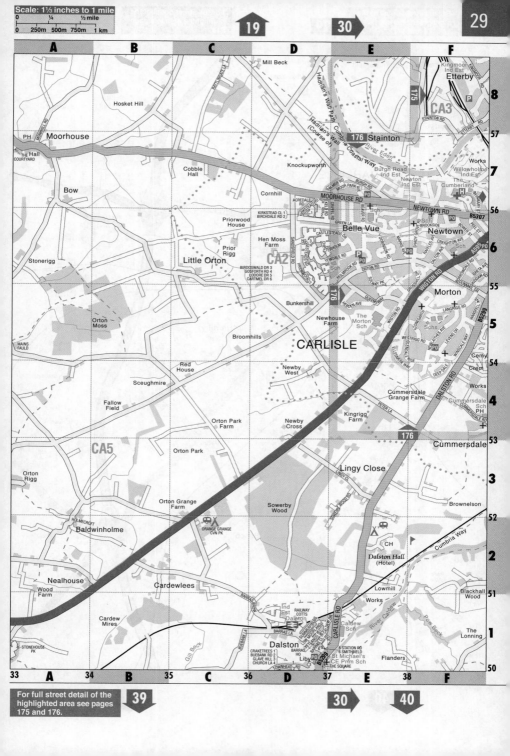

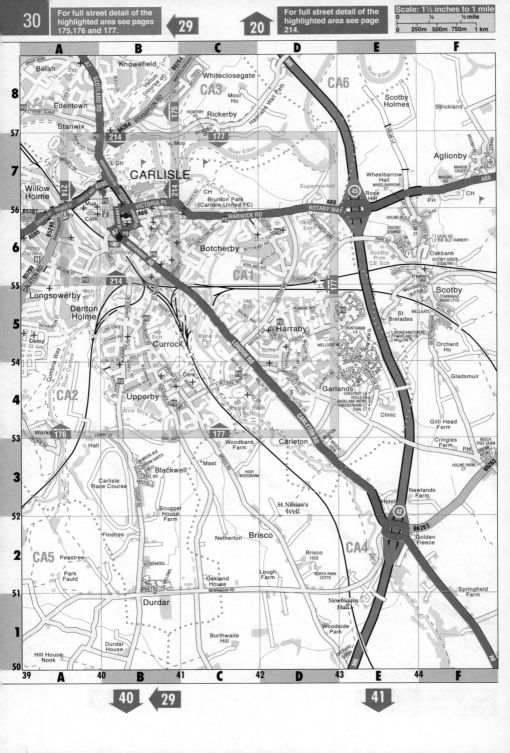

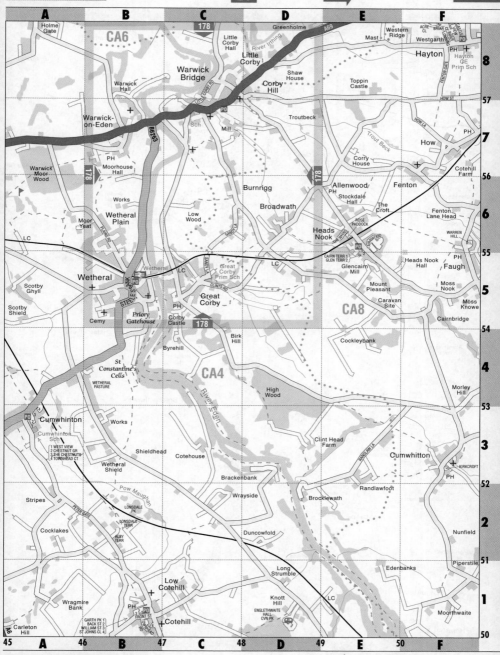

A B C D E F

8
57
7
56
6
55
5
54
4
53
3
52
2
51
1
50

CA6

Holme Gate

Little Corby Hall

Greenholme

River Irthing

A69

Western Ridge

Mast

Westgarthside

ACRE CL

BRIAR CL

CASTLE

Hayton

PH

Hayton CE Prim Sch

Little Corby

Warwick Bridge

Warwick Hall

Shaw House

Corby Hill

Toppin Castle

HOW ST

Warwick-on-Eden

Sch

PO

Mill

Troutbeck

Trout Beck

How

HOW LA

PH

PH

Moorhouse Hall

178

FLAKE RD

B6263

How

Corry House

Cotehill Farm

178

Warwick Moor Wood

Works

Wetheral Plain

Low Wood

Burnrigg

Broadwath

Allenwood

PH

Stockdale Hall

Fenton

The Croft

Fenton Lane Head

WARREN HILL

Moor Yeat

SAND LA

Heads Nook

ROSE PADDOCK

LC

LC

Wetheral

PO

Wetheral

LC

SAND LA

Great Corby Prim Sch

LC

CAIRN TERR 1
GLEN TERR 2

Heads Nook Hall

PH

Faugh

Scotby Ghyll

STEEL BANK

CLINTS RD

Great Corby

PH

Glencairn Mill

Mount Pleasant

Moss Nook

Moss Knowe

Scotby Shield

Cemy

Priory Gatehouse

Corby Castle

178

Caravan Site

CA8

Cairnbridge

Byrehill

Birk Hill

Cockleybank

Morley Hill

St Constantine's Cells

CA4

WETHERAL PASTURE

River Eden

High Wood

LC

Cumwhinton

PO

Cumwhinton Sch

1 WEST VIEW
2 CHESTNUT GR
3 THE CHESTNUTS
4 TOWNHEAD CT

Works

Shieldhead

Cotehouse

Clint Head Farm

RANDLAW LA

Cumwhitton

KIRKCROFT

PH

Wetheral Shield

Brackenbank

Randlawfoot

Stripes

Pow Maughan

PETER GATE

LONSDALE PK

LONSDALE TERR

ALBY TERR

Wrayside

Duncowfold

Brocklewath

Nunfield

Cocklakes

Edenbanks

Piperstile

Long Strumble

Wragmire Bank

Low Cotehill

PH

PO

FRONT ST

TOWNHEAD RD

Cotehill

GARTH PK 1
BACK ST 2
WILLIAM ST 3
ST JOHNS CL 4

Knott Hill

ENGLETHWAITE HALL CVN PK

LC

Moorthwaite

Carleton Hill

45 A 46 B 47 C 48 D 49 E 50 F

For full street detail of the highlighted area see page 178.

41

32

42

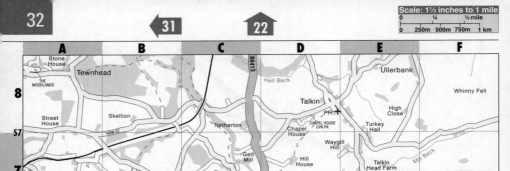

A   **B**   **C**   **D**   **E**   **F**

8
Stone House
Townhead
THE WOODLANDS
Ullerbank
Whinny Fell
Talkin
PH
High Close
Turkey Hall

57
Street House
Skellion
HOW ST
Netherton
Chapel House
CHAPEL HOUSE CVN PK
Waygill Hill
Talkin Head Farm

7
LC
Cowran Side
Cowran
Ring Gate Lodge
The Hill
Gelt Mill
Greenwell
Hill House
Talkin Fell
Kelky Fell

56
The Flatt Farm
River Gelt
Low Hynam

6
Closehead
FENTON LA
Whin Hill
Hayton Moss
Castle Carrock
Castle Carrock Sch
PH
PO
Garth Head
Jockey Shield

55
Faugh Quarry
Sirelands
Tarn Lodge
THE BACK
RECTORY RD
SIDES FELL
Oaktree Hall
Works

5
Park House
North Scales
Long Dyke
Tottergill
Castle Carrock Fell

54
Stonebridge Lees
Carrock Fell
Moor House
CA8
Nixon Head
Mast Roughet Hill
Hespeck Raise
Geltsdale House

4
Longdyke Farm
Brackenthwaite

53
Whitehead Hill
Black Dub

3
Carlatton Demesne
Albyfield
Cardunneth Pike

52
Hallfield
Hall's Tenement
Turnberry House
Cumrew Fell

2
Carlatton Mill
Cairn Beck
Saughtreegate

51
Moorthwaite Moss
Fell End
DEGGY LOANING

1
Chapel Well
Scarrowhill
Foulpool
Cumrew

50
Hornsby
Hornsby Gate
B6413

B6413
Hell Beck
Mill Beck

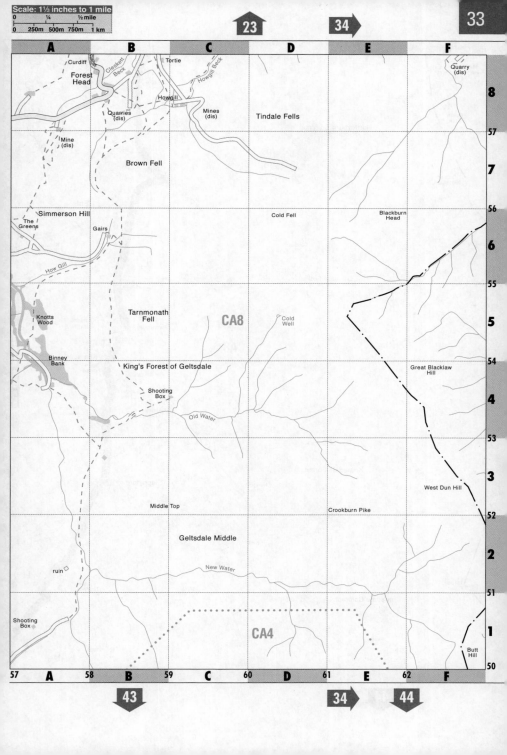

A   B   C   D   E   F

Curdiff   Tortie   Quarry (dis)
Cleskett Beck
Forest Head   Howgill Beck

Howgill   8

Quarries (dis)   Mines (dis)   Tindale Fells   57

Mine (dis)   Brown Fell   7

Simmerson Hill   Cold Fell   Blackburn Head   56

The Greens   Gairs   6

How Gill   55

Knotts Wood   Tarnmonath Fell   CA8   Cold Well   Great Blacklaw Hill   5

Binney Bank   King's Forest of Geltsdale   54

Shooting Box   4

Old Water   West Dun Hill   53

3

Middle Top   Crookburn Pike   52

Geltsdale Middle   2

ruin   New Water   51

Shooting Box   CA4   1

Butt Hill   50

57   A   58   B   59   C   60   D   61   E   62   F

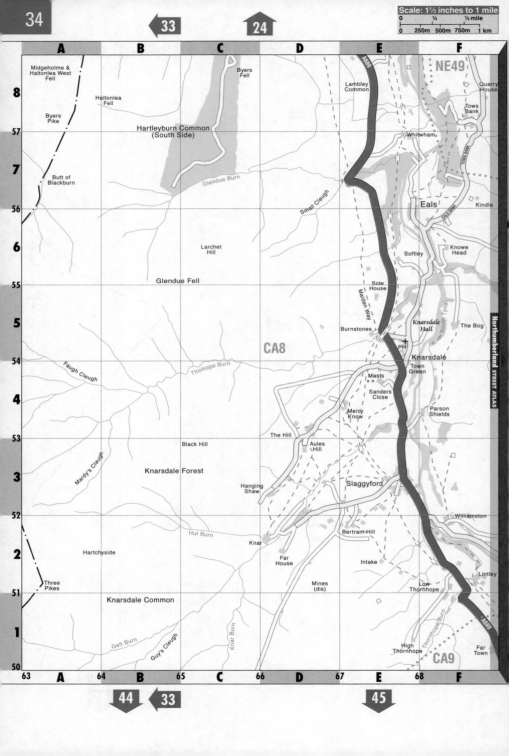

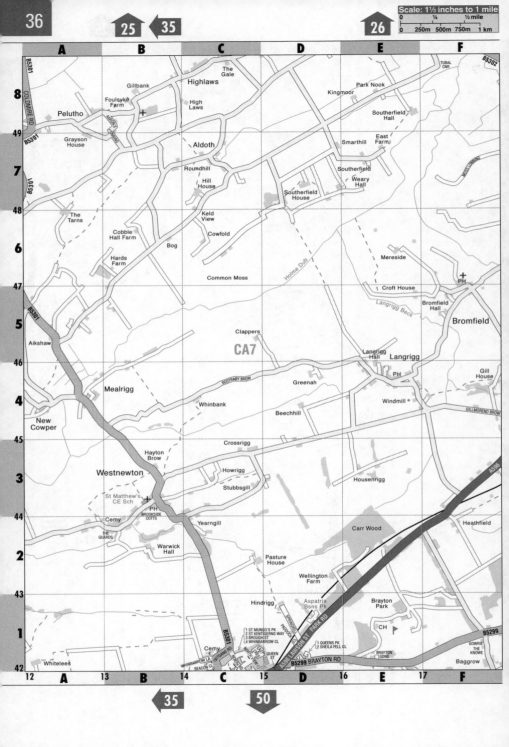

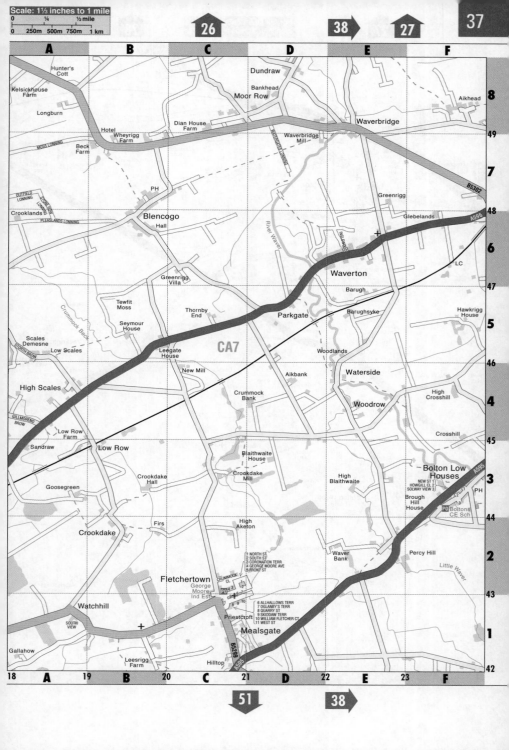

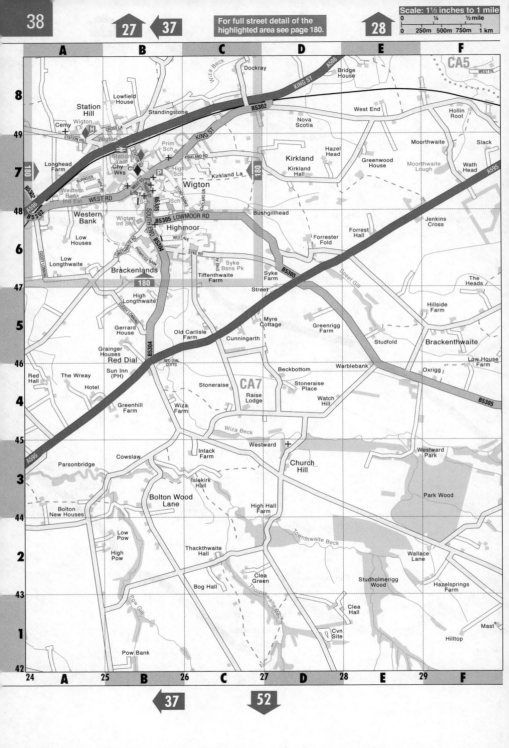

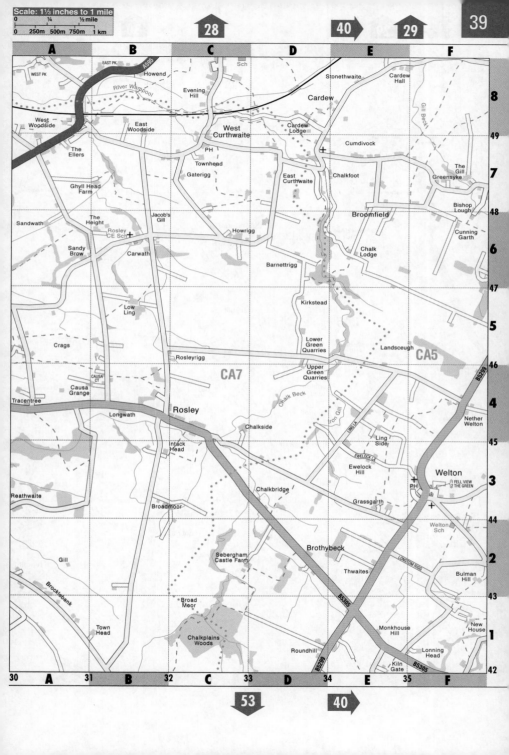

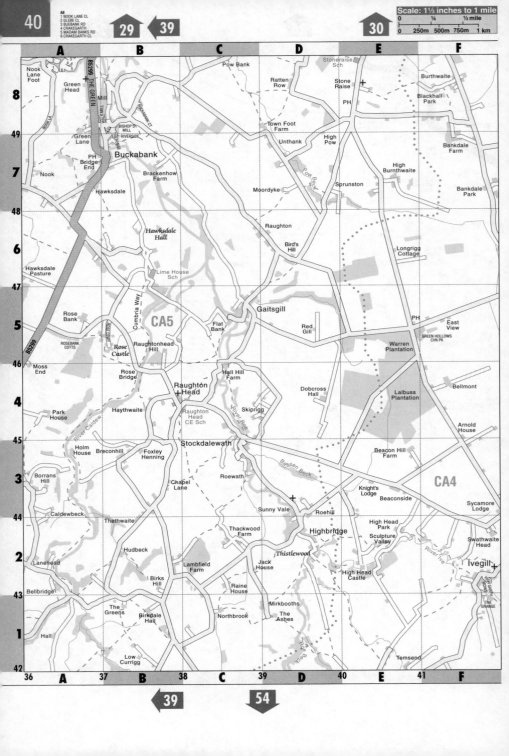

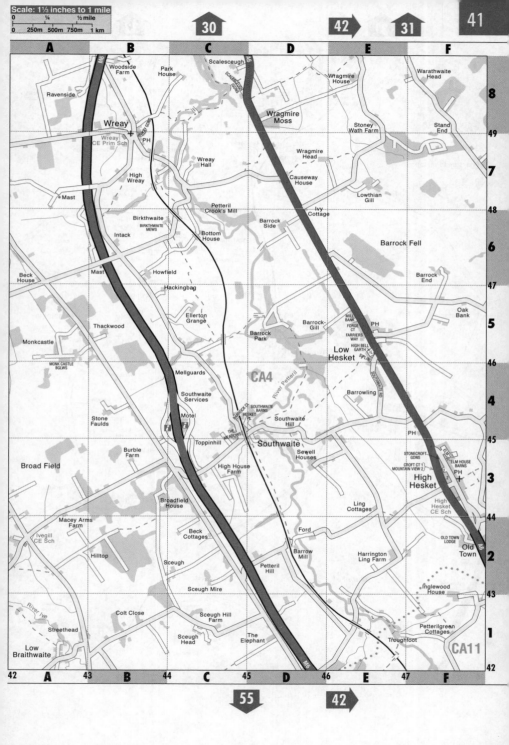

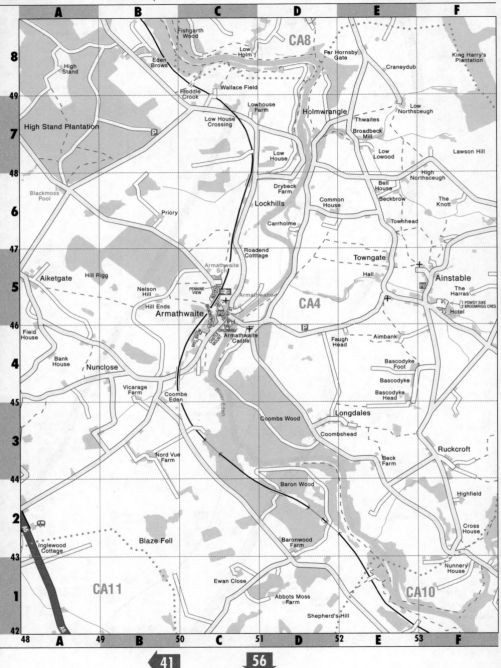

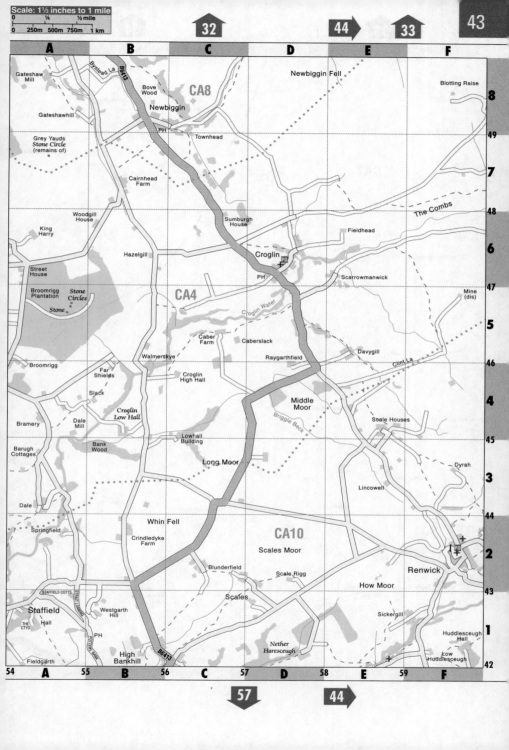

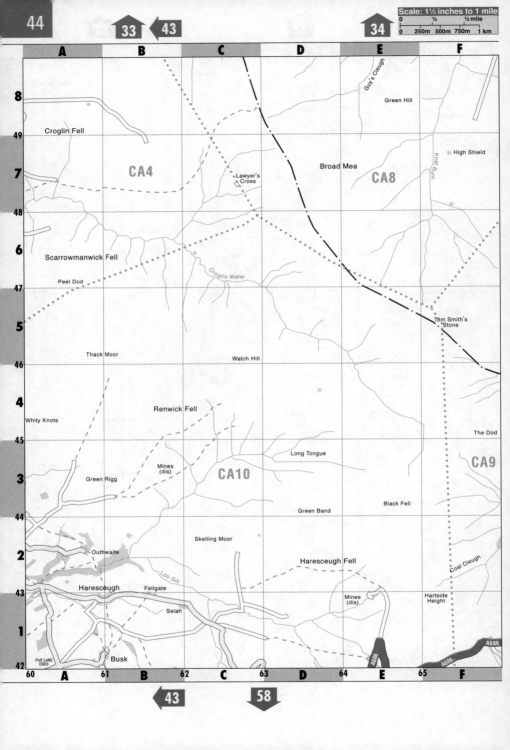

A   B   C   D   E   F

Northumberland STREET ATLAS

CA8

Thornhope
Fell

Thornhope Burn

Ruin

Great
Heaplaw

Kirkhaugh

Kirkhaugh

Middle
Row

8

Underbank   Ruins

Isaac's Tea Trail

Ayle

Ayle Burn

Castle Nook

Kirkside
Wood

181

49

Whitley Castle
ROMAN FORT

Whitlow

Pennine Way

Randalholme

7

Howgill
Rigg

South Tynedale Rly

A689

Newshield

Whitley Common
Black Hill

Wanwood
Hill

Coatlith
Hill
Farm

48

Grey Nag

High
Harbutlaw

Harbut
Lodge

River South Tyne

Loaning

6

THE LOANING

181

47

Gilderdale Burn

Alston

Mus

Alston

A689

Woldgill Burn

Alston
Sch

TH

5

Park Fell

THE WARDWAY

Black
House

Cemy

46

Woldgill Moss

Bridge
End   Fairhill

Sandhill

CA9

Horse
Edge

Hill
House

Annat
Walls

4

Ruin

181

Crosslands

45

Watcher's Hill

Bayles

Scalebank

P

Low Nest

Brownside
Moss

Ghyll
House

3

Brownside

Ameshaugh

Low
Cowgap

44

Scarberry
Hill

Leadgate

AMESHAUGH RD

Hartside
Cottages

Intack
Farm

Bleagate

2

Howburn

Rotherhope
Tower

Benty Hill

Blackburn
Bank

Black Burn

Littlegill

43

Slaggieburn

Meathaw
Hill

Mines
(dis)

Rotherhope Cleugh

Rotherhope
Farm

1

42

66   A   67   B   68   C   69   D   70   E   71   F

For full street detail of the
highlighted area see page 181.

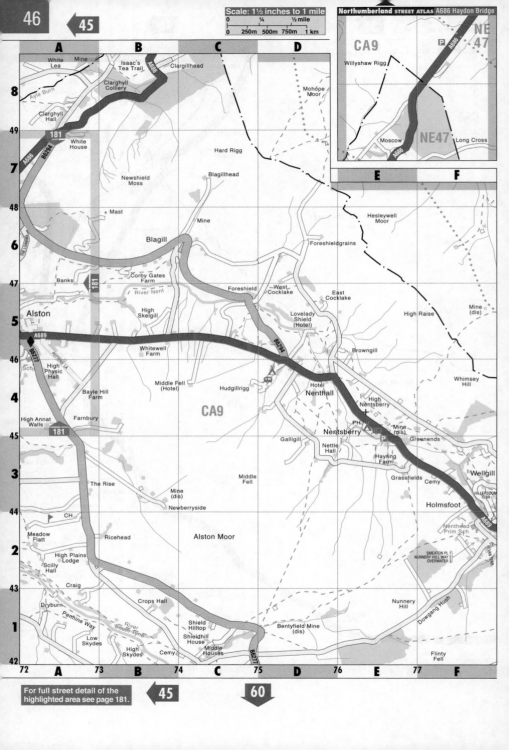

45

Scale: 1⅓ inches to 1 mile

0   ¼   ½ mile
0   250m 500m 750m 1 km

Northumberland STREET ATLAS A686 Haydon Bridge

CA9

NE 47

Willyshaw Rigg

Moscow

NE47   Long Cross

E   F

A

B

C

D

White Lea   Mine

Isaac's Tea Trail   Clargillhead

Clarghyll Colliery

Mohope Moor

8

Ayle Burn

Clarghyll Hall

49

181   White House

Hard Rigg

7

Newshield Moss

Blagillhead

Hesleywell Moor

48

Mast   Mine

Foreshieldgrains

6

Blagill

Corby Gates Farm

River Nent   Foreshield   West Cocklake

East Cocklake

High Raise   Mine (dis)

47

Banks

High Skelgill

Lovelady Shield (Hotel)

5

Alston

A689

Whitewell Farm

BrB6294

Browngill

46

B6277

Sch

POTTER'S LA

High Physic Hall

Middle Fell (Hotel)   Hudgillrigg

Hotel Nenthall

High Nentsberry

Whimsey Hill

4

Bayle Hill Farm

Farnbury

CA9

Mine (dis)

PH

Nentsberry   Greenends

High Annat Walls

181

Galligill

Nettle Hall

Hayring Farm

Wellgill

45

The Rise   Mine (dis)

Middle Fell

Grassfields   Cemy

HILLERSDON TERR

3

Holmsfoot

44

CH

Newberryside

Nenthead Prim Sch

Meadow Flatt

Ricehead

Alston Moor

2

High Plains Lodge

SMEATON PL 1
NUNNERY HILL WAY 2
OVERWATER 3

Scilly Hall

Craig

43

Dryburn

Crops Hall

Pennine Way

River South Tyne

Shield Hilltop

Nunnery Hill

Dowgang Hush

1

Low Skydes

High Skydes   Cemy

Shieldhill House

Middle Houses

Bentyfield Mine (dis)

Flinty Fell

42

72   A   73   B   74   C   75   D   76   E   77   F

For full street detail of the highlighted area see page 181.

45

60

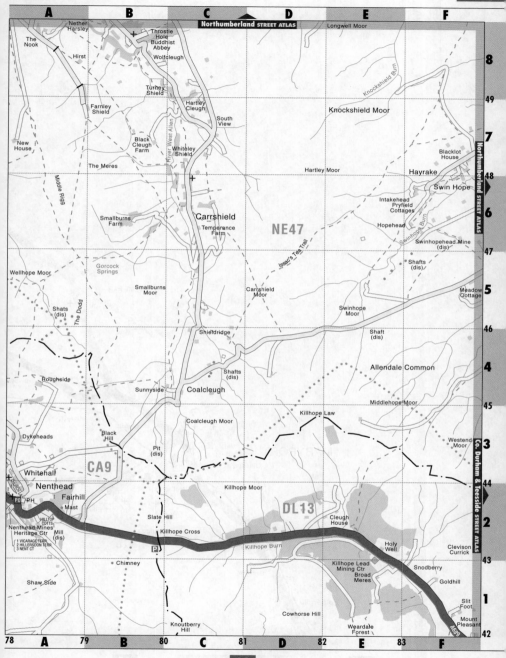

Scale: 1⅓ inches to 1 mile

0   ¼   ½ mile
0   250m 500m 750m 1 km

Northumberland STREET ATLAS

Co. Durham & Teesside STREET ATLAS

Nether Harsley
The Nook
Hirst
Throstle Hole Buddhist Abbey
Wolfcleugh
Longwell Moor
Knockshield Burn
Turney Shield
Hartley Cleugh
New House
Farnley Shield
South View
Knockshield Moor
River West Allen
Black Cleugh Farm
Whiteley Shield
The Meres
Blacklot House
Hartley Moor
Hayrake
Swin Hope
Middle Rigg
Smallburns Farm
Carrshield
Temperance Farm
NE47
Intakehead
Pryfield Cottages
Hopehead
Swinhope Burn
Swinhopehead Mine (dis)
Gorcock Springs
Smallburns Moor
Carrshield Moor
Issac's Tea Trail
Shafts (dis)
Wellhope Moor
Swinhope Moor
Meadow Cottage
Shats (dis)
The Dodd
Shieldridge
Shaft (dis)
Allendale Common
Shafts (dis)
Rougheside
Sunnyside
Coalcleugh
Middlehope Moor
Black Hill
Coalcleugh Moor
Killhope Law
Westend Moor
Dykeheads
Pit (dis)
CA9
Whitehall
Nenthead
Fairhill
Mast
Killhope Moor
DL13
Cleugh House
Nenthead Mines Heritage Ctr
HILLTOP COTTS
Mill (dis)
1 VICARAGE TERR
2 HILLERSDON TERR
3 NENT CT
PO
PH
Slate Hill
Killhope Cross
Holy Well
Clevison Currick
P
Killhope Burn
Killhope Lead Mining Ctr
Broad Meres
Snodberry
Goldhill
Chimney
Shaw Side
Cowhorse Hill
Weardale Forest
Slit Foot
Mount Pleasant
A689
Knoutberry Hill

A   B   C   D   E   F

78 79 80 81 82 83

49 48 47 46 45 44 43 42

8 7 6 5 4 3 2 1

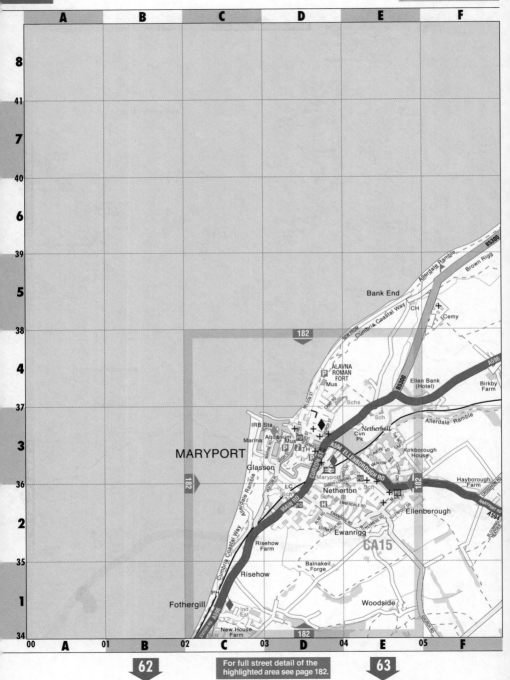

Scale: 1½ inches to 1 mile
0   ¼   ½ mile
0   250m 500m 750m 1 km

A   B   C   D   E   F

8
41
7
40
6
39
5
38
4
37
3
36
2
35
1
34

00   A   01   B   02   C   03   D   04   E   05   F

B5300
Brown Rigg
Allerdale Ramble
Bank End
Cumbria Coastal Way
CH
Cemy
A596
B5300
Ellen Bank (Hotel)
Birkby Farm
NEW ROAD
182
ALAVNA ROMAN FORT
Mus
Schs
Sch
Allerdale Ramble
Netherhall
Cvn Pk
IRB Sta
Aquarium
Mus
Marina
MARYPORT
Glasson
Kirkborough House
Hayborough Farm
182
A594
ELLENBOROUGH RD
SYCAMORE RD
MEADOW VIEW
Sch
Sch
Netherton
Schs
Sch
LC
Sch
MAIN RD
PO
Sch
ENNERDALE RD
H
EWANRIGG RD
PO
MAIN ST
Ellenborough
A594
MARYPORT
Cumbria Coastal Way
Allerdale Ramble
Risehow Farm
EDINAGH RD
Ewanrigg
GLENFORT DR
CA15
Balnakeil Forge
Risehow
Woodside
CHURCH RD
PH
Fothergill
Ind Est
Sch
New House Farm
182

62

For full street detail of the highlighted area see page 182.

63

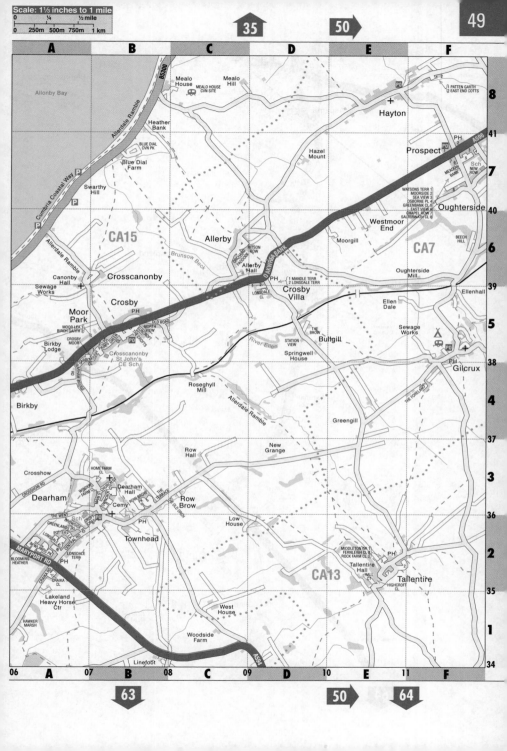

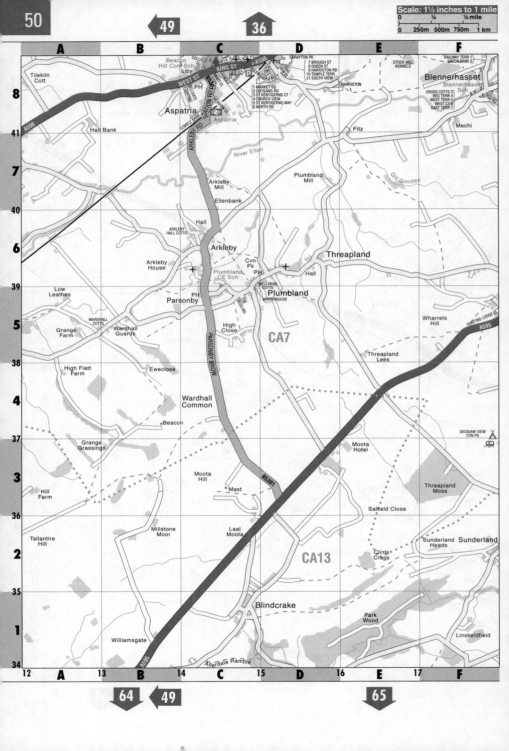

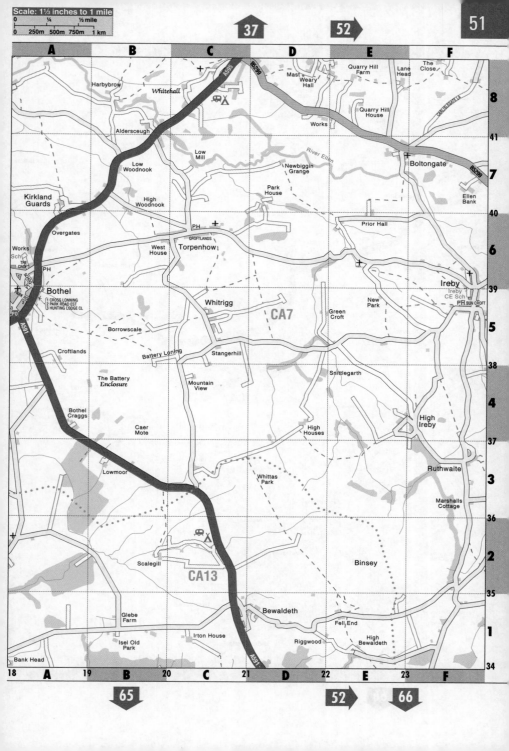

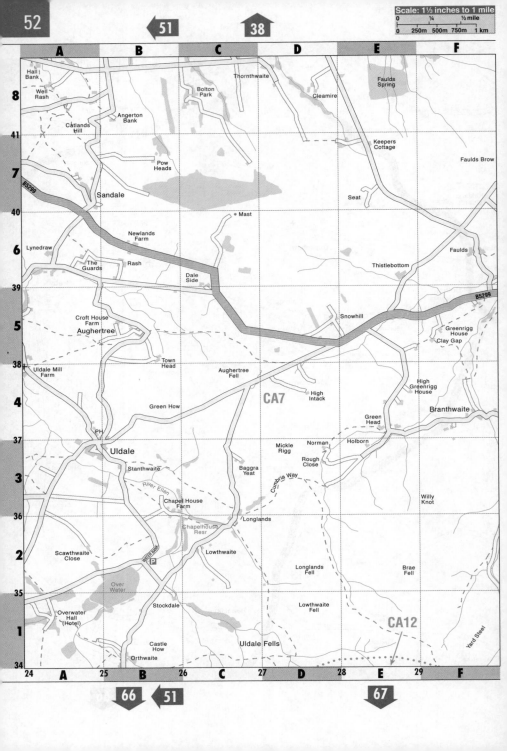

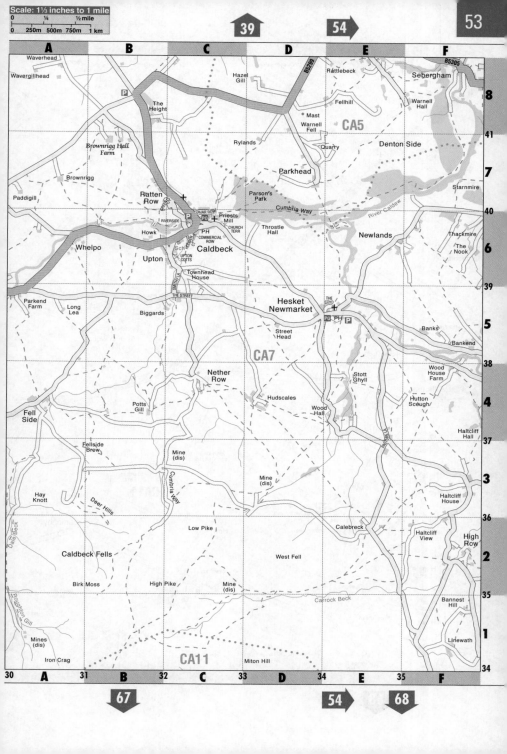

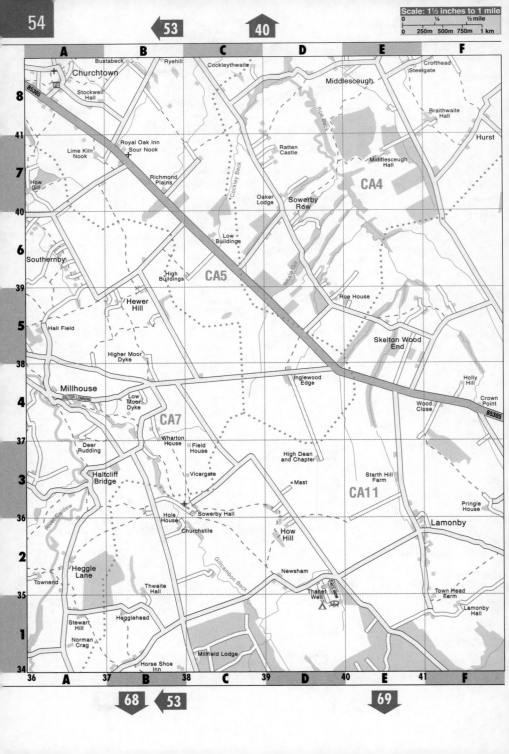

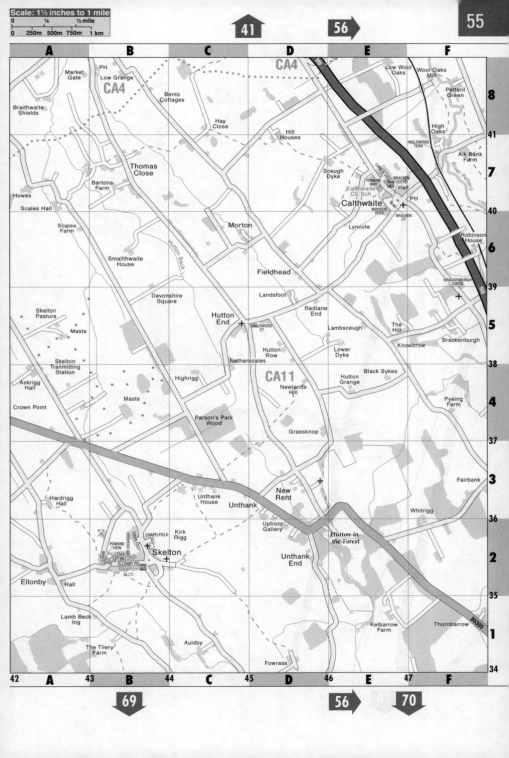

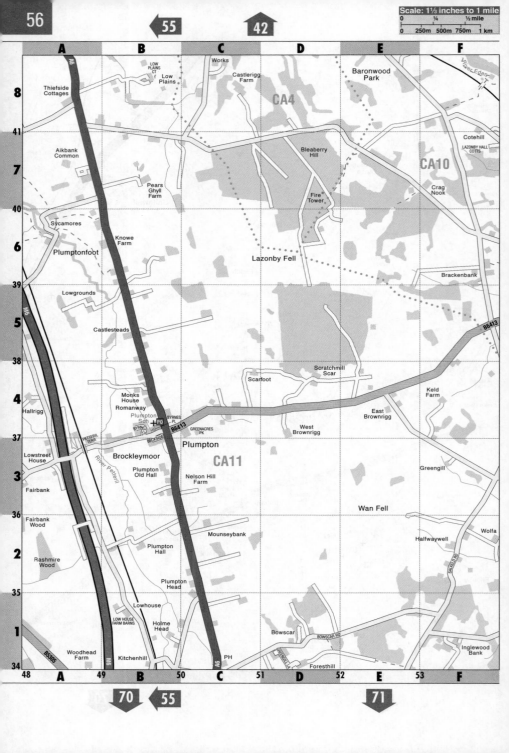

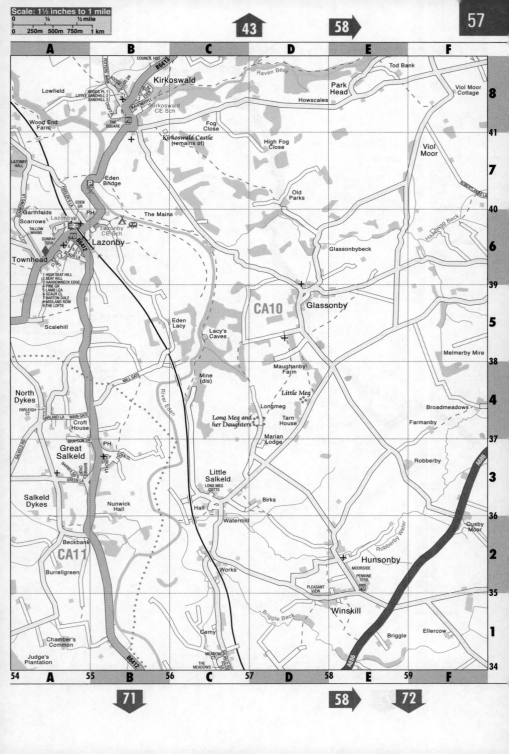

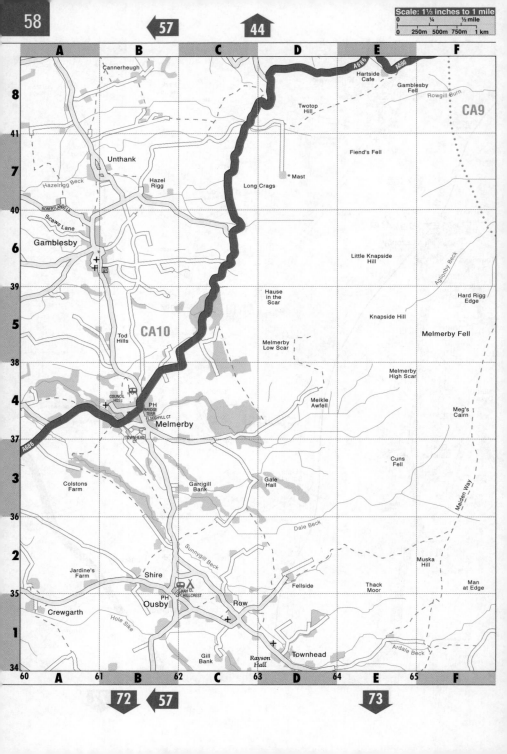

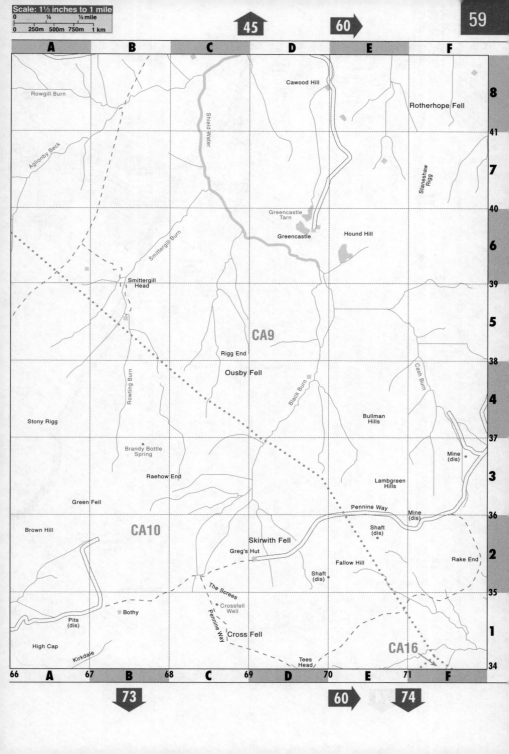

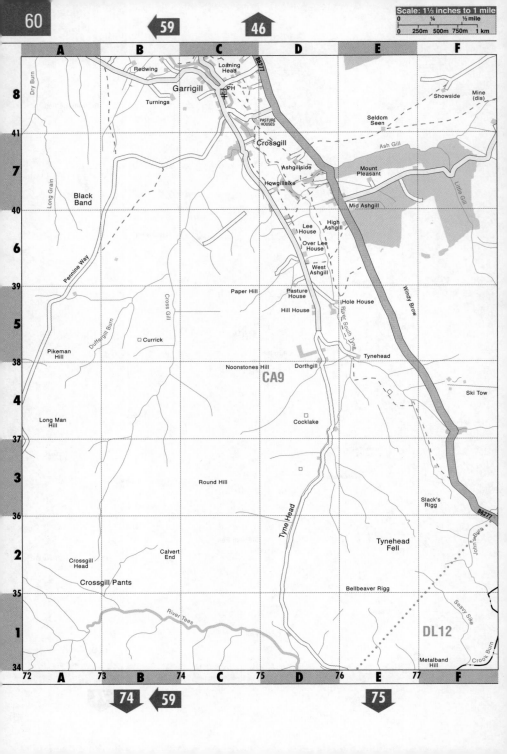

Scale: 1½ inches to 1 mile

0   ¼   ½ mile
0 250m 500m 750m 1 km

A   B   C   D   E   F

Redwing
Loaning
Head

Garrigill   PH

8

Turnings

PASTURE
HOUSES

Showside   Mine
(dis)

Seldom
Seen

41

Crossgill

Ash Gill

7

Ashgillside

Mount
Pleasant

Howgillsike

Black
Band

Mid Ashgill

40

Little Gill

Lee
House

High
Ashgill

6

Over Lee
House

West
Ashgill

Pennine Way

39

Paper Hill

Pasture
House

Hole House

Windy Brow

Hill House

Cross Gill

River South Tyne

5

Duffergill Burn

Currick

Tynehead

Pikeman
Hill

38

Noonstones Hill   Dorthgill

Ski Tow

CA9

4

Long Man
Hill

Cocklake

37

3

Round Hill

Slack's
Rigg

36

B6277

Tyne Head

Calvert
End

Tynehead
Fell

2

Crossgill
Head

John Eplura

Crossgill Pants

Bellbeaver Rigg

35

Seavy Sike

River Tees

1

DL12

Metalband
Hill

Crook Burn

34

A   72   73   B   74   C   75   D   76   E   77   F

74 59   75

Dry Burn

Long Grain

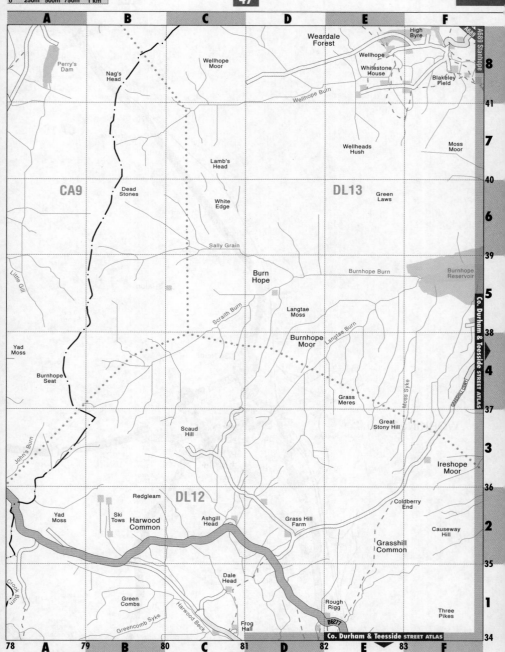

A   B   C   D   E   F

8

41

7

40

6

39

5

38

4

37

3

36

2

35

1

34

Perry's Dam

Nag's Head

Wellhope Moor

Weardale Forest

Wellhope

High Byre

Whitestone House

Blakeley Field

A689 Stanhope

A689

CA9

Dead Stones

Lamb's Head

White Edge

Sally Grain

Wellheads Hush

DL13

Green Laws

Moss Moor

Little Gill

Burn Hope

Burnhope Burn

Burnhope Reservoir

Yad Moss

Scraith Burn

Langtae Moss

Burnhope Moor

Langtae Burn

Moss Syke

GRASSHILL CONT

Co. Durham & Teesside STREET ATLAS

Burnhope Seat

Grass Meres

Great Stony Hill

John's Burn

Scaud Hill

Ireshope Moor

Redgleam

DL12

Yad Moss

Ski Tows

Harwood Common

Ashgill Head

Grass Hill Farm

Coldberry End

Grasshill Common

Causeway Hill

Crook Burn

Green Combs

Greencomb Syke

Harwood Beck

Dale Head

Frog Hall

Rough Rigg

B6277

Three Pikes

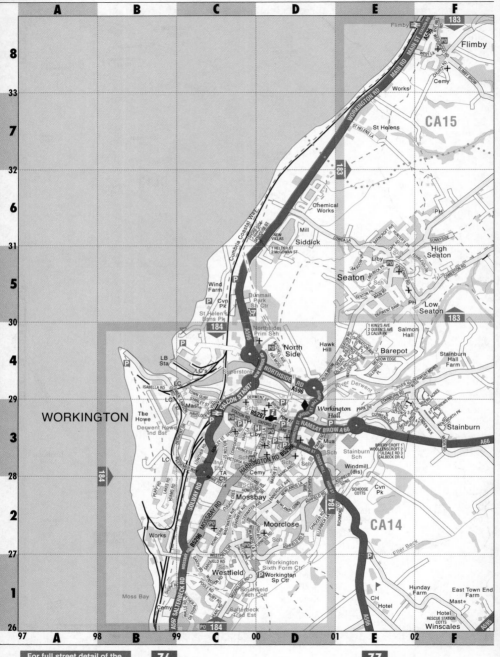

Scale: 1⅓ inches to 1 mile

48

WORKINGTON

For full street detail of the highlighted area see pages 183 and 184.

76

77

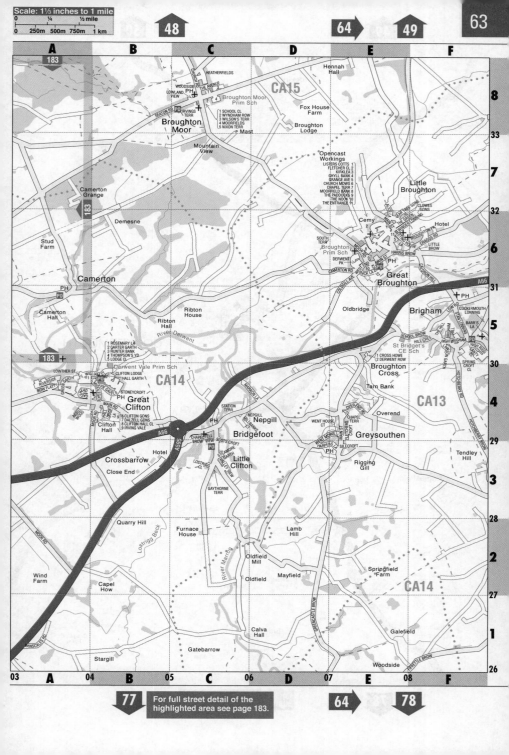

49 63

50

CA15

A594
WOODLANDS GRANGE
PH
Dovenby
Fieldside
Bridekirk
Dovenby Mill
Bridekirk Dovenby CE Prim Sch
Bonnyhill
Dovenby Craggs
A595
Allerdale Ramble
Redmain
Forth House
Anns Hill
Wood Hall Farm
A594
A5086 GOAT BROW
Belle Vue
PH
PO THE VILLAS
DOVERS LA
Hame's Hill
Derwent Mills Commercial Pk (Cockermouth)
River Derwent
Park House Farm
Cockermouth Sch
Allerdale Ramble
Watch Hill
A66
A595
190
Papcastle
Wordsworth Ho
GOTE RD
Castle
CASTLEGATE
OAKTREE CRES
CASTLEGATE DR
MECH LA
H
190
Greenlands
Wyndham House
Low Rd
ELLERBECK BROW
BARRS LA
Brigham
East House
The Fitz
FITZ LA
Mus Liby
CROWN ST
MAIN ST
B5292
PO
Sch
VICTORIA RD
TH
P
MARKET PL
ST HELENS ST
MELBREAM RD
WINDMILL LA
CABLE AVE
HIGHFIELD RD
Annfield Farm
COCKERMOUTH
MAYO ST
BRIGHAM RD
Scales Farm
Ellerbeck
Laketand Bsns Pk
LAMPLUGH RD
A5086
FERN BANK
YH
DE VEW
FITZ VIEW
PASSAGE LA
ROSE LA
SIMONSCALES LA
TOWERS LA
VIOLET BANK
LORTON RD
Cemy
Strawberry How
Strawberry How Bsns Ctr
STRAWBERRY HOWE RD
A66
Bouch House
Wellington Farm
Hotel
Sheep & Wool Ctr
190
Green Bank Farm
River Cocker
Roundclose Hill
Esps Farm
Byerstead
Hotel
HUNDITH HILL RD
Hundith Hill
Shatton Lodge
The Dubbs
Dubbs Moss
CA13
Waterloo
Eaglesfield
HALL TERR
BARKERS LA
PH
BECKSIDE
Hollins
Moorland Close
Southwaite
Green Trees
Stanger
Shatton Hall
Bent Houses
Eaglesfield Crag
Paddle CE Prim Sch
Palace How
Threlkeld Leys
Sneckyeat
Low Hall
MIRK LA
Deanscales
THE HILL
East House
PH
CRAGG CL
High Dyke
Brandlingill
Hill Farm
Wood Farm
Birk Bank
Lanefoot Farm
Crag End Farm
A5086
B5292

For full street detail of the highlighted area see page 190.

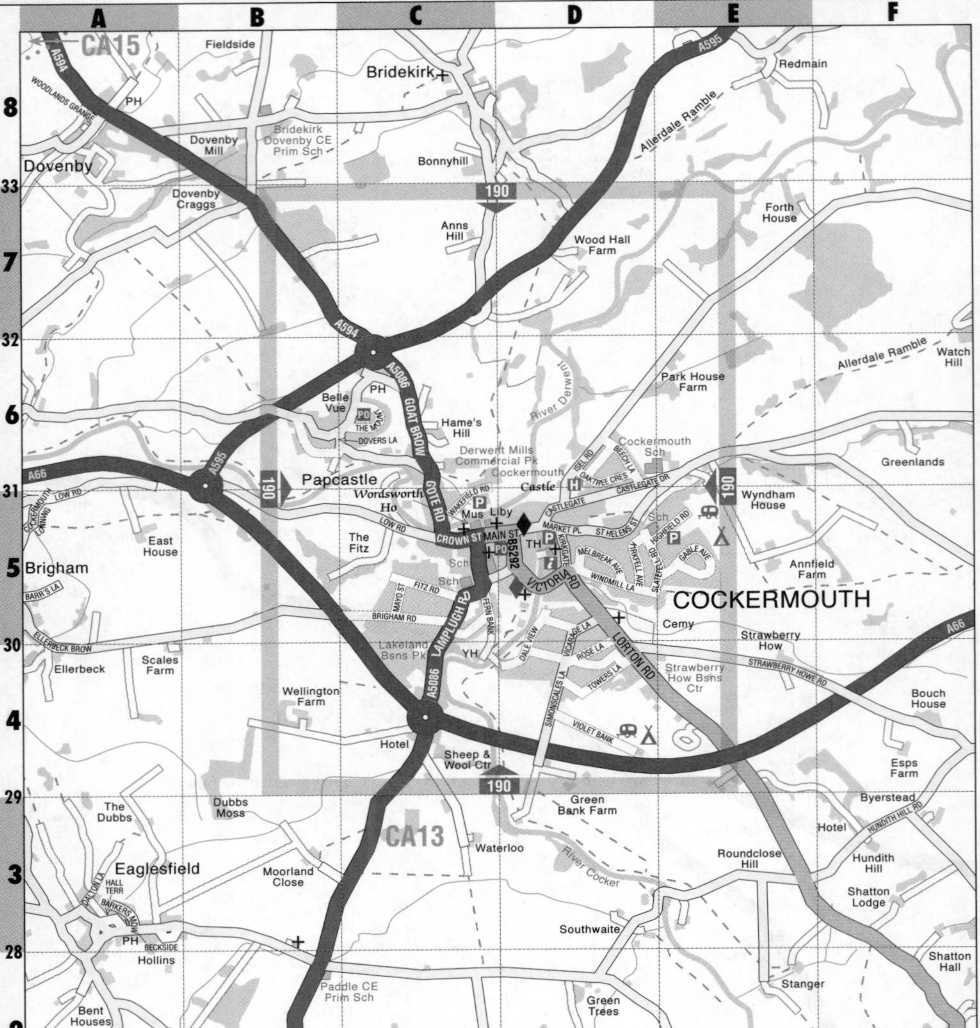

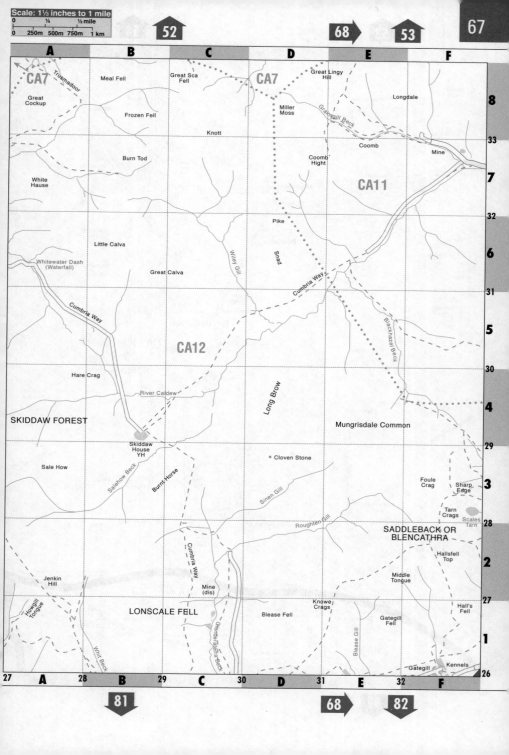

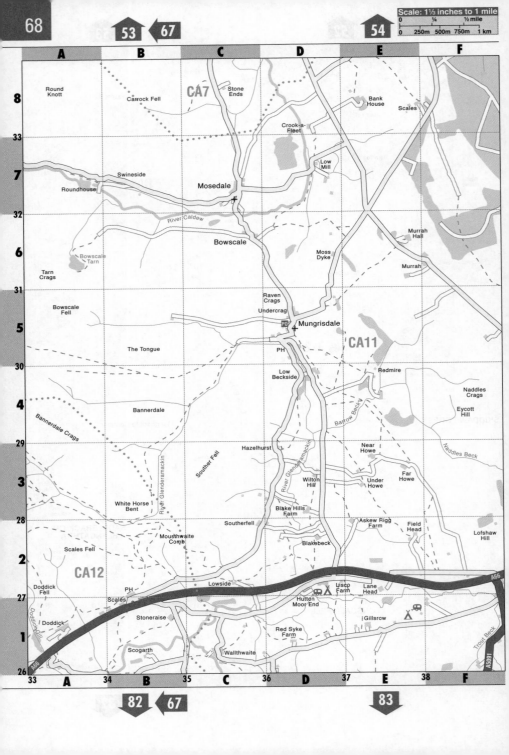

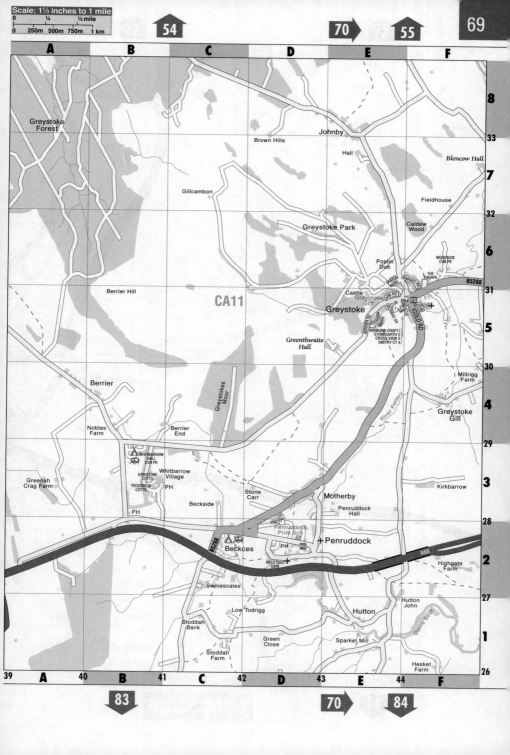

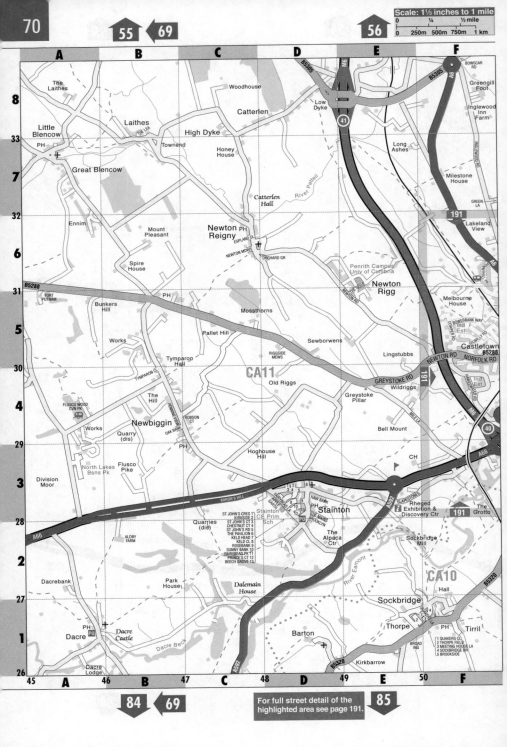

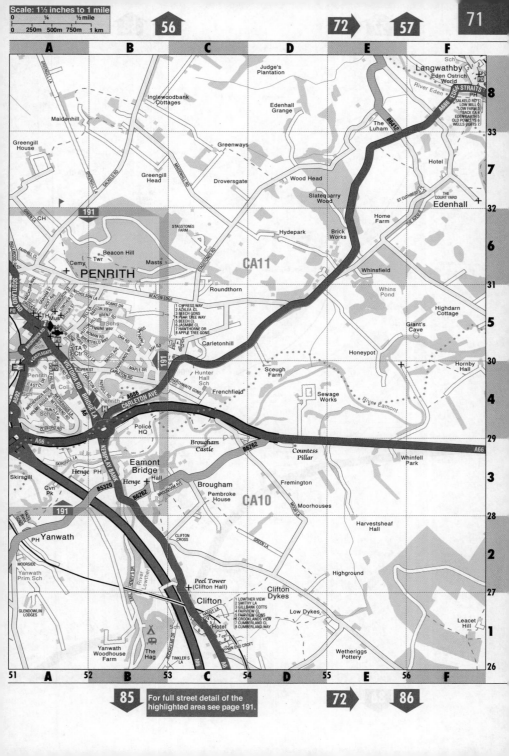

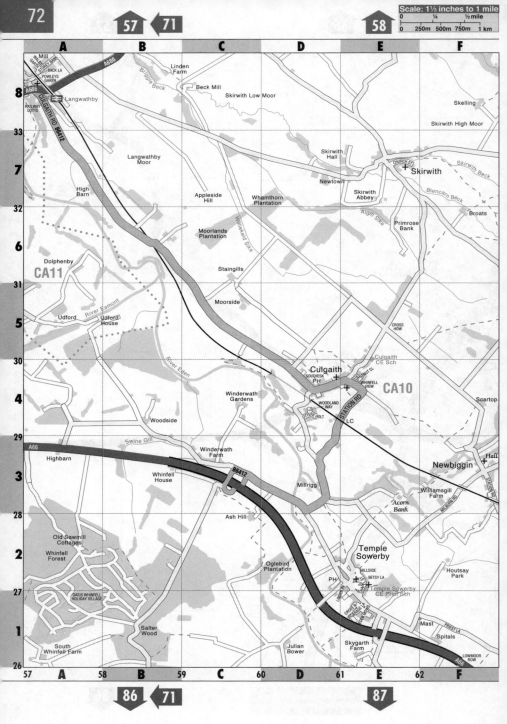

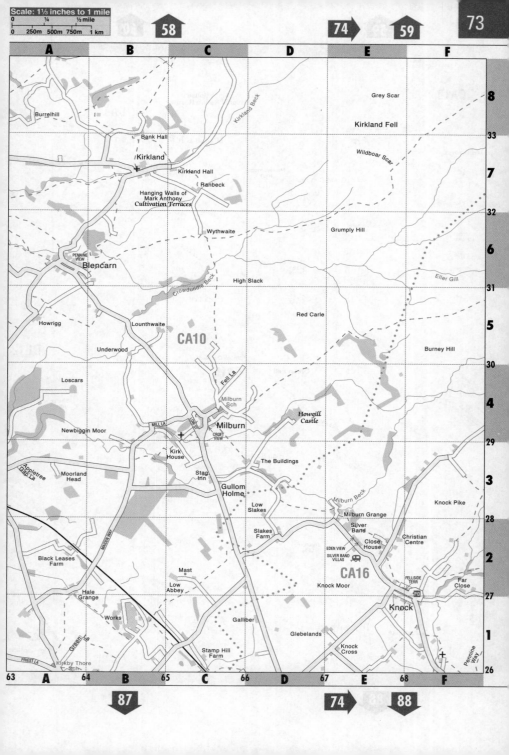

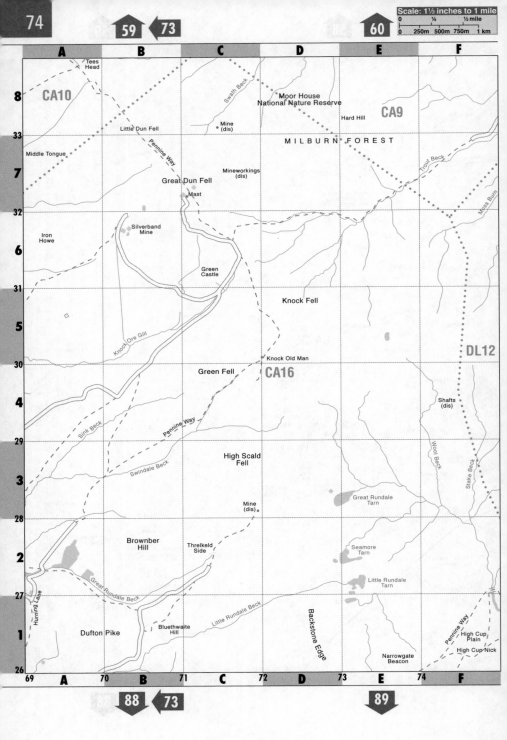

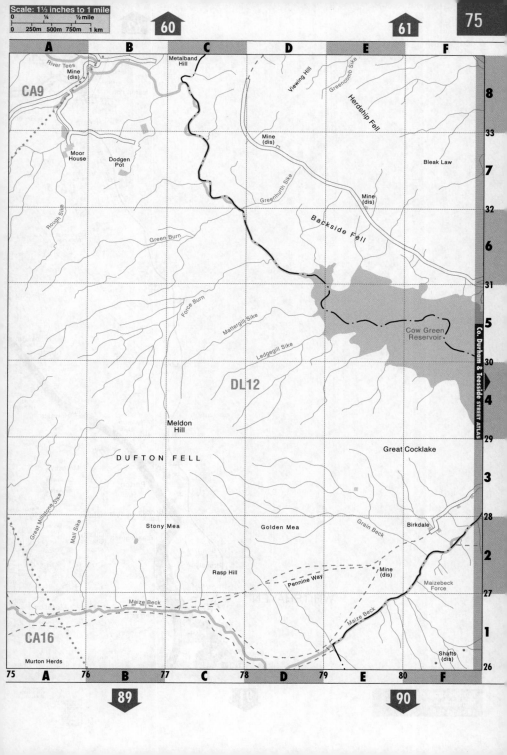

Scale: 1⅓ inches to 1 mile

0   ¼   ½ mile
0   250m 500m 750m 1 km

A | **B** | **C** | **D** | **E** | **F**

River Tees

Mine (dis)

Metalband Hill

CA9

Viewing Hill

Greencomb Sike

Herdship Fell

8

Moor House

Dodgen Pot

Mine (dis)

Bleak Law

33

Greenhurth Sike

7

Rough Sike

Green Burn

Mine (dis)

32

Backside Fell

6

Force Burn

31

Mattergill Sike

Cow Green Reservoir

5

Ledgegill Sike

30

DL12

4

Meldon Hill

Great Cocklake

29

DUFTON FELL

3

Great Millstone Syke

Mail Sike

Stony Mea

Golden Mea

Grain Beck

Birkdale

28

2

Rasp Hill

Pennine Way

Mine (dis)

Maizebeck Force

27

Maize Beck

Maize Beck

CA16

1

Murton Herds

Shafts (dis)

26

75   **A**   76   **B**   77   **C**   78   **D**   79   **E**   80   **F**

Co. Durham & Teesside STREET ATLAS

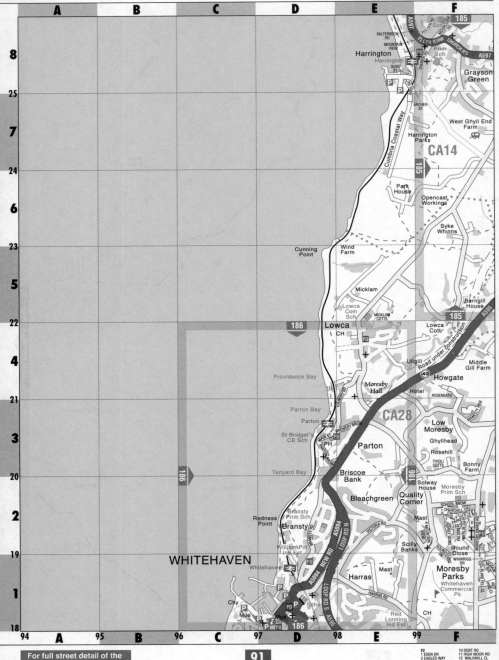

A   B   C   D   E   F

8
25
7
24
6
23
5
22
4
21
3
20
2
19
1
18

94   A   95   B   96   C   97   D   98   E   99   F

185

Harrington
Harrington
QUAY
ST
SALTERBECK
RD
MOUNTAIN
VIEW
Prim
Sch
ELLER BANK
CHURCH RD
A597
A597

Grayson
Green

ARCHER
ST

West Ghyll End
Farm

Harrington
Parks

CA14

185

Park
House

Opencast
Workings

Syke
Whinns

Climbria Coastal Way

Cunning
Point

Wind
Farm

Micklam

Lowca
Com
Sch

MICKLAM
COTTS

Barngill
House

186

Lowca
CH

Lowca
Cotts

185

A595

Ullgill
Middle
Gill Farm

Road under construction

Providence Bay

Moresby
Hall

Hotel

40

Howgate

ROSENEATH

Parton Bay

Parton

St Bridget's
CE Sch

PH

CA28

Low
Moresby

Ghyllhead

Rosehill

Parton

BRANSTY BROW

MAIN ST

MAREST RISE

TIVOLI
COTTS

Bonny
Farm

Tanyard Bay

Briscoe
Bank

Solway
House

981

Moresby
Prim Sch

186

Redness
Point

Bransty
Prim Sch

Bransty

Quality
Corner

Bleachgreen

SCHOOL BROW

CHURCHILL RD

Mast

Scilly
Banks

Mast

MOUNTAIN
VIEW

Round
Close

WHINRIGG
DR

WHITEHAVEN

Whitehaven

William Pitt
Ind Est

A5094 NEW RD

LOOP RD N

VICTORIA RD

LOOP RD S   A595

Harras

Mast

Moresby
Parks

Whitehaven
Commercial
Pk

Chy

Mus

Mus

Sch

186

Red
Lonning
Ind Est

CH

For full street detail of the
highlighted area see pages
185 and 186.

91

F2
1 EDEN DR
2 EAGLES WAY
3 PEREGRINE CL
4 HAWK PL
5 KESTREL GR
6 ROUND CL
7 HARRIER CT
8 ROWNTREE CRES
9 SOLWAY RD
10 DENT RD
11 HIGH MOOR RD
12 WALKMILL CL

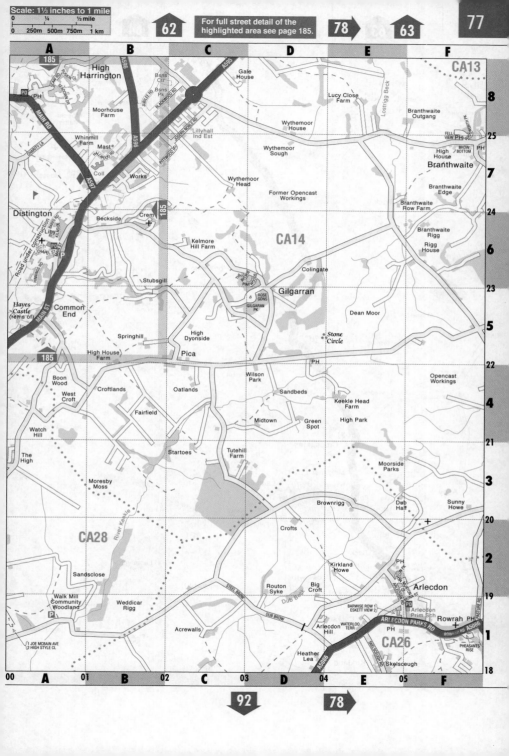

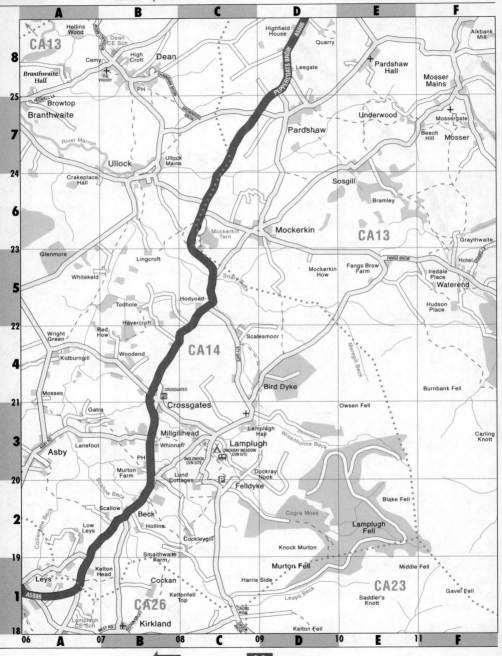

CA13

Hollins Wood
Dean CE Sch
High Croft
Dean
Cemy
Branthwaite Hall
THE PRIORY
PH
Browtop
Branthwaite
River Marron
Ullock
Ullock Mains
Crakeplace Hall
Glenmore
Whitekeld
Lingcroft
Todhole
Havercroft
Red How
Woodend
Wright Green
Kidburngill
Mosses
Gatra
Asby
Lanefoot
Whinnah
PH
Murton Farm
Scallow
Low Leys
Leys
Kelton Head
Kirkland
Lamplugh CE Sch
WEST RD
Cockan
Keltonfell Top
CA26

Highfield House
Quarry
Leegate
Pardshaw Hall
Pardshaw
Underwood
Mossergate
Mosser Mains
Beech Hill
Mosser
Sosgill
Bramley
Mockerkin Tarn
Mockerkin
Mockerkin How
Fangs Brow Farm
FANGS BROW
Graythwaite
Hotel
Iredale Place
Waterend
Hudson Place
Snary Beck
Hodyoad
Scalesmoor
CA14
Bird Dyke
Meregill Beck
Owsen Fell
Burnbank Fell
Carling Knott
CROSSGATES
Crossgates
Millgillhead
Lamplugh Hall
Lamplugh
INGLENOOK CVN SITE
DOCKRAY MEADOW CVN SITE
Wisenholme Beck
Lund Cottages
Dockray Nook
Felldyke
Blake Fell
Cogra Moss
Lamplugh Fell
Beck
Hollins
Cockleygill
Smaithwaite Farm
Knock Murton
Murton Fell
Harris Side
Leaps Beck
CA23
Saddler's Knott
Middle Fell
Gavel Fell
Kelton Fell
CROSS RIGG

A5086

PEPPER'S/OATS BROW A5086

Aikbank Mill

Stallow Beck
Collier gate Beck

06 A 07 B 08 C 09 D 10 E 11 F

77 93

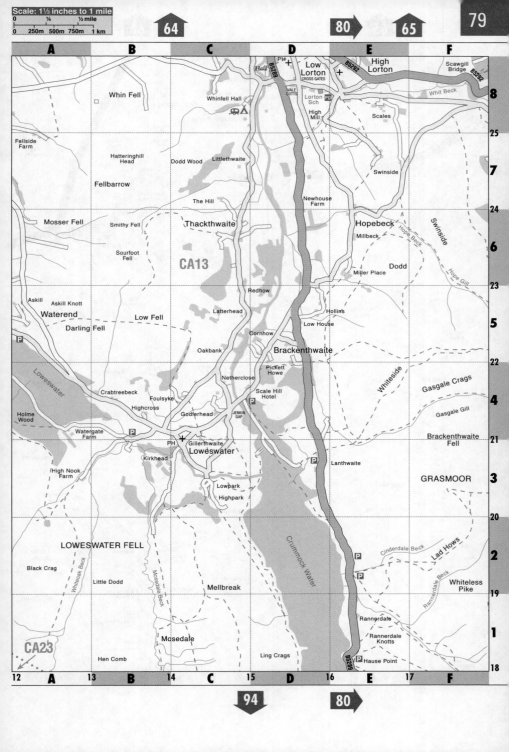

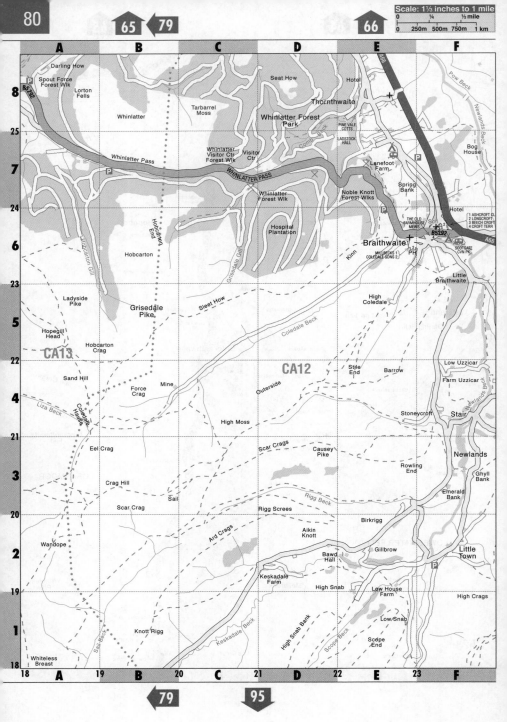

65 79

66

Scale: 1⅓ inches to 1 mile

0   ¼   ½ mile

0   250m 500m 750m   1 km

Darling How
Spout Force
Forest Wlk
Lorton
Fells
Whinlatter
Tarbarrel
Moss
Seat How
Hotel
Thornthwaite
Whinlatter Forest
Park
PINE VALE
COTTS
LADSTOCK
HALL
Comb Beck
Pow Beck
Newlands Beck
Bog
House
Whinlatter Pass
Whinlatter
Visitor Ctr
Forest Wlk
Visitor
Ctr
P
WHINLATTER PASS
P
Lanefoot
Farm
Spring
Bank
Hotel
Hobcarton Gill
Hobcarton
End
Whinlatter
Forest Wlk
Noble Knott
Forest Wlks
THE OLD
FARMHOUSE
MEWS
Sch
1 ASHCROFT CL
2 LONGCROFT
3 BEECH CROFT
4 CROFT TERR
A66
Hospital
Plantation
B5292
Hobcarton
Kinn
Braithwaite
PH
MILLBECKS 1
COLEDALE GDNS 2
SCOTGATE
CVN PK
Little
Braithwaite
Ladyside
Pike
Grisedale
Gill
Sleet How
High
Coledale
Hopegill
Head
Ladyside
Pike
Grisedale
Pike
CA13
Hobcarton
Crag
Coledale Beck
CA12
Stile
End
Barrow
Low Uzzicar
Farm Uzzicar
Newlands Beck
Sand Hill
Liza Beck
Coledale Hause
Force
Crag
Mine
Outerside
Stoneycroft
Stair
Eel Crag
High Moss
Scar Crags
Causey
Pike
Rowling
End
Newlands
Ghyll
Bank
Crag Hill
Sail
Rigg Beck
Emerald
Bank
Scar Crag
Rigg Screes
Birkrigg
Wandope
Ard Crags
Aikin
Knott
Gillbrow
Little
Town
Bawd
Hall
P
Keskadale
Farm
High Snab
Low House
Farm
High Crags
Knott Rigg
Sail Beck
Keskadale Beck
High Snab Bank
Scope Beck
Low Snab
Scope
End
Whiteless
Breast

79

95

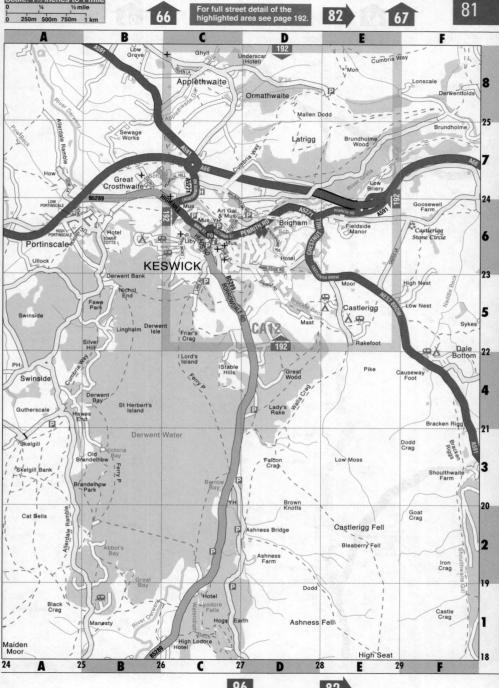

Scale: 1⅓ inches to 1 mile

0   ¼   ½ mile
0   250m 500m 750m 1 km

66

For full street detail of the highlighted area see page 192.

82   67

81

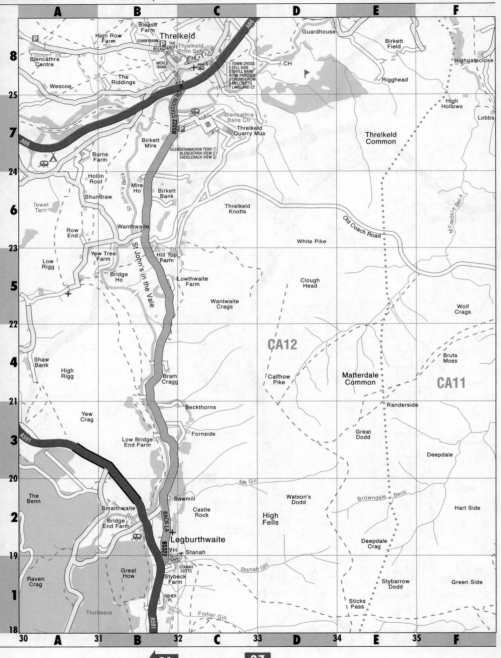

Scale: 1⅓ inches to 1 mile

0 ¼ ½ mile

0 250m 500m 750m 1 km

A **B** **C** **D** **E** **F**

8

P

Blencathra
Centre

High Row
Farm

SUNNYBANK

Blease
Farm

Threlkeld

THE
CROFT

P

Threlkeld
Prim Sch

MERLE
BANK

PH

Guardhouse

Birkett
Field

Highgateclose

CH

1 TOWN CROSS
2 FELL SIDE
3 GHYLL BANK
4 THE PADDOCK
5 CHURCH ROW
6 MELLBUTTS
7 LAKELAND CT

Wescoe

The
Riddings

Rigghead

25

High
Hollows

Lobbs

7

A66

Birkett
Mire

B5322 STATION RD

Blencathra
Bsns Cfr

P

Threlkeld
Quarry Mus

GLENDERAMACKIN TERR 1
BLENCATHRA VIEW 2
SADDLEBACK VIEW 3

Threlkeld
Common

24

Burns
Farm

Hollin
Root

Mire
Ho

Birkett
Bank

Shundraw

St John's Beck

Threlkeld
Knotts

McIredale Beck

6

Tewet
Tarn

Row
End

Wanthwaite

White Pike

Old Coach Road

23

Low
Rigg

Yew Tree
Farm

Bridge
Ho

Hill Top
Farm

Lowthwaite
Farm

St John's in the Vale

5

Wantwaite
Crags

Clough
Head

Wolf
Crags

22

Shaw
Bank

High
Rigg

CA12

Bruts
Moss

4

Bram
Cragg

Calfhow
Pike

Matterdale
Common

CA11

21

Yew
Crag

Beckthorns

Randerside

Great
Dodd

Deepdale

3

A591

Low Bridge
End Farm

Fornside

20

The
Benn

Sawmill

Mill Gill

Watson's
Dodd

Browndale Beck

Hart Side

2

Smaithwaite

Bridge
End Farm

BACK LA

Castle
Rock

High
Fells

Deepdale
Crag

19

B5322

Legburthwaite

YH

Stanah

STANAH

STANAH
COTTS

Stanah Gill

Stybarrow
Dodd

Green Side

1

Raven
Crag

Great
How

Stybeck
Farm

FISHER
PL

Sticks
Pass

Thirlmere

A591

Fisher Gill

18

30 **A** 31 **B** 32 **C** 33 **D** 34 **E** 35 **F**

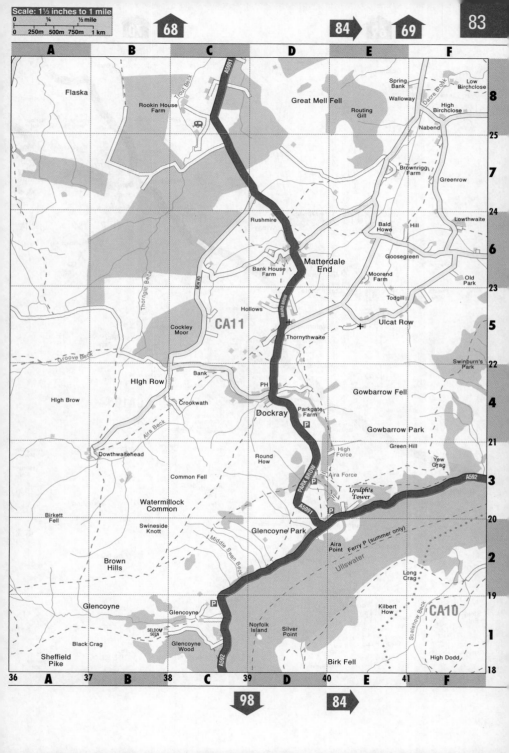

Scale: 1½ inches to 1 mile

0   ¼   ½ mile

0 250m 500m 750m 1 km

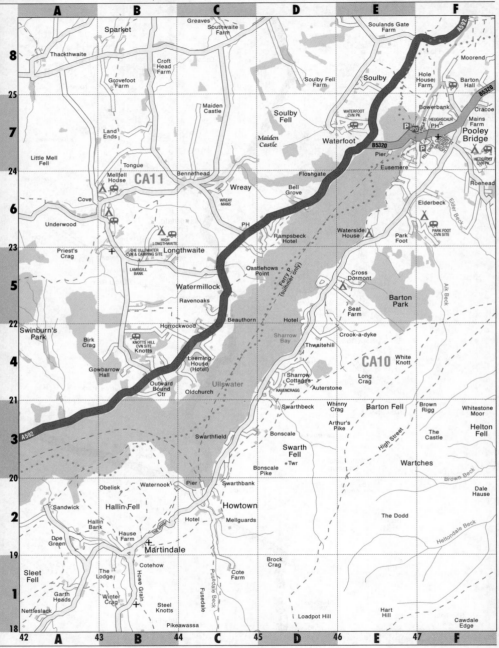

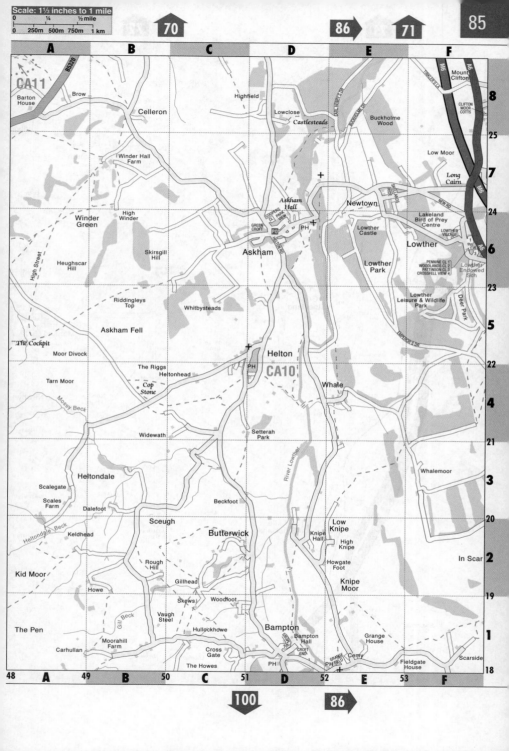

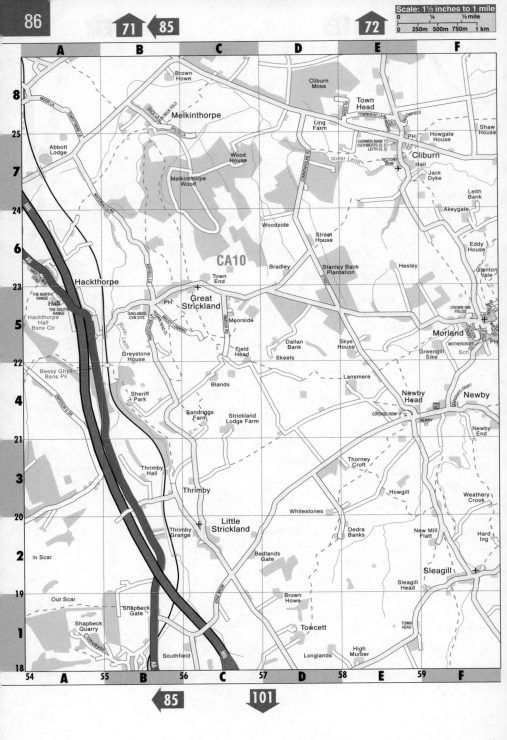

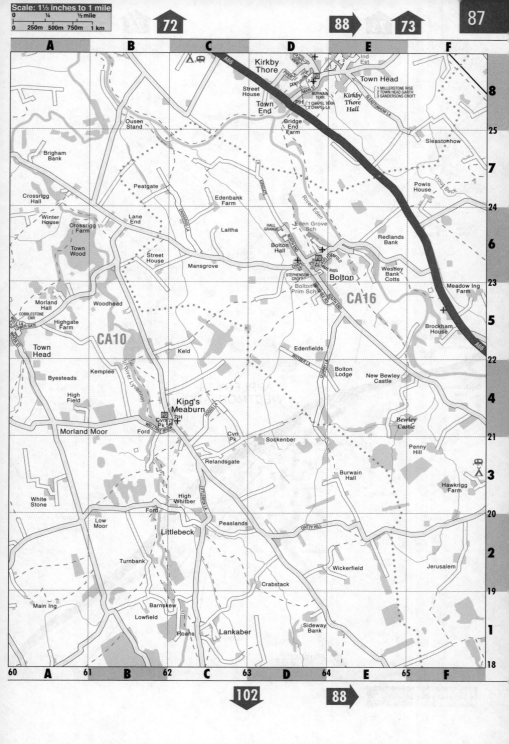

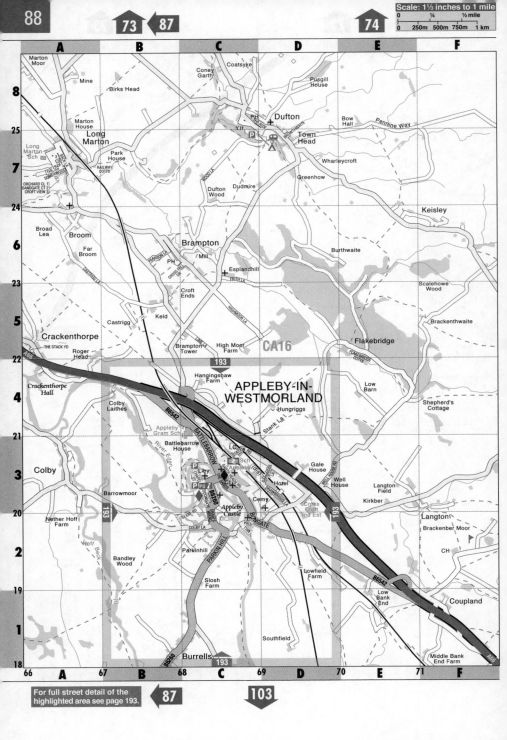

73 87

74

Scale: 1⅓ inches to 1 mile

0   ¼   ½ mile
0   250m   500m   750m   1 km

A   B   C   D   E   F

Marton Moor
Mine
Birks Head
Coney Garth
Coatsyke
Pusgill House
Bow Hall
Pennine Way

Marton House
Long Marton
Park House
RAILWAY COTTS
PH
YH
Dufton
Town Head
Wharleycroft

Long Marton Sch
ORCHARD CL 1
SANDGATE CT 2
CROFT VIEW 3
THE CROFT
SOMERWOOD CL
Dufton Wood
Dudmire
Greenhow
Keisley

Broad Lea
Broom
Far Broom
Brampton
MHL
Esplandhill
Burthwaite
Scalehowe Wood

CASTRIGG LA
PEARSON LA
CROSS FELL
PH
Croft Ends
TRUTE LA
HIGHMOOR LA
Brackenthwaite

Castrigg
Keld
Brampton Tower
High Moor Farm
CA16
Flakebridge
FLAKEBRIDGE COTTS

Crackenthorpe
THE STACK YD
Roger Head
193
Hangingshaw Farm
Low Barn

A66
Crackenthorpe Hall
APPLEBY-IN-WESTMORLAND
Hungriggs
Shepherd's Cottage

Colby Laithes
B6542
BATTLEBARROW
Stank La
Gale House
Well House
Langton Field

Colby
Appleby Gram Sch
Battlebarrow House
River Eden
LC
Appleby
Sch
Hotel
Kirkber
Langton

193
Barrowmoor
P
P
Appleby Castle
Cemy
Cross Croft Ind Est
193
Brackenber Moor
CH

Nether Hoff Farm
Hoff
Back
COLBY LA
BONGATE
Parkinhill
PARKIN HILL
Lowfield Farm
B6542
Coupland

Bandley Wood
Slosh Farm
Low Bank End

Southfield
Middle Bank End Farm
A66

66   A   67   B   68   C   69   D   70   E   71   F

Burrells
193

87

103

For full street detail of the highlighted area see page 193.

8   25   7   24   6   23   5   22   4   21   3   20   2   19   1   18

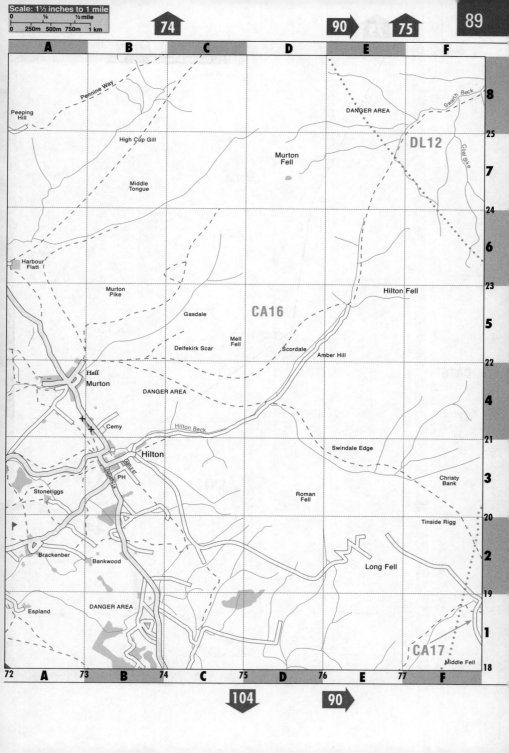

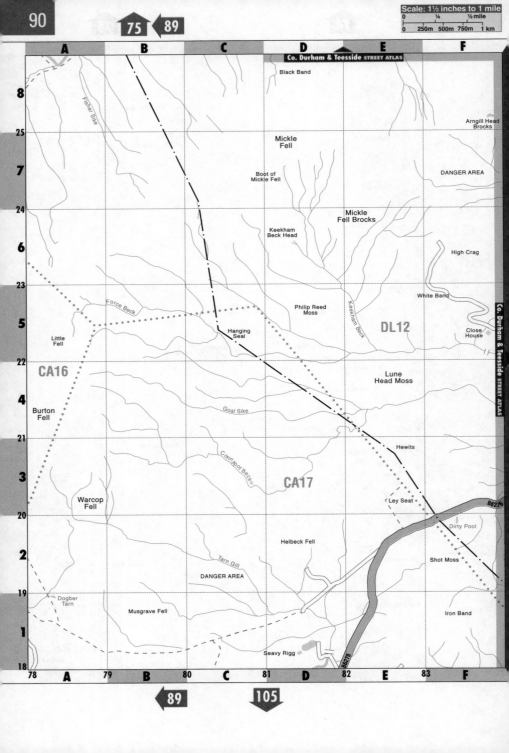

Scale: 1⅓ inches to 1 mile
0   ¼   ½ mile
0   250m 500m 750m 1 km

Co. Durham & Teesside STREET ATLAS

Co. Durham & Teesside STREET ATLAS

A   B   C   D   E   F

Black Band

Arngill Head
Brocks

Mickle
Fell

Boot of
Mickle Fell

DANGER AREA

Mickle
Fell Brocks

Keekham
Beck Head

High Crag

Force Beck

Philip Reed
Moss

White Band

DL12

Hanging
Seal

Close
House

Little
Fell

CA16

Lune
Head Moss

Burton
Fell

Goal Sike

Hewits

Conn pot Beck

CA17

Ley Seat

B627

Warcop
Fell

Dirty Pool

Helbeck Fell

Shot Moss

Tarn Gill

DANGER AREA

Dogber
Tarn

Musgrave Fell

Iron Band

Seavy Rigg

B6276

78   A   79   B   80   C   81   D   82   E   83   F

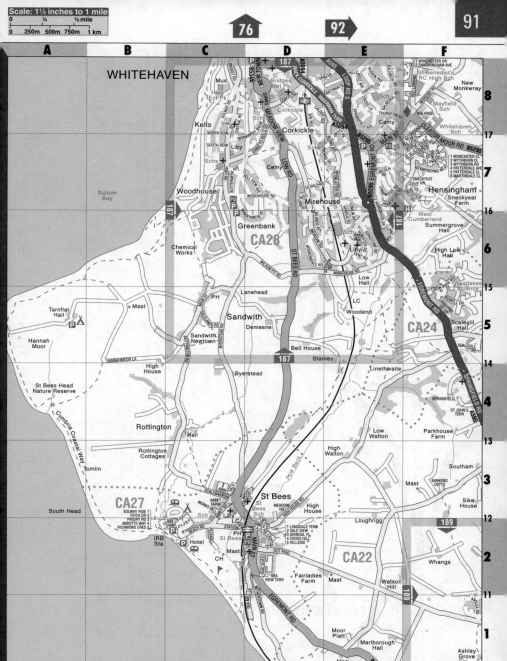

WHITEHAVEN

Kells

Woodhouse

Greenbank

CA28

Corkickle

Mirehouse

Hensingham

West Cumberland

Summergrove Hall

High Low Hall

Westlakes Science Park

Scalegill Hall

CA24

New Monkwray

Chemical Works

Lanehead

Sandwith

Demesne

Low Hall

LC

Woodend

Bell House

Stanley

Linethwaite

Springfield

ST JOHN'S TERR

High House

Byerstead

Sandwith Newtown

High Walton

Low Walton

Parkhouse Farm

Rottington

Rottington Cottages

Hall

Tomlin

CA27

South Head

St Bees

Loughrigg

CA22

Whangs

Southam

Sike House

BANKEND COTTS

Watson Hill

Moor Platt

Marlborough Hall

How Man

Fairladies Farm

Ashley Grove

Saltom Bay

Tarnflat Hall

Hannah Moor

St Bees Head Nature Reserve

Cumbria Coastal Way

IRB Sta

Hotel

94   A   95   B   96   C   97   D   98   E   99   F

For full street detail of the highlighted area see pages 187 and 189.

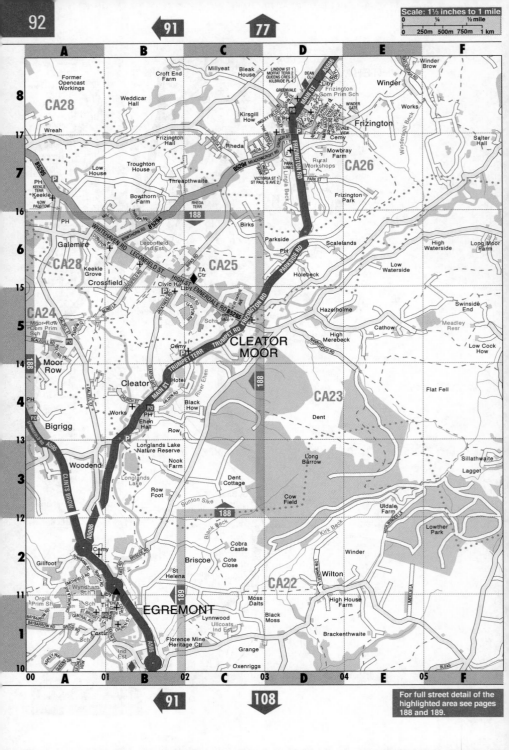

Scale: 1⅓ inches to 1 mile

0   ¼   ½ mile
0   250m 500m 750m   1 km

A   **B**   **C**   **D**   **E**   **F**

8

CA28

Former
Opencast
Workings

Weddicar
Hall

Croft End
Farm

Millyeat

Bleak
House

LINDOW ST 1
MOFFAT TERR 2
QUEENS CRES 3
KILBRIDE PL 4

DEAN
CL 1

Liby
Frizington
Com Prim Sch

Winder

Winder
Brow

17

Wreah

Frizington
Hall

Rheda

Kirsgill
How

GREENVALE
CT 5

PH

P
O

Cemy

WINDER
GATE

Works

Frizington

Salter
Hall

7

PH
KEEKLE
TERR
Keekle

Low
House

Troughton
House

Threapthwaite

B5294

MEADOWCROFT RD

VICTORIA ST 1
ST PAUL'S AVE 2

FRIZINGTON RD

Lingla Beck

PARK
LINKS

Rural
Workshops

Park St

Mowbray
Farm

CA26

Frizington
Park

LOW
PADSTOW

16

PH

Bowthorn
Farm

RHEDA
TERR

188

Birks

Parkside

PH

Scalelands

PARKSIDE RD

Low
Waterside

High
Waterside

Long Moor
Farm

6

CA28

Galemire

WHITEHAVEN RD

BOWTHORN RD

CONISTON ST

LECONFIELD ST

Leconfield
Ind Est

B5294

BIRKS RD

CA25

CROSSFIELD RD

Holebeck

15

Keekle
Grove

Crossfield

HIGH ST

Civic Hall

Liby

TA
Ctr

ENNERDALE RD

B5295

FLEUR HAYNE

FRIZINGTON RD

Hazelholme

Swinside
End

Meadley
Resr

5

CA24

BLIND LA

Moor Row
Com Prim
Sch

SCALEGILL RD

DALZELL ST

Schs

P
O

JACOB'S

CHAPEL ST

CHURCH ST

CHAPS RD

TRUMPET RD

B5295

High
Merebeck

MINNYGATCH RD

Cathow

Low Cock
How

14

188

Moor
Row

Cemy

TRUMPET TERR

CLEATOR
MOOR

4

PH

Cleator

Works

CHURCH ST

MAIN ST

HILDEN RD

Hotel

PH

Black
How

River Ehen

188

CA23

Flat Fell

Bigrigg

A595

P
O

PH
Ehen
Hall

Row

Dent

13

Woodend

SPRINGFIELD RD

P

Longlands Lake
Nature Reserve

Nook
Farm

Long
Barrow

Sillathwaite

Lagget

3

CLINTS BROW

A5086

Longlands
Lake

Row
Foot

Dent
Cottage

Cow
Field

Uldale
Farm

Lowther
Park

12

188

Sunton Sike

Black Beck

Kirk Beck

LIMETREE LA

2

Gillfoot

Cemy

BRISCOE RD

EAST RD

St
Helena

Briscoe

Cobra
Castle

Cote
Close

Winder

HIGH WINDER LA

Wilton

11

Orgill
Prim Sch

HENMAN RD

NORTH RD

SMITHFIELD RD

ST JOHN RD

Wyndham
Sch

Sch

Liby

A595

B5086

Moss
Dalts

CA22

High House
Farm

1

BAYBARROW RD

Castle

ST BRIDGE ST

CENTRAL AVE

GROVE RD

Ind Est

EGREMONT

Lynnwood
Ullcoats
Ind Est

Black
Moss

Grange

Brackenthwaite

10

ASPLEY WAY

QUEENS DR

Florence Mine
Heritage Ctr

Oxenriggs

00   **A**   **01**   **B**   **02**   **C**   **03**   **D**   **04**   **E**   **05**   **F**

For full street detail of the
highlighted area see pages
188 and 189.

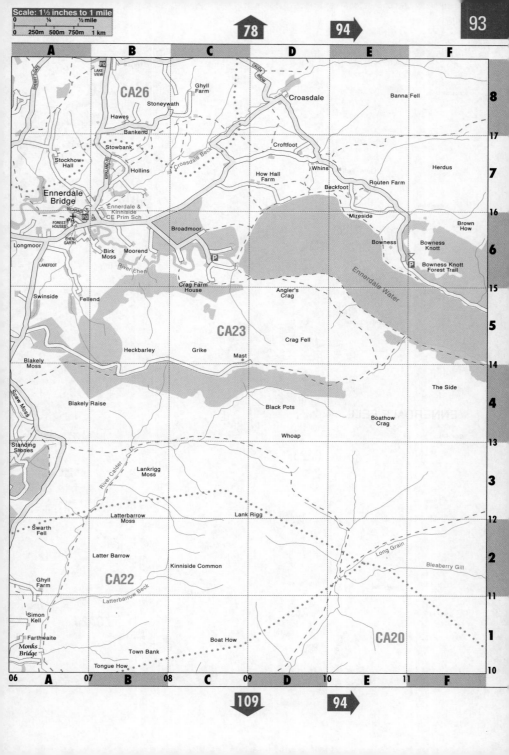

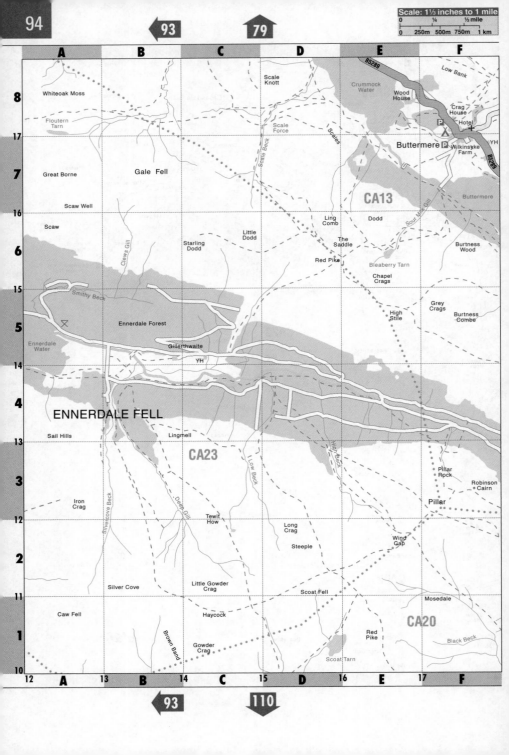

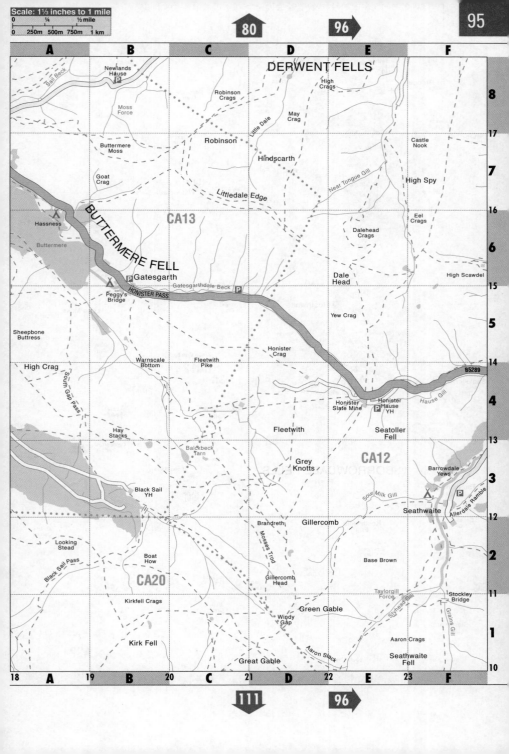

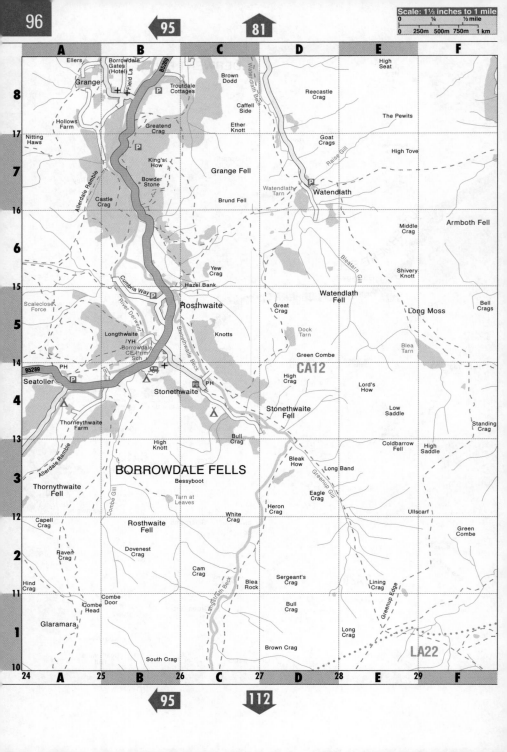

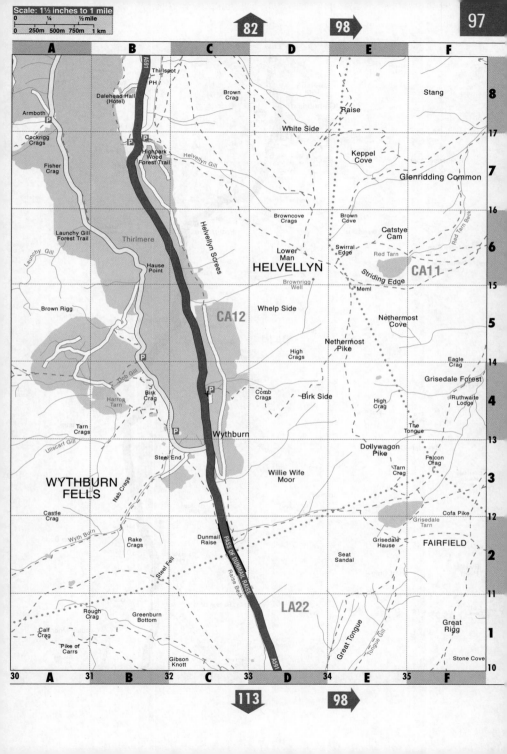

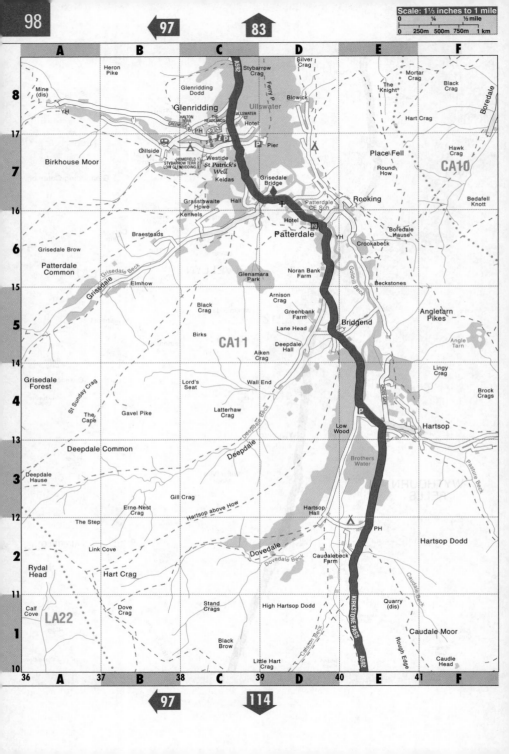

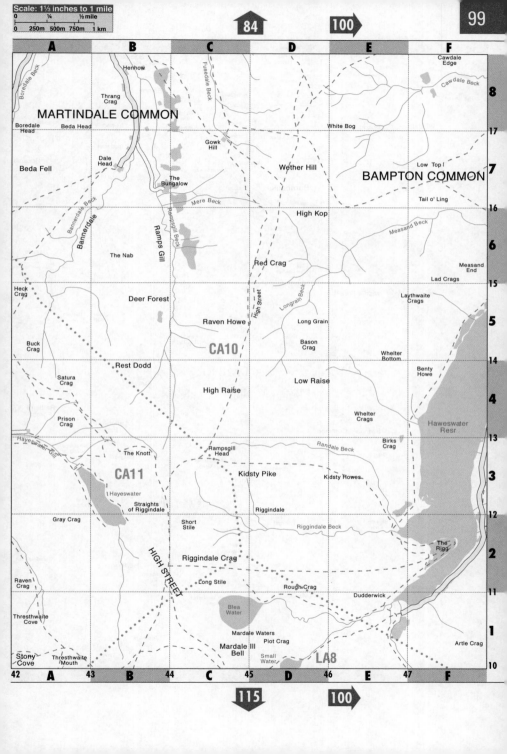

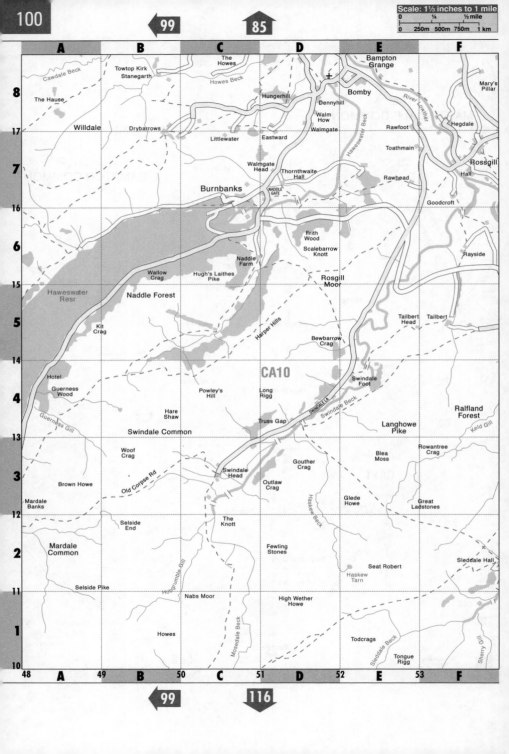

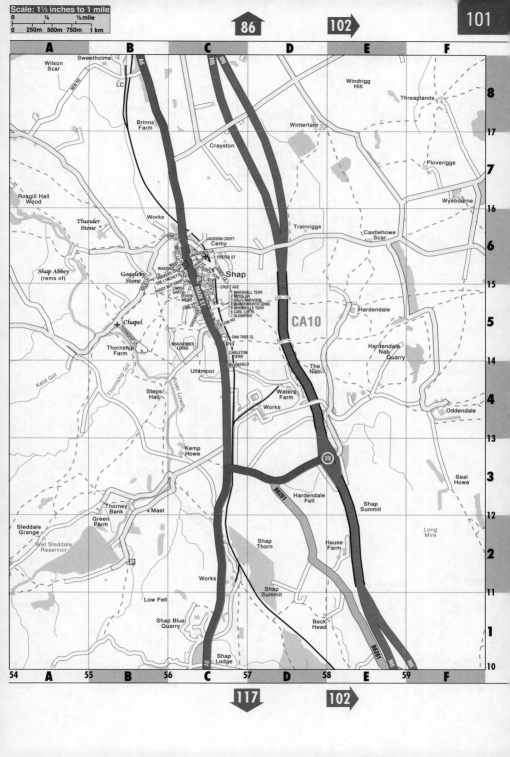

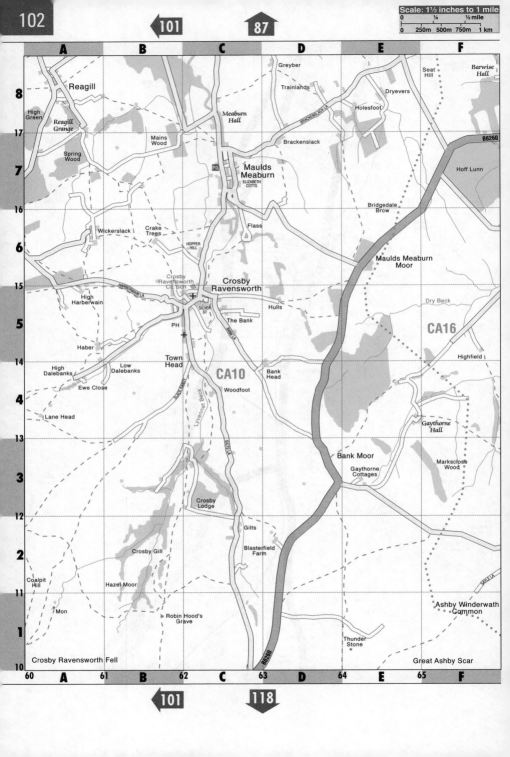

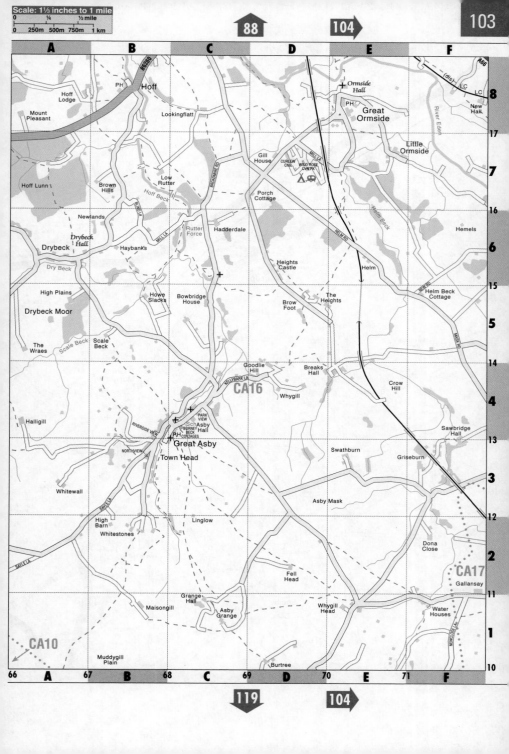

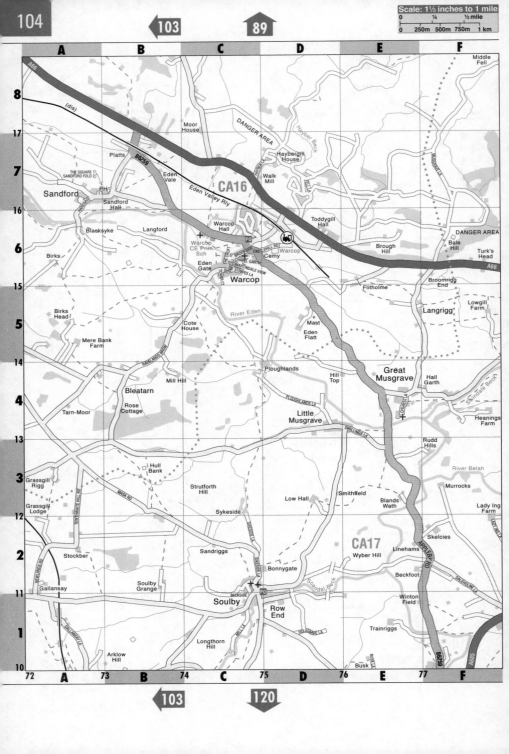

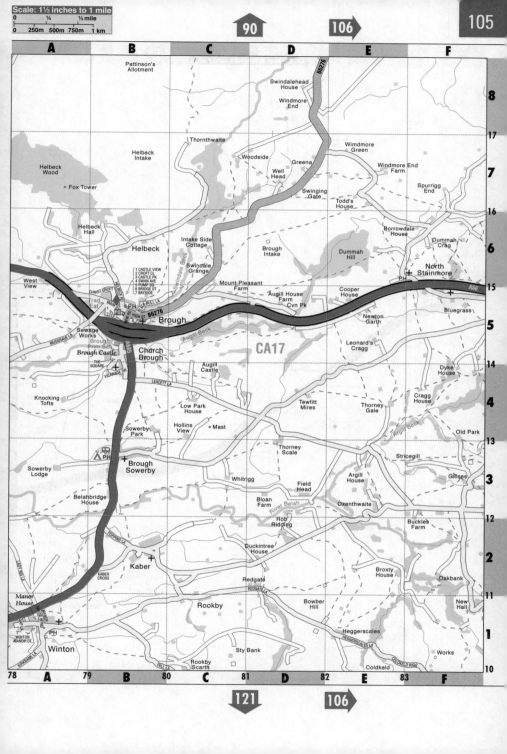

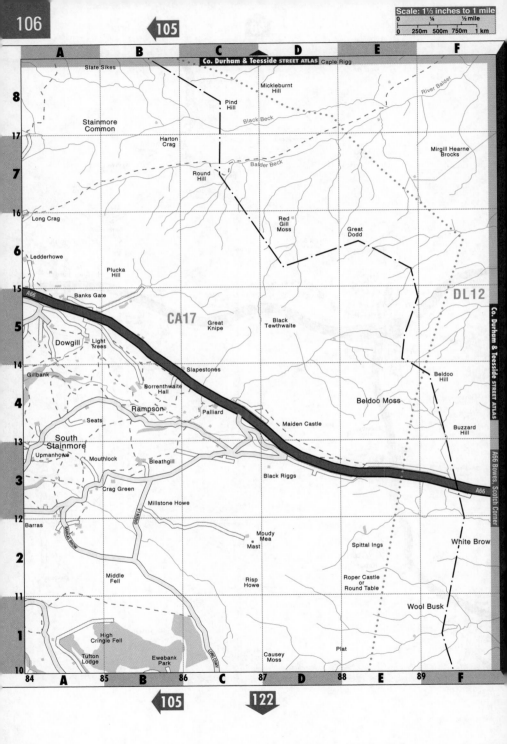

Scale: 1⅓ inches to 1 mile

¼ ½ mile
250m 500m 750m 1 km

For full street detail of the
highlighted area see page 189.

91

108

108

Ghyll Farm

B5345

BLACK LING
COTTS

QUEEN DR

Coneyside
Farm

189

Snellings

B5345

Coulderton

CA22

Middletown

189

Nethertown

LAKELAND
VIEW

Nethertown

Cumbria Coastal Way

CA21

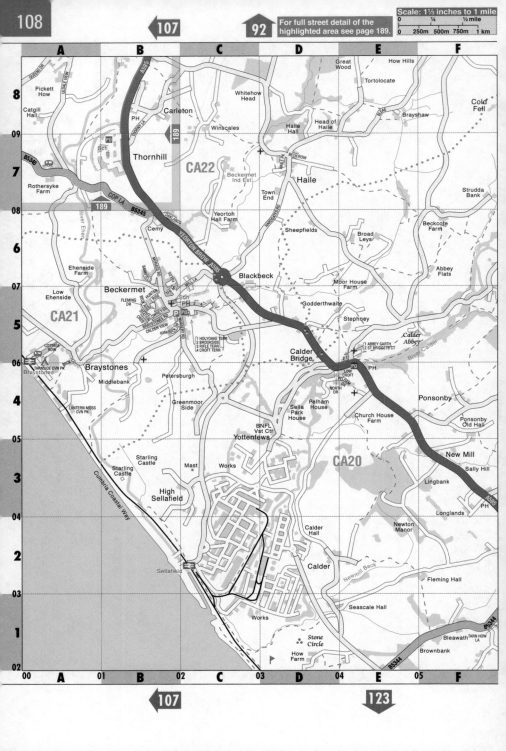

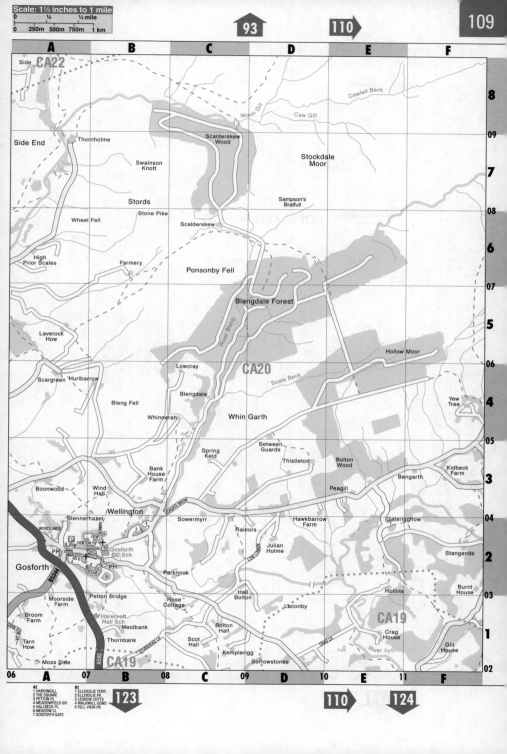

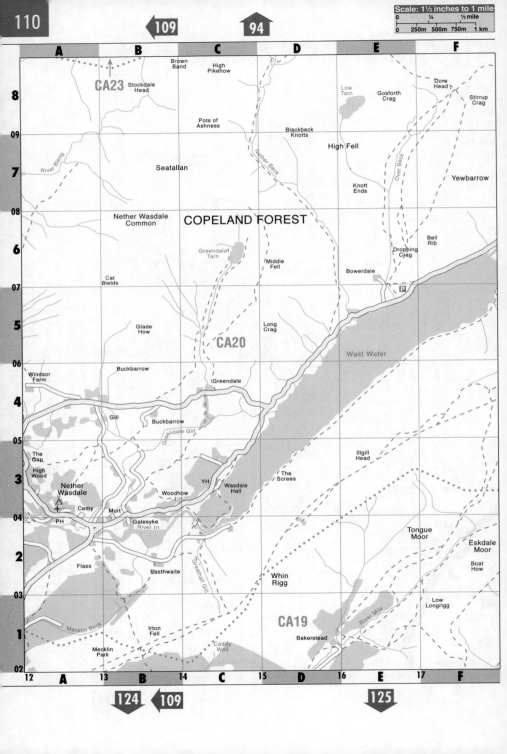

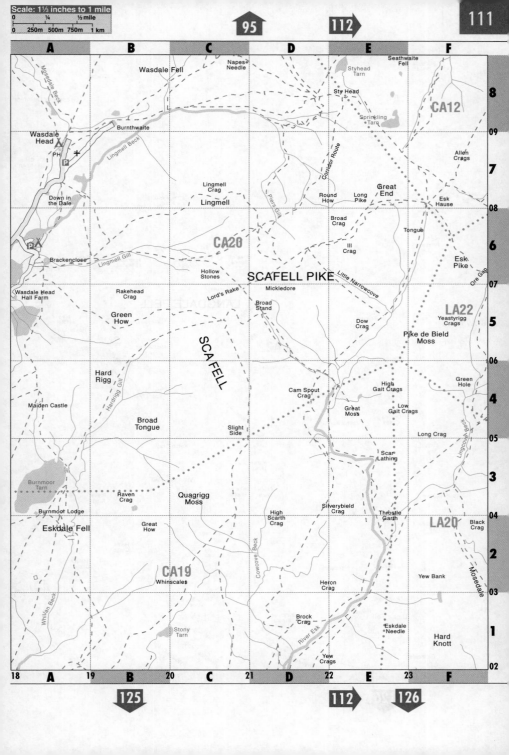

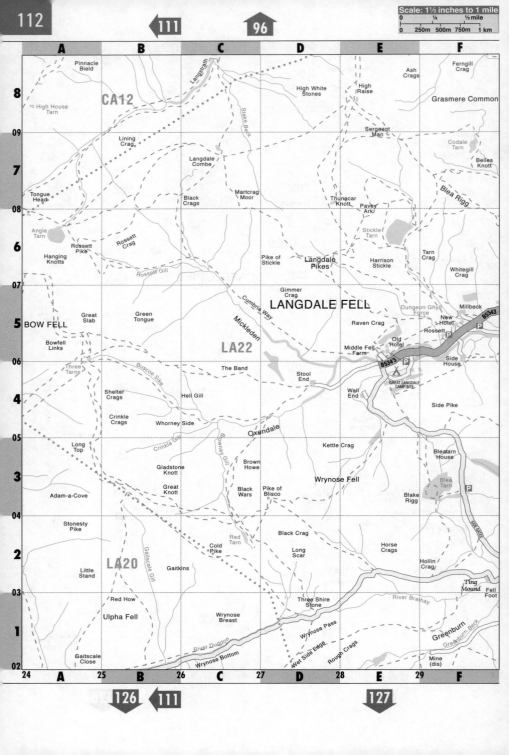

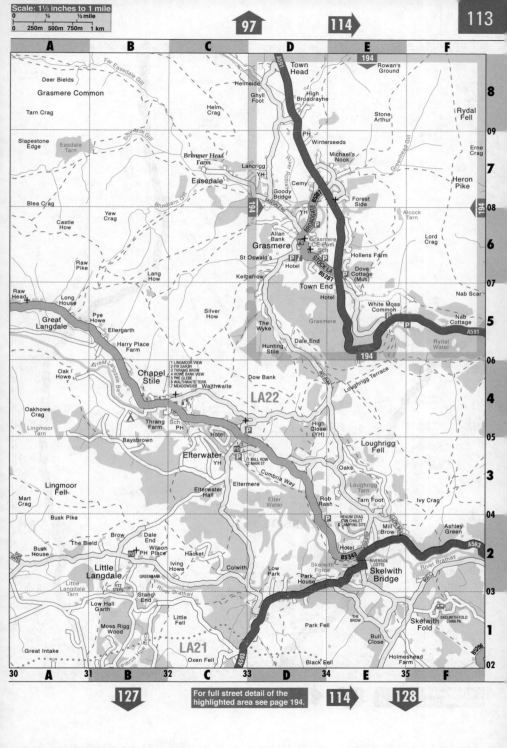

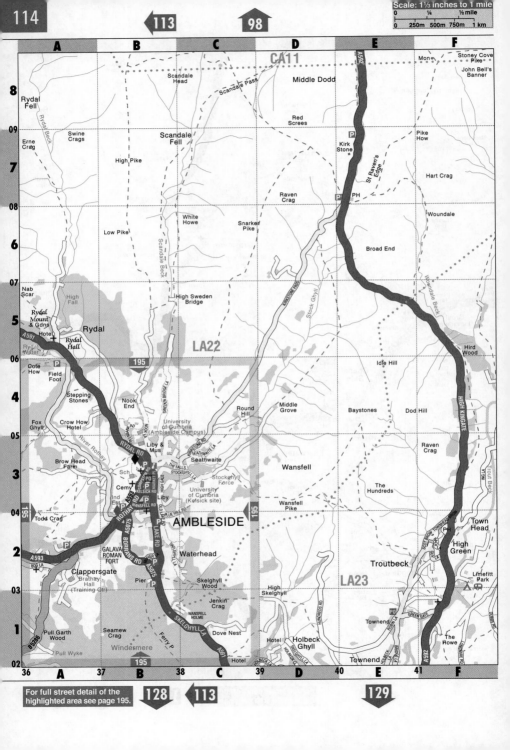

Scale: 1⅓ inches to 1 mile
0   ¼   ½ mile
0   250m 500m 750m 1 km

A   B   C   D   E   F

CA11
Mon →   Stoney Cove Pike
Scandale Head   John Bell's Banner
Middle Dodd

8
Rydal Fell   Scandale Pass
Rydal Beck

09
Erne Crag   Swine Crags   Scandale Fell   Red Screes   Pike How

Kirk Stone

7
High Pike   St Raven's Edge   Hart Crag

08
White Howe   Raven Crag   PH   Woundale
Snarker Pike

6
Low Pike   Broad End

Scandale Beck

07
Nab Scar   High Fall   High Sweden Bridge   Stock Ghyll   Woundale Beck

5
Rydal Mount & Gdns   Rydal   LA22   Hird Wood
A591   Hotel   Rydal Hall
Rydal Water

06
Cote How   Field Foot   195   Idle Hill   HIGH KINGATE

4
Stepping Stones   Nook End   Round Hill   Middle Grove   Baystones   Dod Hill
Fox Ghyll   Crow How Hotel   University of Cumbria (Ambleside Campus)   Raven Crag
River Rothay

05
Brow Head Farm   Liby & Mus   Seathwaite   Wansfell
RYDAL RD

3
Sch   THE FALLS   STOCKGHYLL LA   Stockghyll Force
Cemy   Liby   University of Cumbria (Kelsick site)   The Hundreds
Ind Est

04
Todd Crag   AMBLESIDE   Wansfell Pike   Town Head   PH
ROTHAY RD   A5075   195   High Green
BORRANS RD   LAKE RD

2
A593   GALAVA ROMAN FORT   Waterhead   Troutbeck   Limefitt Park
BOP LA   SCOT BROW

03
Clappersgate   Pier   Skelghyll Wood   LA23   High Skelghyll
Brathay Hall (Training Ctr)   Jenkin Crag

1
Pull Garth Wood   Seamew Crag   WANSFELL HOLME   Dove Nest   Townend   PO   The Howe
B5286   SKELGHYLL LA   Hotel   Holbeck Ghyll   GREEN GATE
Pull Wyke   Ferry P   Hotel   Townend   A592
Windermere

02
A   B   C   D   E   F
36   37   38   39   40   41
195

For full street detail of the highlighted area see page 195.

↓ 128   ← 113   ↓ 129

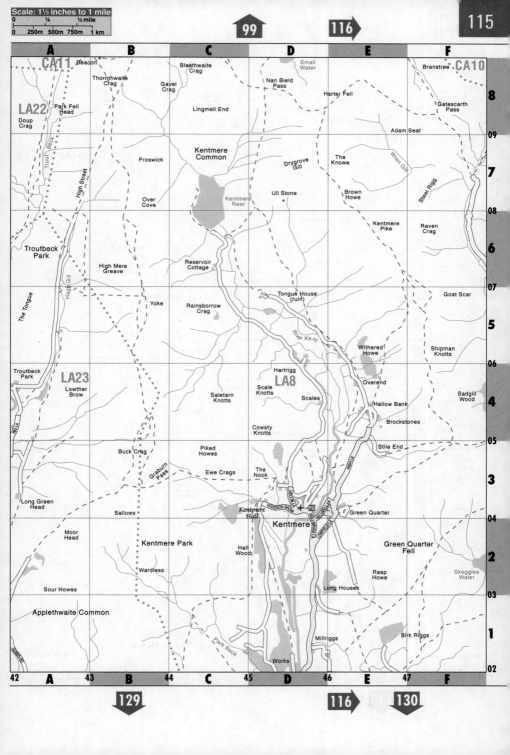

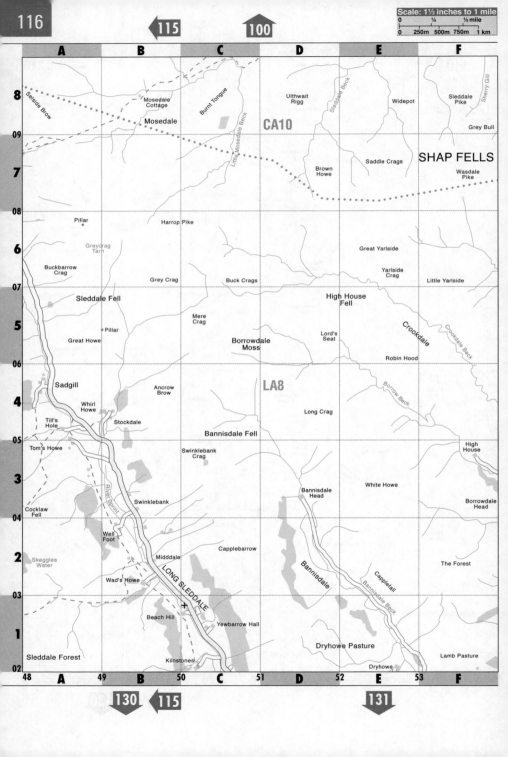

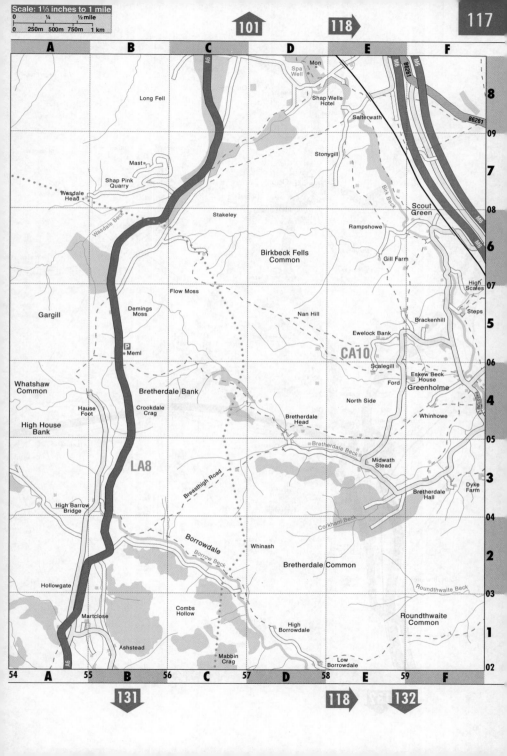

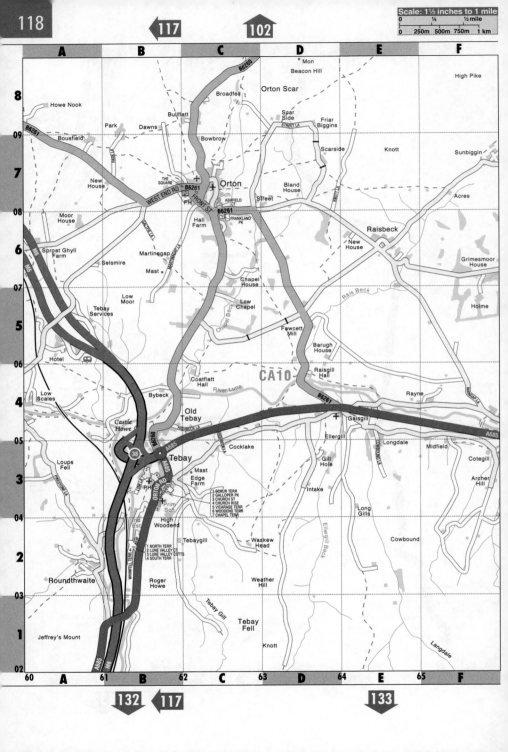

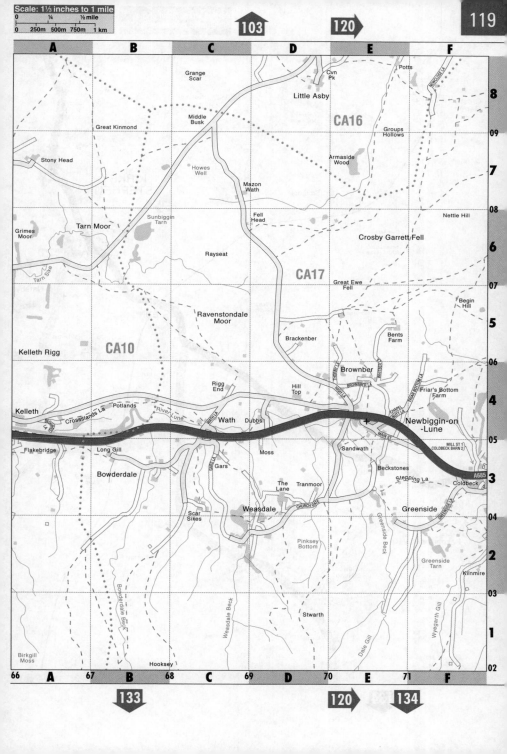

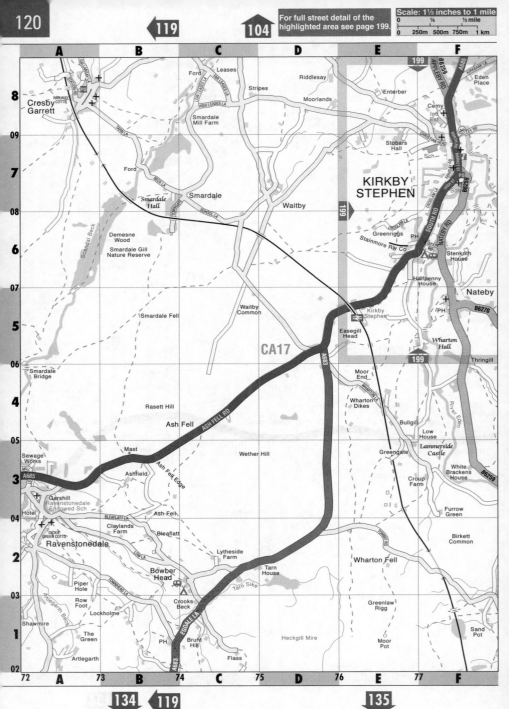

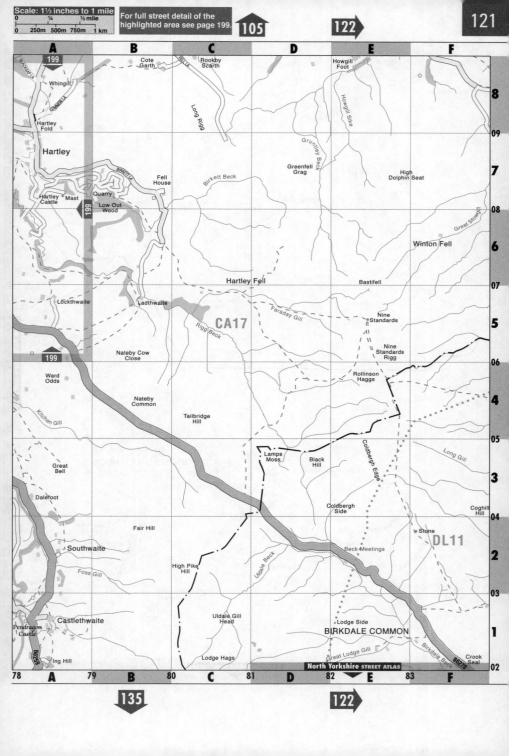

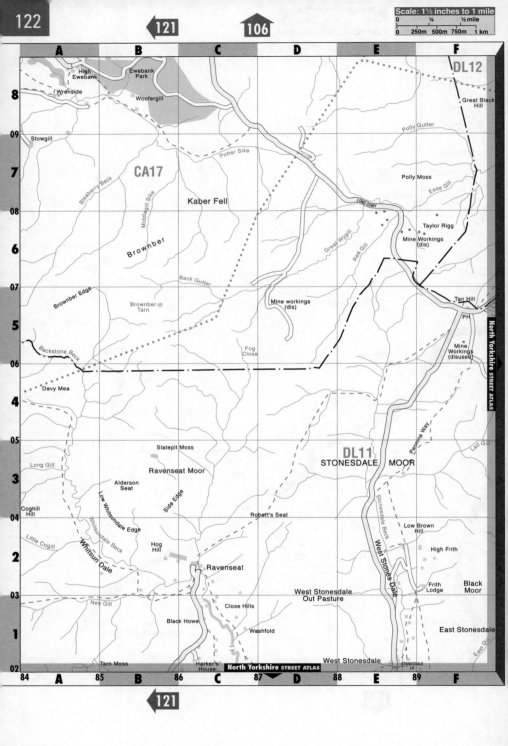

121

106

Scale: 1⅓ inches to 1 mile

0   ¼   ½ mile
0   250m 500m 750m   1 km

DL12

8

High Ewebank

Ewebank Park

Wrenside

Woofergill

Great Black Hill

09

Stowgill

Polly Gutter

7

CA17

Kaber Fell

Bleaberry Beck

Middlagill Sike

Potter Sike

Polly Moss

Ease Gill

08

Brownber

Long Cswy

Taylor Rigg

Mine Workings (dis)

6

Great Wygill

Rea Gill

07

Brownber Edge

Back Gutter

Brownber Tarn

Mine workings (dis)

Tan Hill

PH

5

Backstone Beck

Fog Close

Mine Workings (disused)

06

Davy Mea

4

05

Long Gill

Slatepit Moss

Ravenseat Moor

DL11
STONESDALE   MOOR

Lad Gill

Pennine Way

3

Alderson Seat

Low Whitsundale Edge

Side Edge

Stonesdale Beck

04

Coghill Hill

Whitsundale Beck

Robert's Seat

Low Brown Hill

Little Cogill

High Frith

2

Whitsun Dale

Hog Hill

Ravenseat

West Stonesdale

Frith Lodge

Black Moor

03

Ney Gill

Close Hills

West Stonesdale Out Pasture

1

Black Howe

Washfold

East Stonesdale

East Gill

02

Tarn Moss

Harker's House

West Stonesdale

STONESDALE LA

84   A   85   B   86   C   87   D   88   E   89   F

121

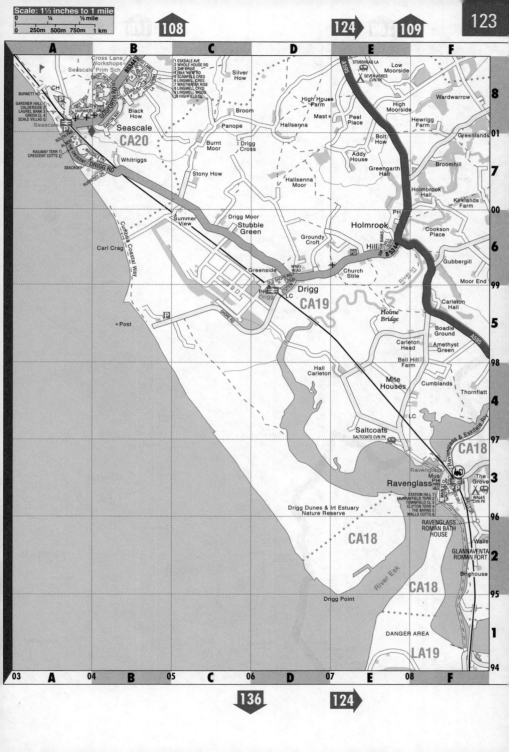

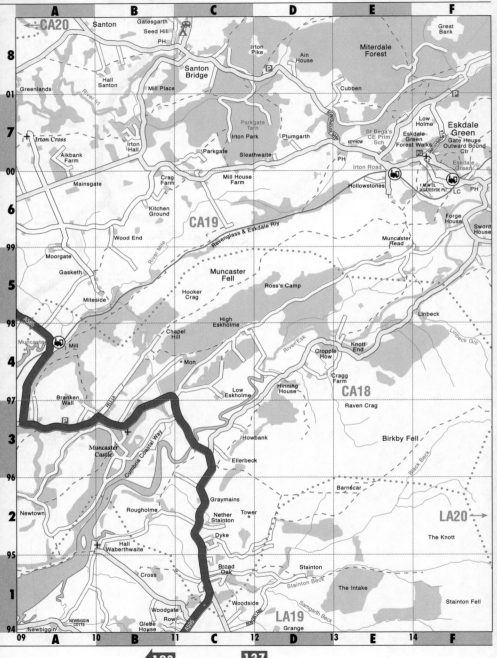

124

109 ← 123

110 →

Scale: 1⅓ inches to 1 mile
0   ¼   ½ mile
0 250m 500m 750m 1 km

CA20

Santon
Gatesgarth
Seed Hill
PH

Irton
Pike

Ain
House

Miterdale
Forest

Great
Bank

8

Santon
Bridge

P

Cubben

Mill Place

01

Greenlands

Hall
Santon

Low
Holme

P

River Irt

Parkgate
Tarn

St Bega's
CE Prim
Sch

Eskdale
Green

7

Irton Cross

Irton
Hall

Irton Park

Parkgate

Plumgarth

KEYHOW

Eskdale
Green
Forest Walks

Gate House
Outward Bound
Ctr

Aikbank
Farm

Sleathwaite

PH

Eskdale
Green

00

Mainsgate

Crag
Farm

Mill House
Farm

Irton Road

Hollowstones

1 NEW CL
2 GATESYDE PL

LC

PH

6

Kitchen
Ground

CA19

Forge
House

Sword
House

Wood End

Ravenglass & Eskdale Rly

Muncaster
Head

99

Moorgate

River Mite

Muncaster
Fell

Linbeck

Gasketh

Hooker
Crag

Ross's Camp

Linbeck Gill

5

Miteside

High
Eskholme

98

Chapel
Hill

River Esk

Knott
End

Muncaster

Mill

Mon

Cropple
How

Cragg
Farm

CA18

4

Branken
Wall

River Esk

Low
Eskholme

Hinning
House

Raven Crag

97

P

Howbank

Birkby Fell

Black Beck

3

Muncaster
Castle

Cumbria Coastal Way

Ellerbeck

96

Barnscar

Newtown

Rougholme

Graymains

Tower

LA20 →

2

Nether
Stainton

The Knott

Dyke

Hall
Waberthwaite

95

Broad
Oak

Stainton

The Intake

Stainton Fell

Cross

Stainton Beck

1

Woodgate
Row

Woodside

LA19

Samgarth Beck

Stainton Fell

NEWBIGGIN
COTTS

Glebe
House

Grange

94

Newbiggin

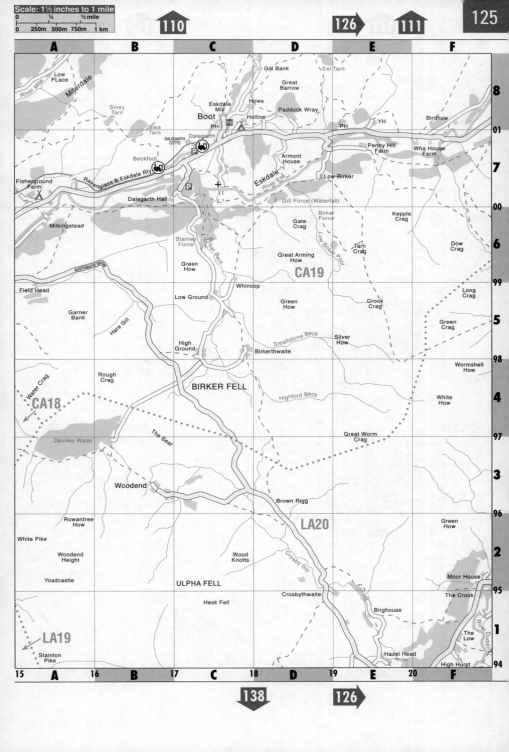

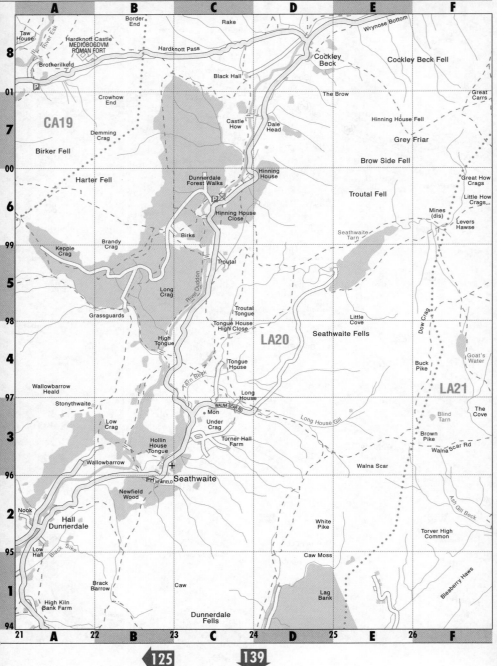

Scale: 1⅓ inches to 1 mile

0   ¼   ½ mile
0   250m 500m 750m 1 km

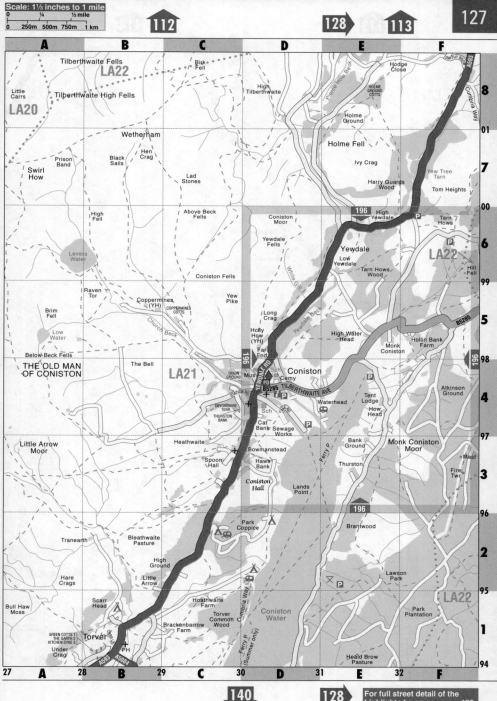

Scale: 1½ inches to 1 mile

0   ¼   ½ mile

0   250m   500m   750m   1 km

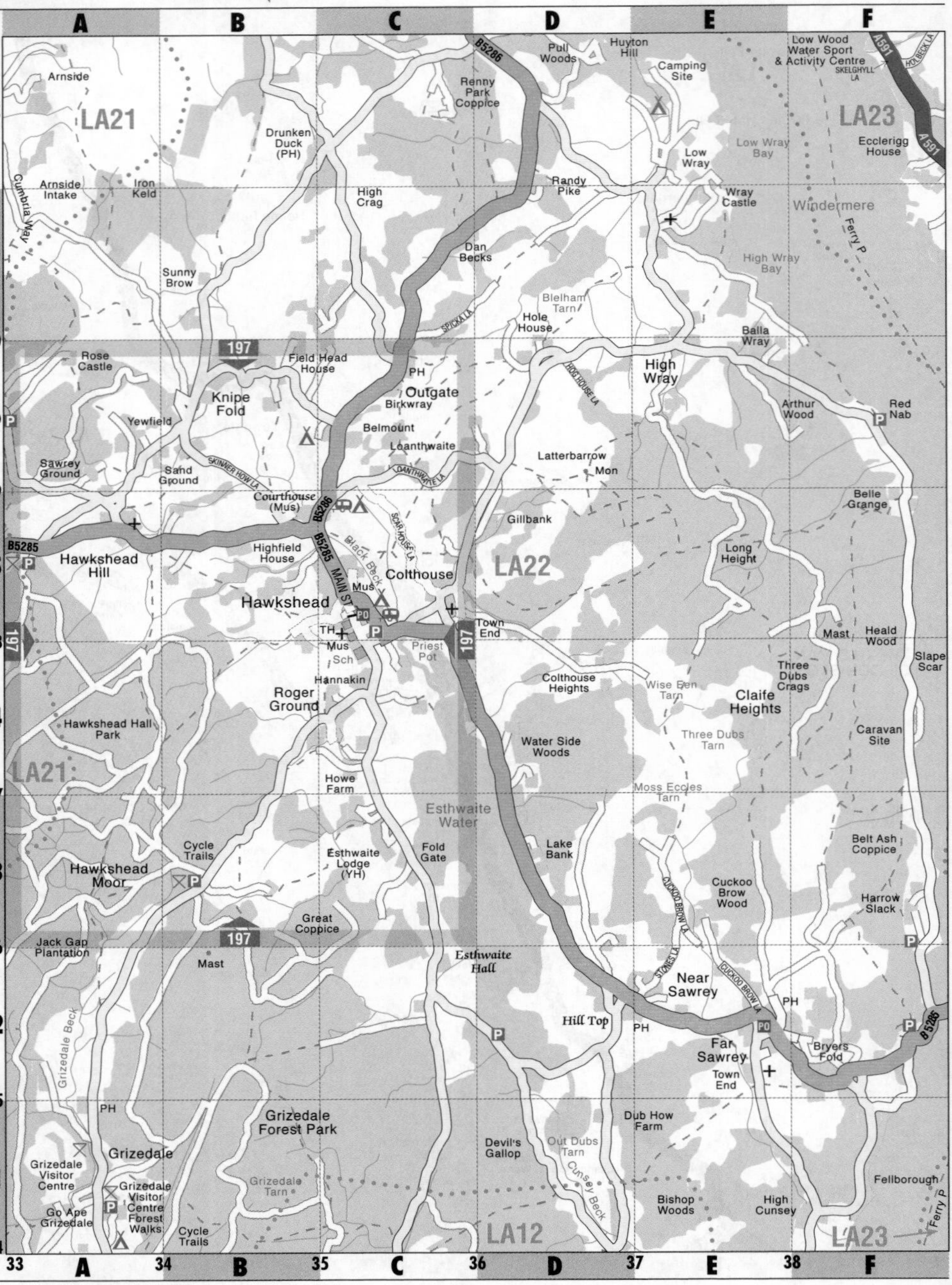

A   B   C   D   E   F

8

Arnside

LA21

Drunken Duck (PH)

Renny Park Coppice

Pull Woods

Huyton Hill

Camping Site

Low Wood Water Sport & Activity Centre
SKELGHYLL LA

LA23

Ecclerigg House

01

Arnside Intake

Iron Keld

High Crag

Randy Pike

Low Wray

Low Wray Bay

Wray Castle

Cumbria Way

7

Sunny Brow

Dan Becks

SPICE LA

High Wray Bay

Windermere

00

Bleiham Tarn

Hole House

Balla Wray

Rose Castle

Field Head House

PH

Outgate

High Wray

6

P

Knipe Fold

Yewfield

Birkwray

Belmount

Loanthwaite

LOANTHWAITE LA

PORT HOUSE LA

Latterbarrow
Mon

Arthur Wood

Red Nab

P

Sawrey Ground

Sand Ground

SKINNER HOWE LA

Courthouse (Mus)

Long Height

Belle Grange

99

Highfield House

SCAR HOUSE LA

Black Beck

Gillbank

LA22

B5285

Hawkshead Hill

MAIN ST

B5285

Colthouse

Heald Wood

Mast

Slape Scar

5

B5285

P

Hawkshead

Mus

TH
Mus
Sch

P20

Town End

Priest Pot

197

Colthouse Heights

Wise Een Tarn

Three Dubs Crags

Claife Heights

Caravan Site

98

197

P

Hannakin

Roger Ground

Water Side Woods

Three Dubs Tarn

4

Hawkshead Hall Park

Howe Farm

Moss Eccles Tarn

Belt Ash Coppice

LA21

97

Esthwaite Water

Lake Bank

Cuckoo Brow Wood

Harrow Slack

3

Hawkshead Moor

Cycle Trails

P

Esthwaite Lodge (YH)

Fold Gate

CUCKOO BROW LA

P

Jack Gap Plantation

Great Coppice

197

Esthwaite Hall

STONY LA

Near Sawrey

PH

96

Mast

Hill Top

PH

Far Sawrey

P20

Bryers Fold

B5285

2

P

P

Grizedale Beck

Town End

95

PH

Dub How Farm

1

Grizedale Visitor Centre

Grizedale

Grizedale Forest Park

Grizedale Tarn

Devil's Gallop

Out Dubs Tarn

Cunsey Beck

Bishop Woods

High Cunsey

Fellborough

Ferry P

Go Ape Grizedale

Grizedale Visitor Centre Forest Walks

Cycle Trails

LA12

LA23

94

33   A   34   B   35   C   36   D   37   E   38   F

For full street detail of the highlighted area see page 197.

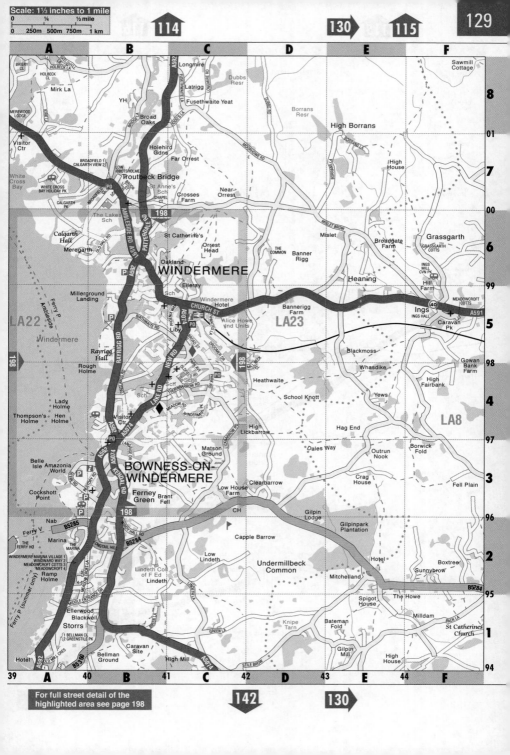

115 129 116
Scale: 1⅓ inches to 1 mile
0 ¼ ½ mile
0 250m 500m 750m 1 km

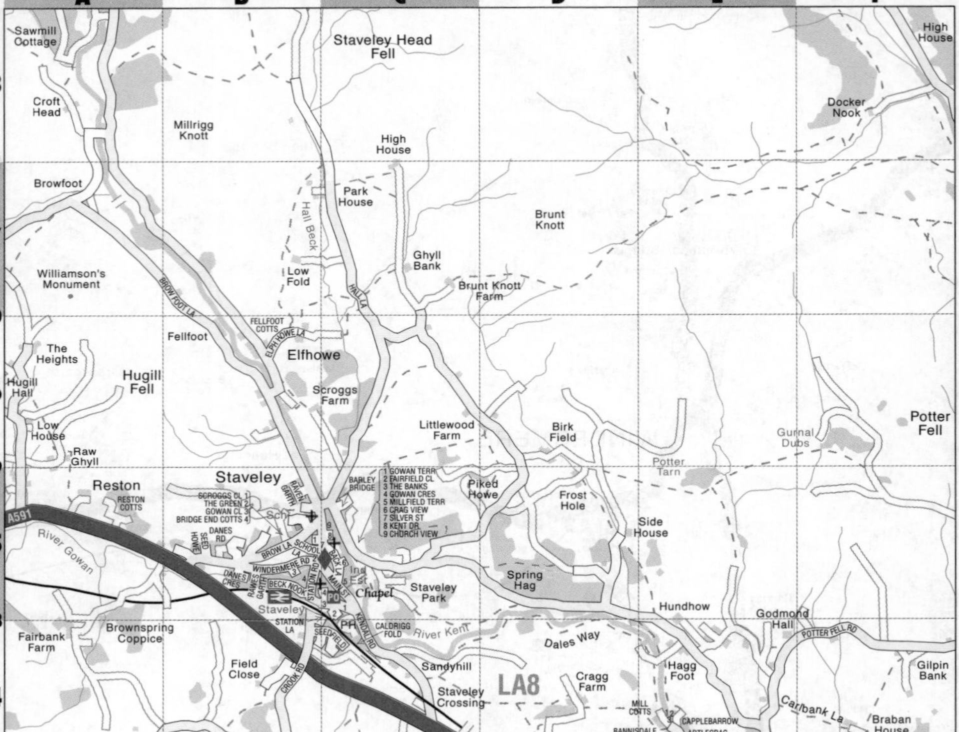

A B C D E F
8 01 7 00 6 99 5 98 4 97 3 96 2 95 1 94
45 46 47 48 49 50
Sawmill Cottage
Staveley Head Fell
High House
Croft Head
Millrigg Knott
Docker Nook
High House
Browfoot
Park House
Hall Beck
Brunt Knott
Ghyll Bank
Williamson's Monument
Low Fold
Brunt Knott Farm
BROW FOOT LA
HALL LA
FELLFOOT COTTS
ELPH HOWE LA
Fellfoot
Elfhowe
The Heights
Hugill Hall
Hugill Fell
Scroggs Farm
Low House
Littlewood Farm
Birk Field
Potter Fell
Gurnal Dubs
Raw Ghyll
Potter Tarn
Staveley
Reston
RESTON COTTS
BARLEY BRIDGE
1 GOWAN TERR
2 FAIRFIELD CL
3 THE BANKS
4 GOWAN CRES
5 MILLFIELD TERR
6 CRAG VIEW
7 SILVER ST
8 KENT DR
9 CHURCH VIEW
Piked Howe
Frost Hole
Side House
SCROGGS CL 1
THE GREEN 2
GOWAN CL 3
BRIDGE END COTTS 4
DANES RD
SEED HOWE
RAVEN GARTH
A591
River Gowan
BROW LA
SCHOOL LA
BACK LA
WINDERMERE RD
DANES CRES
RAWES GARTH
BECK NOOK
STATION RD
MAIN ST
Ind Est
Chapel
Staveley Park
Spring Hag
Hundhow
Staveley
STATION LA
SEEDFIELD
PH
KENDAL RD
CALDRIGG FOLD
River Kent
Dales Way
Godmond Hall
POTTER FELL RD
Fairbank Farm
Brownspring Coppice
Field Close
CROOK RD
Sandyhill
LA8
Cragg Farm
Hagg Foot
Gilpin Bank
Staveley Crossing
MILL COTTS
BANNISDALE
CAPPLEBARROW
ARTLECRAG
Carlbank La
Braban House
Laithwaite Farm
Cowan Head
1 FALCON CRAG
2 GREATHOWE
3 DOCKERNOOK
New Hall
ASHES LA
Ashes
Broadfold
Plantation Bridge
Bowston
WINTER LA
WINSTANLEY PL
KENT CL
MEADOW CL
The Glen
ASHES LA
Fell Plain
Waingap
ASHES LA
Rather Heath
Burneside
Hollin Hall
Garnett House
LC
HOLME HOUSES
Mill
ROGER ROW
Crook End
Tarn Close
SHARPS LA
Burneside
Barn Farm
RATHERHEATH LA
Brow Foot
GOWAN LEA
ELLERGREEN
HOLLINS ROW
Beckside
Yew Tree Farm
RATHERHEATH LANE CAMPING & CVN SITE
Oakbank
Moss Side
Tolson Hall
Crook
Bonning Gate
HOLLINS LA
Hollins
SPRINT HOLME
STEELE'S ROW 1
CHARLES CT 2
IVY CRES 3
HOWGILL HOUSES 4
HOWGILL CL 5
BOURNEVILLE 6
B5284
CROOK BROW
PH
POUND FARM CVN PK
HIGH BRUNDRIGG
Bannel Head
Mon
CROOK RD
HALHEAD BROW
CROOK RD
B5284
WINDERMERE RD
DOBBY LA
Brundrigg
Toadpool
LA9
Ellerbeck Farm
Halhead Hall
Plumgarths
Crook Hall
CAPPLERIGG LA
Madgegill
A5284
Capplerigg
Fell Gate
Cunswick Scar
200
Crag
Ash Spring
A591
Lane Foot
DOLHOLME HILL

129 143
For full street detail of the highlighted area see page 200.

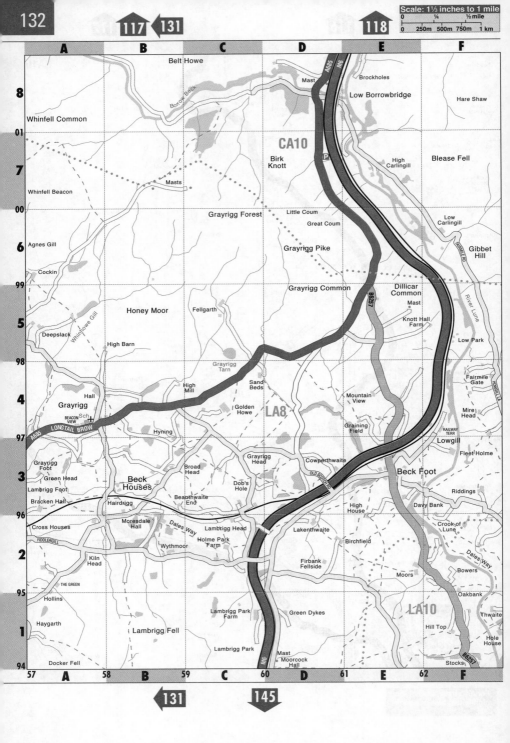

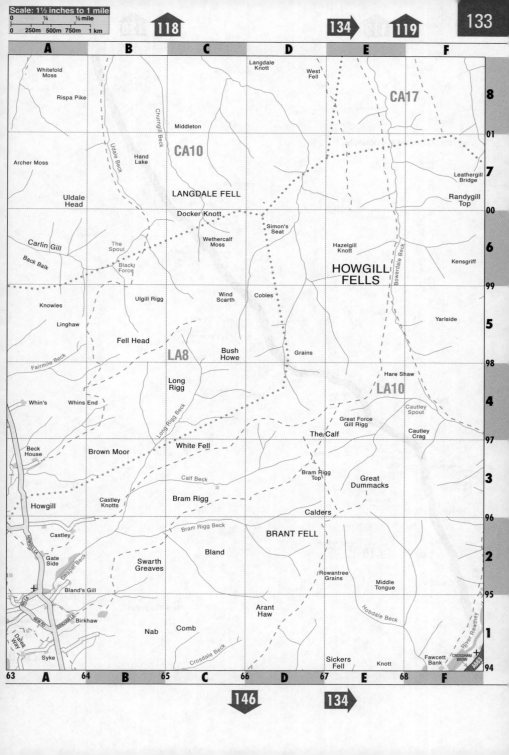

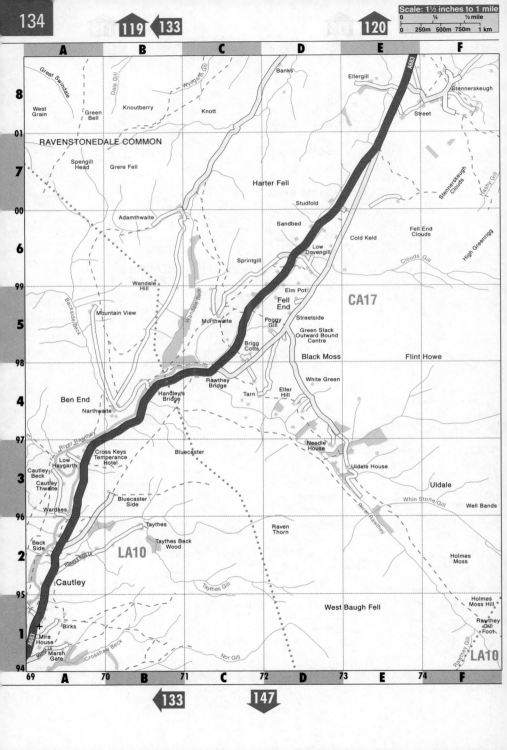

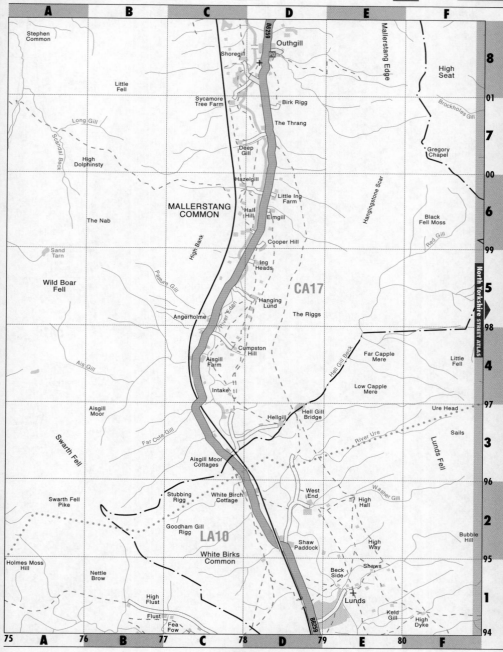

A   B   C   D   E   F

Stephen
Common

Little
Fell

Outhgill

Shoregill

Mallerstang Edge

High
Seat

Brockholes Gill

Long Gill

Sycamore
Tree Farm

Birk Rigg

The Thrang

Gregory
Chapel

Scandal Beck

High
Dolphinsty

Deep
Gill

Hazelgill

Hanginstone Scar

Black
Fell Moss

Red Gill

MALLERSTANG
COMMON

Little Ing
Farm

Hall
Hill   Elmgill

The Nab

High Bank

Cooper Hill

Sand
Tarn

Ing
Heads

Pasture Gill

CA17

Wild Boar
Fell

North Yorkshire STREET ATLAS

Hanging
Lund

The Riggs

Angerholme

River Eden

Cumpston
Hill

Aisgill
Farm

Far Capple
Mere

Little
Fell

Ais Gill

Intake

Low Capple
Mere

Aisgill
Moor

Hellgill

Hell Gill
Bridge

Hell Gill Beck

Ure Head

Sails

Swarth Fell

Far Cote Gill

River Ure

Lunds Fell

Aisgill Moor
Cottages

Swarth Fell
Pike

Stubbing
Rigg

White Birch
Cottage

West
End

Washer Gill

High Hall

Bubble
Hill

Goodham Gill
Rigg

LA10

Shaw
Paddock

High
Way

Holmes Moss
Hill

White Birks
Common

Nettle
Brow

Beck
Side

Shaws

Keld
Gill

High
Dyke

High
Flust

Flust

Fea
Fow

Lunds

75   A   76   B   77   C   78   D   79   E   80   F

123

Scale: 1½ inches to 1 mile

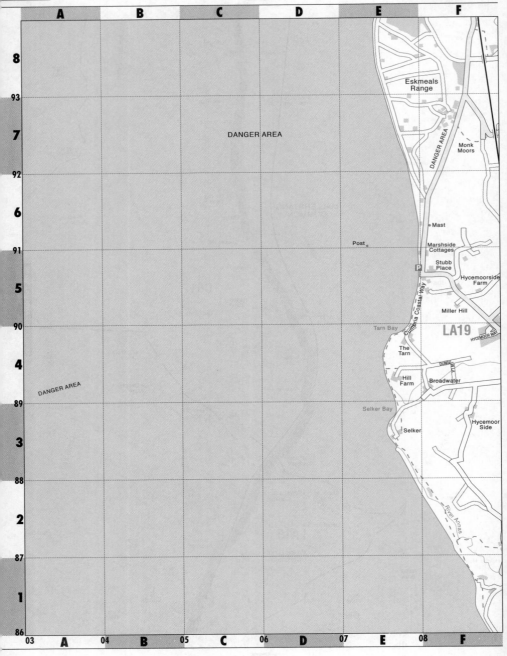

DANGER AREA

Eskmeals
Range

DANGER AREA

Monk
Moors

Mast

Post

Marshside
Cottages

Stubb
Place

Hycemoorside
Farm

Cumbria Coastal Way

Miller Hill

Tarn Bay

LA19

HYCEMOOR WAY

The
Tarn

DUNGA...

DANGER AREA

Hill
Farm

Broadwater

Selker Bay

Hycemoor
Side

Selker

River Annas

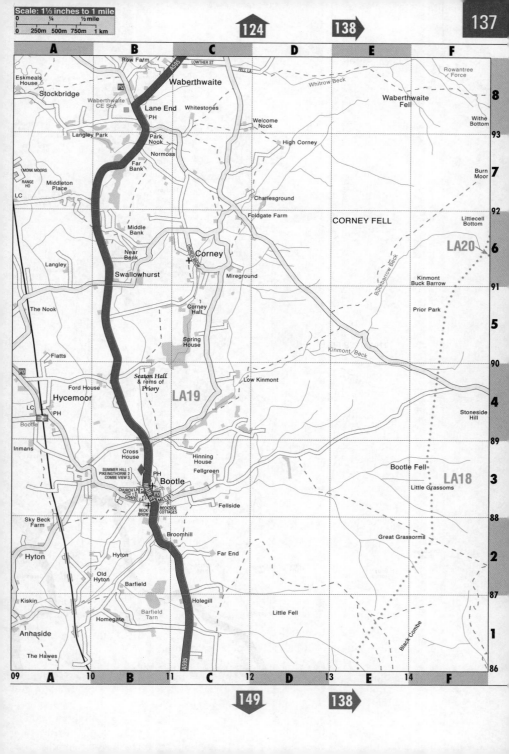

A **B** **C** **D** **E** **F**

LA19

Storthes

Holehouse Gill

Fox Crags

8

Baskell Farm

The Pike

Ulpha

Dunnerdale

Pike Side

GUNSON COTTS

Whitfell

Hole House

Church House

Birks Wood

Stickle Pike

93

Rainsbarrow Wood

Birks

Yew Pike

Bigert Mire

Whistling Green

7

BOBBIN MILL LA

Sella

BELL BROW

Dunnerdale Fells

Millbrow

Long-Garth

92

Sele Bottom

Low Cragnall

P

Booth Holme

Plough Fell

Frith Hall

6

Folds

Ulpha Park

Stonestar

91

Buck Barrow

LA20

River Duddon

Pickthall Ground

Logan Beck

Penn

5

Loganbeck

Whineray Ground

Hutton

THWAITES FELL

Beckstones

Beckfoot

90

Duddon Hall

Mere Crags

4

Rawfold

Fenwick

Lower Bleansley

Windy Slack

Low Moss

89

Thwaite Yeat

Bank End

LA18

TAL CANNING

3

Swinsdale Fell

Swinside

Duddon Bridge

SMITHY BROW

88

Boadhole

Stoupdale Crags

Ash House

Greenslack

2

Gray Stones

Knott Hill

Cragg Hall

Graystone House

Holme

HIGH CROSS BROW

A595

Black Beck

BUCKMAN BROW

Cumbria Coastal Way

PH

CHURCH

A595

87

Broadgate

Hazel Mount

Low Boghouse Cott

LADY HALLA

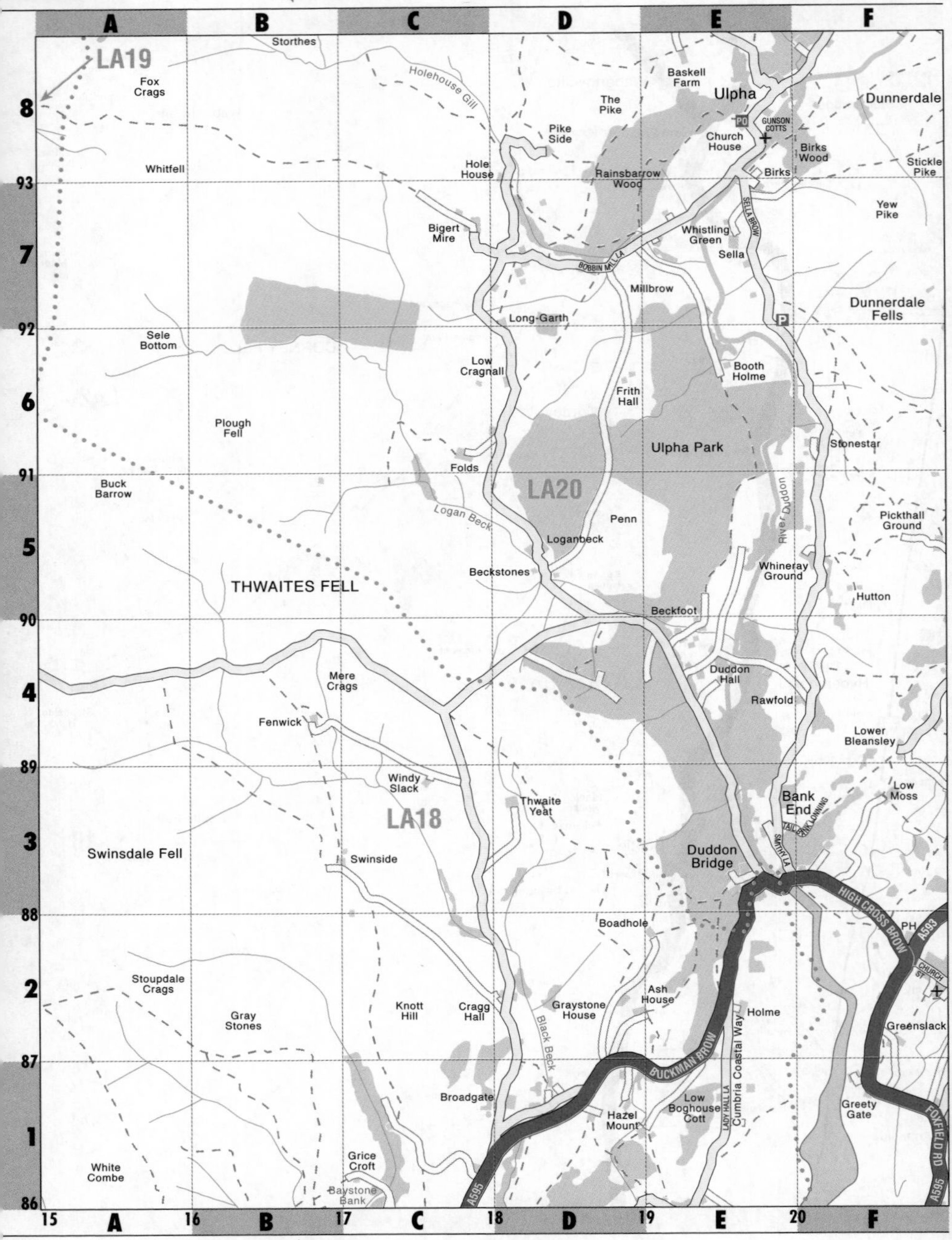

Greety Gate

FOXFIELD RD

1

White Combe

Grice Croft

Greenslack

Baystone Bank

86

15 **A** **16** **B** **17** **C** **18** **D** **19** **E** **20** **F**

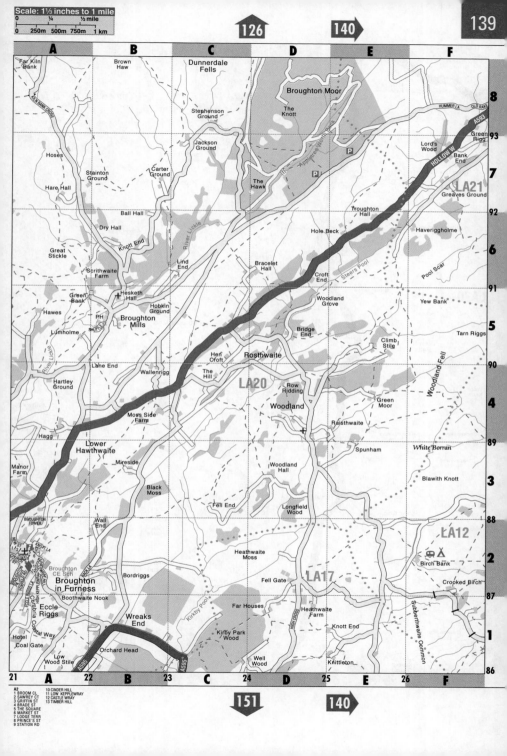

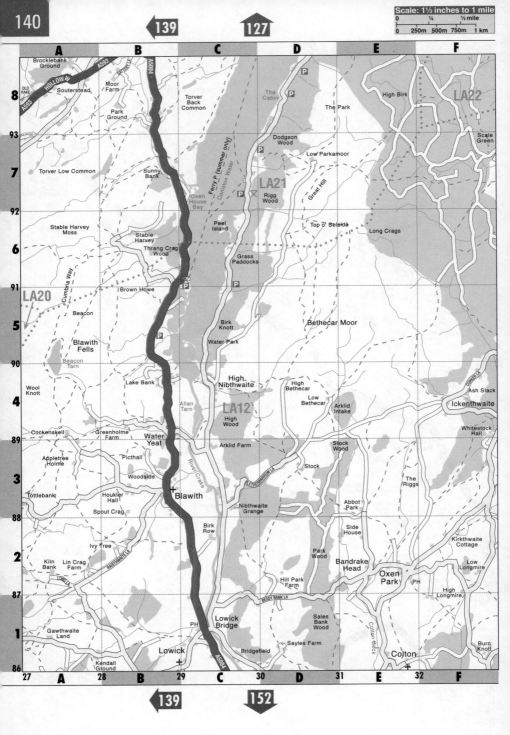

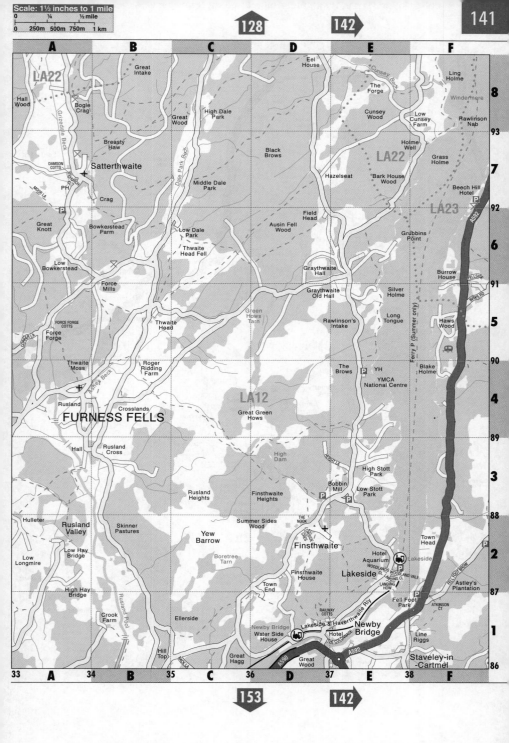

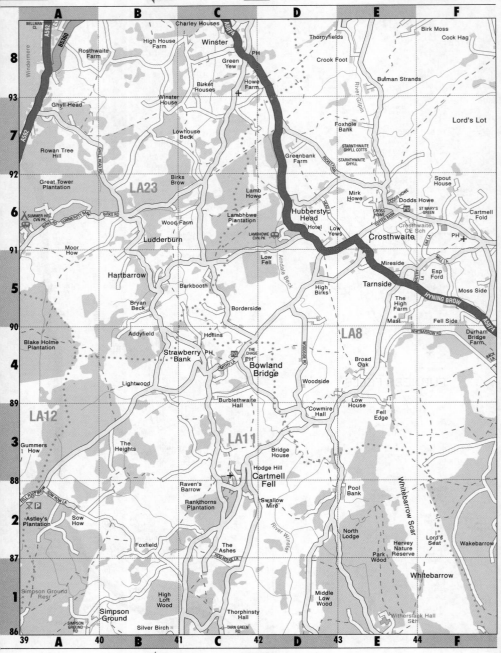

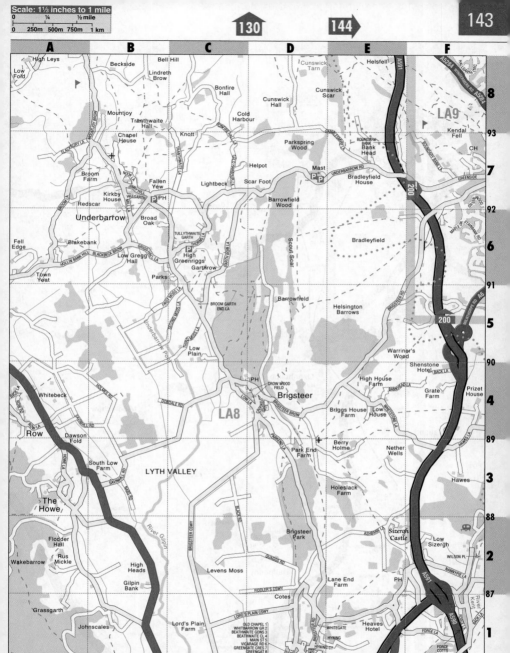

Scale: 1⅓ inches to 1 mile

0   ¼   ½ mile
0 250m 500m 750m 1 km

130
144

High Leys
Low Fold
Beckside
Bell Hill
Lindreth Brow
Bonfire Hall
Cunswick Tarn
Helsfell
LA9
Kendal Fell
CH

Mountjoy
Tramthwaite Hall
Cold Harbour
Cunswick Hall
Cunswick Scar
Chapel House
Knott
Parkspring Wood
BOUNDARY BANK LA
Bank Head

Broom Farm
Fallen Yew
Helpot
Mast
Bradleyfield House
GREENSIDE

Kirkby House
Lightbeck
Scar Foot
Redscar
PH
Barrowfield Wood

Underbarrow
Broad Oak
TULLYTHWAITE GARTH
Bradleyfield

Fell Edge
Blakebank
High Greenriggs
Garthrow
Scout Scar

Town Yeat
Low Gregg Hall
Parks
Barrowfield

Broom Garth End La
Helsington Barrows

Underbarrow Pool
Low Plain
200

Whitebeck
Warriner's Wood
Shenstone Hotel
BACK LA

Row
Dawson Fold
PH
Crow Wood Field
Brigsteer
High House Farm
Grate Farm
Prizet House

LA8
BRIGSTEER BROW
Briggs House Farm
Low House

South Low Farm
Park End Farm
Berry Holme
Nether Wells
Hawes

LYTH VALLEY
Holeslack Farm

The Howe
River Gilpin
BRIGSTEER CSWY
Brigsteer Park
Sizergh Castle
Low Sizergh
WILSON PL

Flodder Hall
Rus Mickle
BLACK RD
DUGGLE RD
Levens Moss
Lane End Farm
PH
Heaves Hotel

Wakebarrow
High Heads
Cotes
FORCE LA
FORCE COTTS

Grassgarth
FIDDLER'S CSWY
LORD'S PLAIN CSWY

Johnscales
Lord's Plain Farm
OLD CHAPEL 1
WHITBARROW GR 2
BEATHWAITE GDNS 3
BEATHWAITE CL 4
MAIN ST 5
VICARAGE RD 6
GREENGATE CRES 7
THE GREEN 8
OAKWOOD CL 10
NETHERCROFT 11
WHITEGATE
HYNING
HYNING CT
Levens

Rawsons
Gilpin Cottage

For full street detail of the highlighted area see page 200.

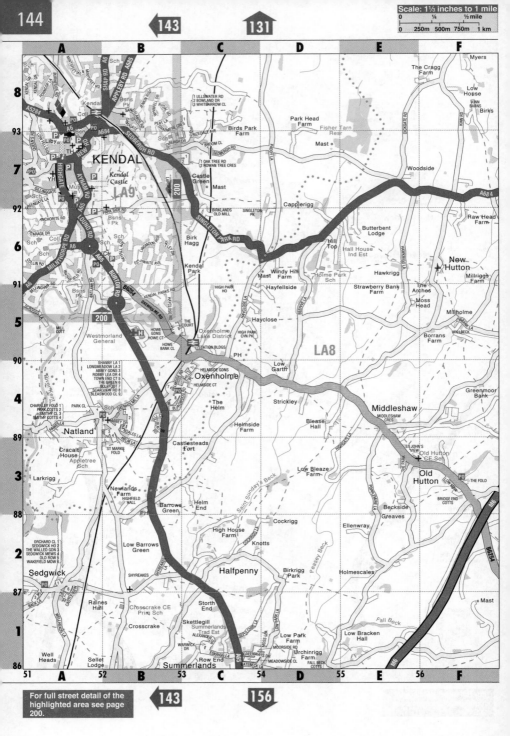

143
131

Scale: 1½ inches to 1 mile

0   ¼   ½ mile
0 250m 500m 750m 1 km

A   **B**   **C**   **D**   **E**   **F**

8

93

7

KENDAL

Kendal
Castle

LA9

92

6

91

Birk
Hagg

Kendal
Park

5

200

Westmorland
General

Oxenholme
Lake District

STATION BLDGS

PH

LA8

90

Oxenholme

4

The
Helm

Strickley

Middleshaw

Helmside
Farm

Bleaze
Hall

89

Natland

Cracalt
House   Appletree
Sch

Castlesteads
Fort

Low Bleaze
Farm

Old Hutton
CE Sch

3

Larkrigg

Newlands
Farm   HIGHFIELD
HALL

Old
Hutton

THE FOLD

Barrows
Green

Helm
End

Beckside
Greaves

88

Low Barrows
Green

High House
Farm

Cockrigg

Ellenwray

BRIDGE END
COTTS

2

Sedgwick

Knotts

Birkrigg
Park

Holmescales

SHYREAKES

Halfpenny

87

Raines
Hall

Crosscrake CE
Prim Sch

Storth
End

Mast

1

Crosscrake

Skettlegill
Summerlands
Trad Est
ALEXANDRA

Low Park
Farm

Urchinrigg
Farm   FALL BECK
COTTS

Low Bracken
Hall

Well
Heads

Sellet
Lodge

WARWICK
DR

Row End

86

Summerlands

A 51 **B** 52 **C** 53 **D** 54 **E** 55 **F** 56

For full street detail of the
highlighted area see page
200.

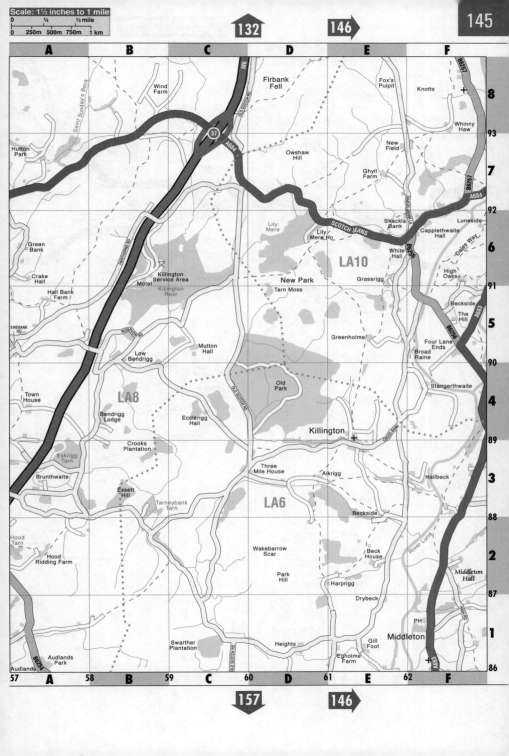

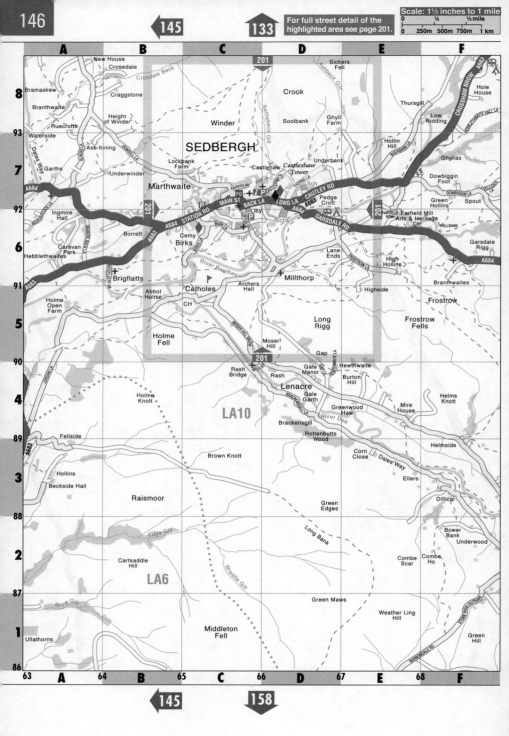

A B C D E F

CA17

Nor Gill
Caphill Moss
Far Askew Gill
West Baugh Fell Tarn
Rawhey Gill

Hebblethwaite Hall
HEBBLETHWAITE HALL LA

8

BAUGH FELL

Blake Mire

93

Haskhaw Gill

Sarthwaite

Near Gill Laids

FELL GATE LA
Fellgate
Dowbiggin

Breaskay Moss
Ringling Keld Gutter
Dry Gill

Gill Head

7

East Tarns

Tarn Hill

92

DOWBIGGIN LA

High Fawes

GARSDALE LA

Garsdale Foot

Knoutberry Haw

East Baugh Fell

6

Potgill Holme
Hole House
Hind Keld

Tarn Rigg Hill

91

Whit Beck

Bellow End
Thwaites Head

P

West Mostard

Birkrigg

Tarn Hill

Whitbeck

Bridge End East

5

GARSDALE

90

Clough River

Cowper Gill

Low House

Camp Site

Copplethwaite

LA10

Far House

P
A684

Garsdale

4

89

Rawidding La

Lunds La

Rawridding
Hining Hill

Aye Gill Pike

Rise Hill

3

Hole House

88

Mon

North Lord's Land

Wood Head Lathe

BARTH LA

Barth

Aye Gill Wold

2

Foulsyke Farm

Gawthrop

GOWLANDS CROSS
High Hall

HALL LA

Hall Bank

Guilmire

Broadmire

STONE HO OUTRAKE

Dent

Dent CE Prim Sch
PH
CE Prim Sch

Backstonegill

Scotchergill

Kirk Bank

High House

GLEBE FOLD 1
FLINTERGILL CL 2
GHYLLSIDE 3

Milt Beck

High Chapel

Cross House

Blands

Gibbs Hall

BORDER LA

P

1

South Lord's Land

Flinter Gill Outrake

DENTDALE

Garic La

Banks

Cage Farm

Coventree
Fell Garth

Dales Way

Birchen Trees

86

69 A 70 B 71 C 72 D 73 E 74 F

159 148

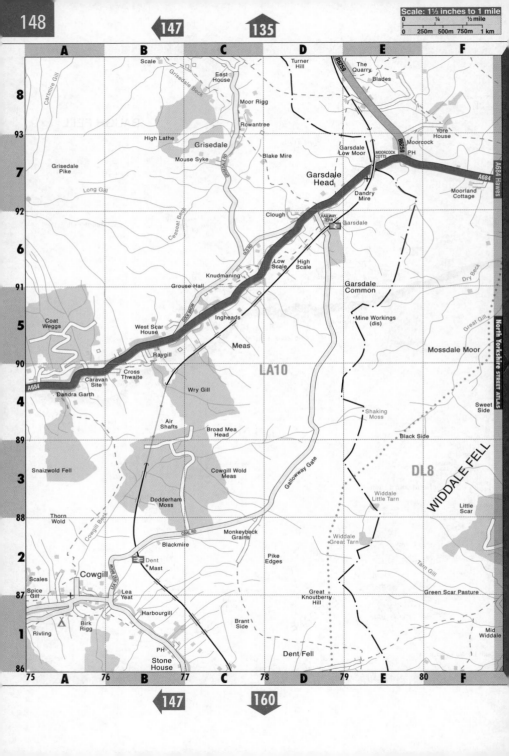

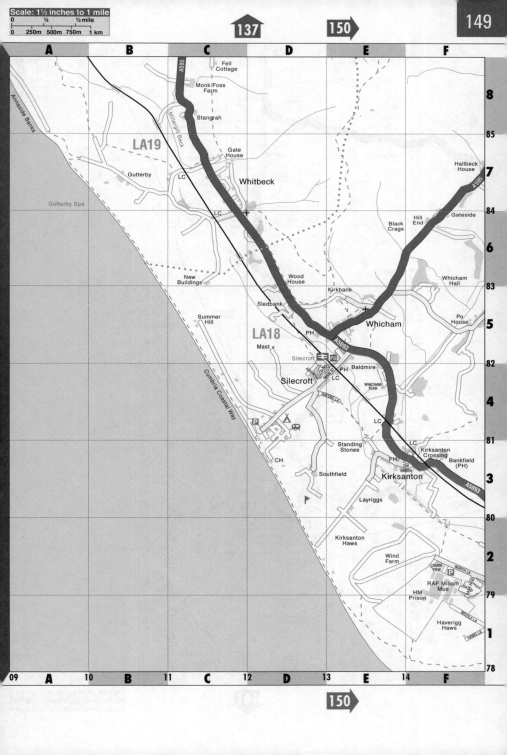

149 138

Scale: 1½ inches to 1 mile
0 ¼ ½ mile
0 250m 500m 750m 1 km

A B C D E F

8
DUDDON MEWS COTTS
Elf Hall
LADY HALL LA
CAUSEY LA
LA20
Baystone Bank Resr
Whirlpippin
Baystone Bank
Bank House
MAINS BROW A595
THWAITES BROW
ROANLANDS BROW
INGLEWOOD TERR
Foxfield
LC
PH
A595
Fore Slack
Thwaites Sch
CHAPEL BROW

85
Whicham Mill
DUBDALE BROW A595
Hallthwaites
Roanlands
Shaw Moss
Ralliss
The Oaks Farm
BECK BROW
MILL BROW
Low Shaw

7
Beckside
Chappels Farm
BROCKWOOD HALL
The Green PH
BECKSIDE
Arnaby
A595
Mire House
Dunningwell
Strands

84
Applehead
Haws House
Green Road
LC
Whicham Beck

6
Spunham
Woods
High Brow
School Ellis
HODGSON TERR
LC
Whicham Valley
Bankside
Mast

83
Park House
The Hill
LC
Millom Park
Hall Bank
Duddon Mount

5
Waterblean
Millom Marsh
High Lowscales

82
202 Burnfield
LA18
Low Scales
Low House
Cumbria Coastal Way

4
Millom Castle (remains of)

81
Beck Wood
Beck Farm
Salthouse

3
Langthwaite Farm
A5093
HUDDLESTON RD
FESTIVAL RD
Sch
WYATT HILL
BAY VIEW
HOLBORN HILL
P PO
202
HORN HILL
HIGH ST
SALTHOUSE RD
Ctr
MILLOM RD
Millom Sch
MILLOM
Ind Est
Borwick Rails Harbour
202

80
Haverigg Crossing
Haverigg Pool
GRAMMARCROFT
ALBERT ST
NEWTON ST
BURNESS ST
Libry PO
Millom Sch
DEVONSHIRE RD
YH
Duddon Villa
Oxenbows
HAVERIGG RD
LONTHERMAN RD
MAINSCALE RD
ARGYLE ST
WASDYKE RD
Ind Est

2
Fox Croft
WAINGATE BRIDGE COTTS
IONA
TARNHEAD
New Hall
Borwick Rails
Red Hills
NORTH LA
Steel Green
Cumbria Coastal Way

79
MIDDLE LA
HARRIS LA
BUTTERFLIES CVN PK
Haverigg

1
Stoup Dub
Hodbarrow Lake Nature Reserve
RB Sta
TIMBER WOOD CL
P
P
Cumbria Coast Way
P
Hodbarrow Point
LA16
DUDDON RD
P

78
Cumbria Coast Way
202

15 A 16 B 17 C 18 D 19 E 20 F

For full street detail of the highlighted area see page 202.

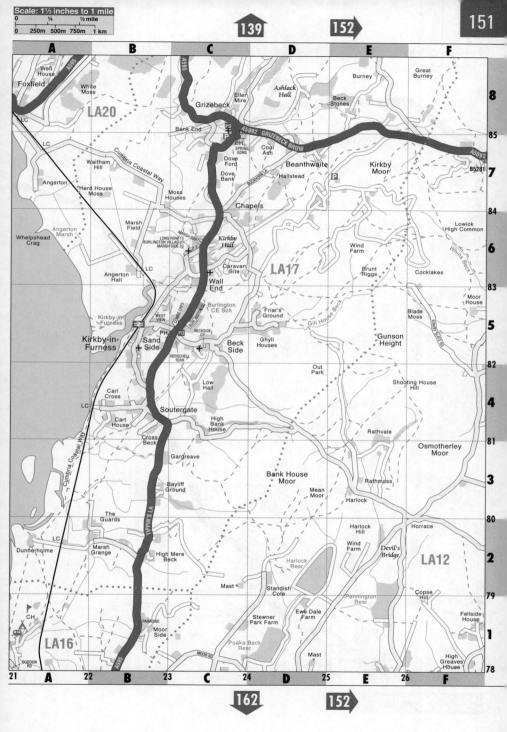

Scale: 1⅓ inches to 1 mile

0   ¼   ½ mile
0   250m 500m 750m 1 km

A   B   C   D   E   F

High Stennerley
Lowick Hall
Colton
CRAGG BROW
Bouth
PH
THE SQUARE

Low Stennerley
Moss Cottage
Ridding Side Farm
Old Hall Farm

Wood Gate
Esps Farm
Lowick Green

Stone Dykes
Lowick Common
BONBIN MILL COTTS
PH
THE ROW
Spark Bridge
CAPPY LA

Gawthwaite
LANE HEAD
CRAKE MOUNT
Thurston Ville
Lane Head
Tottlebank
Hotel
Pool Foot
A590

B5281
Keldray
Beck Bottom
Mast
A5092

Knapperthaw
Nettleslack
Stainton Gap
Summer Hill
Hill Top
Lady Syke

GROFFA CRAG
High Scathwaite
Hall
BEECH COTTS

Hawkswell
Penny Bridge
OAK VALE
PH
Legbarrow Point
A5092

Broughton Beck
BANKSIDE
ELLIS WOOD
MAIN ST
BANK TERR
Greenodd

Whins Beck
Moor House Beck
LA12
Smithy Green
HIGH GARTH
Penny Bridge CE Sch
SHERIFF WELL CL
LA12

Netherhouses
DROFT GARTH
Low Scathwaite
High Farm
THE RAKE
SHERIFF BANK

Cumbria Way
Ben Cragg
Hollin Hall
Mearness Farm

Well House
Rake
Toppin Rays
Mearness Point

Hollowmire
Mansriggs Hall
Gawith Field
Nab Point

Stony Crag
Bowstead Gates
Arrad Foot
Cumbria Coastal Way
P

Mansriggs
The Alps
Hotel
Plumpton Cottage Farm
Ashes Point

Newbiggin
Crag
Great Oath Hill

Higher Lath Farm
Beck Side
Newland Bottom
The Falls

Bortree Stile
203
Newland
Newland Beck

Gamswell
Old Hall Farm
TOWN BANK RD
ULVERSTON
Mon
Oubus Hill
203
Causeway End
Plumpton Hall
Leven Viaduct
LA11

203
Rosside
CHITTER LA
TEBAY LA
Next Ness
NEXT NESS COTTS
THE OLD BARN

Ulverston
H
Mus
CHURCH ST
B5281
The Uakes Glass Ctr
STEEL ST

Stone Cross
P
PO
Liby
Dale Street Inf Sch
Plumpton Bight

Hotel
A590

A   B   C   D   E   F
27 28 29 30 31 32

For full street detail of the highlighted area see page 203.

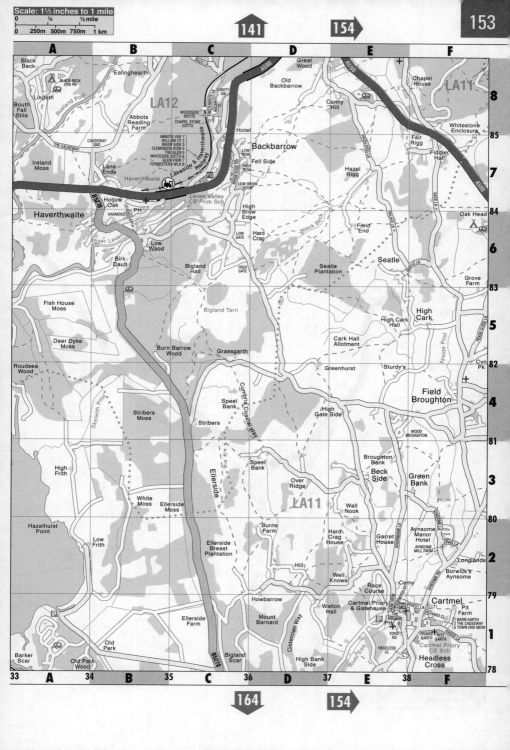

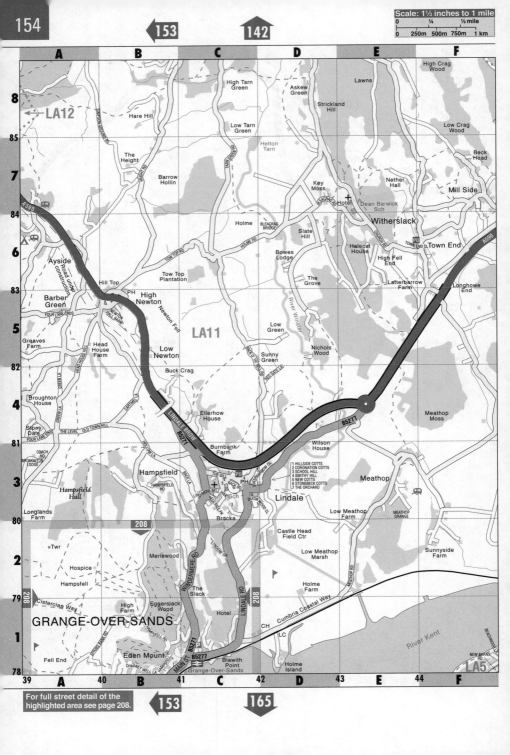

Scale: 1⅓ inches to 1 mile

0   ¼   ½ mile
0   250m 500m 750m 1 km

A   B   C   D   E   F

White Scar
Raven's Lodge
Gilpin Farm
Caravan Park
Sampool Bridge
Causeway End
PH
Whitbarrow View
CHURCH
ST NELSON SQ
LEVENS
CE Sch
Levens Park
Lawrence House Farm
GREENGATE

A5074
A5074
Low Levens Farm
A6
Levens Bridge
High Barns

Stakes Moss
River Gilpin
LA8
River Kent
Levens Hall
P
Hall
PARSON'S WAY

Low Fell End
80
Sampool
Ninezergh
Eversley
Hincaster

Moorcock Hall
Bellart How Moss
High Foulshaw
Halforth
College Green
Leasgill
211
Heversham St Peter's CE Prim Sch
Mabbin Hall

LA11
LA7
Moss Side Farm
MOSS SIDE RD
Hotel
P
Heversham
WOODHOUSE LA
Dallam Sch

Foulshaw Moss
211
Cumbria Coastal Way
MARSH RD
Hall
Park House
St Anthony's
LA7
Haverflatts

Middle Foulshaw
Park Hill
Cragg Yeat
Ackenthwaite
211

209
Low Foulshaw
Bsns Pk
Park Side
CHURCH ST
Sch
B6385

Ulpha Fell
Ulpha
P PARK RD
Dallam Tower
B5282
MAIN ST
B6384
Liby
Milnthorpe
Milnthorpe Prim Sch
B6384

Milnthorpe Sands
PH
Sandside
Quarry
Deer Park
Whasset

Storth
YANG LA
PO
Haverbrack
Knott Hill
HANGBRIDGE LA

Wray Cottage
211
Mills & Mus
PARSONAGE FOLD
Cemy
P
Beetham Ho
River Bela
Beetham

Kent Viaduct
Arnside
SANDSIDE RD
Underlaid Wood
Wood Edge
MEADOW BANK
BLACKBERRY HILL
Beetham CE Prim Sch
Hall
Pye's Bridge Farm

Arnside
Ash Meadow
B5282
THE PROMENADE
Sch
Arnside Moss
LA5
Carr Bank
Tower
Hazelslack
Fairy Steps
High Cote
209
DEEPDALE CL
Slack Head
Deepdale Farm
PH
HALE GREEN FARM

YH
RED HILLS RD
HIGH KNOTT RD
LC
LC
209
COLD WELL LA
Major Woods
SILVER RIDGE CVN PK
Hale
A6
Fell End Farm

8
85
7
84
6
83
5
82
4
81
3
80
2
79
1
78

45   A   46   B   47   C   48   D   49   E   50   F

For full street detail of the highlighted area see pages 209 and 211.

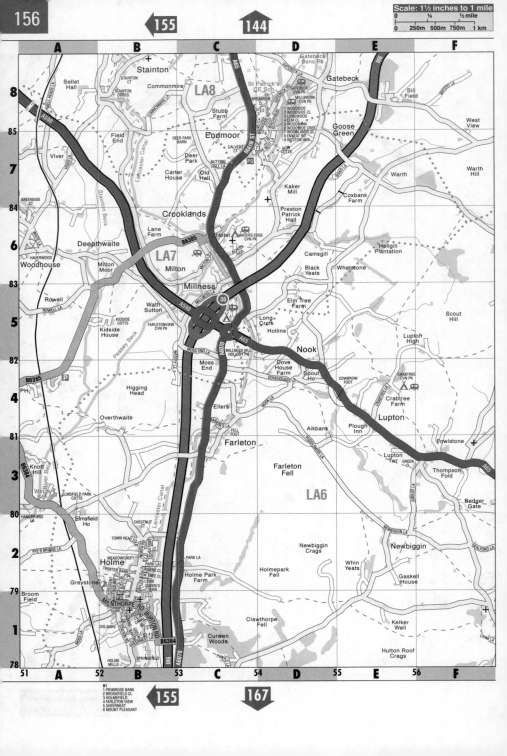

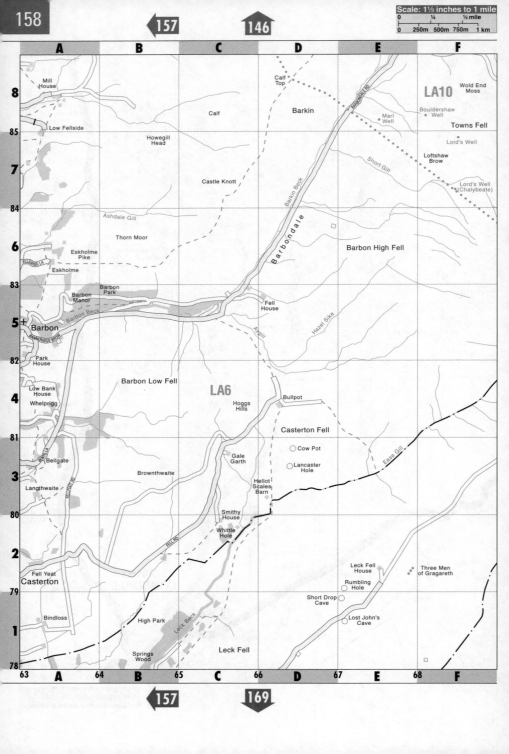

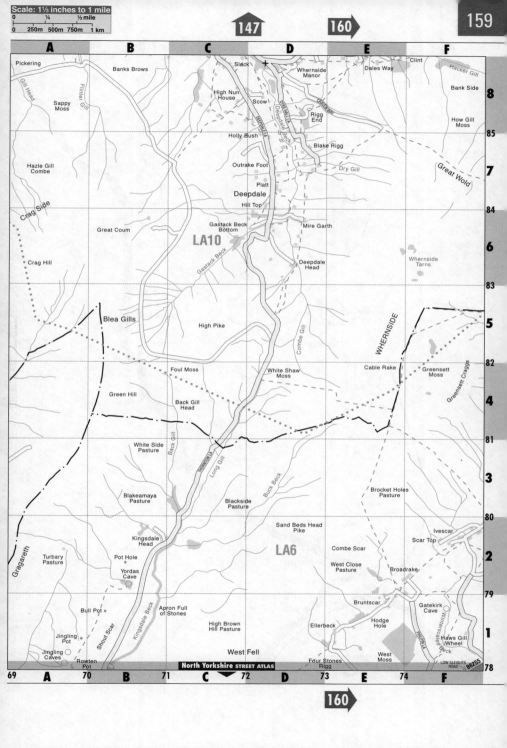

A   B   C   D   E   F

Pickering
Gill Head
Flinter Gill
Sappy Moss
Banks Brows
Slack
Whernside Manor
Dales Way
Clint
Hacker Gill
Bank Side

High Nun House
Scow
Rigg End
How Gill Moss

Deepdale Beck
Great Way
Dike Holl

Holly Bush
Blake Rigg

Hazle Gill Combe
Outrake Foot
Dry Gill
Great Wold

Crag Side
Platt
Deepdale
Hill Top

Great Coum
Gastack Beck Bottom
Mire Garth

LA10

Crag Hill
Gastack Beck
Deepdale Head
Whernside Tarns

Blea Gills
WHERNSIDE

High Pike
Combe Gill

Foul Moss
White Shaw Moss
Cable Rake
Greensett Moss
Greensett Craggs

Green Hill
Back Gill Head

White Side Pasture
Back Gill
Thornton La
Long Gill
Buck Beck
Brocket Holes Pasture

Blakeamaya Pasture
Blackside Pasture
Sand Beds Head Pike

Graggareth
Kingsdale Head
LA6
Combe Scar
Ivescar
Scar Top

Turbary Pasture
Pot Hole
West Close Pasture
Broadrake

Yordas Cave
Kingsdale Beck
Bruntscar
Gatekirk Cave

Bull Pot
Apron Full of Stones
High Brown Hill Pasture
Ellerbeck
Hodge Hole
Winterscales Beck
The Hill
Haws Gill Wheel

Jingling Pot
Shout Scar

Jingling Caves
Rowten Pot
West Fell
Four Stones Rigg
West Moss
Low Sleights Road
B6255

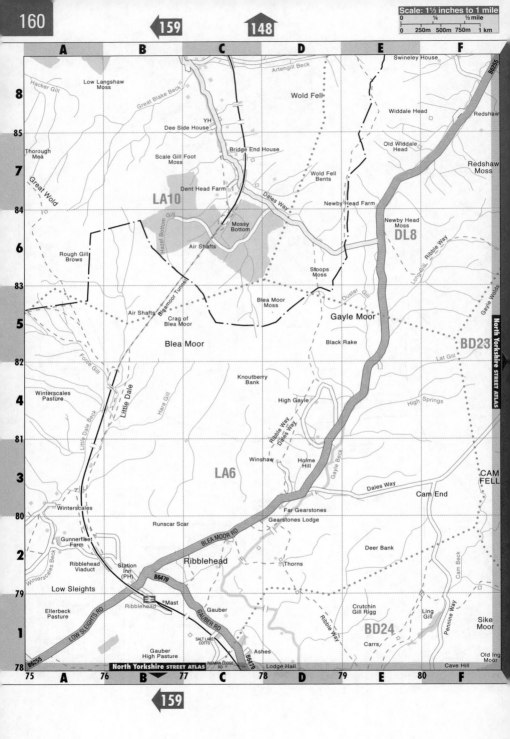

A B C D E F

Bullstone Bed

Askam in Furness

Askam Pier

LB Sta

TEAL CL 1
TURNSTONE CRES 2
PARKLANDS DR 3
PLOVER CL 4
CASPIAN RD 5
AVOCET CRES 6

The Lots

LA16

8

77

7

204

76

Cumbria Coastal Way

Roanhead Farm

Sandscale Haws

Mines (dis)

6

Sandscale Haws Nature Reserve

75

HAWTHWAITE LA

The Moors

5

DALTEA RD

Lowsy Point

Scarth Bight

204

A590

74

Scarth Channel

LC

LA14

4

BOUNWOOD RD

SCARTH RD

Sowerby Woods Bsns Pk

PARK RD

North End Haws

Sowerby Cottages

RAVENSCROFT RD

Park Road Ind Est

73

Shope Tree Scar

Works

Sowerby Hall

CH

3

BANK LA

BANK LA

Keswick Ave

Hawcoat

North Walney Nature Reserve

Sowerby Lodge

WHINFIELD AVE

MIDDLEFIELD

QUARRY BROW

DALTON LA

Sch

North End Marsh

206

Ind Ests

ANGL...

72

Works

Quarry (dis)

CLIFFE RD

206

LA14

Ormsgill

Works

MILL BANK

Sch

DARE RD

NEWLAND AVE

WHEATCLOSE RD

2

ST FRANCIS GDNS

Crem
Schs

THORNCLIFFE RD

Walney Airfield

Cemy

Schs

Walney Meetings

WALNEY RD

CEDAR RD

SCHNEIDER RD

DEVONSHIRE RD

71

1

Benny Hill

COMBE VIEW

PHOENIX RD

HARDCASTLE RD

PROSPECT RD

FAIRFIELD LA

LYNDALE AVE

North Scale

TEASDALE RD

A590

ANCHOR RD

WEST VIEW RD

HORNBEAM RD

LA13

70

BARROW-IN-FURNESS

For full street detail of the highlighted area see pages 204, 206 and 207.

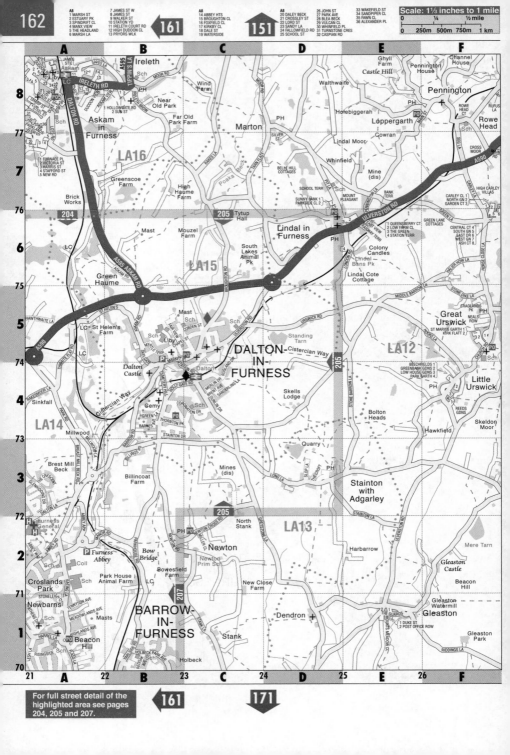

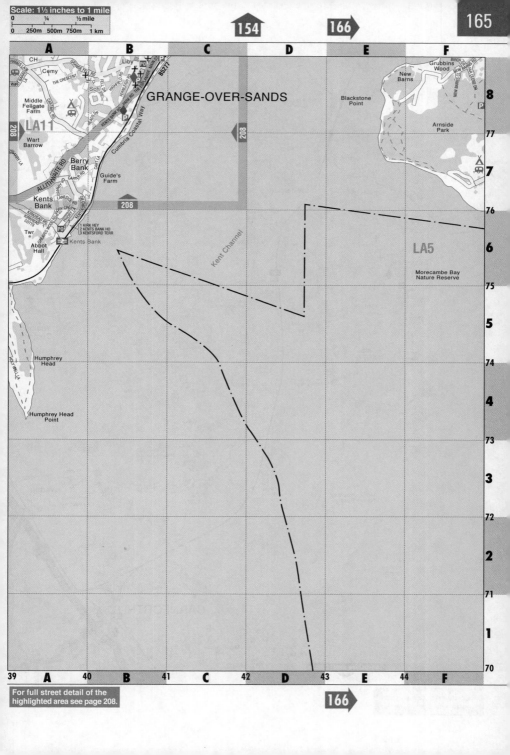

GRANGE-OVER-SANDS

LA11

CH
Cemy
THE CRESCENT
Liby
PO
B5277
Sch
Middle
Fellgate
Farm
Wart
Barrow
Berry
Bank
Cumbria Coastal Way
ALLITHWAITE RD
Guide's
Farm
208
Kents
Bank
1 KIRK HEY
2 KENTS BANK HO
3 KENTSFORD TERR
Twr
Abbot
Hall
Kents Bank
208

Kent Channel

Blackstone
Point

Grubbins
Wood
New
Barns
Arnside
Park
P

LA5

Morecambe Bay
Nature Reserve

Humphrey
Head

Humphrey Head
Point

For full street detail of the
highlighted area see page 208.

165 155

Scale: 1½ inches to 1 mile

0   ¼   ½ mile
0   250m 500m 750m 1 km

A **B** **C** **D** **E** **F**

Coldwell Farm
Leighton House
BEETHAM CVN PK
FELL END CVN PK
Lakeland Wildlife Oasis

Red Hills
Cemy
Arnside Hagg Wood
Arnside Knott
LA7
Silverdale Moss
Gait Burrows Nature Reserve
Brackenthwaite Farm
Leighton Beck
Hale Moss
HALLMORE CVN PK

Arnside Tower Farm
LC
Arnside Tower (remains of)
Middlebarrow Wood
Quarry
Challan Hall
Hawes Water
Waterslack
Thrang End Farm
White Moss
Hazel Grove

Eaves Wood
Red Bridge
Yealand Storrs
TEMPLE CT

Cemy
The Row
Brow Foot Farm
Yealand Redmayne
EIGHT ACRE LA
NINETEEN ACRE LA
1 HILL TOP CL
2 MEADOWS CL

Silverdale
Sch
Liby
Bottoms Farm
Cringlebarrow Wood
Yealand CE Prim Sch

Bank House Farm
CH
Silverdale
Visitor Ctr
Grisedale Farm
Leighton Moss Nature Reserve
Yealand Manor
PH

PH
Know Hill
Silverdale Green
Slackwood Farm
LC
Grisedale Wood
Leighton Hall
Yealand Conyers

Lindeth Tower
Heald Brow
SNAPE LA

Lancashire Coastal Way
Crag Foot
Chy
LA5
Three Brothers
Hyning Priory

Jack Scout
Jenny Brown's Point

Scar Close
Warton Crag Nature Reserve
213
LA6

Morecambe Bay Nature Reserve
Ings Point
Scout Crag
P
PH
Sch
Liby
Warton
Warton Old Rectory

Cotestones Farm
Millhead
Lorry Pk
35a

Warton Sands
Galley Hall
213
CARNFORTH
Carnforth

Hunting Hill
Schs
Ind Est
Cemy
B6254

Marsh House Farm
DANGER AREA

45 **A** 46 **B** 47 **C** 48 **D** 49 **E** 50 **F**

For full street detail of the highlighted area see pages 210 and 213.
165

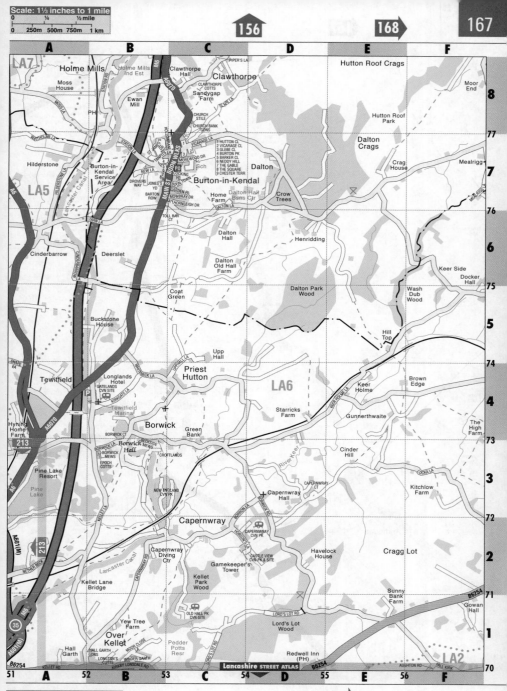

LA7

Holme Mills
Moss House
Holme Mills Ind Est
Clawthorpe Hall
PIPER'S LA
Hutton Roof Crags
Moor End

Clawthorpe
CLAWTHORPE COTTS
Sandygap Farm
Ewan Mill
CHURCH STILE
CHURCH BANK GDNS
Hutton Roof Park

Hilderstone
PH
8

77

Dalton Crags

LA5
Burton-in-Kendal Service Area

1 HUTTON CL
2 VICARAGE CL
3 GLEBE CL
4 BURTON PK
5 BARKER CL
6 NEDDY HILL
7 THE GABLE
8 THE SQUARE
9 CHESTER TERR

Dalton
Crag House
Mealrigg
7

Burton-in-Kendal
DROVERS WAY
JONES ST
BARTON ROW
MOWBRAY DR
DOWNLEIGH DR
Home Farm
Dalton Hall Bsns Ctr
Crow Trees
76

Cinderbarrow
Deerslet
TOLL BAR CT
DALTON LA

Dalton Hall
Henridding
6

Dalton Old Hall Farm

Coat Green
Dalton Park Wood
Keer Side
Docker Hall
75

Buckstone House
Wash Dub Wood
Hill Top
5

Upp Hall

74

Tewitfield
Longlands Hotel
GATELANDS CVN SITE
Tewitfield Marina
BECK LA
UPPHALL LA
Priest Hutton
LA6
Keer Holme
Brown Edge
4

Hyning Home Farm
213
Borwick
Green Bank
Starricks Farm
Gunnerthwaite
The High Farm
73

Pine Lake Resort
Pine Lake
BORWICK CT
BORWICK LA
Borwick Hall
BORWICK MEWS
EPOCH COTTS
CROFTLANDS
BECKSIDE
River Keer
Cinder Hill
Kitchlow Farm
COCKA LA
3

NEW ENGLAND CVN PK
Capernwray Hall
CAPERNWRAY CT
72

Capernwray
CAPERNWRAY CVN PK
Cragg Lot
2

Capernwray Diving Ctr
Gamekeeper's Tower
CASTLE VIEW CVN PK & SITE
Havelock House
Sunny Bank Farm
B6254
Gowan Hall

Kellet Lane Bridge
Lancaster Canal
Kellet Park Wood
OLD HALL PK CVN SITE
LORD'S LOT RD
1

M6
35
Yew Tree Farm
Over Kellet
Pedder Potts Resr
Lord's Lot Wood
Redwell Inn (PH)
LA2

Hall Garth
HALL GARTH GDNS
LONGTAIN'S COTTS
MOOR CLOSE
WINDER GARTH
KIRKBY LONSDALE RD
B6254
AUGHTON RD
FELL KIRK

A   52   B   53   C   54   D   55   E   56   F

For full street detail of the highlighted area see page 213.

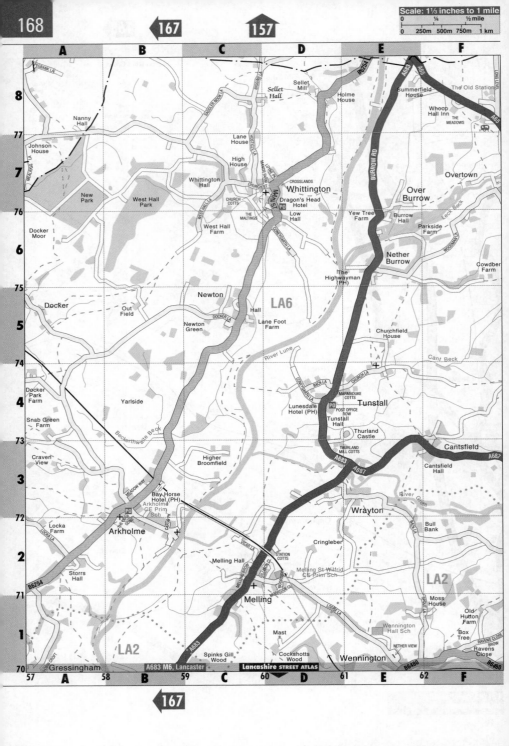

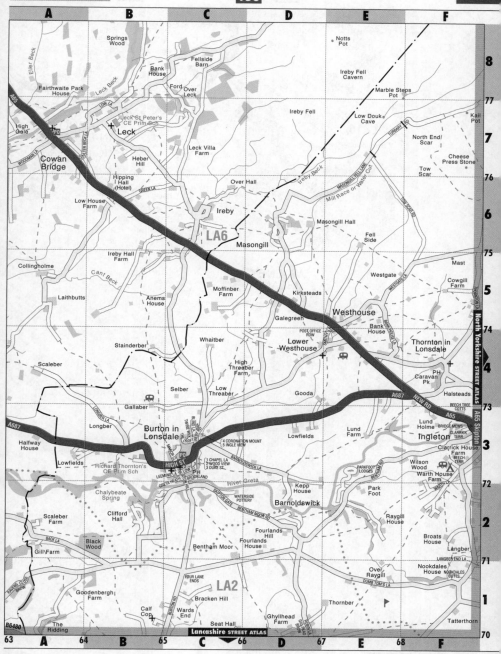

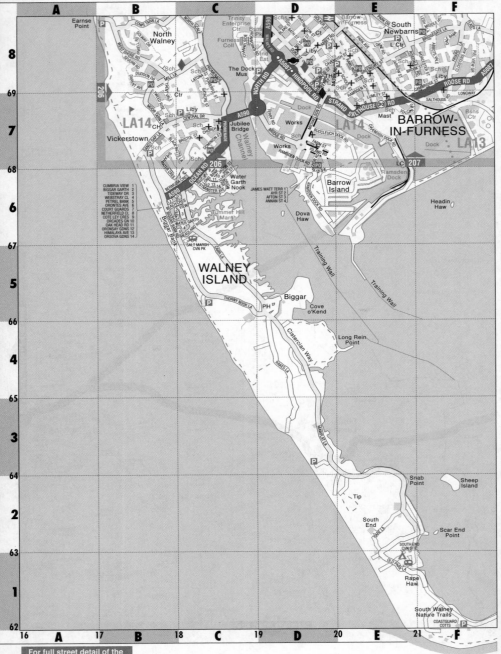

161
162

Scale: 1⅓ inches to 1 mile

| 0 | ¼ | ½ mile |
| 0 | 250m | 500m 750m | 1 km |

8

69

7

68

6

67

5

66

4

65

3

64

2

63

1

62

Earnse Point

North Walney

Trinity Enterprise Ctr

Furness Coll

The Dock Mus

206

LA14 CH

Vickerstown

Liby

Central Dr

Jubilee Bridge

Walney Channel

Barrow-in-Furness

South Newbarns

BARROW-IN-FURNESS

LA14

LA13

LC 207

Water Garth Nook

206

OCEAN RD

Biggar Bank

SALT MARSH CVN PK

Dova Haw

Ramsden Dock

Barrow Island

Headin Haw

WALNEY ISLAND

Biggar

PH

Cove o'Kend

Long Rein Point

Cistercian Way

Training Wall

Training Wall

CUMBRIA VIEW 1
BIGGAR GARTH 2
TIDEWAY DR 3
WEBSTRAY CL 4
PETREL BANK 5
ORONTES AVE 6
COURT GUARDS 7
NETHERFIELD CL 8
COTE LEY CRES 9
ORCADES GN 10
OAK HEAD RD 11
ORONSAY GDNS 12
HIMALAYA AVE 13
ORSOVA GDNS 14

JAMES WATT TERR 1
AYR ST 2
AFTON ST 3
ANNAN ST 4

Snab Point

Sheep Island

Tip

South End

Scar End Point

SOUTHEND CVN SITE

Rape Haw

South Walney Nature Trails

COASTGUARD COTTS

16   A   17   B   18   C   19   D   20   E   21   F

For full street detail of the highlighted area see pages 206 and 207.

For full street detail of the
highlighted area see page 207.

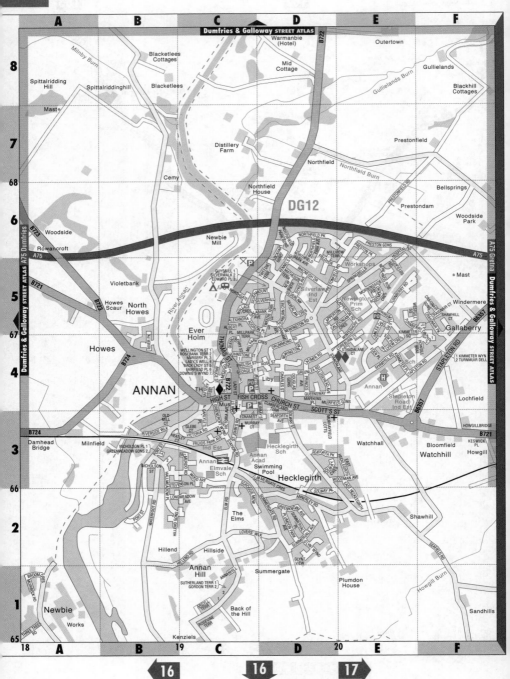

Dumfries & Galloway STREET ATLAS

Warmanbie (Hotel)
Outertown
Blacketlees Cottages
Mid Cottage
Gullielands
Spittalridding Hill
Spittalriddinghill
Blacketlees
Gullielands Burn
Blackhill Cottages
Mast
Distillery Farm
Prestonfield
Cemy
Northfield
Northfield Burn
Northfield House
Bellsprings
DG12
Prestondam
Woodside Park
Woodside
Newbie Mill
Workshops
Mast
Rowancroft
Northfield Pk
Millview Terr
Violetbank
Silverla Ind Est
Windermere
Howes Scaur
North Howes
Silverhill
Newington Prim Sch
Gallaberry
Ever Holm
Alexandra Pl
Albert Pl
Millpark Terr
Kimmeter
Shawhill Ct
1 Kimmeter Wyn
2 Turnmuir Dell
Howes
Standalane Ct
Annan
Liby
Lochfield
ANNAN
High St
Fish Cross
Church St
Scott's St
Stapleton Road Ind Est
Mus
Howgillbridge
Old Mill Ct
Riverside Wlk
Glebe Ct
Victoria Rd
Damhead Bridge
Milnfield
Nicholson Pl 1
Greenmeadow Gdns 2
Ind Est
Hecklegirth Sch
Watchhall
Bloomfield
Keswick Pl
Howgill
Nicholson St
Annan Acad
Watchhill
Annan Swimming Pool
Elmvale Sch
Hecklegirth
Longmeadow Ave
The Elms
Woodman Ave
Shawhill
Hillend
Hillside
Lovers Wlk
Annan Hill
Summergate
Plumdon House
Newbie
Works
Sutherland Terr 1
Gordon Terr 2
Back of the Hill
Sandhills
Kenziels
Howgill Burn

16   16   17

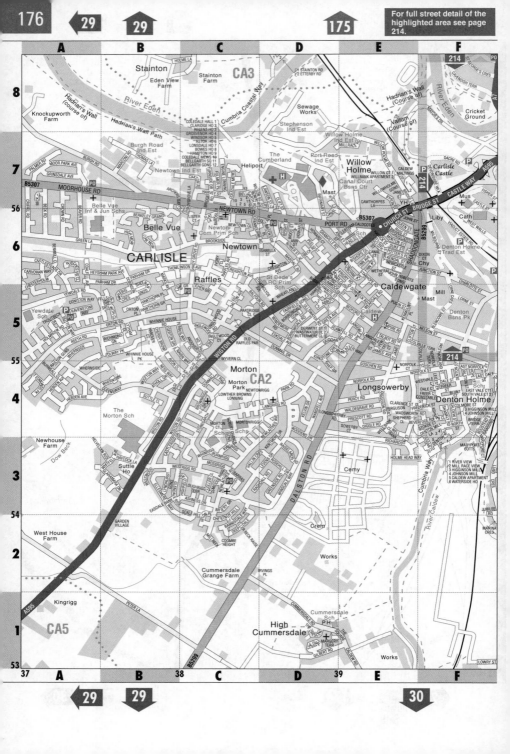

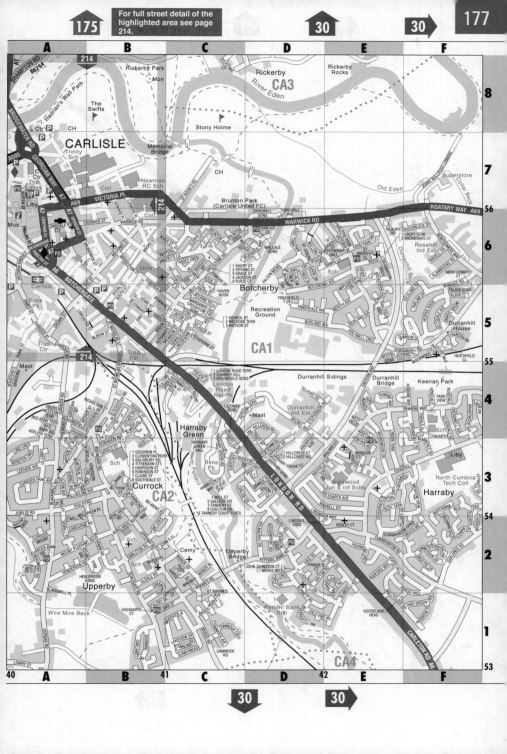

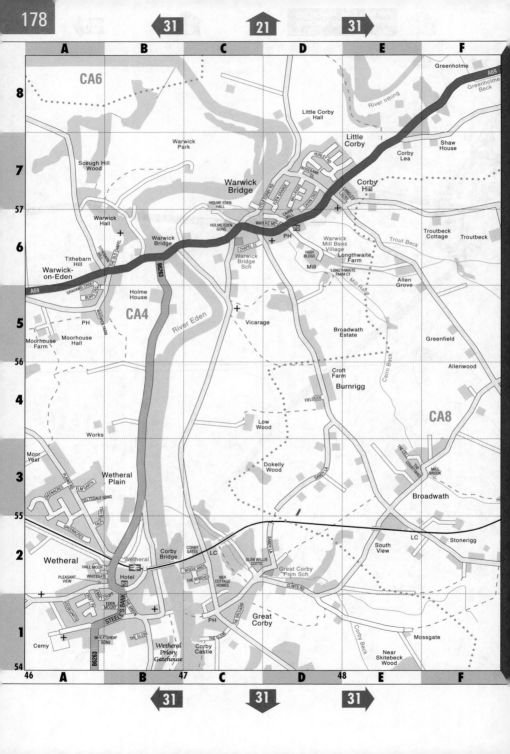

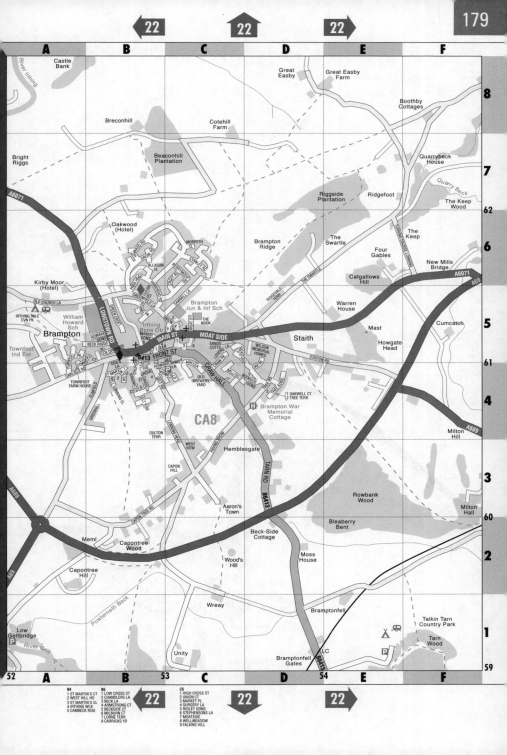

B4
1 ST MARTIN'S CT
2 WEST HILL HO
3 ST MARTIN'S CL
4 IRTHING WLK
5 CAMBECK RISE

B5
1 LOW CROSS ST
2 CHANDLERS LA
3 BECK LA
4 ARMSTRONG CT
5 BECKSIDE CT
6 MILBURN CT
7 LORNE TERR
8 CARRICKS YD

C5
1 HIGH CROSS ST
2 UNION CT
3 MARKET PL
4 SURGERY LA
5 RIDLEY GDNS
6 STEPHENSONS LA
7 MOATSIDE
8 WELLMEADOW
9 FALKINS HILL

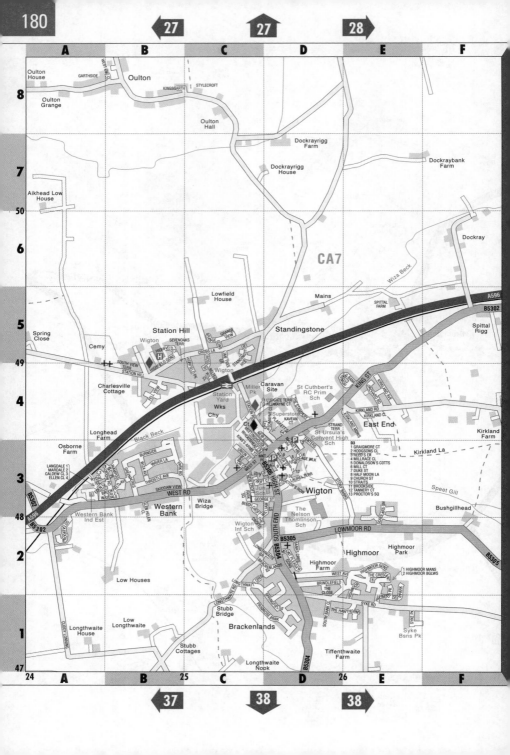

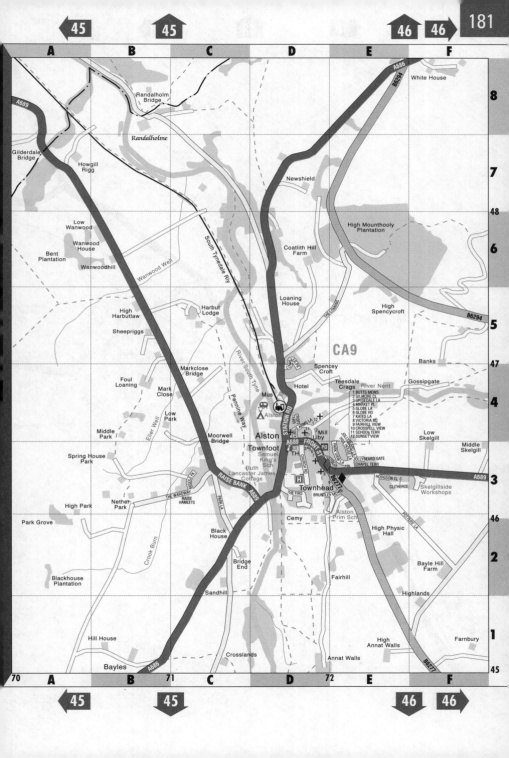

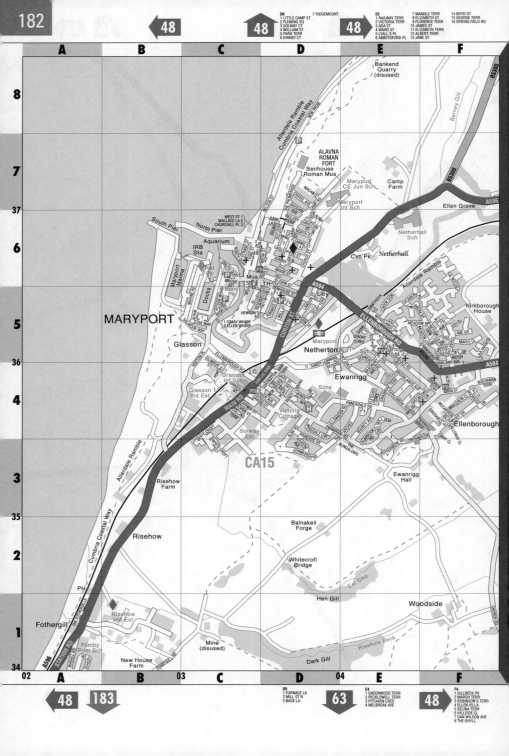

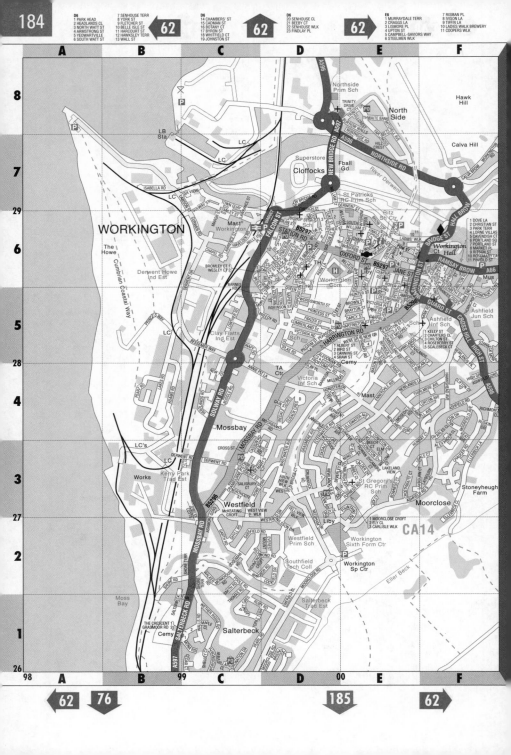

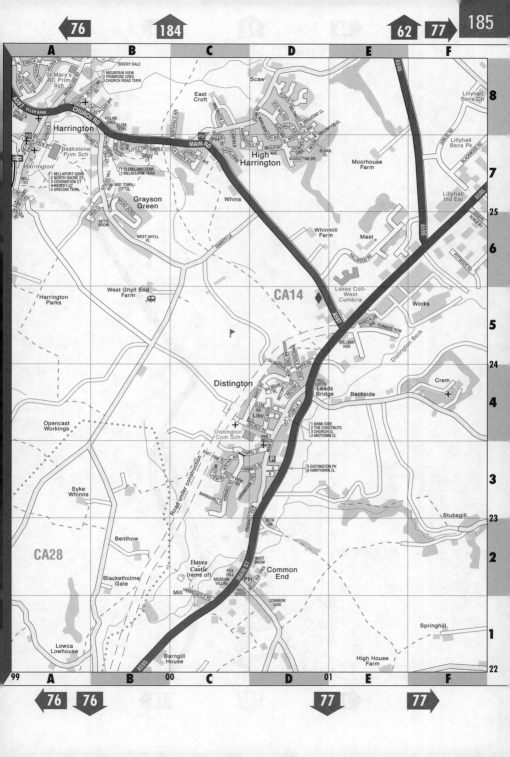

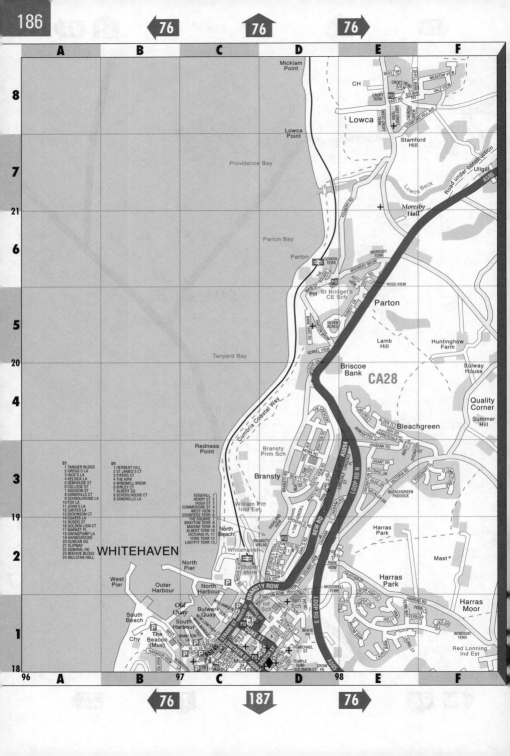

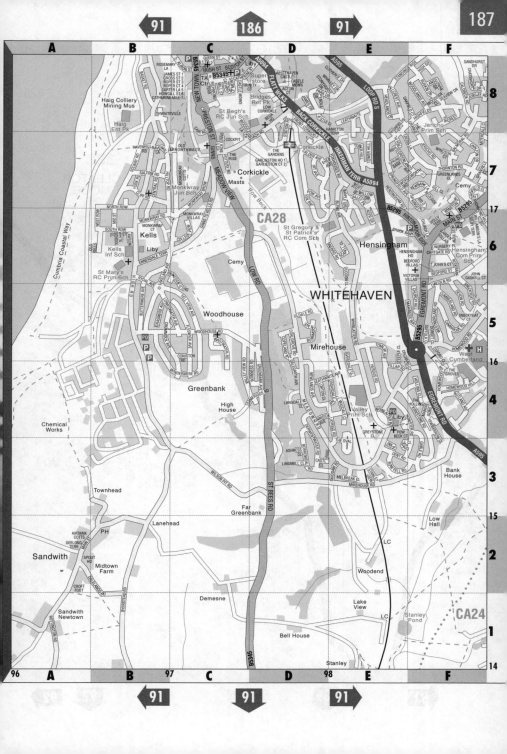

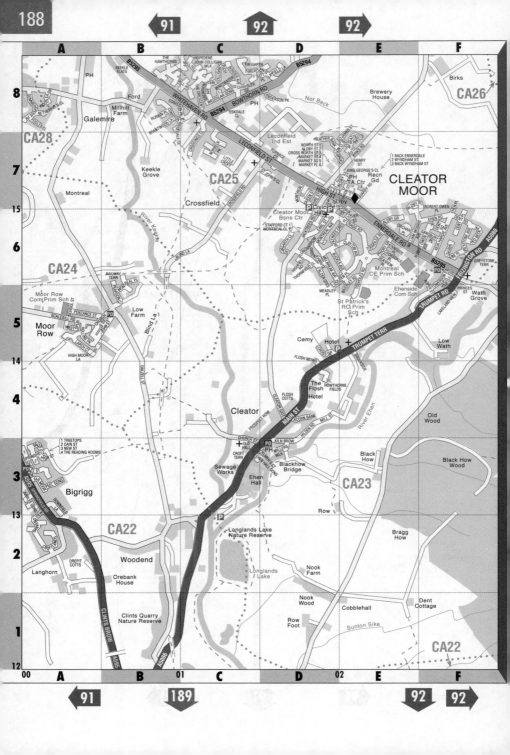

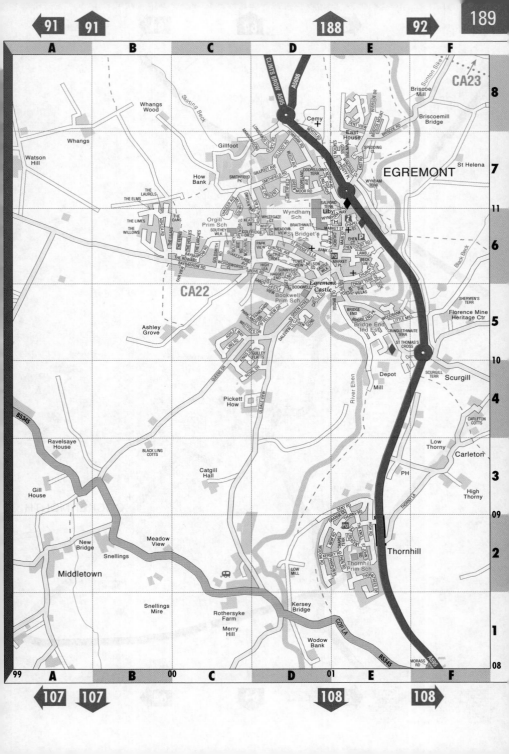

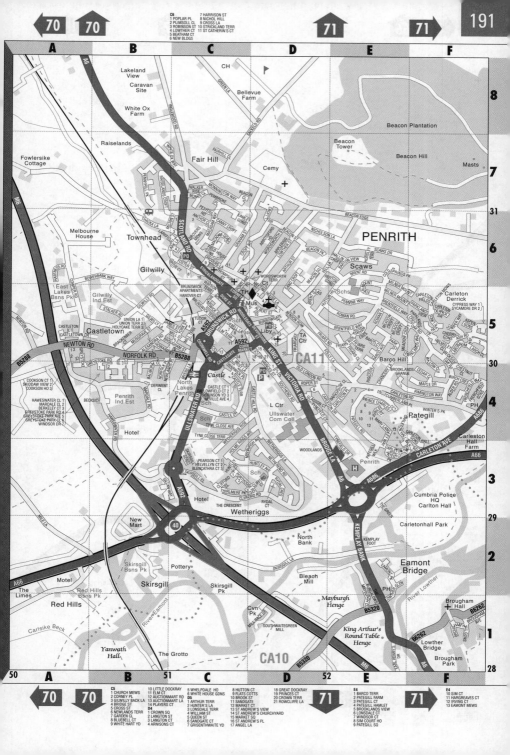

C6
1 POPLAR PL
2 PLIMSOLL CL
3 ROBINSON ST
4 LOWTHER CT
5 BEATHAM CT
6 NEW BLDGS
7 HARRISON ST
8 NICHOL HILL
9 CROSS LA
10 STRICKLAND TERR
11 ST CATHERIN'S CT

PENRITH

CA11

CA10

C5
1 CHURCH MEWS
2 CORNEY PL
3 GILWILLY BACK LA
4 BRIDGE ST
5 CROSS ST
6 NEWLANDS TERR
7 GARDEN CL
8 BLUEBELL CT
9 WHITE HART YD
10 LITTLE DOCKRAY
11 ELM CT
12 AUCTIONMART RD
13 AUCTIONMART LA
14 PLAYERS CT
D4
1 ARTHUR TERR
2 HUNTER'S LA
3 LONSDALE TERR
4 WILLIAM ST
5 QUEEN ST
6 SANDGATE CT
7 GRISENTHWAITE YD

5 WHELPDALE HO
6 WHITE HOUSE GDNS
D5
1 CROWN SQ
2 LANGTON ST
3 LANGTON CT
4 ARNISONS CT

8 HUTTON CT
9 FLATS COTTS
10 BROOK ST
11 SANDGATE
12 MARKET CT
13 ST ANDREW'S VIEW
14 ST ANDREW'S CHURCHYARD
15 MARKET SQ
16 ST ANDREW'S PL
17 ANGEL LA

18 GREAT DOCKRAY
19 PRINCES CT
20 CROWN TERR
21 ROWCLIFFE LA

E4
1 BARCO TERR
2 PATEGILL FARM
3 PATEGILL CT
4 PATEGILL HAMLET
5 BROOKLANDS VIEW
6 LONSDALE CT
7 WINDSOR CT
8 SIM COURT HO
9 PATEGILL SQ

E4
10 SIM CT
11 HARGREAVES CT
12 IRVING CT
13 EAMONT MEWS

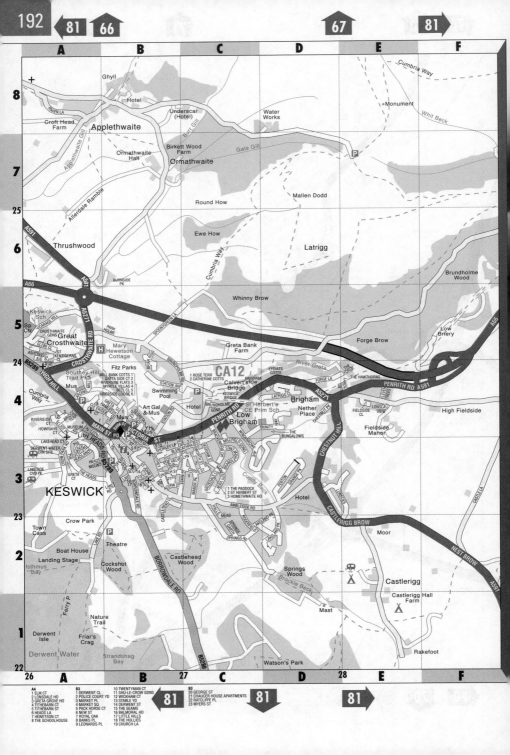

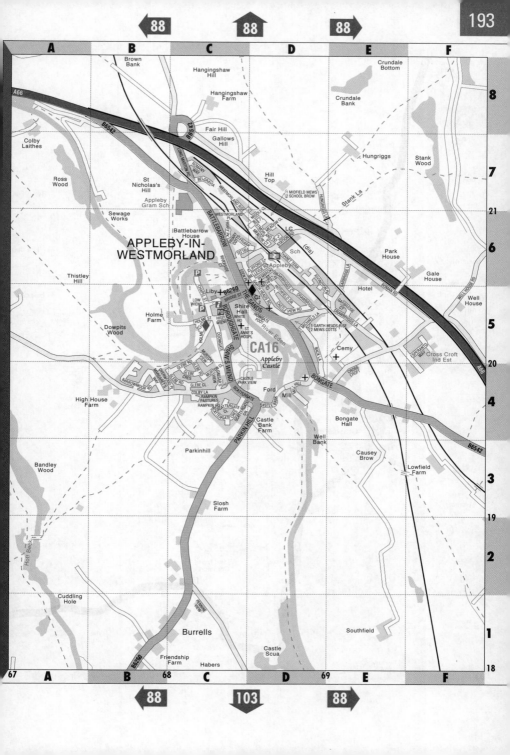

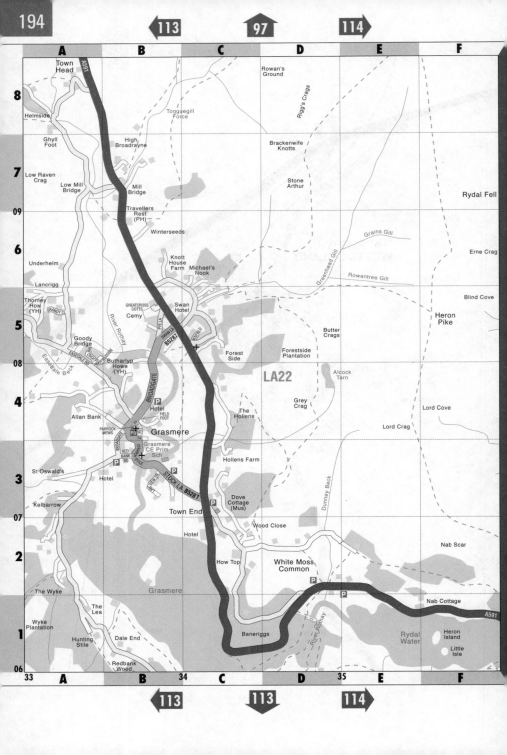

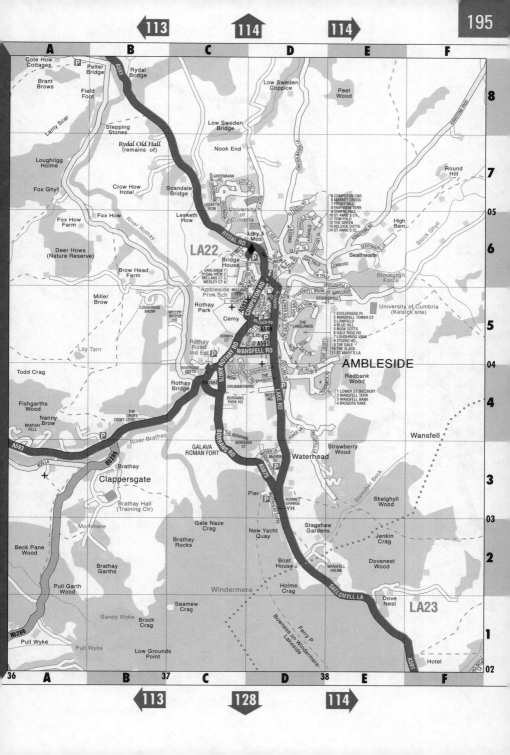

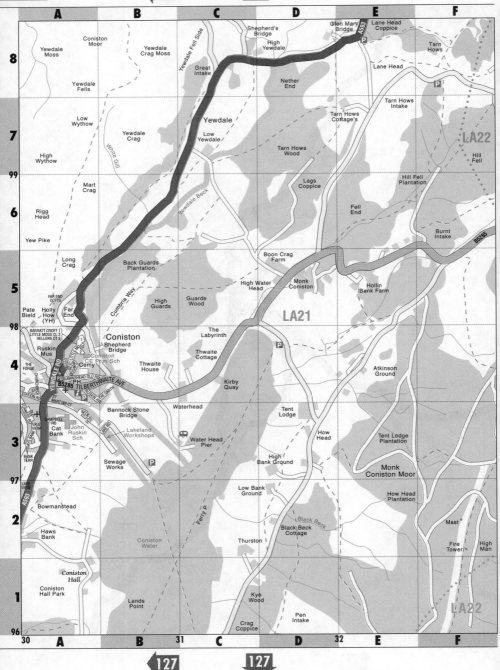

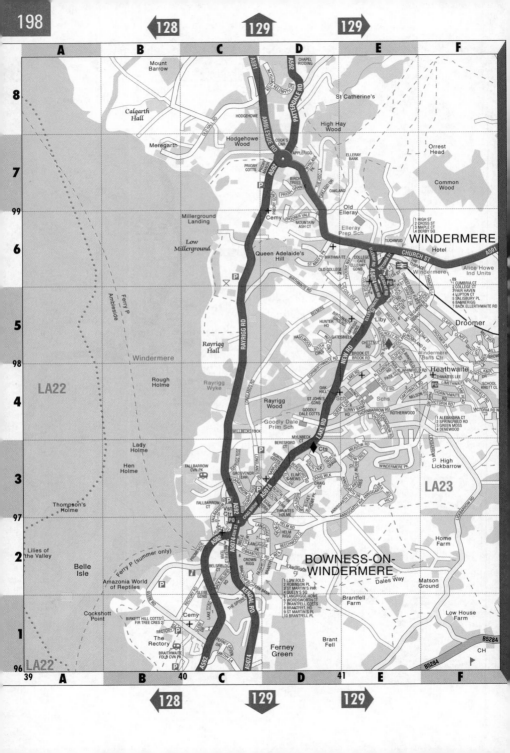

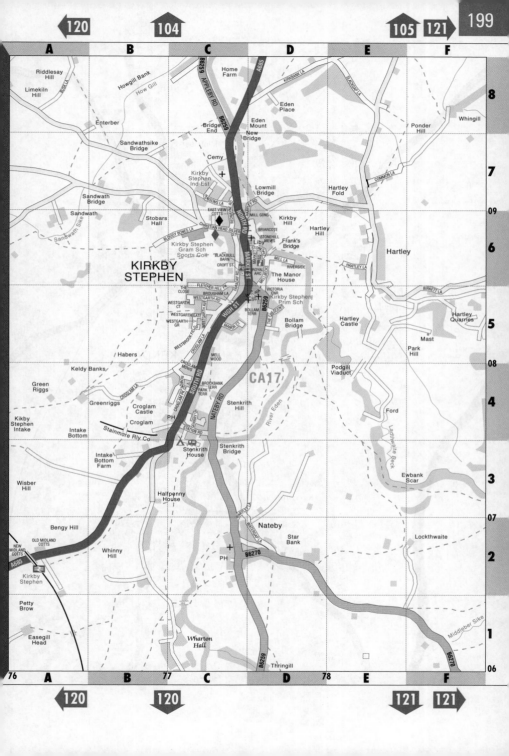

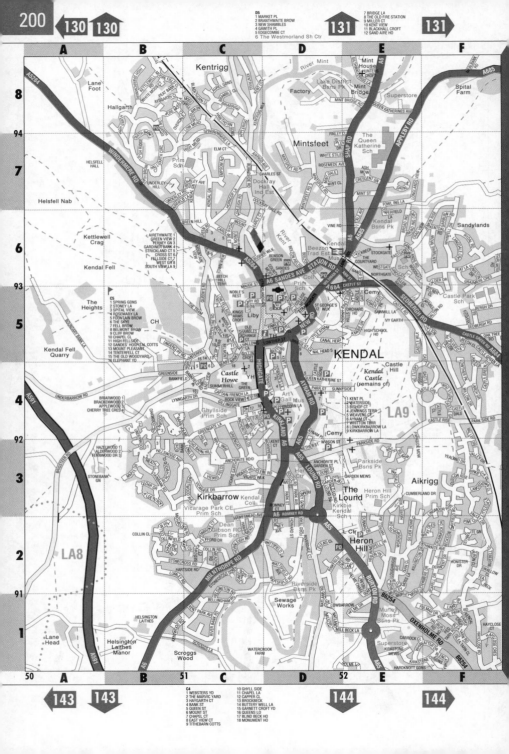

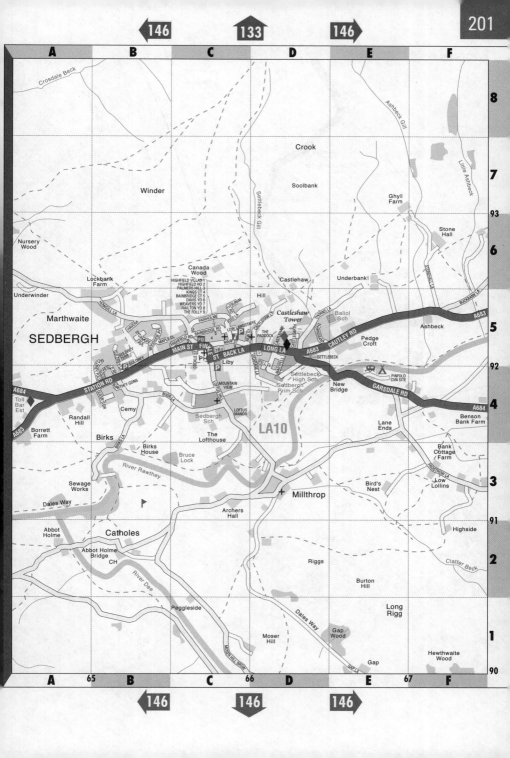

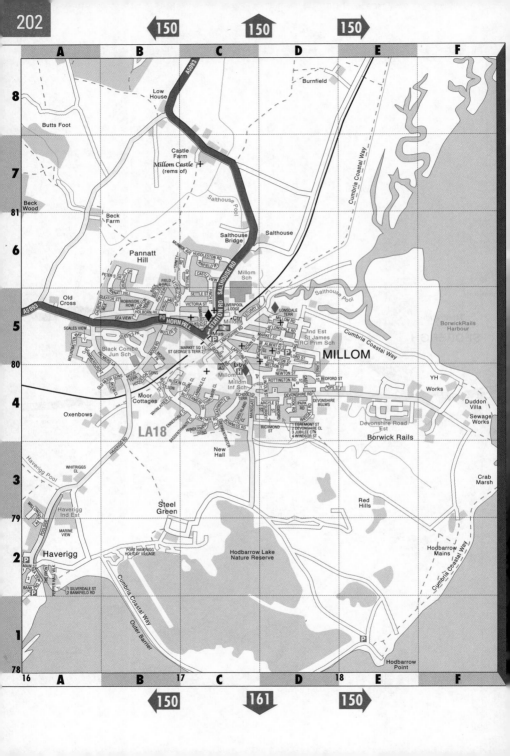

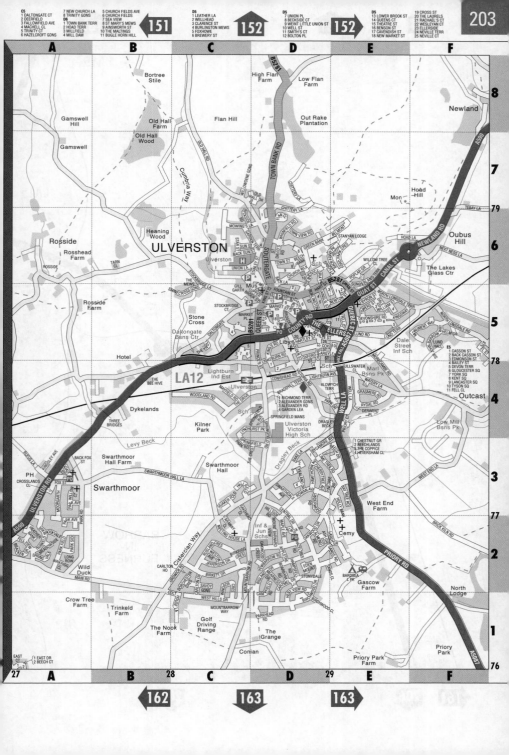

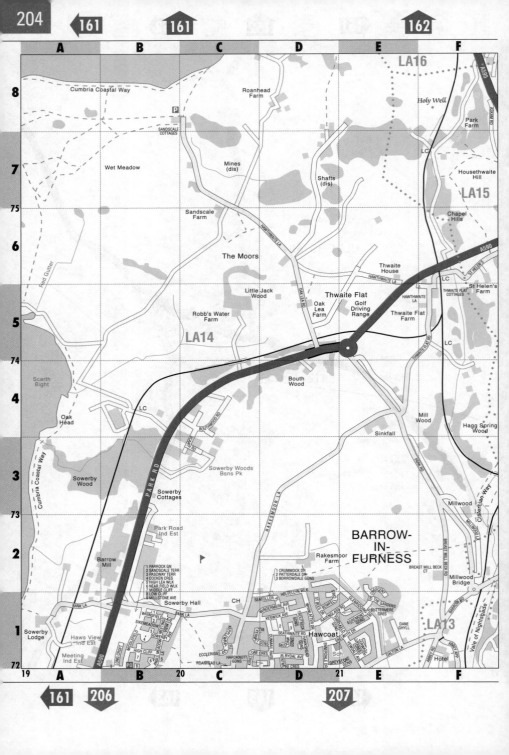

← 161
161
162 ↑

Map Labels

LA16

Cumbria Coastal Way

Roanhead Farm

Holy Well

Park Farm

P

SANDSCALE COTTAGES

8

Wet Meadow

Mines (dis)

Shafts (dis)

LC

Housethwaite Hill

7

LA15

75

Sandscale Farm

Chapel Hills

HAWTHWAITE LA

6

The Moors

OAK LEA RD

Thwaite House

A590

HAWTHWAITE LA

Red Gutter

Little Jack Wood

Thwaite Flat

LC

Oak Lea Farm

Golf Driving Range

Thwaite Flat Farm

HAWTHWAITE LA

THWAITE FLAT COTTAGES

St Helen's Farm

ST HELEN'S

5

Robb's Water Farm

LA14

LC

74

Scarth Bight

Bouth Wood

Mill Wood

Hagg Spring Wood

4

Oak Head

LC

Sinkfall

BOLTHWOOD RD

PARK RD

Millwood

Cistercian Way

Cumbria Coastal Way

3

Sowerby Wood

Sowerby Woods Bsns Pk

RAKESMOOR LA

PARK RD

Millwood

MILLWOOD LA

73

Sowerby Cottages

BREAST MILL BECK RD

Park Road Ind Est

BARROW-IN-FURNESS

Rakesmoor Farm

BREAST MILL BECK CT

Millwood Bridge

2

Barrow Mill

1 PARROCK GN
2 SANDSCALE TERR
3 PASCWAY TERR
4 COCKEN CRES
5 HIGH LEA WLK
6 NEAR FIELD WLK
7 MIDDLE CLIFF
8 LOW CLIFF
9 MILLSTONE AVE

1 CRUMMOCK DR
2 PATTERDALE DR
3 BORROWDALE GDNS

SEATOLLER

HELVELLYN WLK

ST ENOCHS

THE TCH GARDENS

BUTTERMERE CRES

Vale of Nightshade

LA13

Sowerby Hall

CH

BANK LA

BANK LA

Sowerby Lodge

Haws View Ind Est

KESWICK AVE

SEATHWAITE RD

FREDERICK AVE

DUNMAIL RD

HAWKSMOOR

DANE GHYLL

Hawcoat

Sch

1 LOW GREY DESK

Meeting Ind Est

A590

HIGH CLIFF

ECCLERIGGS AV

HARDKNOTT GDNS

ROANHEAD LA

RYDAL AVE

THE CRES

DALTON LA

GREYSTONE GDNS

Hotel

C5
1 HOPE ST
2 LANCASTER ST
3 ASHWORTH ST
4 JAMES TERR
5 BRIDGE HO
6 CAMBRIDGE CT

7 WESLEY CT
8 DEVONSHIRE ST
9 PORTER ST
10 BROUGHTON LODGE
11 FELL CROFT
12 TUDOR SQ
13 CROWN MEWS

14 VICTORIA TERR
15 STOREY SQ

162
162

LA16

Mast

Green
Haume

GREEN HAUME
COTTAGES

Rakes
Cottage

Elliscale
Farm

Mouzel
Farm

Mouzell
House

Rickett
Hills

Mast

Tytup
Hall

Tytup
Farm

South Lakes
Wild Animal
Park

P

Lindal in
Furness

EMPLANDS
COTTS

LA12

LA15

Standing
Tarn

Hill
Farm

Cistercian Way

Hagg
Hills

Dowdales
Sch

George
Romney
Jun Sch

Gill
Dub

Sch

Briarcliffe Gdns

1 CROOKLANDS TERR
2 CROOKLANDS BROW

L Ctr

Lib

Thomas
Wood

Dalton
Castle

P

COURT No 5

LITTLE
FIELDS

Dalton

DALTON-
IN-
FURNESS

Cemy

Anty
Cross

Nursery

Dalton
St Mary's
CE Prim
Sch

Highfield
Farm

Skells
Lodge

Cistercian Way

Dalton
Junction

LA14

SCHOOLWATERS

Green
Hills
Farm

Longlands
Cottages

Longlands
Farm

Quarry

Sunnymead

Stainton with
Adgarley

PENNINGTON CL 1
DENDRON CL 2

BAYCLIFFE DR

Tithe Barn
Cottages

Minikin
Hall
Farm

SUNNY
BANK STONE CL   PH

Adgarley
Farm

Abbots
Way

Billincoat
Farm

Halfway
House

Mine
(dis)

Mine
(dis)

Mine
(dis)

Stainton
Head
Farm

Stainton
Green
Farm

The
Billings

Home
Farm

LA13

162
162
207

B4
1 CASTLE ST
2 MARKET PL
3 GOOSE GN
4 GLENFIELD RD
5 HAMILTON TERR
6 GARDEN LEA
7 OLIVE CL
8 JUNIPER CL
9 DEVOKE WATER GDNS

10 DALTON FIELDS LA

C4
1 STATION TERR
2 GROVE ST
3 STATION CL
4 FILBERT CL
5 BRIDGE CL
6 RAILWAY TERR
7 SISKIN AVE
8 GRAYTHWAITE CL

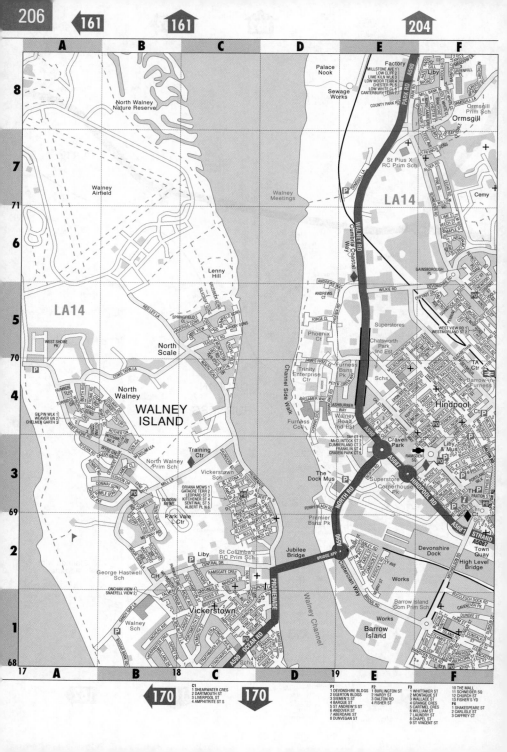

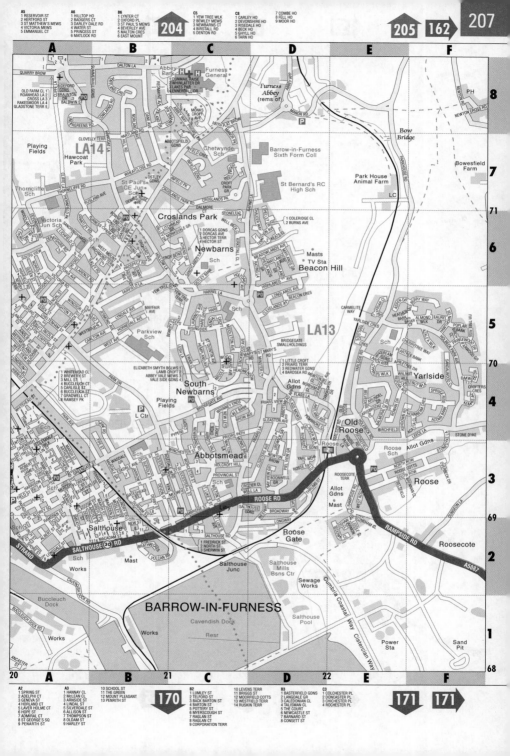

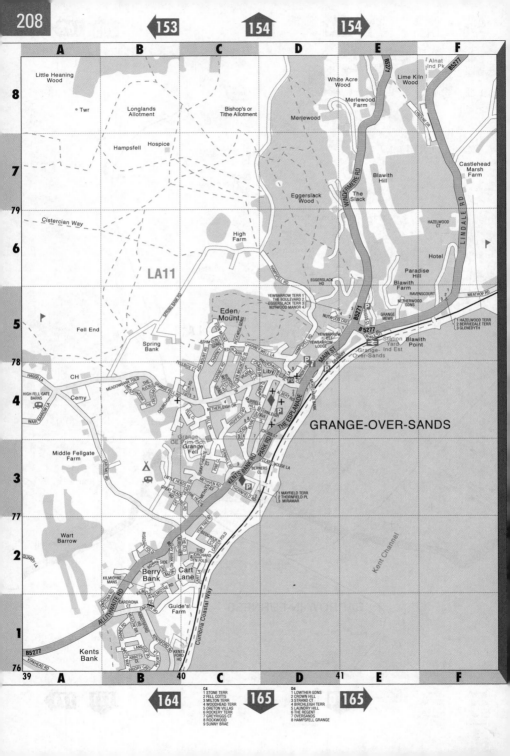

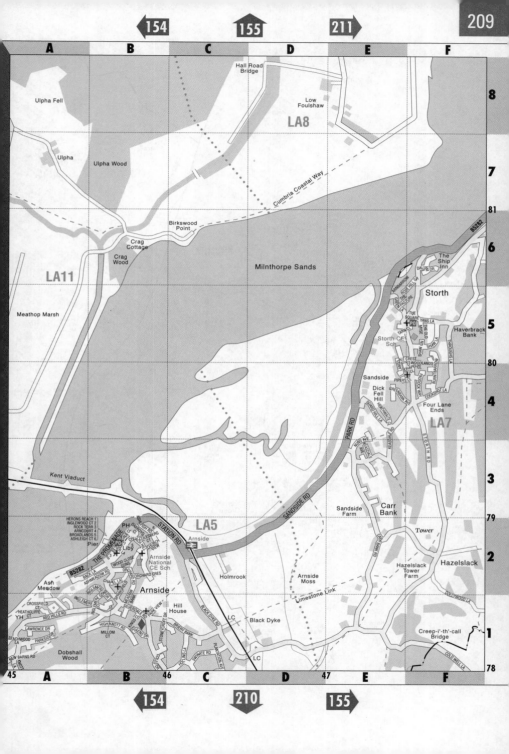

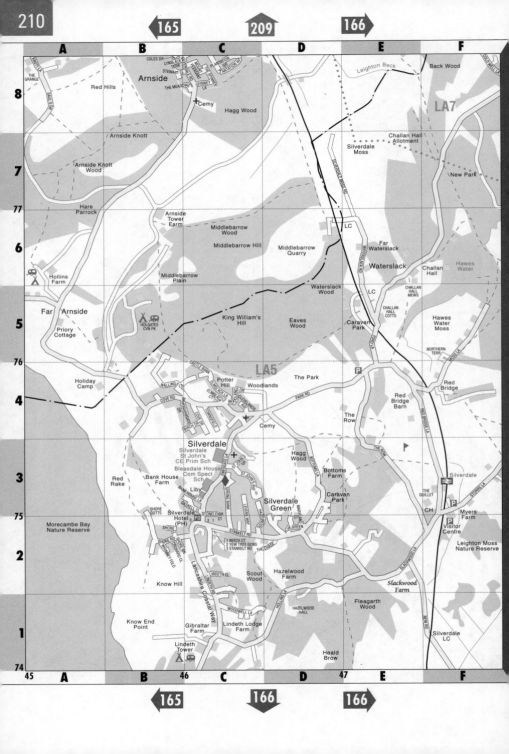

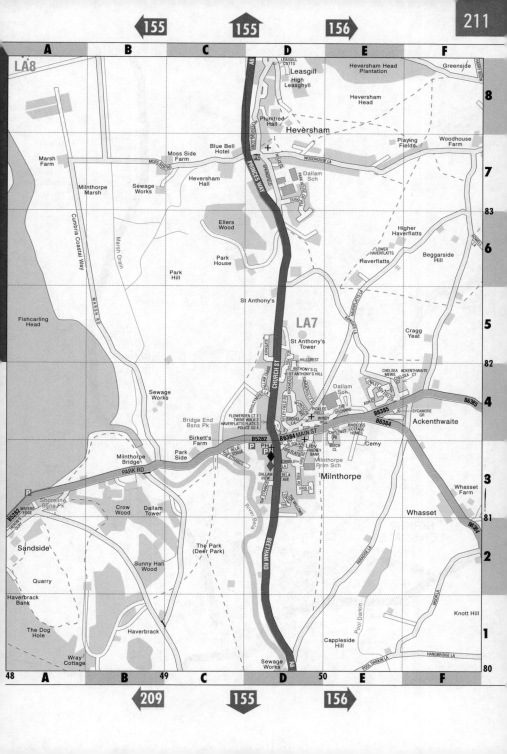

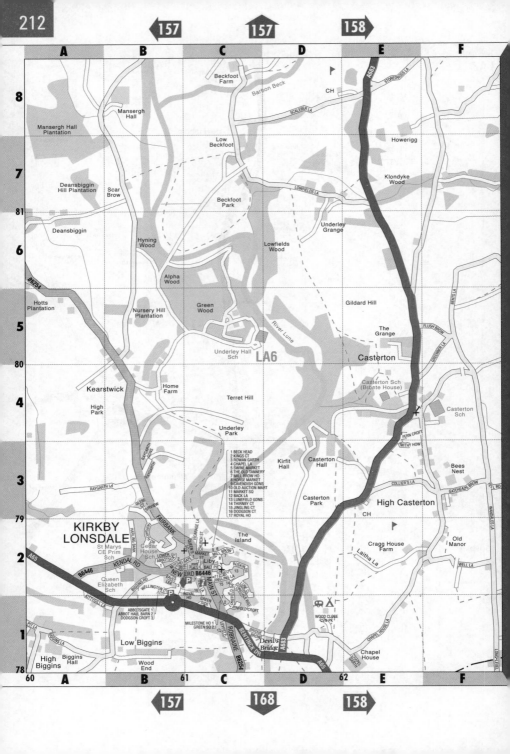

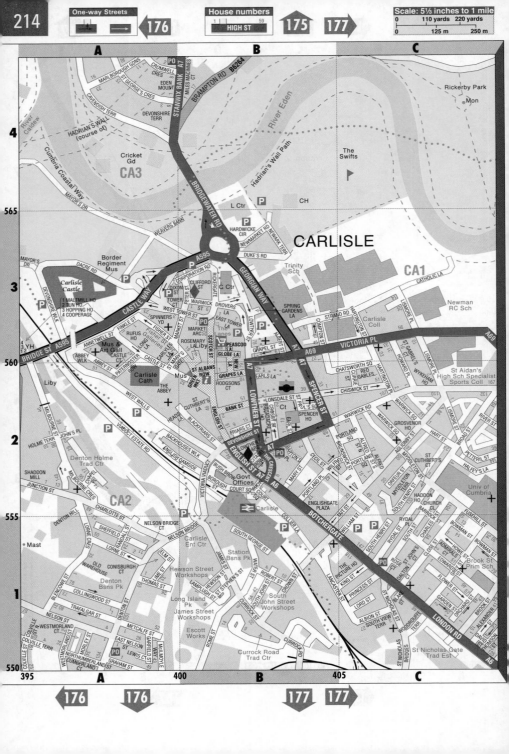

Index

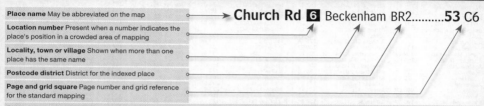

Place name May be abbreviated on the map

Location number Present when a number indicates the place's position in a crowded area of mapping

Locality, town or village Shown when more than one place has the same name

Postcode district District for the indexed place

Page and grid square Page number and grid reference for the standard mapping

Church Rd 6 Beckenham BR2.........53 C6

Cities, towns and villages are listed in CAPITAL LETTERS   Public and commercial buildings are highlighted in magenta
Places of interest are highlighted in blue with a star★

Abbreviations used in the index

Acad	Academy	Comm	Common	Gd	Ground	L	Leisure	Prom	Promenade
App	Approach	Cott	Cottage	Gdn	Garden	La	Lane	Rd	Road
Arc	Arcade	Cres	Crescent	Gn	Green	Liby	Library	Recn	Recreation
Ave	Avenue	Cswy	Causeway	Gr	Grove	Mdw	Meadow	Ret	Retail
Bglw	Bungalow	Ct	Court	H	Hall	Meml	Memorial	Sh	Shopping
Bldg	Building	Ctr	Centre	Ho	House	Mkt	Market	Sq	Square
Bsns, Bus	Business	Ctry	Country	Hospl	Hospital	Mus	Museum	St	Street
Bvd	Boulevard	Cty	County	HQ	Headquarters	Orch	Orchard	Sta	Station
Cath	Cathedral	Dr	Drive	Hts	Heights	Pal	Palace	Terr	Terrace
Cir	Circus	Dro	Drove	Ind	Industrial	Par	Parade	TH	Town Hall
Cl	Close	Ed	Education	Inst	Institute	Pas	Passage	Univ	University
Cnr	Corner	Emb	Embankment	Int	International	Pk	Park	Wk, Wlk	Walk
Coll	College	Est	Estate	Intc	Interchange	Pl	Place	Wr	Water
Com	Community	Ex	Exhibition	Junc	Junction	Prec	Precinct	Yd	Yard

Index of towns, villages, streets, hospitals, industrial estates, railway stations, schools, shopping centres, universities and places of interest

A

Aaron's Lonning CA7 ...36 B8
Abbey App LA13 .... 207 D8
Abbey Caldew Hospl
CA2 ....176 E5
Abbey Cl LA14.........184 E3
Abbey Ct CA14.........185 B7
Abbey Dr LA9..........144 B4
Abbey Farm CA27......91 C3
Abbey Garth CA20 ....108 E5
Abbey Gdns LA9 ....144 B4
Abbey Hts 4 LA16.... 162 A8
Abbey Park Hospl
LA14. .... 207 C8
Abbey Rd
Abbeytown CA7 ....26 C1
Barrow-in-F LA13, LA14....207 B6
Dalton-in-F LA15 ....205 B4
St Bees CA27............91 C3
Abbey St CA3 ....214 A2
Abbey The CA3 ....214 A2
ABBEYTOWN...........26 C1
Abbey Vale CA27 ....91 C3
Abbey Vale Mews
LA13. .... 207 C4
Abbey Way LA14........207 C8
Abbey Wlk CA3 ....214 A3
Abbot Hall Art Gallery★
LA9. ....200 D4
Abbot Hall Barn LA6 ...212 B2
Abbots Cl
Abbeytown CA7 ....26 C1
Grange-o-S LA11 ....208 B1
Abbotsfield Gdns LA13..207 C7
Abbotsford Dr CA3.....175 D3
Abbotsford Ho
Grange-o-S LA11.......208 B1
Penrith CA11 ....191 D6
Abbotsford Pl 6 CA15 .182 E5
Abbotsgate LA6.........212 B2
ABBOTSMEAD...........207 C3
Abbotsmead App LA13 .207 D4
Abbots Rd CA2 ....176 E5
Abbots Vale LA13 ......207 C3
Abbots Vue LA12.......153 C7
Abbots Way LA11......208 B1
Abbot Way CA27 ....91 C2
Abbot Wood CA14 .....63 A4
Abercorn St LA14......206 F1
Aberdare St 7 LA14 ...206 F1

Aberdeen St LA14......206 F1
Acacia Cl LA13 ....207 F4
Acacia Rd LA12 ....203 D2
Acer Gr CA28..........187 E6
ACKENTHWAITE........211 F4
Ackenthwaite Ct LA7...211 F4
Acorn Bank
Barrow-in-F LA13 ......207 F4
Cleator CA23 ....188 D4
Acorn Bank Garden &
Water Mill★ CA10.....72 E3
Acorn Bsns Pk CA3 ....175 B6
Acorn St CA12.........192 B3
Acrebank Cl CA7.......174 E8
Acre Cl CA8 ....31 F8
Acredale Rd CA2.......29 D7
Acre Dales CA7 ....177 C5
Acremire La CA7........17 B5
Acre Moss La LA9......200 B8
Acre The CA7 ....26 E6
Acton Ct CA28 ....187 D8
Adams Rd CA14........184 B4
Ada St 3 CA15 ....182 E5
Addison Pl DG12 ......172 C5
Addison St 7 CA28 ....186 C1
Adelaide St
Barrow-in-F LA14 ......206 E4
Carlisle CA1............177 C5
Adelphi Ct 2 LA14.....207 A2
Adelphi Terr CA2.......177 A4
Adgarley Way LA15 ....205 C3
Admiral Ct 4 LA14 ....207 A2
Admiral Ho 22 CA28....186 C1
Admirals Ct CA1 ....214 C1
Africanda Rd DG16. ...173 D3
Afton St LA14..........170 D6
AGLIONBY 30 F7
Aglionby St CA1 ....214 C2
Aikbank Cotts CA28 ...187 A2
Aikbank Rd CA28 ......186 E3
AIKETGATE.............42 A5
AIKRIGG...............200 F3
Aikrigg Ave LA9 ....200 B3
AIKTON................28 A4
Ainslie Dale LA15.....205 C5
Ainslie St
Barrow-in-F LA14 ......206 F5
Dalton-in-F LA15 ......205 C5
AINSTABLE.............42 F5
Ainsworth St 8 LA12 ..203 D6
Aira Force★ CA11......83 D3
Airethwaite LA9 ....200 C6

Airfield Approach Bsns Pk
LA11..................164 D6
Airygill La CA10........86 B6
Alamein Rd LA5 ....213 D3
Alanbrooke Rd CA1 ....177 F6
Alan Ct CA14 ....184 F5
Alauna Dr CA15........182 D6
Albemarle St CA13....190 B3
Albert Pl N LA14.......206 C3
Albert Pl S LA14 ......206 D3
Albert Rd LA11 ....208 D4
Albert Sq 7 CA28 .....186 D1
Albert St
Barrow-in-F LA14 ......207 A2
Carlisle CA1............214 B3
3 Carnforth LA5........213 C5
Carnforth, Millhead LA5 ..213 C5
Dalton-in-F LA15 ......205 C5
Longtown CA6 ....10 C3
Millom LA18............202 D5
Penrith CA11 ....191 D5
Seascale CA20.........123 A7
Workington CA14......184 D5
Albert Terr
12 Maryport CA15......182 E5
Whitehaven CA28 ......186 D2
Albion St
Carlisle CA1............214 C1
Whitehaven CA28 ......187 C8
ALBYFIELD.............32 D3
Alby Farm CA11 ....70 B2
Alby Gr CA25 ....188 E6
Alby St CA25 ....188 F7
Alder Ave CA15 ....182 E5
Alder Cl CA28 ....186 E4
Aldercroft LA9 ....200 B3
Alder Rd
Barrow-in-F LA14 .....206 F7
Penrith CA11 ....191 F4
Alderwood LA9 ....200 B3
Aldery Bank 5 DG14...3 D3
Aldery Terr 3 DG14....3 D3
ALDINGHAM 163 A2
ALDOTH................36 C7
Aldwych Terr LA12....203 E4
Alexander Cl LA14 ....184 E3
Alexander Dr LA8 .....144 C1
Alexander Gdns LA12 .203 D4
Alexander Pl 38 LA16 ..162 A8
Alexander Rd LA12....203 D4

Alexander St CA1 .....214 C1
Alexandra Ct LA23 ....198 E4
Alexandra Dr CA1......177 F5
Alexandra Pl DG12....172 C5
Alexandra Rd
Carnforth LA5 ....213 C3
Penrith CA11 ....191 B5
Windermere LA23 .....198 E4
Alfred Barrow Sch The
LA14..................206 F2
Alfred St N CA1........214 C2
Alfred St S CA1 ....214 C2
Alice Howe Ind Units
LA23..................198 F6
Alice La CA13..........63 E6
Albany Ct CA15 ....183 C8
Albany St CA15 ....183 C8
Allandale Rd CA1......177 F3
Allan Hill CA15 ....183 D7
Allason Cl CA8.........179 B6
ALLENWOOD...........31 E6
ALLERBY...............49 C6
Allerdale Gr CA13.....190 B2
Allhallows La LA9......200 C5
Allhallows Terr CA7....37 C1
Allison St 6 LA14 .....207 A3
ALLITHWAITE..........164 E7
Allithwaite CE Prim Sch
LA11..................164 F7
Allithwaite Rd
Flookburgh LA11 ......164 E6
Grange-o-S LA11 ......208 B1
ALLONBY..............35 C2
Allonby Cl LA14........206 B4
Allonby Prim Sch CA15...35 C2
All Saints' CE Prim Sch
CA13 ....190 E4
Alma Terr CA7 ....174 C5
Almery Dr CA2.........177 B4
Almhouses The LA20...138 E8
Almond Rd LA12 ......203 D2
Almond Wlk LA14 .....207 F5
Alnat Ind Pk LA11.....208 F8
Alne Rd CA15..........182 D4
Alpaca Ctr The★ CA11...70 D2
ALSTON 181 D4
Alstonby Ct CA6 ......20 B8
Alstonby Hall Farmstead
CA6 ....20 B8
Alston Prim Sch CA9...181 E3
Alston Sta CA9 ....181 D4
Alston Watermill★
CA9 ....181 D4

	Aar–Ans

Alton St CA2 ....177 A3
Amazonia World of
Reptiles★ LA23.......198 B2
AMBLESIDE............195 E5
Ambleside Prim Sch
LA22..................195 C5
Ambleside Rd
Keswick CA12 ....192 C3
Windermere LA23 .....198 D7
Ameshaugh Rd CA9....45 E2
Amphitrite St S 4
LA14..................206 C1
Amphitrite St LA14....206 C1
Ancaster St LA14......206 F1
Anchor Cl CA11........191 C6
Anchor Ct LA15........205 B5
Anchorite Fields LA9..200 D4
Anchorite Pl LA9 .....200 D3
Anchorite Rd LA9......200 C3
Anchor Rd LA14 ......206 F1
Andover Cl CA2........176 C5
Andover St 6 LA14 ...206 F1
Andreas Ave LA14.....206 B1
Andrews Ct LA14 .....206 D5
Andrews Way LA14....206 D6
Angel La 17 CA11 .....191 D5
Angle Meadow La
LA14..................204 B1
ANNAN.................172 B4
Annan Acad DG12.....172 C3
ANNAN HILL...........172 C1
Annanhill DG12........172 C1
Annan Hospl DG12....172 E4
Annan Rd DG16........173 C3
Annan St LA14 ....170 D6
Annan Sta DG12 ......172 C3
ANNASIDE 137 A1
Annerley Rd DG12 ....172 D2
Annetwell St CA3 .....214 A3
Ann Terr Pal La LA14 .184 C4
Annisgarth Ave LA23 .198 E3
Annisgarth Cl LA23 ...198 E3
Annisgarth Dr LA23 ..198 E3
Annisgarth Pk LA23...198 E3
Ann St
Carlisle CA2............176 D6
Dalton-in-F LA15 .....205 A5
Kendal LA9.............200 E6
Anson St LA14.........206 F4

ANTHORN 16 E1
Antonine Way CA3 .... 20 C1
ANTY CROSS 205 C4
Anvil Cl CA6 .... 21 E5
Anzac Ave LA14 .... 206 C1
Appleby Gram Sch CA16 .... 193 C7
APPLEBY-IN-WESTMORLAND 193 C6
Appleby Prim Sch CA16 .... 193 D6
Appleby Rd
Kendal LA9 .... 131 C1
Kirkby Stephen CA17 .... 104 F2
Appleby Sta CA16 .... 193 D6
Apple Garth
Cargo CA6 .... 19 D2
Stainton CA11 .... 70 D3
Applerigg
Kendal LA9 .... 200 C8
Penrith CA11 .... 191 D6
Windermere LA23 .... 198 D7
APPLETHWAITE 192 B8
Appletree Dr LA13 .... 207 E5
Apple Tree Gdns CA11 .... 71 C5
Appletree Rd LA12 .... 203 D2
Appletree Sch LA9 .... 144 A3
Applewood LA9 .... 200 B4
Applewood Cl CA1 .... 177 E6
Aquarium of the Lakes* LA12 .... 141 E2
Archer Hill LA5 .... 213 C6
Archers Garth CA2 .... 176 C7
Archers Mdw LA9 .... 200 E3
Archer St CA14 .... 185 A7
Arches The CA15 .... 182 E4
Argyle Pl LA14 .... 207 B3
Argyle St
Barrow-in-F LA14 .... 207 B3
Millom LA18 .... 202 D4
Ulverston LA12 .... 203 E5
Argyll Dr CA1 .... 177 E4
Argyll Terr DG12 .... 172 C1
ARKHOLME 168 B2
Arkholme CE Prim Sch LA6 .... 168 B3
Arkholme Cl LA5 .... 213 D4
ARKLEBY 50 C6
Arkleby Hall Cotts CA7 .... 50 C6
Arkleby Rd CA7 .... 50 C7
Arkwright Way CA1 .... 177 D3
ARLECDON 77 F2
Arlecdon Parks Rd CA26 .... 77 F1
Arlecdon Prim Sch CA26 .... 77 F1
Arlecdon Rd CA26 .... 77 E2
ARMATHWAITE 42 C5
Armathwaite Sch CA4 .... 42 C5
Armathwaite Sta CA4 .... 42 C5
Armitt Liby & Mus The* LA22 .... 195 D6
Armon Cl LA13 .... 207 E2
Armstrong Ct 4 CA8 .... 179 B5
Armstrong St 4 CA14 .... 184 D6
ARNABY 150 D7
Arnbarrow LA7 .... 209 E6
Arncourt LA5 .... 209 B2
Arnhem Rd LA5 .... 213 D3
Arnisons Ct 4 CA11 .... 191 D4
ARNSIDE 209 B2
Arnside Ct CA1 .... 177 E3
Arnside National CE Sch LA5 .... 209 B2
Arnside Rd CA1 .... 177 E3
Arnside St 3 LA14 .... 207 A3
Arnside Sta LA5 .... 209 C2
ARRAD FOOT 152 D3
Arras Ave LA11 .... 164 D6
Arthuret Dr CA6 .... 10 C3
Arthuret Rd CA6 .... 10 B3
ARTHUR SEAT 5 B5
Arthur St
Barrow-in-F LA14 .... 207 A3
Carlisle CA2 .... 177 A4
Penrith CA11 .... 191 D6
Arthur Terr 1 CA11 .... 191 D5
Artlecrag LA8 .... 130 E4
Arundel Dr LA13 .... 207 E4
ASBY 78 A3
Asby Endowed Sch CA16 .... 103 C4
Asby Rd CA14 .... 78 A3
Ash Bank LA18 .... 149 D4
Ashbank La LA8 .... 143 E2
Ashburn Croft CA11 .... 69 E5
Ashburner Way LA14 .... 206 E4
Ashby St CA15 .... 182 E5
Ash Cl CA15 .... 182 F5
Ashcroft Cl CA12 .... 80 F6
Ash Ct
Milnthorpe LA7 .... 211 E4
Ulverston LA12 .... 162 F6
Ashdown Rd LA13 .... 207 E4
Ash Dr LA5 .... 213 D8
Ashes La LA8 .... 130 C3
Ashes The LA7 .... 211 D3
Ash Fell Rd CA17 .... 120 C4
Ashfield Ct CA10 .... 118 C7
Ashfield Gdns CA14 .... 184 F4
Ashfield Inf Sch CA14 .... 184 F5
Ashfield Jun Sch CA14 .... 184 F5
Ashfield Rd CA14 .... 184 F4
Ashfield Rd S CA14 .... 184 E3
Ashford Way CA1 .... 177 E2
Ash Gr
Carlisle CA3 .... 175 C2
Ulverston LA12 .... 203 D2
Whitehaven CA28 .... 186 E4
Ashgrove CA13 .... 190 D3
Ash Lea CA8 .... 179 C5
Ashlea Rd CA22 .... 189 B6
Ashleigh Ct LA5 .... 209 B2
Ashleigh Pl CA28 .... 187 E7
Ashleigh Rd
Arnside LA5 .... 209 B2
Kendal LA9 .... 200 C7
Ashley St CA2 .... 176 E6
Ashley Way CA22 .... 189 C5
Ashman Cl CA2 .... 176 F4
Ash Mdw LA9 .... 200 E7
Ashmeadow Rd LA5 .... 209 B2
Ashmore Gdns CA14 .... 184 C3
Ashmount Gdns LA11 .... 208 C5
Ash Mount Rd LA11 .... 208 C5
Ashness Cl CA28 .... 187 D3
Ashness Dr CA2 .... 176 C3
Ash Rd CA11 .... 191 F5
Ash St LA23 .... 198 C2
Ashton St CA14 .... 184 E5
Ashtree Ave CA12 .... 192 A5
Ash Tree Sq CA5 .... 18 F1
Ashtrees Way 2 LA5 .... 213 C4
Ashwell Pl TD9 .... 1 B6
Ashworth St 3 LA15 .... 205 C5
ASKAM IN FURNESS 162 A8
Askam Rd LA15 .... 205 A7
Askam Sta LA16 .... 162 A8
Askam View LA16 .... 162 B8
Askam Village Sch LA16 .... 162 A8
Askerton Cl CA3 .... 175 D3
ASKHAM 85 D6
Askham Cres CA11 .... 191 E5
ASPATRIA 50 C8
Aspatria Bsns Pk CA7 .... 36 D1
Aspatria Richmond Hill Sch CA7 .... 36 D1
Aspatria Sta CA7 .... 50 C8
Aspen Dr LA13 .... 207 E5
Aspen Gdns CA11 .... 191 F5
Assembly Sq CA7 .... 26 C1
Astor Ho CA2 .... 176 C7
Athens Dr LA13 .... 207 C6
Atholl Gr CA2 .... 176 B4
Athol St LA14 .... 206 F1
Atkinson Cres CA1 .... 177 D2
Atkinson Ct LA12 .... 141 F1
Atkinson St LA18 .... 150 A1
Auchinleck Dr CA1 .... 177 F6
Auctionmart La 13 CA11 .... 191 C5
Auctionmart Rd 12 CA11 .... 191 C5
AUGHERTREE 52 A5
Aughton Rd LA2 .... 167 F1
Austhwaite Brow CA19 .... 125 A6
Austin Friars Sch CA3 .... 175 C1
Avenue The
Bassenthwaite CA12 .... 66 C7
Broughton Moor CA15 .... 63 C8
Edenhall CA11 .... 71 F6
Gilgarran CA14 .... 77 C6
Grange-o-S LA11 .... 208 B4
Avocet Cres LA16 .... 161 F8
Avon Cl CA2 .... 176 B4
Avon St LA14 .... 170 C6
AYLE 45 F8
Aynam Ct LA9 .... 200 D4
Aynam Pl LA9 .... 200 D4
Aynam Rd LA9 .... 200 D4
Aynsome La LA11 .... 153 F2
Aynsome Mill Farm LA11 .... 153 F2
Aynsome Rd LA11 .... 153 F2
Ayr St LA14 .... 170 D6
Aysgarth Cl LA9 .... 200 B8
AYSIDE 154 A6
Azalea Cl CA11 .... 71 C5
Azalea Wlk LA13 .... 207 F5

B

BACKBARROW 153 D7
Back Barton St 3 LA14 .... 207 B2
Back Bay View LA18 .... 202 B5
Back Belsfield Rd LA23 .... 198 C2
Back Casson St 2 LA12 .... 203 E5
Back Corkickle CA28 .... 187 D8
Back Ellerthwaite Rd 7 LA23 .... 198 E5
Back Ennerdale CA25 .... 188 E7
Back Ford Pk LA12 .... 203 D6
Back Fox St LA12 .... 203 A3
Back Ginns CA28 .... 187 C7
Backhouses Wlk CA2 .... 214 B2
Back Hunter St 1 LA5 .... 213 C4
Back La
Appleby-in-W CA16 .... 193 D5
Arnside LA5 .... 209 B2
Backbarrow LA12 .... 153 C8
Beetham LA7 .... 155 F1
Bowness-on-W LA8 .... 129 F1
3 Brampton CA8 .... 179 B5
Brigsteer LA8 .... 143 F4
Broughton-in-F LA20 .... 139 A2
Carnforth LA5, LA6 .... 213 D2
Cockermouth CA13 .... 190 C5
Flookburgh LA11 .... 164 C6
Back La *continued*
Great Broughton CA13 .... 63 E6
Kendal, Garth Row LA8 .... 131 D4
Kendal LA9 .... 200 E5
Kirkby Lonsdale LA6 .... 212 C2
Langwathby CA10 .... 72 A8
Legburthwaite CA12 .... 82 B1
Levens LA8 .... 143 F1
Lindale LA11 .... 154 C3
Long Marton CA16 .... 88 A7
3 Maryport CA15 .... 182 D5
Melkinthorpe CA10 .... 86 B8
Newby Bridge LA11, LA12 .... 153 F7
Row LA8 .... 143 A4
Sedbergh LA10 .... 201 C5
Sedgwick LA8 .... 144 A1
Shap CA10 .... 101 C6
Staveley LA8 .... 130 C5
Troutbeck LA23 .... 114 F2
Tunstall LA6 .... 168 D4
Ulverston LA12 .... 203 D6
Warton LA5 .... 213 C7
Wrayton LA6 .... 168 E2
Back Lady St DG12 .... 172 C4
Back New St 5 LA5 .... 213 C4
Back O' Th' Fell Rd LA11 .... 154 C5
Back Rd LA11 .... 154 C3
Back St CA4 .... 31 B1
Back Sun St LA12 .... 203 C6
Back Wyndham St CA25 .... 188 E7
Baden Powell St LA14 .... 206 C3
Badgers Ct 2 LA14 .... 207 A6
Badgers Rake LA22 .... 195 D4
BAILEY 5 D6
Bailey Rd CA3 .... 175 C3
Bailey St 4 LA12 .... 203 E5
Bainbridge Ct LA10 .... 201 C5
Bainbridge Rd LA10 .... 201 C5
Baird Rd CA1 .... 177 D2
Baker Cl LA15 .... 205 C6
Baldwin Ave LA15 .... 205 B5
BALDWINHOLME 29 A2
Baldwin St LA14 .... 207 A8
Balfour Rd CA2 .... 176 C5
Baliol Sch LA10 .... 201 E5
Balmoral Cl CA11 .... 191 B4
Balmoral Ct 1 CA3 .... 175 B1
Balmoral Dr LA13 .... 207 E4
Balmoral Ho 16 CA12 .... 192 B3
Balmoral Rd CA28 .... 187 F7
BAMPTON 85 D1
BAMPTON GRANGE 100 E8
BANDRAKE HEAD 140 E2
BANK END
Broughton in Furness 138 E3
Maryport 48 E5
Bank End LA18 .... 202 A2
Bankend Cotts CA24 .... 91 F3
Bankend Rd CA3 .... 175 B5
Bankend View CA22 .... 188 A2
Bankfield
Beckermet CA21 .... 108 B6
Kendal LA9 .... 200 B4
Bankfield Gdns LA14 .... 206 C5
Bankfield Rd
Haverigg LA18 .... 202 A2
Kendal LA9 .... 200 C4
Bank Hall CA8 .... 23 B2
Bank Head LA18 .... 149 F2
Bankhead La LA8 .... 143 E4
Bank House La
Silverdale LA5 .... 210 C3
Westhouse LA6 .... 169 E4
Bank La
Barrow-in-F LA14 .... 204 A1
Crosby Ravensworth CA10 .... 102 C5
Egremont CA22 .... 189 E6
Maryport CA15 .... 182 D6
Banklands CA14 .... 184 E5
Banklands Ct CA14 .... 184 E5
BANK MOOR 102 E3
Bank Rd
Whitehaven CA28 .... 186 D3
Windermere LA23 .... 198 D3
Workington CA14 .... 184 F5
BANKS 22 F7
Banks Cres CA7 .... 180 D2
Banks Ct 11 CA13 .... 190 D4
Banks Hill Turret 52a* CA8 .... 23 A7
Bankside LA12 .... 152 D5
Bank Side CA14 .... 185 D4
Banks La
Carlisle CA1 .... 177 E6
Dent LA10 .... 147 B1
Banks Pl 8 CA12 .... 192 B3
Bank St
Annan DG12 .... 172 C4
Carlisle CA3 .... 214 B2
4 Kendal LA9 .... 200 C4
Keswick CA12 .... 192 B4
Longtown CA6 .... 10 B3
Banks The LA8 .... 130 C5
Bank Terr
Bowness-on-W LA23 .... 198 D3
Coniston LA21 .... 196 A3
Lindal in F LA12 .... 162 E7
Maryport CA15 .... 182 D4
Penny Bridge LA12 .... 152 E5
Bank Top LA11 .... 164 D7
Bank Top Cl LA11 .... 164 D7
Bank Yard Rd CA28 .... 186 D5
Bannatyne Dr CA14 .... 185 D7
Bannerigg 6 LA23 .... 198 E5
Banneriggs Brow LA6 .... 158 A5
Bannisdale LA8 .... 130 E4
Bannisdale Way CA2 .... 176 C2
BARBER GREEN 154 A5
BARBON 157 F5
Barbondale Rd LA6, LA10 .... 158 E8
BARCLOSE 20 F5
Barco Ave CA11 .... 191 E5
Barco Ct CA11 .... 191 E5
Barco Terr 1 CA11 .... 191 E4
BARDSEA 163 C5
Bardsea Cl LA15 .... 205 B3
BARDSEA GREEN 163 C5
Bardsea L Pk LA12 .... 203 E2
Bardsea Rd LA13 .... 207 D4
Bardsley St CA2 .... 176 C6
BAREPOT 62 E4
Barfs Rd CA14 .... 185 D4
Barker Cl LA6 .... 167 B7
Barker's La LA6 .... 156 C4
Barkers Mdw CA13 .... 64 A3
Barkhouse Cl CA11 .... 191 E4
Barley Bridge LA8 .... 130 C5
Barnard St 7 LA13 .... 207 B3
Barncroft Ave CA14 .... 183 B3
Barncroft Cl CA14 .... 183 A2
Barnes Ave LA15 .... 205 B3
Barnes Croft CA11 .... 57 A3
Barnes Gn CA11 .... 57 A3
Barnes Rd CA14 .... 184 C5
Barnett Dr CA14 .... 183 B3
Barnfield LA22 .... 197 E5
Barnfield La LA14 .... 206 F8
Barn Garth LA11 .... 153 F1
Barnghyll Pl CA14 .... 185 C3
Barn Holme LA9 .... 200 B4
BARNOLDSWICK 169 D2
Barnoldswick La LA6 .... 169 D3
Barnrigg LA6 .... 157 F5
Barnsdale Rd CA14 .... 184 D4
Barns The CA18 .... 123 F3
Baron's Hill CA11 .... 70 C3
Baron Way CA6 .... 175 A7
Barque St 4 LA14 .... 206 F1
Barras Brow
Dalston CA5 .... 29 D1
South Stainmore CA17 .... 106 A2
Barras Cl
Carlisle CA2 .... 176 C3
Dalston CA5 .... 29 D1
Barras Ho CA5 .... 29 D1
Barras La CA5 .... 29 D1
Barratt Croft LA21 .... 196 A4
Barrock Cl CA4 .... 41 C4
Barrock St CA1 .... 214 C2
BARROW-IN-FURNESS 207 C1
Barrow-in-Furness Sixth Form Coll LA13 .... 207 D7
Barrow-in-Furness Sta LA14 .... 206 F4
BARROW ISLAND 206 E1
Barrow Island Com Prim Sch LA14 .... 206 F1
Barrowmoor Rd CA16 .... 193 B4
Barrow Rd
Barrow-in-F LA13 .... 204 F1
Dalton-in-F LA13 .... 205 A3
Barr's La CA13 .... 64 A5
Barth La LA10 .... 147 A3
BARTON 70 D1
Barton Dale CA10 .... 57 A6
Barton Row LA6 .... 167 B7
Barton's Pl CA1 .... 214 B2
Barton St 4 LA14 .... 207 B2
Barton View CA11 .... 191 E6
Barwise Brow CA7 .... 17 A5
Barwise Row CA26 .... 77 E1
Barwood Gr LA13 .... 207 F5
Basket Rd CA28 .... 187 B8
BASSENTHWAITE 66 C7
Bassenthwaite Cl LA18 .... 202 C4
Bassenthwaite Prim Sch CA12 .... 66 B6
Bassenthwaite St CA2 .... 176 D5
Basterfield Gdns 1 LA13 .... 207 B3
Bath St LA14 .... 206 E4
Battery St DG12 .... 172 C4
Battlebarrow CA16 .... 193 C6
BATTLEHILL 17 A8
Baybarrow Rd CA22 .... 189 C6
BAYCLIFF 163 B3
Baycliffe Dr LA15 .... 205 C2
BAYLES 181 B1
Baysdale Cl LA14 .... 206 F7
Bayside CA17 .... 105 B5
Baystone Bank La LA18 .... 150 B8
Bay Stones Cl LA12 .... 163 B3
Bay Tree Rd LA12 .... 203 E3
Bay View
Millom LA18 .... 202 B5
St Bees CA27 .... 91 C2
Bay View Gr LA13 .... 207 D3
Beach Cres LA14 .... 170 B6
Beach Rd CA27 .... 91 C2
Beach St
Askam in F LA16 .... 162 A8
Workington CA14 .... 184 C3
Beachwood La LA5 .... 209 A1
Beacon Cl
Aspatria CA7 .... 36 C1
Penrith CA11 .... 191 C7
Beacon Cres LA13 .... 207 D5
Beacon Edge CA11 .... 191 E6
BEACON HILL 207 D6
Beacon Hill Com Sch CA7 .... 50 C8
Beacon Pk CA11 .... 191 D6
Beaconsfield St CA2 .... 177 A4
Beaconsfield Terr CA7 .... 174 B3
Beaconside CE Inf Sch CA11 .... 191 E6
Beaconside CE Jun Sch CA11 .... 191 E5
Beacon Sq CA11 .... 191 D6
Beacon St CA11 .... 191 D6
Beacon The (Mus)* CA28 .... 186 B1
Beacon View LA8 .... 132 A4
BEANTHWAITE 151 D7
Beast Banks LA9 .... 200 C5
Beatham Ct 5 CA11 .... 191 C6
Beathwaite Cl LA8 .... 143 D1
Beathwaite Gdns LA8 .... 143 D1
Beatrix Potter Gallery* LA22 .... 197 E5
Beatty Cl CA28 .... 186 D3
Beatty Rd CA28 .... 186 D3
Beaufort Ave CA14 .... 185 D7
BEAUMONT 19 B2
Beaumont Rd CA2 .... 177 A2
Beaver Rd CA2 .... 176 A6
BECK 78 B2
BECK BOTTOM 152 C7
Beck Brow LA19 .... 137 B3
BECKCES 69 C2
Beck Cl
Braystones CA21 .... 108 A5
Carlisle CA2 .... 176 A7
BECKERMET 108 B5
Beckermet CE Sch CA21 .... 108 B5
Beckermet Gdns LA14 .... 204 C1
Beckermet Ind Est CA22 .... 108 C7
BECKFOOT 35 D8
BECK FOOT 132 E3
Beckfoot Sta* CA19 .... 125 B7
Beckgate LA6 .... 157 F5
Beck Gn
Distington CA14 .... 185 D2
Egremont CA22 .... 189 E6
Beck Head LA6 .... 212 C2
Beck Ho 4 LA14 .... 207 C8
BECK HOUSES 132 B3
Beck La
Brampton CA8 .... 179 B5
Crosby Garrett CA17 .... 120 B7
Old Town LA6 .... 157 A6
Beck Nook LA8 .... 130 B5
Beck Orchard CA8 .... 179 B5
Beck Rd CA2 .... 176 A6
Beck Riggs CA8 .... 179 B5
Beck Rise CA21 .... 108 B5
Beck Row CA22 .... 108 D7
BECK SIDE
Cartmel 153 E3
Kirkby-in-Furness 151 C5
Beckside
Eaglesfield CA13 .... 64 A3
Flimby CA15 .... 183 C7
Hallthwaites LA18 .... 150 C7
High Harrington CA14 .... 185 B7
Kendal LA9 .... 200 F2
Penrith CA11 .... 191 B4
Penrith, Scaws CA11 .... 191 F5
Plumpton CA11 .... 56 B3
Soulby CA17 .... 104 C1
Whitehaven CA28 .... 187 F7
Beckside Cl CA13 .... 190 E4
Beckside Cotts LA19 .... 137 B3
Beckside Ct
5 Brampton CA8 .... 179 B5
Kirkby-in-F LA17 .... 151 C5
8 Ulverston LA12 .... 203 D5
Beckside Gdns CA8 .... 179 D4
Beckside Mews LA6 .... 167 B3
Beckside Rd
Dalton-in-F LA15 .... 205 C4
Ulverston LA12 .... 203 C6
Beckstone Cl CA14 .... 185 A8
Beckstone Prim Sch CA14 .... 185 A7
Beck Yeat LA21 .... 196 A3
Bective Rd LA6 .... 212 C2
Bedford Rd CA2 .... 176 E5
Bedford St
Barrow-in-F LA14 .... 207 A5
Hensingham CA28 .... 187 F6
Millom LA18 .... 202 D4
Bedford Villas CA28 .... 187 F6
Beeby Ct 21 CA14 .... 184 D6
Beeby St CA14 .... 184 D6
Beech Ave CA22 .... 189 D7
Beech Bank LA12 .... 203 D6
Beech Cl
Clifton CA11 .... 71 C5
Kendal LA9 .... 200 F5
Milnthorpe LA7 .... 211 E3
Beech Cotts LA12 .... 152 E6
Beech Croft
Braithwaite CA12 .... 80 F6
Burgh by S CA5 .... 18 F2
Wigton CA7 .... 180 C3
Beech Ct
Silverdale LA5 .... 210 C2
Swarthmoor LA12 .... 203 A1
Workington CA14 .... 184 E3
Beech Dr LA12 .... 203 E3
Beeches The
Great Corby CA4 .... 178 C2
Maryport CA15 .... 182 F6
Beechfields LA12 .... 162 F4

Beech Gdns CA11 71 C5
Beech Gr
  Carlisle CA3 175 E2
  Houghton CA3 20 C2
  Seaton CA14 183 B1
  Stainton CA11 70 D3
  Warton LA5 213 C7
  Whitehaven CA28 186 E3
Beech Hill
  Dent LA10 147 B2
  Oughterside CA7 49 F6
Beech Hill Terr LA9 200 C6
Beech La CA13 190 E5
Beechlands LA12 203 D3
Beech Lea CA7 27 B7
Beech Rd LA11 208 C4
Beech St
  Barrow-in-F LA14 206 F6
  Windermere LA23 198 E6
Beech Terr LA6 169 F3
Beech Tree Cotts LA6 169 F3
Beech Tree Ct CA6 20 F8
Beech Tree Farm CA4 30 F3
Beechwood Ave CA3 175 E2
Beechwood Cl
  Bowness-on-W LA23 198 D2
  Maryport CA15 182 F5
Beehive Bldgs 23 CA28 186 C1
Beehive La LA8 144 D5
Bee Hive The LA12 203 B4
Beemire LA23 198 D5
BEETHAM 155 F2
Beetham CE Prim Sch LA7 155 E2
Beetham Cvn Pk LA5, LA7 166 E8
Beetham Ho LA7 155 E2
Beetham Rd LA7 211 D2
Beezon Fields LA9 200 D6
Beezon Rd LA9 200 D6
Beezon Trad Est LA9 200 D6
Bega Ho CA28 187 D8
Beggars La CA10 119 A4
Bela Ave LA7 211 D3
Bela Forge LA7 211 C3
BELAH 175 C2
Belah Cres CA3 175 D2
Belah Prim Sch CA3 175 D2
Belah Rd CA3 175 C2
Belfry Cl CA3 175 B1
Belgravia CA16 193 C7
Bellaport Gdns CA14 185 A7
Bellbrigg Lonning CA13 190 E3
Bell Cl CA12 192 B4
Belle Hill Cotts LA12 162 D7
Belle Isle Pl CA14 184 C6
Belle Isle St 10 CA14 184 D6
Belle Isle View LA23 198 C2
BELLE VUE 176 B6
Belle Vue Cres CA14 185 D2
Belle Vue Inf Sch CA2 176 A6
Belle Vue Jun Sch CA2 176 A6
Belle Vue La LA22 195 D6
Bellevue Rd CA16 193 D6
Bellgarth Gdns CA2 176 C7
Bellgarth Rd CA2 176 C7
Bellgarth Sq CA2 176 C7
Bellgate Steading CA7 50 C8
Bell Hill LA11 154 C3
Bell Hill Pk LA11 154 C3
Bellingham Rd LA9 200 C1
Bell La CA10 86 F5
Bellman Cl LA23 129 A1
Bellsfield CA6 10 C3
Belmont
  Kendal LA9 200 C5
  Ulverston LA12 203 E6
Belmont Brow 8 LA9 200 C5
Belmont Rd CA2 177 B3
Belsfield LA13 207 E3
Belsfield Ct LA23 198 C2
Belsfield Terr LA23 198 C2
Belted Will Cl CA7 180 C4
Belvedere Rd LA13 207 E4
Belvedere St CA14 184 E6
Benfield LA22 194 C5
Bensmoore Rd DG16 173 D5
Benson Gn LA9 200 D6
Benson Lane LA19 124 C1
Benson Row CA11 191 D5
Benson St 16 LA12 203 D5
Bentham Moor Rd LA6 169 D2
Bentham Rd LA6 169 E3
Bents La LA6 158 A3
Benwell Cl CA2 176 A6
Beresford Ct LA23 198 D3
Beresford Rd LA23 198 D3
Berkeley Ct CA11 191 B4
Berkeley Grange CA2 176 B6
Berlin St CA1 177 C4
Bermuda Cres LA14 170 C6
Berners Cl LA11 208 C3
Berriedale Terr LA11 208 F5
BERRIER 69 B4
Berrier Rd CA11 69 E5
BERRY BANK 208 B2
Berry Bank Rd LA11 208 B2
Berrymoor Rd CA8 179 C6
Berwick St CA14 184 E5
Bessamer Way LA14 206 D4
Bessemer Way CA14 184 C5
Bessy Bank La LA12 140 D1
Bessy Ghyll Bsns Pk CA10 86 A4
Betsy La CA10 72 E2
Betweengates La LA6 157 F7
Bevan Terr CA9 46 F2
Beveridge Rd CA2 176 F4
Beverley Ave 4 LA14 207 B6
Beverley Cl CA14 184 D3
Beverley Rise CA1 30 E5
BEWALDETH 51 D1
BEWCASTLE 6 C1
Bewcastle Cl CA3 175 C3
Bewcastle Sch CA6 5 E4
Bewley Mews 2 LA13 207 C5
Bewley Stps LA13 207 C5
Bideford Gdns LA14 207 A8
BIGGAR 170 D5
Biggar Bank Rd LA14 170 B6
Biggar Garth LA14 170 C6
Biggins La
  Kirkby Lonsdale LA6 212 A1
  Whittington LA6 168 C8
Biggins Rd LA6 212 B2
Bigland Dr LA12 203 D2
BIGLANDS 27 E4
BIGRIGG 188 A3
Billings Rd LA13 205 A2
Bindloss Cottage Homes LA7 211 E4
Binfold Croft LA6 212 C1
Birch Cl
  Barrow-in-F LA13 207 F5
  Workington CA14 184 D3
Birch Cres CA11 191 F4
Birchdale Rd CA2 29 D6
Birch Dr LA5 210 C4
Birchfield LA8 156 D8
Birchfields LA13 207 E4
Birch Gr LA5 165 F8
Birch Hill La CA7 27 C8
Birchleigh Terr 4 LA11 208 D4
Birch Rd LA22 195 D5
Birch St LA23 198 E5
Birch Trees LA23 198 D7
Birchwood Cl
  Kendal LA9 200 B3
  Ulverston LA12 203 D1
Birchwood Dr LA12 203 D1
Birdcage Wlk CA7 180 D3
BIRD DYKE 78 D4
Birdoswald Dr CA2 29 D6
Birdoswald Roman Fort (mus)★ CA8 14 B1
Bird St CA14 184 D5
Birkbeck Cl LA9 200 F3
BIRKBY 49 A4
Birkett Dr LA12 203 C2
Birkett Hill Cotts LA23 198 C1
Birkett La CA17 199 F5
Birkfield Rd LA23 198 E4
Birkhaw La LA10 133 A1
Birklands Old Mill LA8 144 C6
Birkrigg Cl LA12 203 A2
Birkrigg Cres LA12 203 C2
BIRKS 201 B4
Birks La
  Endmoor LA7 156 E7
  Sedbergh LA10 201 B4
Birks Rd
  Cleator Moor CA25 188 E7
  Ludderburn LA23 142 B6
  Windermere LA23 142 A6
Birkthwaite Mews CA4 41 B6
Birky La CA6 20 E3
Birley Ct 6 CA28 186 D1
Birstall Rd 4 LA13 207 C5
Birthwaite LA23 198 D6
Birthwaite Ground LA23 198 E5
Birthwaite Rd LA23 198 D6
Bishop Ct LA9 200 D4
Bishop Harvey Goodwin Sch The CA2 177 B3
Bishops Cl CA2 176 E6
Bishop's Mill CA5 40 B8
Bishop St CA14 184 D6
Biskey Howe Pk LA23 198 D3
Biskey Howe Rd LA23 198 D3
Bisland Ct CA1 177 E3
BLACKBECK 108 C6
Blackbeck Brow LA8 143 B6
Black Beck Cvn Pk LA12 153 A8
Black Beck Rd LA22 197 E5
Blackberry Hill LA7 155 E2
Blackbull Barn CA17 199 C6
Black Bull La CA17 105 B5
Blackburn Dr CA1 177 F2
Blackburn St CA14 184 D5
Black Butts La LA14 206 C1
Black Combe Jun Sch LA18 202 B5
BLACKDYKE 25 F3
Blackdyke Rd CA3 175 B5
Black Dyke Rd LA5 209 C1
BLACKFORD 20 A5
Blackford CE Prim Sch CA6 20 A5
Blackfriars St CA3 214 B2
Blackhall Croft 11 LA9 200 D5
Blackhall Rd LA9 200 D5
Black Ling Cotts CA22 189 B3
Black Rd LA8 143 C3
Blacksike Sq DG16 173 D5
Blackthorn Cl LA9 200 C8
BLACKWELL 30 B3
Blackwell Pl CA2 177 A2
Blackwell Rd CA2 177 A3
Blackwood Rd CA14 185 F7
BLAGILL 46 B6
Blake Fell Cl CA28 76 F1
Blake St
  Barrow-in-F LA14 206 E4
  Carlisle CA1 214 C1
BLAWITH 140 C3
Blea Beck 28 LA16 162 A8
BLEACHGREEN 186 E4
Bleachgreen Paddock CA28 186 E3
Bleacrag Bridge LA11 154 D6
Bleacrag Rd LA11 154 D7
Bleaflatt La CA17 120 B3
Blea Moor Rd LA6 160 C2
Bleas
  Egremont CA22 92 F1
  Haile CA22 108 E8
Bleasdale House Com Specl Sch LA5 210 C3
Blease Rd CA12 82 B8
Bleaswood Cl LA9 144 B4
Bleaswood Rd LA9 144 B4
BLEATARN 104 B4
Blea Tarn Cl LA9 200 F1
Blea Tarn Rd LA9 200 F1
BLENCARN 73 B6
Blencarn Pk CA6 19 C4
Blencathra Bsns Ctr CA12 82 C7
Blencathra Ct
  Cockermouth CA13 190 F4
  Penrith CA11 191 C3
Blencathra Gdns LA9 200 F1
Blencathra St CA12 192 C3
Blencathra View CA12 82 C7
BLENCOGO 37 B6
Blencowe St CA2 214 A1
Bleng Ave CA28 187 E6
Blenket Cl LA11 164 F7
Blenkinsopp Castle Home Pk CA8 24 D7
Blenkinsopp Terr CA8 24 D7
BLENNERHASSET 50 F8
Blennerhasset Sch CA7 50 F8
Bletherbarrow La LA12 140 C3
Blind Beck Ho 17 LA9 200 C4
BLINDCRAKE 50 D1
Blind La
  Burton in L LA6 169 C3
  Cleator Moor CA24, CA25 188 C6
  Great Asby CA16 103 B7
BLITTERLEES 174 C1
Bloody Bones La CA17 199 C6
Bloomfield Pk LA5 213 C3
Blooming Heather CA15 49 A2
Bluebell Cl LA9 200 F2
Bluebell Ct 8 CA11 191 C5
Bluebell La CA11 191 C5
Blue Dial Cvn Pk CA15 49 B7
Blue Hill LA22 195 D5
Blue Hill Rd LA22 195 D4
Blundell Rd CA1 177 E2
Blunt St CA2 176 F4
Blyth Rise LA14 206 A4
BNFL Vst Ctr★ CA20 108 D4
Boarbank Farm LA11 164 F7
Boarbank La LA11 164 F7
Boarbank Rd LA12 203 D2
Bobbin Mill Cotts LA12 152 D7
Bobbin Mill La LA20 138 D7
Bog La
  Ambleside LA22 195 A3
  Skelwith Bridge LA22 113 F2
Bogle Crag Forest Wlk★ LA12 141 A8
Bolefoot LA9 144 B4
Bollam Terr CA17 199 D5
BOLTON 87 E6
BOLTONFELLEND 11 F3
BOLTONGATE 51 F7
Bolton Hall CA16 87 D6
BOLTON LOW HOUSES 37 F3
Bolton Pl 12 LA12 203 D5
Bolton Prim Sch CA16 87 D5
Boltons CE Sch CA7 37 F3
Bolton St
  Barrow-in-F LA13 207 C3
  Workington CA14 184 D5
BOLTON WOOD LANE 38 B3
BOMBY 100 E8
Bonfire Hall La LA8 143 C7
Bongate CA16 193 D4
BONNING GATE 130 D2
Bookwell CA22 189 D5
Bookwell Prim Sch CA22 189 D5
Boon Town LA6 167 C7
Boonwell Gr LA13 207 D3
Boon Wlks LA6 167 C7
BOOT 125 C8
Boot Brow CA14 185 D2
Booth St LA5 213 C3
BOOTLE 137 B3
Bootle Sta LA19 137 A4
Border Ave CA25 188 C8
Border Cl CA1 177 F2
Border Cres DG16 173 D2
Border Regiment Mus★ CA3 214 A3
Borders Bsns Pk CA6 10 C3
Borland Ave
  Carlisle CA1 177 D5
  Carlisle CA1 177 E5
Boroughgate CA16 193 C5
Borough St CA3 214 B2
Borrans Ct LA22 195 C3
Borrans La LA23 129 E7
Borrans Park Ho LA22 195 C4
Borrans Rd LA22 195 C3
Borrans The LA22 195 C4
Borron La LA6 167 C3
Borrowdale CE Prim Sch CA12 96 B4
Borrowdale Gdns
  Barrow-in-F LA14 204 D1
  Carlisle CA2 176 D5
Borrowdale Rd
  Carlisle CA2 176 D5
  Keswick CA12 192 B2
  Whitehaven CA28 187 D3
BORWICK 167 B4
Borwick Ave LA5 213 D8
Borwick Cl LA5 213 D8
Borwick Ct LA6 167 B4
Borwick La LA6 167 B3
Borwick Mews LA6 167 B3
BORWICK RAILS 202 E4
Borwick Rd LA6 167 D3
Boston Ave CA2 177 A3
Botany Ct 16 CA14 184 D6
BOTCHERBY 177 D5
Botcherby Ave CA1 177 D5
Botcherby Hall CA1 177 E6
Botchergate CA1 214 B1
BOTHEL 51 A5
Bottoms La LA5 210 D3
Boulevard The LA11 208 E5
Boundary Bank LA9 143 E7
Boundary Bank La LA9 200 A5
Boundary Rd CA2 177 B3
Bounty Ave CA15 182 E4
Bourne Gdns LA14 206 A4
Bourneville LA9 130 F2
BOUSTEAD HILL 18 C1
Boustead's Grassing CA2 176 F4
BOUTH 152 F8
Bouthwood Rd LA14 204 C4
BOW 29 A7
BOWBER HEAD 120 B2
Bow Bridge★ LA13 207 E7
Bowder Stone★ CA12 96 B7
Bowerbank Way CA11 191 B6
Bowerhouse Bank CA19 124 D7
Bower St CA2 176 D6
Bowes Ho CA2 176 C7
Bowfell Cres
  Barrow-in-F LA14 204 D1
  Windermere LA23 198 F5
Bow Fell Rd CA28 187 E3
Bow Flatts CA14 63 A4
BOWLAND BRIDGE 142 D4
Bowland Cl LA5 213 B3
Bowland Dr LA9 144 C8
Bowling Green Cvn Pk LA5 213 B3
Bowman St CA1 214 C1
Bowness Ct CA14 184 E3
Bowness Knott Forest Trail★ CA23 93 F6
BOWNESS-ON-SOLWAY 17 B5
Bowness-on-Solway Prim Sch CA7 17 B5
BOWNESS-ON-WINDERMERE 198 D2
Bowness Rd
  Barrow-in-F LA14 207 B6
  Dalton-in-F LA15 205 B3
  Millom LA18 202 C4
  Whitehaven CA28 187 D4
BOWSCALE 68 C6
Bowscale Cl CA3 175 C1
Bowscar Rd
  Penrith CA11 70 F8
  Plumpton CA11 56 D1
BOWSTON 130 E3
Bowthorn Rd CA25 188 C8
Bow Window Ave LA13 171 B5
Box Tree LA6 157 F5
Boyd St 14 CA15 182 E5
Bracken Bed La LA12 171 C8
Brackenber Ct CA11 191 B5
Brackenber Lodge CA10 101 C5
Brackenburgh Cotts CA11 55 F6
Bracken Cl CA3 175 C2
Bracken Cotts CA11 55 E7
Bracken Ct CA11 55 E7
Brackenfield LA23 198 C2
Bracken Gr LA12 203 A2
Brackenhill La CA13 190 B3
BRACKENLANDS 180 C1
Brackenlands CA7 180 D2
Bracken Ridge CA3 175 C2
Brackenrigg CA4 42 C5
Brackenrigg Dr CA12 192 C3
Brackensgill La LA10 146 D4
Brackenslack La CA10 102 D8
Brackenthaite Rd LA5, LA7 166 D8
BRACKENTHWAITE
  Castle Carrock 32 D4
  Loweswater 79 D5
  Wigton 38 F5
Brackenwood LA9 200 B4
Bradbury Ave CA15 182 E4
Braddyll Terr LA12 203 D4
Brade St 4 LA20 139 A2
Bradford St LA14 206 F8
Bradshawgate Dr LA5 210 C4
Braeside CA14 183 B1
Braisgate CA11 55 B2
BRAITHWAITE 80 E6
Braithwaite Ct CA22 189 E6
Braithwaite Fold Cvn Pk LA23 198 B1
Braithwaite Prim Sch CA12 80 F6
Brakeside Gdns CA28 187 C6
Bramble Cl LA9 200 C8
Bramerton Orch CA1 177 E6
BRAMPTON
  Appleby-in-Westmorland 88 C6
  Carlisle 179 A5
Brampton Junc Sta CA8 22 E2
Brampton Jun & Inf Sch CA8 179 C5
Brampton Old Rd CA3, CA6 20 C1
Brampton Rd CA3 175 F1
Brampton War Memorial Cottage Hospl CA8 179 D4
Brandlehow Cres CA12 192 C3
BRANDLINGILL 64 C1
Brandrith The LA22 195 D4
BRANSTY 186 D3
Bransty Prim Sch CA28 186 D3
Bransty Rd CA28 186 D3
Bransty Row CA28 186 C2
Bransty Villas CA28 186 D2
Brantfell Cotts LA23 198 D2
Brantfell Ho LA23 198 C2
Brantfell Pl LA23 198 C2
Brantfell Rd LA23 198 C2
Brantfell Wlk LA23 198 D2
BRANTHWAITE
  Caldbeck 52 F4
  Workington 77 F7
Branthwaite Brow 2 LA9 200 D5
Branthwaite La CA14 183 B1
Brantwood★ LA21 127 E2
Brantwood Ave CA1 177 F4
Brantwood La CA25 188 B8
Brathay Cres LA14 207 B2
Brathay Fell LA22 195 A4
Brathay Hall (Training Ctr) LA22 195 B3
Braunton Dr LA14 207 A8
BRAYSTONES 108 A4
Braystones Rd CA21 108 B5
Braystones Sta CA21 108 A5
Brayton Gdns CA7 36 E1
Brayton Pk CA7 50 D8
Brayton Rd
  Aspatria CA7 36 D1
  Whitehaven CA28 186 D3
Brayton St CA14 184 E5
Brayton Terr CA28 186 D2
Breast Mill Beck Ct LA14 204 F2
Breast Mill Beck Rd LA14 204 F2
Breen La LA23 129 B1
Brennan Cl LA13 207 F3
Brent Ave LA15 205 C4
Brentfield Way CA11 191 E5
Brent Gdns CA11 191 D5
Brent Rd CA11 191 E6
Brewery Brow CA28 186 E6
Brewery La 4 CA13 190 D4
Brewery St
  Allonby CA15 35 C1
  Barrow-in-F LA14 207 A4
  6 Ulverston LA12 203 D5
Brewery Terr CA15 35 C1
Briar Bank
  Carlisle CA3 175 C2
  Cockermouth CA13 190 E2
Briar Cl CA8 31 F8
Briarcliffe Gdns LA15 205 D6
Briarcote CA17 199 D6
Briar Ct LA13 207 F5
Briar Lea Ct CA6 10 C3
Briarrigg LA9 200 C8
Briar Rigg CA12 192 B5
Briarscroft LA5 213 D8
Briarwood LA9 200 B4
Brick Kiln Rd LA12 203 F2
BRIDEKIRK 64 C8
Bridekirk Dovenby CE Prim Sch CA13 64 B8
Bridge App LA14 206 D2
Bridge Brow LA6 212 C1
Bridge Cl 5 LA15 205 C4
Bridge End CA22 189 E5
Bridge End Bsns Pk LA7 211 C4
Bridge End Cotts
  Old Hutton LA8 144 F3
  Staveley LA8 130 B5
Bridge End Ind Est CA22 189 E5
Bridge End Pk CA22 189 E5
BRIDGEFOOT 63 C4
Bridgegate Ave LA13 207 C4
Bridgegate Smallholdings LA13 207 D5
Bridge Ho 5 LA15 205 C5
Bridge House★ LA22 195 D6
Bridge La
  Carlisle CA2 176 E7
  7 Kendal LA9 200 D5
  Penrith CA11 191 E3

Bridge La *continued*
  Troutbeck Bridge LA23 129 B8
  Troutbeck LA23 114 E1
Bridge Mews LA6 169 F3
BRIDGEND 98 E5
Bridge Rd
  Barrow-in-F LA14 206 E1
  Carlisle CA2 176 C7
Bridge St Cl 3 CA13 190 C4
Bridgeside LA5 213 C3
Bridges Ret Pk CA28 187 D8
Bridge St
  Appleby-in-W CA16 193 C5
  Brough CA17 105 B5
  Burneside LA9 130 F2
  Carlisle CA2, CA3 214 A3
  Cockermouth CA13 190 C4
  Kendal LA9 200 D5
  Longtown CA6 10 B3
  Maryport CA15 182 C6
  4 Penrith CA11 191 C5
  Workington CA14 184 F6
Bridge Terr
  Carlisle CA2 176 F4
  Keswick CA12 192 A4
  Melmerby CA10 58 B4
Bridge View CA7 174 B3
Bridgewater Rd CA1, CA3 214 B4
Brierley Rd CA25 188 E6
Brier Lonning CA8 21 F1
Briery Acres CA14 62 F3
Briery Bank LA5 209 C1
Briery Cl LA23 129 A8
Briery Croft CA14 62 E4
Brierydale CA14 184 D1
Brierydale La CA14 62 E3
Briery Gr CA2 176 C3
Brigbourne Dr CA14 183 B2
BRIGFLATTS 146 B6
Brigflatts La LA10 146 B6
Brigg's St 11 LA14 207 B2
BRIGHAM
  Cockermouth 63 F5
  Keswick 192 D4
Brigham Hill CA13 63 F5
Brigham Rd CA13 190 B3
Brigham Row CA12 192 C4
Brighton Pl 7 DG14 3 D3
Brighton St LA14 207 A5
Bright St CA2 176 D6
Brig St LA14 206 F1
BRIGSTEER 143 D4
Brigsteer Brow LA8 143 D4
Brigsteer Cswy LA8 143 C2
Brigsteer Rd
  Kendal LA8 143 E5
  Levens LA8 143 D1
Brindlefield CA7 180 D2
Brisbane Park Inf Sch LA14 206 E4
BRISCO 30 D2
BRISCOE 92 C2
BRISCOE BANK 186 E4
Briscoe Cres CA28 186 D4
Briscoe Mount CA22 189 E8
Briscoe Rd CA22 189 E8
Brisco Mdws CA2 177 C1
Brisco Rd CA2, CA4 30 C3
Brisco View CA1 30 D3
Bristol St LA14 206 C1
Broadacre Ho CA3 214 B2
Broad Acres CA14 185 B7
Broad Cl LA14 206 F8
Broadfield LA23 129 B7
Broadfield Cl LA23 129 B7
Broadfield La LA10 147 E1
Broadgate LA22 194 B4
Broadguards CA2 176 E6
Broad Ing
  Kendal LA9 200 E6
  Sockbridge CA10 70 E1
Broad Ing Cres LA9 200 E6
Broadlands LA5 209 B2
Broadmire Rd CA16 103 C7
Broadoaks Ct CA1 177 E6
Broadoaks Grange CA1 177 E5
Broad St
  Carlisle CA1 214 C2
  Windermere LA23 198 E5
Broadstairs La LA14 206 C2
BROADWATH 178 F3
Broadway LA13 207 D3
Brockbank Terr CA17 199 C4
Brockbeck 13 LA9 200 C4
BROCKLEYMOOR 56 B3
Brockleymoor CA11 56 B3
Brockwood Hall LA18 150 B7
Brogden St LA12 203 D5
Bromley Ct CA14 184 C6
Bromley St CA14 184 D6
Brook Bank CA28 187 F6
Brook Cl 6 CA5 28 F1
Brook Ct LA23 198 E5
Brookfield CA10 101 C4
Brookfield Ave CA7 180 B3
Brookfield Cl 2 LA6 156 B1
Brookfield Gdns CA1 177 C4
Brookfields CA7 180 A2
Brookland LA6 169 C3
Brooklands Ave CA15 182 E4
Brooklands Grange CA11 191 E4
Brooklands View 5 CA11 191 E4
Brooklyn CA11 70 D3
Brook Rd LA23 198 E5
Brook St Prim Sch CA1 214 C1
Brookside
  Beckermet CA21 108 C5
  Carlisle CA2 176 C6
  Cleator CA23 188 E5
  Seaton CA14 183 B2
  Sockbridge CA10 70 F1
  Warcop CA16 104 C6
  11 Wigton CA7 180 D3
Brook Side CA15 182 E5
Brookside Cotts CA7 36 B3
Brookside Pl CA2 176 D6
Brook St
  Barrow-in-F LA13 207 C3
  Carlisle CA1 214 C1
  Flimby CA15 183 C8
  10 Penrith CA11 191 D5
  Troutbeck Bridge LA23 129 B7
  Workington CA14 184 D6
Brookvale LA12 203 A2
BROOM 88 A6
Broom Bank CA28 186 E1
Broom Cl
  1 Broughton-in-F LA20 139 A2
  Kendal LA9 144 C7
Broom Cres DG12 172 A1
Broome Ct CA1 177 D3
Broomfallen Rd CA4 30 F5
BROOMFIELD 39 E6
Broom Garth CA2 30 B3
Broom Garth End La LA8 143 C5
Broom Ind Est DG12 16 B8
Broom La LA8 143 A7
Broomrigg Cres CA4 42 F5
Broomy Hill CA4 30 F7
BROTHYBECK 39 D2
BROUGH 105 C5
BROUGHAM 71 C3
Brougham Ave CA10 71 C3
Brougham Castle* CA11 71 C3
Brougham Hall* CA10 191 F1
Brougham Hall Gdns CA10 191 F1
Brougham La CA17 199 C5
Brougham St CA11 191 C5
Brough Castle* CA17 105 B5
Brough Prim Sch CA17 105 B5
BROUGH SOWERBY 105 B3
Brough St CA7 50 C8
BROUGHTON BECK 152 B5
Broughton CE Sch LA20 139 A2
Broughton Cl 15 LA16 162 A8
BROUGHTON CROSS 63 E4
BROUGHTON-IN-FURNESS 139 A2
Broughton Lodge
  10 Dalton-in-F LA15 205 C5
  Grange-o-S LA11 154 A3
BROUGHTON MILLS 139 B5
BROUGHTON MOOR 63 C8
Broughton Moor Prim Sch CA15 63 C8
Broughton Pk
  Broughton-in-F LA20 139 A2
  Great Broughton CA13 63 F6
Broughton Prim Sch CA13 63 E6
Broughton Rd LA15 205 D7
Broughton Tower LA20 139 A2
Brow Ave LA13 207 D4
Brow Bottom CA14 77 F7
Brow Cl LA23 198 E3
Brow Cres LA23 198 E3
Brow Edge Rd LA12 153 C7
Browfield Cl CA11 98 C7
Browfoot Cl LA5 213 E4
Brow Foot La LA8 130 B7
Browhouses DG12 18 A8
Brow La LA8 130 B5
BROWNBER 119 E4
Brownber La CA17 119 E4
Brownrigg Brow CA14 78 C7
Brownrigg Dr CA2 176 C4
Brown's Pl CA14 183 B2
Brown St
  Barrow-in-F LA14 207 A2
  Workington CA14 184 E5
Browsholme Cl LA5 213 B3
Brow Side LA12 153 C7
Browside Rd CA15 49 A2
Brow St CA15 182 D6
Brow The
  Bullgill CA15 49 D5
  Skelwith Bridge LA22 113 E1
Browthwaite CA16 88 D7
BROWTOP 78 A7
Brow Top CA14 184 E6
Bruce St DG12 172 C4
Brundholme Gdns CA12 192 C4
Brundholme Rd CA12 192 B4
Brunel Way CA1 177 D4
Brunlea Dr CA28 186 E3
BRUNSTOCK 20 D2
Brunstock Cl CA3 175 C3
Brunstock La CA3, CA6 175 F6
Brunstock Mews CA6 20 C2
Brunswick Apartments CA11 191 C5
Brunswick Rd CA11 191 C5
Brunswick Sch CA11 191 C5
Brunswick Sq CA11 191 C5
Brunswick St CA1 214 C2
Brunswick Terr CA11 191 C5
Brunthill Rd CA3 175 B5
Bruntley Mdws CA9 181 E3
Brunton Ave CA1 177 C6
Brunton Cres CA1 177 C6
Brunton Park (Carlisle United FC) CA1 177 C7
Buccleuch Ct LA14 207 A4
Buccleuch Dock Rd LA14 206 F1
Buccleuch St
  Barrow-in-F LA14 206 F3
  Dalton-in-F LA15 205 B5
Buccleuch Terr TD9 1 B6
Buchanan Pl CA2 177 B3
Buchanan Rd CA2 177 B2
Buchanan Terr CA15 182 F4
BUCKABANK 40 B7
Buckabank Ct CA5 40 B8
Buckbank La LA10 146 E7
Buckholme Dr
  Askham CA10 85 E8
  Clifton CA10 71 C1
Buckhorn La LA17 151 D7
Buckle Ave CA25 188 D6
Buckman Brow LA18, LA20 138 E1
Buddle Rd CA14 184 C4
Buebank La CA5 29 C1
Buebank Rd 3 CA5 40 A8
Buffs Croft CA4 178 A5
Bugle Horn Hill 11 LA12 203 D6
Buildings Farm Cl CA14 183 A3
Buller St LA14 206 C2
BULLGILL 49 D5
Bungalows The
  Eamont Bridge CA10 191 E1
  Keswick CA12 192 D4
  Maryport CA15 182 E3
BURGH BY SANDS 18 F2
Burgh by Sands Sch CA5 18 F1
Burgh Rd CA2 176 A7
Burgh Road Ind Est CA2 176 B7
Burland Gr LA9 200 E2
Burlington CE Sch LA17 151 C5
Burlington Cl LA17 151 C5
Burlington Mews 4 LA12 203 D5
Burlington St
  1 Barrow-in-F LA14 206 F2
  Ulverston LA12 203 D5
Burlington Villas LA17 151 C6
Burnaby St LA14 206 E2
BURNBANKS 100 C7
BURNESIDE 130 F3
Burneside Rd LA9 200 C7
Burneside Sta LA9 130 F2
Burnett Ho CA20 123 A8
Burnett Rd CA1 177 D1
Burney Beck Cotts CA16 103 C4
Burnfoot Gr CA3 175 B2
Burnmoor Ave CA28 187 D5
BURNRIGG 178 E4
Burnrigg CA2 176 C3
Burnsall Cl CA2 176 A4
Burns Ave LA13 207 D6
Burnside
  Harrington CA14 185 A8
  Longtown CA6 10 C3
  Wigton CA7 180 B3
Burnside Ct CA3 175 D1
Burnside Pk CA12 192 B6
Burnside Rd DG16 173 C3
Burn St CA6 10 C3
Burnswalk Terr CA7 174 C4
Burntbarrow LA7 209 F4
BURRELLS 193 C1
Burrowgate CA11 191 D5
Burrow Rd LA6 168 E7
Burrow Walls CA14 184 E8
BURTHOLME 22 D6
Burton High Cl CA28 186 E2
Burton Hill LA6 169 C3
BURTON-IN-KENDAL 167 C7
BURTON IN LONSDALE 169 B3
Burton Morewood CE Prim Sch LA6 167 C7
Burton Pk LA6 167 B7
Burton Rd
  Holme LA6 156 B1
  Kendal LA9 200 E2
  Oxenholme LA9 144 B4
Burwain Terr CA10 87 D8
Bush Brow CA3 214 B2
Busher Wlk LA9 200 C6
Bushfield CA6 4 F7
BUSK 44 B1
Busk Cotts LA22 195 D5
Busk La
  Kirkby Stephen CA17 199 A8
  Sedbergh LA10 201 B4
Butler St LA18 202 B5
Butterburn Cl CA3 175 C2
Butterflies Cvn Pk LA18 150 A1
BUTTERMERE 94 F7
Buttermere Ave CA28 187 B5
Buttermere Cl
  Carlisle CA2 176 D5
  Cockermouth CA13 190 F3
Buttermere Cres LA14 204 E1
Buttermere Dr
  Dalton-in-F LA15 205 C3
  Kendal LA9 200 F2
  Millom LA18 202 C4
Buttermere Rd CA15 182 E3
Butter Well La LA9 200 C4
BUTTERWICK 85 C2
Buttery Well La 14 LA9 200 C4
Buttery Well Rd LA9 200 C4
Butts Beck LA15 205 C6
Butts Fold CA13 190 E4
Butts Mdw CA12 66 B6
Butts Mews CA9 181 D4
Butts St DG12 172 C4
Buxton St LA14 206 F1
Byerstead Rd CA28 187 B1
BYREBURNFOOT 3 D4
Byreburnfoot DG14 3 C4
Byreburnfoot Trail* DG14 3 D4
Byrnes Cl CA11 56 B4
Byrnes Pl CA11 56 B4
Byron St
  Barrow-in-F LA14 206 F4
  Carlisle CA2 176 E7
  Ulverston LA12 203 E5
  17 Workington CA14 184 D6
Byron Terr CA8 24 D7

C

Cadgill Rd DG16 173 C2
Cadman St 15 CA14 184 D6
Caesar's View CA16 193 C4
Caffrey Ct 3 LA14 206 F4
Cain St
  Bigrigg CA22 188 A3
  Workington CA14 184 D4
Caird Ave CA3 175 C2
Cairn Cres CA4 178 D7
Cairn Mill CA4 178 D6
Cairn Terr CA8 31 E6
Cairnwood CA8 31 E6
Calbeck Dr CA14 62 F3
Calcutta St LA14 206 E4
CALDBECK 53 C6
Caldbeck Rd
  Carlisle CA2 176 D6
  Whitehaven CA28 187 F8
Caldcotes CA2 176 E6
Caldecote Ave CA13 190 D2
CALDER 108 D2
Calder Ave CA28 187 D7
CALDER BRIDGE 108 D5
Calder Cl LA5 213 A3
Calder Cres CA25 188 D6
Calder Dr
  Dalton-in-F LA15 205 B3
  Kendal LA9 200 F6
  Workington CA14 184 E3
Calder Gn LA14 206 B3
Calderside CA20 123 A8
Calder View CA21 108 B5
Caldew Apartment CA2 176 F3
Caldew Cl CA7 180 A3
Caldew Ct CA3 175 D2
Caldew Dr CA5 29 D1
CALDEWGATE 176 E5
Caldew Lea Sch CA2 176 E6
Caldew Maltings CA2 176 E7
Caldew Rd CA2 176 E1
Caldew Sch CA5 29 E1
Caldew St
  Carlisle CA2 176 F4
  Silloth CA7 174 C4
Caldrigg Fold LA8 130 C4
Caldron Hill CA13 63 F6
Caledonian Bldgs 12 CA3 175 B1
Caledonian Cl 3 LA14 207 B3
Caledonian Cres DG12 172 E5
Caledonian Rd CA14 184 D5
Calgarth Pk LA23 129 A7
Calgarth View LA23 129 B7
California La CA3 175 D5
California Rd CA3 175 D5
CALTHWAITE 55 E7
Calthwaite CE Sch CA11 55 E7
Calva Brow CA14 184 F7
Calva Pk CA14 62 E4
Calva Rd CA14 62 E4
Calvert Ct LA8 156 C7
CALVO 25 F4
Cambeck Cl CA8 179 B4
Cambeck Rise 5 CA8 179 B4
Camborne Ave LA5 213 B2
Cambridge Ct 6 LA15 205 C5
Cambridge Prim Sch LA13 207 C3
Cambridge Rd CA28 187 F5
Cambridge St
  Barrow-in-F LA13 207 C3
  Millom LA18 202 C5
Cameron St LA14 206 E2
CAMERTON 183 F3
Camerton Rd
  Great Broughton CA13 63 E6
  Seaton CA14 183 D2
Cammock Ave CA2 177 C1
Cammock Cres CA2 177 C1
Cammock Rd CA2 177 C1
Campbell Ho LA21 196 A3
Campbell-Saviors Way 5 CA14 184 E6
Campers' Cnr CA6 10 A7
Campfield Marsh Nature Reserve* CA7 16 F5
Campfield Rd LA12 203 D2
Camp Rd CA15 182 D7
Camp St CA15 182 D6
Canal Cl LA6 156 B1
Canal Court Bsns Ctr CA2 176 D7
Canal Ct CA2 176 D6
Canal Head N LA9 200 E5
Canal Head S LA9 200 D5
Canal Pl LA5 213 D3
Canal Side LA12 152 D1
Canal St
  Carlisle CA2 176 E6
  Ulverston LA12 203 E6
Canberra Rd DG16 173 D3
Candle La LA7 211 D3
Canning St CA14 184 D5
Cannon Field CA6 5 E2
Canny Croft CA11 191 C6
CANONBIE 3 C3
Canonbie Sch DG14 3 D3
Cant Cres CA2 177 B2
Canterbury Terr LA14 206 E8
CANTSFIELD 168 F3
Cape Rd CA14 183 B3
CAPERNWRAY 167 C2
Capernwray Ct LA6 167 D3
Capernwray Cvn Pk LA6 167 D2
Capernwray Diving Ctr* LA6 167 B2
Capernwray Rd LA6 167 B2
Capon Hill CA8 179 C3
Capon Tree Rd CA8 179 B3
Capper Cl 12 LA9 200 C4
Capplebarrow LA8 130 E4
Capplerigg La LA8 130 C1
Cappy La LA12 152 E7
Captain French La LA9 200 C4
Captain Shaw's CE Sch LA19 137 B3
Caraway Cl LA12 203 C2
CARDEW 39 D8
CARDEWLEES 29 C2
Cardiff St LA14 206 C1
Carding Mill La CA12 192 A4
Cardrona Ct LA11 208 B1
Cardrona Rd LA11 208 B1
CARDURNOCK 16 C1
CARGO 19 D2
Carisbrooke Cres LA13 207 E4
CARK 164 D7
Cark & Cartmel Sta LA11 164 D7
Cark Ho LA11 164 D7
Cark House Ct LA11 164 D7
Cark Ind Est LA11 164 D7
CARLETON
  Carlisle 30 D3
  Egremont 189 F3
Carleton Ave CA10 191 F3
Carleton Cl CA1 30 D3
Carleton Cotts CA22 189 F4
Carleton Derrick Dr CA11 191 F5
Carleton Dr CA11 191 E4
Carleton Fields CA11 191 F5
Carleton Hall Gdns CA10 191 F3
Carleton Hall Rd CA10, CA11 191 E3
Carleton Hall Wlk CA11 191 E4
Carleton Hill Rd CA11 71 C5
Carleton Mdws CA11 191 F5
Carleton Pl CA11 191 E4
Carleton Rd
  Carlisle CA1 177 F1
  Penrith CA11 191 E4
Carleton Terr CA10 101 C5
Carley Cl LA12 162 F7
Carley Ho 1 LA14 207 C8
Carley La LA12 162 F7
Carlingdale LA9 130 F2
Carliol Cl CA1 177 D3
Carliol Dr CA1 177 C3
CARLISLE 214 B3
Carlisle Airport CA6 21 D3
Carlisle Castle* CA3 214 A3
Carlisle Cath* CA3 214 A2
Carlisle Coll CA1 214 C3
Carlisle Ent Ctr CA1 214 B1
Carlislegate La CA7 51 F8
Carlisle Race Course CA2 30 B3
Carlisle Rd
  Brampton CA8 179 A4
  Dalston CA5 29 E1
  Longtown CA6 10 C3
Carlisle St 2 LA14 206 F4
Carlisle Sta CA1 214 B2
Carlisle Terr LA5 213 C5
Carlisle Wlk CA14 184 E3
Carl Lofts CA10 101 C5
Carlton Ave LA13 207 B5
Carlton Dr
  Ulverston LA12 203 C2
  Whitehaven CA28 187 F7
Carlton Gdns CA3 175 D1
Carlton Ho LA12 203 C2
Carlton Rd CA14 184 F6

Car–Cli 219

Carlyles La CA3 214 A3
Carlyle's Pl DG12 172 C3
Carmelite Way LA13 207 E5
CARNFORTH 213 C2
Carnforth Brow LA5 213 E4
Carnforth Christ Church CE Prim Sch LA5 213 C3
Carnforth High Sch LA5 213 D3
Carnforth Sta LA5 213 C4
Caroline St LA9 200 C6
CARR BANK 209 E3
Carr Bank Rd LA7 209 E2
Carricks Ct CA8 23 B5
Carricks Yd 8 CA8 179 B5
Carr La
  Torver LA21 127 B1
  Walney Island LA14 170 C5
Carrock Cl LA9 200 E1
CARRSHIELD 47 C6
Cars of the Stars Motor Mus★ CA12 192 B3
Carter Fold LA11 208 C2
Carter Garth CA14 63 B4
Carter La 12 CA28 186 C1
Carter Rd LA11 208 B1
Cartgate Rd CA28 187 F6
Cart La LA11 208 C2
CART LANE 208 C2
CARTMEL 153 F1
Cartmel CE Prim Sch LA11 153 F1
Cartmel Cres 5 LA14 206 F3
Cartmel Dr
  Carlisle CA2 29 D6
  Ulverston LA12 203 D2
Cartmel La LA11 154 B4
CARTMELL FELL 142 D3
Cartmel Priory CE Sch LA11 153 F1
Cartmel Priory & Gatehouse★ LA11 153 E1
Cartmel Rd
  Allithwaite LA11 164 F8
  Grange-o-S LA11 208 B3
Cart Rd CA28 187 C7
Carus Pk LA6 168 B2
Carvoran Roman Army Mus★ CA8 24 D8
Carvoran Way CA2 176 A6
CARWINLEY 10 E8
Caspian Rd 32 LA16 162 A8
Casson Rd CA14 184 C3
Casson St 1 LA12 203 E5
CASTERTON 212 E5
Casterton Sch LA6 212 F4
Castle Bank
  Appleby-in-W CA16 193 D4
  Silverdale LA5 210 C4
CASTLE CARROCK 32 D6
Castle Carrock Sch CA8 32 D6
Castle Circ LA9 200 F4
Castle Cl
  Egremont CA22 189 D5
  High Harrington CA14 185 B7
  Kendal LA9 200 F4
  Whitehaven CA28 187 D8
Castle Cres LA9 200 E5
Castle Croft CA22 189 D6
Castle Ct
  Carlisle CA3 214 A3
  Penrith CA11 191 C4
Castle Dale LA9 200 F4
Castle Dr
  Kendal LA9 200 E4
  Penrith CA11 191 C4
Castle Field LA22 195 C7
Castlegarth LA10 201 D5
Castle Garth LA9 200 E5
Castlegate
  Cockermouth CA13 190 D4
  Penrith CA11 191 C5
Castlegate Dr CA13 190 E4
Castle Gdns
  Cockermouth CA13 190 B5
  Greystoke CA11 69 E6
  Kendal LA9 200 D4
Castle Gr LA9 200 F4
Castle Green Cl LA9 200 F4
Castle Green La LA9 200 F5
Castle Green Rd LA9 200 F5
Castlehaw LA10 201 D5
Castlehaw La LA10 201 D5
Castlehead Cl CA12 192 B3
Castlehill Rd CA16 104 C6
Castle Hill Rd CA11 191 D4
Castle La CA12 192 F3
Castle Mdws CA28 187 C8
Castle Mews CA28 187 D8
Castle Mount CA4 42 C4
Castle Oval LA9 200 F4
Castle Park Sch LA9 200 F5
Castle Park View CA16 193 C4
Castle Pk CA17 105 B5
Castle Rd LA9 200 E5
CASTLERIGG 192 E2
Castlerigg Brow CA12 192 E2
Castlerigg Cl CA28 187 D3
Castlerigg Dr CA2 176 B3
Castle Riggs LA9 200 F4
Castlerigg Stone Circle★ CA12 81 F6
Castle Rise LA9 200 F4
CASTLERTHWAITE 121 A1
Castle St
  Carlisle CA3 214 A3
  1 Dalton-in-F LA15 205 B4
  Hilton CA16 89 B3
Castle St *continued*
  Kendal LA9 200 E6
  Millom LA18 202 D4
Castlesteads Dr CA2 176 A6
Castle Terr CA11 191 C4
Castleton Cl CA11 191 A5
CASTLETOWN 191 B5
Castletown Dr CA11 191 A5
Castle View
  Brough CA17 105 B5
  Egremont CA22 189 D5
  Hayton CA8 31 F8
  Millom LA18 202 C6
  Sedgwick LA8 144 A2
  Walney Island LA14 170 C6
Castle View Cvn Pk & Site LA6 167 D2
Castle View Rd CA16 193 D5
Castle Way CA3 214 A3
Castle Wlk
  Egremont CA22 189 D6
  Kendal LA9 200 E5
Castle Wray 12 LA20 139 A2
Castrigg La CA16 88 A6
Catherine Cotts CA12 192 C4
Catherine Mews CA28 187 C8
Catherine Mill CA28 187 C8
Catherine St
  Maryport CA15 182 D5
  Whitehaven CA28 187 C8
CATHOLES 201 B2
Catholic La CA1 214 C3
CATLOWDY 4 D3
Caton La LA11 164 C7
Caton St LA18 150 A1
CATTERLEN 70 C8
Cat Tree Rd LA11 208 C3
Catty Crook La LA12 171 C7
Cauda Brow CA26 93 D8
CAULSIDE 4 B6
Causa Ct CA7 39 B4
CAUSEWAY END 155 D8
Causeway End LA12 153 B7
Causeway Rd CA14 183 B2
Causeway The
  Cartmel LA11 153 F1
  Haverthwaite LA12 153 A7
Causey La LA18 150 E8
CAUTLEY 134 A2
Cautley Rd LA10 201 E5
Cautley Spout★ LA10 133 F4
Cavendish Ct CA14 184 F6
Cavendish Dock Rd LA14 207 A2
Cavendish Gdns LA6 212 C2
Cavendish Pk LA14 206 F1
Cavendish St
  Barrow-in-F LA14 206 F3
  Barrow-in-F LA14 207 A3
  Cartmel LA11 153 E1
  Dalton-in-F LA15 205 C5
  17 Ulverston LA12 203 D5
  Workington CA14 184 F6
Cavendish Terr CA3 214 A4
Cawflands CA2 30 B2
Cawthorpes La CA2 176 E7
Caxton Rd CA2 176 C7
Cecil St
  Barrow-in-F LA13 207 B3
  Carlisle CA1 214 B2
Cedar Cl CA11 191 F4
Cedar Cres CA15 182 F5
Cedar Ct CA14 184 C1
Cedar Gr
  Carlisle CA3 175 E2
  Kendal LA9 200 B3
Cedar House Sch LA6 212 B2
Cedar La CA13 190 E5
Cedar Rd LA14 206 F7
CELLERON 85 B8
Cemetery Hill LA15 205 B4
Central Ave
  Carlisle CA1 177 E3
  Distington CA14 185 C3
  Egremont CA22 189 D6
  Gretna DG16 173 C3
Central Ct LA12 162 F6
Central Dr
  Ulverston LA12 203 D2
  Walney Island LA14 206 C2
Central Rd
  Dearham CA15 49 A2
  Whitehaven CA28 187 B7
Central Sq CA14 184 E6
Central Way CA14 184 E6
Centurion Pk CA10 87 D8
Centurions Wlk CA3 20 C1
Challan Hall Cotts LA5 210 E5
Challan Hall Mews LA5 210 E5
Challoner Ct CA13 190 D4
Challoner St CA13 190 D4
Chambers Ct LA9 200 B2
Chambers' St 14 CA14 184 D6
Chancel Pl LA9 131 B1
Chancery La CA11 191 E4
Chandlers La 2 CA8 179 B5
Chandler Way CA3 175 B6
Changford Villas CA15 182 F5
Channelside LA14 206 D4
CHAPEL 66 B6
Chapel Brow
  Bridgefoot CA14 63 C4
  Carlisle CA1 177 F5
  Hallthwaites LA18 150 D8
Chapel Butt La CA17 119 E4
Chapel Cl
  10 Kendal LA9 200 C5
Chapel Cl *continued*
  Storth LA7 209 F4
  Warwick Bridge CA4 178 C6
  Whitehaven CA28 187 E3
Chapel Ct
  10 Cockermouth CA13 190 C4
  7 Kendal LA9 200 C4
  Troutbeck Bridge LA23 129 B7
Chapel Ctyd CA4 21 E1
Chapelfield CA11 55 B2
Chapel Field
  Burneside LA9 130 F2
  Kirkbampton CA5 28 E7
Chapelfield La CA5 28 E7
Chapel Fld LA14 206 C5
Chapel Garth
  Kirkby Lonsdale LA6 212 E1
  Warcop CA16 104 C6
Chapel Gdns CA14 183 B1
Chapel Hill LA22 195 D6
Chapel House Cvn Pk CA8 32 D8
Chapel House La LA6 212 E1
CHAPELKNOWE 9 B8
Chapel La
  Arnside LA5 209 B2
  Bootle LA19 137 B3
  Burton in L LA6 169 C3
  11 Kendal LA9 200 C4
  Kirkby Lonsdale LA6 212 C2
  Kirkby Thore CA10 87 D8
Chapel Pl CA2 214 A2
Chapel Rd CA14 184 C6
Chapel Ridding LA23 198 D8
Chapel Row CA7 49 F7
CHAPELS 151 C7
Chapel St
  Appleby-in-W CA16 193 C5
  8 Barrow-in-F LA14 206 F3
  Bigrigg CA22 188 A3
  Bolton CA16 87 D6
  Carlisle CA1 214 B3
  Dalton-in-F LA15 205 B5
  Distington CA14 185 D3
  Egremont CA22 189 E6
  Flimby CA15 183 C8
  Temple Sowerby CA10 72 E2
  Ulverston LA12 203 D5
  Whitehaven CA28 186 C1
  Workington CA14 184 E6
CHAPEL STILE 113 B4
Chapel Stone Cotts LA12 153 C8
Chapel Street Inf Sch LA15 205 C5
Chapel Terr
  Alston CA9 181 E3
  Great Broughton CA13 63 E6
  Greysouthen CA13 63 E4
  Kirkby Thore CA10 87 D8
  Tebay CA10 118 B3
  Thornhill CA22 189 E2
Chapel Wlk LA5 213 D8
Charity La CA14 185 C6
Charles Cl CA14 184 F4
Charles Ct LA9 130 F2
Charles St
  Annan DG12 172 D4
  Carlisle CA1 214 C1
  Kendal LA9 200 C7
Charlotte St CA2 214 A2
Charlotte Terr CA1 177 E6
Charney Ct LA11 208 C5
Charney Rd LA11 208 C4
Charney Well La LA11 208 D5
Charnley Fold LA9 144 A4
Charters Cl CA14 184 E5
Chase The
  Bowland Bridge LA11 142 C4
  Silverdale LA5 210 D2
Chatsworth Dr CA28 187 F8
Chatsworth Park Ind Est LA14 206 E4
Chatsworth Sq
  Abbeytown CA7 26 C1
  Carlisle CA1 214 C2
Chatsworth St LA14 206 E5
Chaucer Ave CA22 189 C7
Chaucer House Apartments 20 CA12 192 B3
Chaucer Rd CA14 184 F3
Chaucer Way LA13 207 D6
Cheapside LA22 195 D5
Chelmer Garth LA14 206 A4
Chelsea Ct LA7 211 E4
Chelsea Mews LA7 211 E4
Cheltenham St LA14 207 A5
Cherry Brow CA2 176 B5
Cherry Garth CA6 19 D2
Cherry Gdns CA11 191 F5
Cherry La
  Carlisle CA1 30 E4
  Cockermouth CA13 190 E5
Cherrytree Ave LA12 203 D3
Cherry Tree Cres LA9 200 B4
Cherry Tree Dr CA15 182 F5
Cherry Tree Pk DG16 173 C2
Cherrytree Way LA13 207 F5
Chertsey Bank CA1 177 C3
Chertsey Gr CA1 177 D3
Chertsey Mount CA1 177 C4
Chesterholm CA2 176 A6
Chester Pl LA14 206 F8
Chester St LA14 206 F8
Chester Terr LA6 167 B7
Chestnut Cl
  Culgaith CA10 72 E4
  Holme LA6 156 B2
Chestnut Cl *continued*
  Penrith CA11 191 F4
Chestnut Ct
  Holme LA6 156 B2
  Stainton CA11 70 D3
Chestnut Gr
  Cumwhinton CA4 31 A3
  Kirkbride CA7 27 B7
  Linstock CA6 20 D1
  Ulverston LA12 203 D3
Chestnut Hill
  Carlisle CA2 176 C2
  Keswick CA12 192 D3
Chestnut La CA1 30 E4
Chestnut Pk
  Keswick CA12 192 D4
  Milnthorpe LA7 211 E4
Chestnut Rd LA23 198 E5
Chestnuts The
  Cumwhinton CA4 31 A3
  Distington CA14 185 D4
  Longtown CA6 20 A7
Chestnut Wlk LA13 207 F4
Chetwynde Sch LA13 207 C7
Cheviot Gn LA14 206 F5
Cheviot Rd CA3 175 E1
Chichester Pl 3 LA13 207 C3
Chiltern Cres LA14 206 F5
Chilton St CA14 184 E5
Chiswick St CA1 214 C2
Chittery La LA12 203 D7
Chitty Hill CA10 87 D2
Christ Church Terr CA13 190 C3
Christ Croft CA17 105 B5
Christian Head CA17 199 C6
Christian St
  Maryport CA15 182 D6
  Workington CA14 184 F6
Christy Pl CA22 189 E7
Chrysler Gr CA25 188 C8
Church Bank Gdns LA6 167 C7
Churchbeck Cl LA21 196 A4
CHURCH BROUGH 105 B5
Church Brow LA19 137 C6
Church Cl
  Carlisle CA1 214 C2
  Distington CA14 185 D4
  Irthington CA6 21 E4
  Levens LA8 155 D8
  Lindal in F LA12 205 F8
  Satterthwaite LA12 141 A7
Church Cotts LA6 168 C7
Church Croft CA10 84 F7
Church Fields 6 LA12 203 D6
Church Fields Ave 5 LA12 203 D6
Churchgate LA11 208 B4
Church Gate CA17 119 D3
CHURCH HILL 38 D3
Church Hill
  Arnside LA5 209 B2
  Grange-o-S LA11 208 D4
  Hensingham CA28 187 F5
Church Hill Ave LA5 213 C7
Church Hos CA6 20 F6
Churchill Ct LA9 130 F2
Churchill Dr
  Millom LA18 202 B6
  Moresby Parks CA28 76 F2
Churchill Pl CA15 182 C6
Church La
  Bootle LA19 137 B3
  Brampton CA8 179 B5
  Carlisle CA3 175 E1
  Great Musgrave CA17 104 E4
  Great Salkeld CA11 57 B3
  19 Keswick CA12 192 B3
  Keswick, Great Crosthwaite CA12 81 B7
  Morland CA10 86 F5
  Nenthead CA9 47 A2
  Thursby CA5 28 F1
  Tunstall LA6 168 E4
  Walney Island LA14 206 D1
  Whitehaven CA28 187 F6
Church Mdws CA13 63 E6
Church Mews 1 CA11 191 C5
Church Pl 2 CA3 175 E1
Church Rd
  Allithwaite LA11 164 F7
  Alston CA9 181 D3
  Broughton Moor CA15 63 C8
  Distington CA14 185 D4
  Flimby CA15 183 C7
  Great Urswick LA12 162 F5
  Greystoke CA11 69 F5
  Harrington CA14 185 A7
  Kirkbride CA7 27 B8
  Levens LA8 155 D8
  Seaton CA14 183 B2
  Witherslack LA11 154 E6
Church Rise CA10 118 B3
Church Road Terr CA14 185 A8
Church Row CA12 82 C8
Church St
  Ambleside LA22 195 D5
  Annan DG12 172 D4
  Barrow-in-F LA14 207 A2
  Beetham LA7 155 E2
  Bowness-on-W LA23 198 C2
  Broughton-in-F LA20 138 F2
  Carlisle CA2 176 E6
  Carlisle, Stanwix CA3 175 E1
  Cleator CA23 188 C3
  Dalton-in-F LA15 205 B4
Church St *continued*
  Dearham CA15 49 B3
  Egremont CA22 189 E6
  Frizington CA26 92 D7
  Keswick CA12 192 B3
  Kirkby Lonsdale LA6 212 C2
  Langwathby CA10 72 E7
  Maryport CA15 182 D6
  Milnthorpe LA7 211 D4
  Moor Row CA24 188 B5
  Shap CA10 101 C6
  Tebay CA10 118 B3
  Whitehaven CA28 186 C1
  Whittington LA6 168 C7
  9 Wigton CA7 180 D3
  Windermere LA23 198 E6
  Workington CA14 184 D7
Church Stile
  Clawthorpe LA6 167 C8
  Grasmere LA22 194 B3
Church Terr
  Caldbeck CA7 53 C6
  4 Carlisle CA3 175 E1
  Maryport CA15 182 F4
  Shap CA10 101 C6
  Silloth CA7 174 C4
CHURCHTOWN 54 A8
Church View
  Arnside LA5 209 B2
  Egremont CA22 189 D6
  Lowca CA28 186 E8
  Staveley LA8 130 C5
Church Went 7 CA13 190 D4
Church Wlk
  Flookburgh LA11 164 D6
  Millom LA18 202 A5
  Ulverston LA12 203 D6
Cinderbarrow La LA5, LA6 167 A6
Cinder Hill 10 LA20 139 A2
Citadel Row CA3 214 B2
Claife Ave LA23 198 F5
Claife Cl LA23 198 F5
Claire St CA2 177 B3
Clairmont Dr CA6 10 C3
CLAPPERSGATE 195 B3
Clapperton Rd DG12 172 D5
Clare House La LA11 208 D3
Clarence Rd LA14 207 A6
Clarence St
  Carlisle CA2 176 E4
  3 Ulverston LA12 203 D5
Claridge Ho CA2 176 C7
Clarkside Bsns Pk LA12 152 E5
Clarrick Terr LA6 169 F3
CLAWTHORPE 167 C8
Clawthorpe Cotts LA6 167 C8
Clay Flatts Ind Est CA14 184 C5
Clay St CA14 184 D6
Clayton Ave CA25 188 E6
Cleater St LA15 205 C5
CLEATOR 188 C4
Cleator Gate CA23 188 D4
CLEATOR MOOR 188 E7
Cleator Moor Bsns Ctr CA25 188 D6
Cleator Moor Rd CA28 91 F7
Cleator St LA18 202 B5
Clementina Terr CA2 177 B4
Cleminson Row LA12 153 C7
Clevelands Ave
  Barrow-in-F LA13 207 D5
  Silverdale LA5 210 C4
CLIBURN 86 F7
Cliff Brow 9 LA9 200 C5
Cliffe La
  Barrow-in-F LA14 207 A7
  Barrow-in-F LA14 207 A8
Clifford Cl CA11 191 C3
Clifford Ct
  Carlisle CA3 175 B7
  Penrith CA11 191 D3
Clifford Dr LA9 200 C2
Clifford Rd CA11 191 D3
Clifford St
  Appleby-in-W CA16 193 D6
  Barrow-in-F LA14 206 F3
  Carlisle CA3 214 B3
Cliff Rd
  Longtown CA6 20 A8
  Whitehaven CA28 187 B7
Cliff Terr LA9 200 C5
CLIFTON 71 C1
Clifton Cross CA10 71 C2
Clifton Ct CA14 184 F4
CLIFTON DYKES 71 D2
Clifton Gdns CA14 63 B4
Clifton Hall Cl CA14 63 B4
Clifton Lodge CA14 63 B4
Clifton Moor Cotts CA10 85 F8
Clifton Prim Sch CA10 71 C1
Clifton St CA2 176 E5
Clifton Terr CA18 123 F3
Clift St CA2 176 D7
Clints Brow
  Bigrigg CA22 188 B1
  Egremont CA22 189 D8
Clints Quarry Nature Reserve★ CA22 188 B1
Clints Rd CA4 178 D2
Clintz Rd CA22 189 D7
Clitheroe CA9 181 E3
Clitheroe Dr CA28 187 E8

Clive St LA14 206 E4
CLOFFOCKS 184 D7
Cloisters Ave LA13 207 D3
Closehead Ave DG12 172 D4
Close St CA1 214 C1
Close The
Kirkby Stephen CA17 199 C5
Whitehaven CA28 186 D3
Wigton CA7 180 D2
Clovelly Terr LA14 207 B7
Clowes Gdns CA13 63 E6
Coach Ho LA11 154 A3
Coach Rd
Warton LA5 166 E4
Whitehaven CA28 187 D7
COALCLEUGH 47 C4
Coalfell CA8 23 C2
Coalfell Ave CA2 176 A6
Coalgrove Rd CA28 187 D5
Coal Rd LA10 148 C2
COANWOOD 24 F1
Coastguard Cotts LA14 170 F1
Coast Rd
Baycliff LA12 163 B3
Newbiggin LA12, LA13 171 E7
Coates La 14 CA28 186 C1
Cobblestone Cnr CA10 87 A5
Cobden St LA15 205 C5
COCKAN 78 B1
Cock Brow LA10 148 C5
Cocken Cres LA14 204 B1
Cocker La CA13 190 D4
COCKERMOUTH 190 E3
Cockermouth Hospl CA13 190 D5
Cockermouth Lonning CA13 63 F5
Cockermouth Sch CA13 190 E5
Cockfield Dr CA14 184 D2
Cocking Yd LA6 167 C7
Cockle St LA10 201 C5
COCKLEY BECK 126 D8
Cockpit CA28 187 C7
Cockrigg La LA8 144 C2
Cockshot La LA7 209 F4
Cockton's Yard 4 CA13 190 C4
COLBY 88 A3
Colby La CA16 193 C4
Colchester Pl 1 LA13 207 C3
Coldbeck Barn CA17 119 F3
Coldgill Ave CA13 63 E6
Cold Harbour La LA8 143 C7
Coldkeld Rigg CA17 105 E1
Coldmire Rd CA7 25 C1
Cold Springs Pk CA11 191 E6
Cold Well La
Arnside LA7 209 F1
Silverdale LA7 210 F8
Coledale Gdns CA12 80 E6
Coledale Hall CA2 176 C7
Coledale Mdws CA2 176 C7
Coledale Mews CA2 176 C7
Coleridge Cl LA13 207 D6
Coleridge Ct CA12 192 A4
Coleridge Dr CA22 189 D6
Colesberg Ct LA5 209 B2
Coles Dr LA5 209 B1
College Cl CA7 50 C8
College Ct 2 LA23 198 E5
College Gate LA23 198 E6
College Mews LA9 200 D5
College Rd LA23 198 E5
College St
Grasmere LA22 194 B4
6 Whitehaven CA28 186 C1
College View CA28 187 C6
Collier La CA1 214 B1
Collier's La LA6 212 E3
Collin Cl LA9 200 B2
Collin Croft LA9 200 C5
Collinfield LA9 200 B2
Collingwood Cl LA21 196 A4
Collingwood St
Barrow-in-F LA14 206 F4
Carlisle CA2 214 A1
Collin Hill LA9 200 B2
Collin Pl CA2 176 D6
Collin Rd LA9 200 C2
Collins Terr CA15 182 C4
Colmore St CA2 176 F4
Colonnade The LA12 141 D1
Colony Candles★ LA12 162 E6
COLTHOUSE 197 F5
Colt House La LA12 203 C1
COLTON 140 E1
Colton Hill LA12 152 D8
Colville St N CA2 214 A1
Colville St CA2 214 A1
Colville Terr CA2 176 E5
Combe Cres LA17 151 C5
Combe Ho 7 LA14 207 C8
Combe View
Bootle LA19 137 B3
Haverigg LA18 149 F2
Walney Island LA14 206 C5
Comely Bank CA7 50 C8
Commercial Row CA7 53 C6
Commodore St CA28 186 D2
COMMON END 185 D2
Commonholme Rd CA10 86 D7
Common La CA17 199 E7
Commonmire La LA8 156 B8
Common Side CA14 185 D1
Common The LA23 129 D6
Compston Cnr LA22 195 D6
Compston Rd LA22 195 D5
Compston St LA22 195 D5
Compton St CA1 214 B3
Concle Terr LA13 171 B5
Conder Brow LA5 213 D4
Coneygarth La
Tunstall LA6 168 D4
Whittington LA6 168 D6
Coney St CA2 177 A3
Conisburgh Ct CA2 214 A1
Conishead Ho LA12 163 D7
Conishead Priory★ LA12 163 D6
Conishead Rd LA12 203 D4
CONISTON 196 B4
Coniston Ave
Dalton-in-F LA15 205 B3
Flimby CA15 183 C7
Seascale CA20 123 B8
Coniston CE Prim Sch LA21 196 A4
Coniston Cl CA14 184 E3
Coniston Cres CA14 184 E4
Coniston Dr
Cockermouth CA13 190 F3
Kendal LA9 200 F6
Workington CA14 184 E3
Coniston Pk CA25 188 B8
Coniston Rd
Barrow-in-F LA14 207 B6
Carnforth LA5 213 D2
Whitehaven CA28 187 C5
Coniston Way CA2 176 A5
Consett St 8 LA13 207 B3
Constable St CA2 176 F4
Conway Gdns LA14 206 B3
Conyers Ave LA14 207 C8
Coogan Cl CA2 176 F3
Cook Rd LA18 202 D4
Cook's Cnr LA23 198 D7
Cookson Ct CA11 191 A5
Cookson Ho CA11 191 A5
Cook St LA14 206 F4
Coombe Height CA2 176 C2
Cooperage CA3 214 A3
Co-operative Terr CA15 183 C8
Cooper La LA12 163 D5
Coopers Cl CA10 85 D6
Coopers Garth CA11 55 B2
Coopers Wlk 11 CA14 184 E6
Cooper Way CA3 175 B6
Coophouse La CA5 19 E1
Copeland Ave
Egremont CA22 189 D7
Whitehaven CA28 187 D5
Copeland Ind Est LA18 202 D5
Cop La CA22 189 E1
Copperfield La LA9 200 E6
Coppermines Cotts LA21 127 C5
Coppice Brow LA5 213 E4
Coppice The LA12 203 D3
Copshaw Pl TD9 1 B6
Corby Gates CA4 178 C2
CORBY HILL 178 E7
Corker La LA12 140 F4
CORKICKLE 187 C7
Corkickle Sta CA28 187 D7
Cornbirthwaite Rd LA23 198 D4
Cornerhouse Pk LA14 206 E3
CORNEY 137 C6
Corney Pl 2 CA11 191 C5
Corney Sq CA11 191 C5
Corn Market CA11 191 D5
Cornwallis St LA14 206 F3
Coronation Ave CA14 62 E4
Coronation Cotts LA11 154 C3
Coronation Cres CA14 185 D3
Coronation Ct CA14 185 A7
Coronation Dr
Dalton-in-F LA15 205 C3
Frizington CA26 92 D8
Whitehaven CA28 186 E3
Workington CA14 184 C1
Coronation Mount LA6 169 C3
Coronation St CA15 182 D4
Coronation Terr CA7 37 C2
Corporation Rd
Carlisle CA3 214 B3
Workington CA14 184 D5
Corporation Terr 9 LA14 207 B2
COTEHILL 31 C1
Cote Ley Cres LA14 170 C6
Cote Lighthouse★ CA7 174 C6
Cotswold Cres LA14 206 F5
Cottage Cvn Pk CA7 17 D3
Cottage Row
Braystones CA21 108 A5
Morland CA10 86 E4
COULDERTON 107 E7
Coulter Beck La LA6 169 A7
Coulton Ho CA1 177 C3
Coulton St LA14 206 F3
Council Hos
Kirkoswald CA10 57 B8
Melmerby CA10 58 B4
Countess Rd CA28 186 D2
Countess Terr CA28 186 D2
County Mews LA9 200 D6
County Park Rd LA14 206 E8
County Rd LA12 203 D5
COUPLAND 88 F1
Court Guards LA14 170 C6
Court No 5 LA15 205 B5
Court Sq CA1, CA3 214 B2
Court Square Brow CA1, CA3 214 B2
Court The
5 Barrow-in-F LA14 207 B3
Oxenholme LA8 144 B5
Courtyard The
Broadwath CA8 178 E3
Kendal LA9 200 E6
Moorhouse CA5 29 A7
Rockcliffe CA6 19 D4
Court Yard The CA11 71 F7
Cove Dr LA5 210 C4
Cove Pl DG16 173 C2
Cove Rd LA5 210 B4
COWAN BRIDGE 169 A7
COWAN HEAD 130 E4
Cowbound La CA10 118 E3
Cowbrow Foot LA6 156 E4
COWGILL 148 A2
Cowlarns Rd LA14 207 B8
Cowper Rd CA11 191 A5
Cows Tarn La LA14 206 B4
Cox's La CA8 179 B5
Cox St LA12 203 D5
Crabtree Cvn Pk LA6 156 E4
Crabtree La LA6 156 E4
CRACKENTHORPE 88 A5
Cracrop Farm Trail★ CA8 12 E5
CRAG BANK 213 B2
Crag Bank Cres LA5 213 B2
Crag Bank La LA5 213 A3
Crag Bank Rd LA5 213 B2
Crag Brow LA23 198 C3
CRAG FOOT 166 C4
Cragg Brow LA12 152 F8
Cragg Cl CA13 64 A1
Cragg Dr LA11 208 C4
Cragg Rd CA25 188 E6
Craggs La 2 CA14 184 E6
Craggs Rd CA13 63 F6
Cragg St LA14 207 A5
Crag La
Cartmel LA11 153 F2
Gosforth CA19 109 E1
Hutton Roof LA6 156 F1
Craglands Pk LA12 162 F5
Crag Rd LA5 213 B7
Crag View
Kendal LA9 200 E6
Staveley LA8 130 C5
Craig Ct LA23 198 D3
Craig Dr CA28 186 E3
Craigholme House Pk LA5 213 A3
Craignair Ct DG12 172 F5
Craignair Gdns DG12 172 F5
Craignair Pk DG12 172 F5
Craig Rd CA14 184 E4
Craigs Bank NE49 24 D3
Craig Wlk LA23 198 D3
Craika Cl CA15 49 A2
Craika Rd CA15 49 A2
Crakegarth 4 CA5 40 A8
Crakegarth Cl 6 CA5 40 A8
Crake Mount LA12 152 D7
Crake Rd LA14 206 A4
Craketrees CA5 29 D1
Cranbourne Rd CA2 176 C6
Cranbourne St CA14 184 C3
Craven Park (Barrow RLFC) LA14 206 E3
Craven Park Ct LA14 206 E4
Craven Way LA10 159 D8
Craw Hall CA8 179 C4
Craw Pk CA8 179 C5
Creighton Ave CA2 176 C6
Crellin St LA14 207 A3
Crerar Cl CA15 182 F4
Crescent Cotts CA20 123 A7
Crescent Gn LA9 200 E7
Crescent Rd LA23 198 E5
Crescent The
Barrow-in-F LA14 204 E1
Carlisle CA1 214 B2
Cleator Moor CA25 188 C8
Eastriggs DG12 17 D8
Egremont CA22 189 D7
Grange-o-S LA11 208 B4
High Cummersdale CA2 176 D1
Holme LA6 156 B2
Keswick CA12 192 A3
Kirkbride CA7 27 B7
Kirkby Stephen CA17 199 D5
Penrith CA11 191 C3
Seascale CA20 123 A7
Thornhill CA22 189 E2
Whitehaven CA28 186 D4
Wigton CA7 180 E2
Workington CA14 184 C1
Cresswell Ave CA1 177 F4
Crest The
Ulverston LA12 203 D3
Whitehaven CA28 187 F8
CREWGARTH 58 A1
Criffel Ave CA15 182 D7
Criffel Rd
Carlisle CA2 176 A6
Parton CA28 186 E6
Criffel St CA7 174 C4
Crindledyke Cl CA6 175 A8
Crindledyke Est CA6 175 A8
Cringlethwaite Terr CA22 189 E5
Croadalla Ave CA22 189 D6
CROASDALE 93 D8
Croasdale Ave CA28 187 E4
Croasdale Cl LA5 213 B3
Croasdale Pl CA25 188 E6
Croft Ave
Penrith CA11 191 C6
Shap CA10 101 C5
Croft Cl
Brough CA17 105 B5
Lazonby CA10 57 A6
Croft Cres CA15 49 B2
Croft Ct
High Hesket CA4 41 F3
Wigton CA7 180 C3
Croft Ctyd LA22 195 B4
Croft End CA10 85 D1
Crofters Cres LA13 207 F4
Croftfield Rd CA14 183 B3
Croft Foot CA28 187 A2
Croft Garth LA12 152 B5
Croft Gdns LA15 205 B5
Croft Head Rd CA20 123 B8
Croft Head View CA28 186 E8
Croft House Gdns CA5 28 F5
Croftlands
Bigrigg CA22 188 A2
Borwick LA6 167 B3
Bothel CA7 51 C6
Warton LA5 213 D8
Croftlands Dr CA18 123 F3
Croftlands Inf & Jun Schs LA12 203 D2
CROFTON 28 D1
Crofton Est CA7 28 B2
Croft Park Gr LA13 207 C7
Croft Pk CA4 178 A1
Croft Pl
Kirkoswald CA10 57 B8
Temple Sowerby CA10 72 E1
Croft Rd
Brampton CA8 179 C6
Carlisle CA3 175 F1
Gretna DG16 173 D3
Croftside CA13 190 D4
Croft St CA17 199 C6
Crofts The
Crosby CA15 49 B5
Silloth CA7 174 C2
St Bees CA27 91 D2
Wigton CA7 180 C2
Croft Terr
Alston CA9 181 D4
Beckermet CA21 108 C5
Braithwaite CA12 80 F6
Carlisle CA1 177 E6
Cleator CA23 188 C3
Cockermouth CA13 190 D4
Egremont CA22 189 E6
Lowca CA28 186 E8
Penrith CA11 191 D6
Croft The
Ambleside LA22 195 B4
Bothel CA7 51 A6
Burton in L LA6 169 C3
Flookburgh LA11 164 D6
Grasmere LA22 194 A5
Long Marton CA16 88 A7
Stainton w A LA13 205 F1
Threlkeld CA12 82 B8
Warcop CA16 104 C6
Warton LA5 213 D8
Croft View
Long Marton CA16 88 A7
Milburn CA10 73 C4
Croglam La
Kirkby Stephen CA17 199 B4
Kirkby Stephen CA17 199 C5
Croglam Mdws CA17 199 C4
Croglam Pk CA17 199 C4
CROGLIN 43 D6
Crompton Dr LA15 205 B3
Cromwell Cres
Carlisle CA3 214 A4
High Harrington CA14 185 D7
Cromwell Rd CA11 191 C5
CROOK 130 B2
Crook Brow LA8 130 A2
Crookburn Cl CA3 175 B2
CROOKDAKE 37 B2
Crooked Gate LA8 143 D4
Crookey CA7 50 C8
CROOKLANDS 156 C6
Crooklands CA14 185 C7
Crooklands Brow LA15 205 D5
Crooklands Terr LA15 205 D5
Crooklands View CA10 71 C1
Crook Rd
Burneside LA9 130 D2
Kendal LA8 130 E1
Staveley LA8 130 B4
CROSBY 49 B5
CROSBY GARRETT 120 A8
Crosby Grange CA6 21 A2
Crosby Moor CA15 49 A5
CROSBY-ON-EDEN 21 B2
Crosby on Eden CE Sch CA6 20 F2
CROSBY RAVENSWORTH 102 C5
Crosby Ravensworth CE Sch CA10 102 C5
Crosby St
Carlisle CA1 214 B2
Maryport CA15 182 D6
CROSBY VILLA 49 D5
Crosfield Rd CA28 186 D2
CROSLANDS PARK 207 C6
Croslands Park Rd LA13 207 C7
Croslands Pk LA13 207 C7
Cross Bank LA6 145 E4
CROSSBARROW 63 B3
CROSSCANONBY 49 B6
Crosscanonby St John's CE Sch CA15 49 B5
Cross Cotts CA7 50 F8
Crosscrake CE Prim Sch LA8 144 B1
Cross Croft CA16 193 E4
Cross Croft Ind Est CA16 193 F5
Cross Fell Dr CA16 88 C6
Crossfell View
Alston CA9 181 E3
Hackthorpe CA10 85 F6
CROSSFIELD 188 C7
Crossfield CA3 175 D2
Crossfield Ct LA5 209 A1
Crossfield Rd CA25 188 C7
Cross Garth CA10 101 C6
Cross Gate CA11 98 E4
CROSSGATES 78 C5
Crossgates CA14 78 B4
Cross Gates CA13 79 D8
Crossgates Rd CA8 23 B2
CROSSGILL 60 D7
Cross Gr
Cleator CA23 188 D5
Wigton CA7 180 C5
Crosshaw Brow LA10 146 F8
Cross Hill
St Bees CA27 91 D2
Workington CA14 184 F5
Crosshill Dr CA2 176 C5
Cross How CA10 72 E5
Cross Howe
Brigham CA13 63 E5
Crosthwaite LA8 142 E6
Crosshow Rd CA15 49 A3
Crossings Cl CA25 188 C7
Cross La
Barrow-in-F LA14 207 A8
Kendal LA9 200 C4
9 Penrith CA11 191 C6
Ulverston LA12 163 D8
Whitehaven CA28 187 E7
Wigton CA7 180 C5
Crosslands LA6 168 D7
Crosslands Cl LA12 203 A3
Cross Lane Ct LA12 163 D8
Cross Lanes CA20 123 B8
Cross Lane Workshops CA20 123 B8
Crossley St 21 LA16 162 A8
Cross Lonning CA7 51 A6
Cross Moor LA12 162 F7
Cross North St CA25 188 D7
Cross Rigg CA26 78 C1
Crossrigg La CA16 87 C6
Cross Side CA22 189 E6
Cross St
Barrow-in-F LA14 207 A2
Carlisle CA3 175 D2
Grange-o-S LA11 208 D4
Kendal LA9 200 C6
Keswick CA12 192 C3
5 Penrith CA11 191 C5
19 Ulverston LA12 203 D5
Whitehaven CA28 187 C8
Windermere LA23 198 E6
Workington CA14 184 C3
Cross View CA11 69 E5
Crossways CA1 177 E3
CROSTHWAITE 142 E6
Crosthwaite CE Sch LA8 142 F6
Crosthwaite Ct CA14 184 E3
Crosthwaite Gdns CA12 192 A5
Crosthwaite Rd CA12 192 A5
Crowgarth Cl CA25 188 D6
Crown Hill 2 LA11 208 D4
Crown Inn Fields CA10 86 F5
Crown Mews 13 LA15 205 C5
Crown Rd CA2 176 A6
Crown Rigg LA23 198 C2
Crown Sq 1 CA11 191 D4
Crown St
Carlisle CA1, CA2 214 B1
Cockermouth CA13 190 C4
Millom LA18 202 C5
Crown Terr 20 CA11 191 D5
Crow Park Rd CA12 192 A3
Crow Park Way CA24 91 F6
Crow Pk CA28 186 D1
Crow Wood Field LA8 143 D4
Crozier Cl LA13 207 C3
Crummock Ave
Cockermouth CA13 190 E4
Whitehaven CA28 187 B5
Crummock Cl CA7 37 C2
Crummock Dr
Barrow-in-F LA14 204 D1
Kendal LA9 200 F2
Crummock Rd
Maryport CA15 182 E3
Workington CA14 184 D3
Crummock St CA2 176 D5
Ctyd The
Hesket Newmarket CA7 53 E5
Staffield CA10 43 A1
Cuckoo Brow La LA22 128 E2
Cuddy Lonning
Wigton CA7 180 A1
Wigton, Red Dial CA7 38 B5

CULGAITH 72 D4
Culgaith CE Sch CA10.....72 E5
Culgaith Rd CA10.........72 A8
Culgarth Ave CA13......190 D3
Culgarth Cl CA13 ....190 E3
Cumberland Bird of Prey Ctr★ CA5 ....28 F7
Cumberland Cl
Clifton CA10..............71 C1
Millom LA18............202 C4
Cumberland Ct
Barrow-in-F LA14 ....206 E4
Carlisle CA2............214 A1
Cumberland Dr LA9......200 E3
Cumberland Infmy The CA2 ....176 D7
Cumberland Pencil Mus★ CA12 ....192 A4
Cumberland Pl CA11.....191 E4
Cumberland Rd CA28......187 F5
Cumberland St
Carlisle CA2.............176 F4
Workington CA14.........184 D5
Cumberland Terr DG12 ....172 D4
Cumberland Way CA10....71 C1
Cumbria Ct 1 LA23......198 E5
Cumbria View LA14 ......170 B6
CUMMERSDALE 29 F3
Cummersdale Rd CA2...176 D1
Cummersdale Sch CA2 ....176 D1
CUMREW 32 E1
Cumrew Cl CA1..........177 F5
Cumwhinton Dr CA1 ......30 E4
Cumwhinton Gdns CA1 ....177 E2
Cumwhinton Rd CA1.....177 E2
Cumwhinton Sch CA4.....31 A3
CUMWHITTON 31 A3
Curdiff CA8...............23 A1
Curlew Cnr CA16 ....103 D7
Curlew Rise DG16.......173 D3
Curlew Wlk CA1 ....177 D6
Currah Cl CA10 ....58 C2
Currie St CA1.............214 C2
CURROCK...................177 B3
Currock Bank Rd CA2....177 A2
Currock Mount CA2......177 A2
Currock Park Ave CA2 ..177 A3
Currock Rd CA2 ....177 A4
Currock Road Trad Ctr CA2 ....214 B1
Currock St CA2 ....214 B1
Curson Rise LA9.........200 F3
Curwen Bank CA10 ....86 E7
Curwendale CA14.........62 E3
Curwen Gr 12 CA13 ......190 C4
Curwen Rd CA14.........184 C6
Curwen St CA14 ....184 F6
Curzon St CA15..........182 D5
Cusack Cres CA14 ....184 D4
Custy Steps CA5..........28 F5
Cuthberts Cl CA10 ....86 E7
Cypress Way CA11........191 F5
Cypress Wlk LA13.........207 E4

D

DACRE.......................70 A1
Dacre Rd
Brampton CA8...........179 B6
Carlisle CA3............214 A3
Hethersgill CA6...........11 F2
Dairy Cotts CA8.............23 B5
Dale Ave LA9..............200 E6
Dale Bank LA13...........207 C4
DALE BOTTOM 81 F4
Dale Cl CA13 ....190 D2
Dale Ct CA2 ....176 F4
Dale-End Rd CA1 ....177 D1
Dalegarth LA12...........171 C8
Dalegarth Ave
Carlisle CA1..............177 E3
Whitehaven CA28 ....187 D4
Dalegarth Cotts CA19 ...125 C7
Dalegarth Sta★ CA19 ....125 C7
Daleholme La CA17.......104 F2
Dalelands Rd CA28.......187 B2
Dalemain House★ CA11...70 C2
Dalesman Dr CA1.........177 F2
Dale St
18 Askam in F LA16 .....162 A8
Carlisle CA2..............176 F4
Ulverston LA12 ....203 E5
Dale Street Inf Sch LA12.....................203 E5
Dale Terr LA15...........205 C5
Dale View
Carlisle CA2.............177 A2
Cockermouth CA13 ......190 D2
Laversdale CA6 ....21 C5
Daleview Cl CA22........189 D5
Daleview Gdns CA22.....189 D5
Daley Beck 20 LA16.....162 A8
Dalkeith St LA14..........206 F3
Dallam Chase LA7........211 D4
Dallam Dr LA7............209 F6
Dallam Sch
Heversham LA7 ....211 D7
Milnthorpe LA7 ....211 E4
Dallam View LA7.........211 D3
Dalmeny Rd CA3.........175 D1
Dalmore Ct LA13.........207 C7
DALSTON 29 D1
Dalston Rd
Carlisle CA2.............176 D3
Dalston Rd *continued*
Workington CA14.........184 E5
Dalston St CA2 ....176 F4
Dalston Sta CA5 ....29 D1
DALTON 167 D7
Dalton Ave CA2...........176 C5
Dalton Castle★ LA15......205 B4
Dalton Ct CA1 ....214 C1
Dalton Dr LA9 ....200 F5
Dalton Fields La
Dalton-in-F LA15 ....205 B3
10 Dalton-in-F LA15 ......205 B4
Daltongate LA12..........203 C5
Daltongate Bsns Ctr LA12....................203 C5
Daltongate Ct 1 LA12 ..203 C5
Dalton Hall Bsns Ctr LA6......................167 C7
DALTON-IN-FURNESS..................205 D4
Dalton La
Barrow-in-F LA14 ....207 B8
Burton-in-K LA6 ....167 C7
Eaglesfield CA13 ....64 A3
Dalton Rd
Askam in F LA16 ....162 A8
3 Barrow-in-F LA14 ......206 F2
Kendal LA9................200 F5
Dalton St Mary's CE Prim Sch LA15.................205 C3
Dalton St CA13 ....190 B3
Dalton Sta LA15 ....205 C4
Dalzell Gdns CA14 ....63 B4
Dalzell St CA22, CA24, CA23 ....188 B4
Damson Cotts LA12 ......141 A7
Dandy Dinmont Cvn Pk CA6 ....20 A5
Dane Ave LA14 ....207 B8
Dane Ghyll LA14 ....204 E1
Dane Ghyll Sch LA14....204 D1
Danes Cres LA8...........130 B5
Danes Rd LA8 ....130 B5
Danny Brow LA10.......147 A6
Dan Wilson Ave 7 CA15 ....182 F4
Darcy St CA14 ....184 E5
Darent Ave LA14..........206 A3
Darley Dale Rd 3 LA14....................207 A6
Dartmouth St 2 LA14....206 C1
David St CA1 ....214 C1
Davies Rd CA14...........184 D3
Davis Yd LA10 ....201 C5
Dawson St CA25..........188 E7
Days Bank LA21 ....196 A3
Deal Ave LA14 ....206 C1
DEAN........................78 D8
Dean Barwick Sch LA11.....................154 E7
Dean CE Sch CA14.........78 B8
Dean Cl CA26...............92 D8
Dean Gibson RC Prim Sch LA9......................200 C2
DEANSCALES 64 A1
Dean St CA14..............184 D6
Dearden Cl LA11..........208 D4
DEARHAM 49 A3
Dearham Bridge Rd CA15 ....49 A4
Dearham Prim Sch CA15 ....49 A3
Dee Cl CA2.................176 B4
Deep Dale CA2 ....176 C2
Deepdale Cl LA7..........155 E1
Deepdale La LA10 ....159 D8
DEEPTHWAITE 156 A6
Deerfield 2 LA12.........203 C5
Deer Orchard Cl CA13....190 E4
Deerpark CA7 ....180 E1
Deer Park Barn LA7......156 C7
Deer Park Rd CA3 ....175 C2
Delagoa St CA1...........177 C5
Delhi Rd DG12..............17 D8
Delhi St LA14.............206 C1
Dell The CA8 ....178 E3
Demainholm Forest Walks★ TD9..................1 A4
DENDRON 162 D1
Dendron Cl LA15.........205 B2
Dene Ave CA14...........185 B7
Dene Cres CA3 ....175 D2
Denewood LA23 ....198 E4
Dennis Rose Ave LA13 ..207 B7
DENT.......................147 B2
Dent CE Prim Sch LA10.....................147 B2
Denton Bsns Pk CA2.....214 A1
Denton Cres CA8 ....23 B6
Denton Hill CA2 ....214 A2
DENTON HOLME 176 F4
Denton Holme Trad Ctr CA2 ....214 A2
Denton Mill Cl CA2 ......176 F4
Denton Mill La CA2......176 F4
Denton Park Ct CA20 ....109 B2
Denton Pk CA20 ....109 B2
Denton Rd 5 LA13 ......207 C5
Denton St CA2............176 F4
Dent Pl CA25..............188 F6
Dent Rd
Cleator Moor CA25 ....188 F6
10 Moresby Parks CA28 ....76 F2
Thornhill CA22............189 E3
Whitehaven CA28 ....187 E3
Dent Sq CA25..............188 F6
Dent Sta LA10 ....148 B2
Dent View CA22..........189 E8
Derbyshire Rd LA14.....207 A6
Derby Sq LA23............198 E6
Derby St LA13 ....207 B3
Derry St LA14.............207 A2
Dertern La LA5 ....213 A1
Derwent Ave
Maryport CA15 ....182 E5
Seaton CA14 ....183 A1
Workington CA14........184 D4
Derwent Bank
Seaton CA14 ....183 B1
Walney Island LA14.......206 B3
Derwent Cl
1 Keswick CA12..........192 B3
Penrith CA11 ....191 B4
Seaton CA14 ....183 B1
Derwent Ct 8 CA13.....190 C4
Derwent Dr
Kendal LA9...............200 F2
Workington CA14.........184 C6
Derwent Howe Ind Est CA14 ....184 B6
Derwent Mdws CA14......62 F4
Derwent Mills 1 CA13..190 C4
Derwent Mills Commercial Pk CA13 ....190 C5
Derwent Pk CA13.............63 E6
Derwent Pl LA12...........203 E4
Derwent Rd CA14 ....184 C3
Derwent Ridge CA14.....183 B1
Derwent Row CA13 ....63 E5
Derwentside Gdns CA13 ....190 C4
Derwent St
Carlisle CA2.............176 D5
Cockermouth CA13 ......190 C4
14 Keswick CA12.........192 B3
Workington CA14........184 E7
Derwent Vale Prim Sch CA14 ....63 B4
Derwentwater Cl LA18 ..202 C4
Derwent Water Cvn Site CA12 ....192 A3
Derwentwater Rd CA28 ....187 D3
Devoke Water Gdns 9 LA15.....................205 B4
Devon Rd CA28............187 F5
Devonshire Bglws LA18.....................202 D4
Devonshire Bldgs 1 LA14.....................206 F1
Devonshire Cl LA18 .....202 D4
Devonshire Ho 2 LA14.....................207 C8
Devonshire Rd
Barrow-in-F LA14 ....206 F5
Millom LA18..............202 E4
Ulverston LA12 ....203 E5
Devonshire Road Est LA18.....................202 E4
Devonshire St
Carlisle CA3..............214 B2
8 Dalton-in-F LA15 ......205 C5
Penrith CA11 ....191 D5
Workington CA14.........184 E5
Devonshire Terr
Carlisle CA3.............214 A4
Coniston LA21 ....127 C4
Kirkby-in-F LA17 ....151 B5
Devonshire Wlk CA3 ....214 A3
Devon St LA13............207 B3
Devon Terr 5 LA12 .....203 E5
Dickgate Rd LA8..........144 E8
Dickie Green Cotts CA17 ....120 A2
Dickinson Ct 13 CA28 ...186 C1
Dick Trod La CA7 ....25 D7
Diggle Rd CA2.............176 E4
DISTINGTON 185 C4
Distington Com Sch CA14 ....185 D4
Distington Pk CA14 .....185 D3
Dixon Ct CA2 ....176 E6
Dixon Ground LA21 .....127 C4
Dixon Pl CA3 ....175 C2
Dixon Rd CA3.............175 C2
Dixon St CA3 ....214 A3
Dixon Wood Cl LA11 .....154 C3
Dobbie Bank LA11 ....164 D7
Dobby La LA8 ....130 B1
Dobdale Rd LA8 ....143 C4
Dobies Bsns Pk CA3 .....175 C6
Dobinson Rd CA2.........176 B5
DOCKER 168 A5
Docker Brow LA8 ....131 F3
Docker La
Kendal LA8...............131 F1
Whittington LA6..........168 C5
Dockernook LA8...........130 E4
Docker Park Farm★ LA6......................168 A4
Dock Mus The★ LA14 ...206 D3
DOCKRAY 83 D4
Dockray Hall Ind Est LA9......................200 D7
Dockray Hall Rd LA9.....200 C7
Dockray Meadow Cvn Site CA14 ....78 C3
Dodding Holme LA8 .....131 C2
Dodds Howe LA8 ....142 E6
Dodd's La LA23 ....129 C8
Dodgson Croft LA6 ....212 B2
Dodgson Ct LA6 ....212 C2
Dolholme Hill LA8 ....130 B1
Dollywood La CA7 ....209 F1
Dominion Rd DG16 ....173 C3
Dominion St LA14 ....206 C1
Donald Rd CA14 ....183 B3
Donaldson's Cotts 5 CA7 ....180 D3
Doncaster Pl 2 LA13 ....207 C3
Doncaster St TD9..........1 B6
Doomgate CA16 ....193 C5
Dora Cres CA14...........184 D6
Dorcas Ave LA13.........207 C6
Dorcas Gdns LA13 ....207 C6
Dorchester Cres LA12...203 C2
Doris St LA14.............206 C3
Dorset Cl CA28............187 F5
Dorset St LA14 ....206 F5
Douglas Gdns DG12.....172 D4
Douglas Pl DG16.........173 C2
Douglas Rd CA14 ....184 D5
Douglas Sq TD9 ....1 B6
Douglas St LA14 ....206 C3
Dove Cottage & Wordsworth Mus★ LA22.....................194 C3
Dovehouses La LA6.......156 D4
Dove La CA14.............184 F6
DOVENBY....................64 A8
Dove Nest La LA8........156 D7
Dover Mews CA10 ....101 C6
Dovers La CA13...........190 B5
Dover St LA14............206 C1
Dowbeck Rd CA2 ....176 E5
DOWBIGGIN................147 A7
Dowbiggin La LA10 ......146 F7
Dowdales Sch LA15.......205 B5
DOWGILL 106 A5
Dowie Cl LA13............207 E2
Dowker's La LA9.........200 D4
Downfield La CA22.......188 A3
DOWN HALL 28 B3
Downie's Wynd DG12 ....172 C4
Dragley Beck LA12.......203 E4
Drake St LA14 ....206 F4
Drawbriggs Ct CA16 .....193 D6
Drawbriggs La CA16 .....193 E5
Drawbriggs Mount CA16 ....193 D5
DRIGG.......................123 D5
Drigg Dunes & Irt Estuary Nature Reserve★ CA19 ....123 D3
Drigg Rd CA20............123 B7
Drigg Sta CA19 ....123 D5
Drive The
Crag Bank LA5............213 A3
Newton Rigg CA11.........70 E5
Seascale CA20............123 B8
Ulverston LA12 ....203 C4
DROOMER 198 F5
Droomer Dr LA23 ....198 F5
Droomer La LA23 ....198 F5
Drover La CA11 ....191 C6
Drovers La
Carlisle CA3..............214 B3
Penrith CA11 ....191 C6
Drovers Mews CA11......191 C6
Drovers Way LA6 ....167 B7
DRUMBURGH 17 F2
Drumburgh Ave CA3 ....175 E4
Drummermire LA22......195 C5
Drummond Rd DG12 .....172 D4
Drury La CA6...............10 D6
DRYBECK 103 A6
Dryden St LA14...........206 F4
Dryden Way CA22........189 D6
Dry La LA8 ....131 C4
Dub Brow CA26.............77 D1
Dubbs Rd LA23 ....129 D8
Dubdale Brow LA18......150 C8
DUBWATH 65 E6
Duchess Ave CA6 ....175 A7
DUDDON BRIDGE.........138 E3
Duddon Cl CA28...........187 E6
Duddon Dr LA14..........206 B3
Duddon Mews LA14......206 B3
Duddon Mews Cotts LA20.....................150 F8
Duddon Rd LA16..........162 A8
Duddon View LA16.......162 A8
Dudley St LA14 ....206 F6
DUFTON......................88 D8
Dugg Hill LA7 ....211 D7
Dukes Dr CA6 ....175 A6
Dukes Mdw CA11..........54 D2
Duke's Rd CA1............214 B3
Duke St
Askam in F LA16 ....162 A8
Barrow-in-F, Hindpool LA14 ....206 F3
Barrow-in-F LA14 ....206 F2
Burton in L LA6 ....169 C3
Carlisle CA2..............176 E6
Cleator Moor CA25 ....188 D7
Dalton-in-F LA15 ....205 C5
Gleaston LA12............162 E1
Holme LA6...............156 B1
Millom LA18..............202 C5
Penrith CA11 ....191 C5
Whitehaven CA28 ....186 C1
7 Wigton CA7.............180 D3
Workington CA14.........184 D6
Dukes Wood Rd CA6.......10 C4
Dumb Tom's La LA2, LA6......................169 E1
Dumfries St LA14 ....207 A3
Dunbar St LA14...........206 F1
Duncan Sq 20 CA28......186 C1
Duncan St LA14...........206 F3
Dundalk St LA14..........206 F1
Dundas St LA14...........206 F5
Dundee St LA14 ....206 F1
Dundonald St LA14 ......206 F4
DUNDRAW...................37 D8
Dunfell View CA10 ....87 D8
Dungeon Ghyll Force★ LA22.....................112 F5
Dungeon La
Barrow-in-F LA13 ....207 F3
Bootle LA19 ....136 F4
Dunkirk Ave LA5.........213 D2
Dunlin Dr LA15 ....205 C4
Dunmail Cres CA13 ......190 B3
Dunmail Dr
Carlisle CA2..............176 D5
Kendal LA9...............200 E2
Dunmail Park Sh Ctr CA14 ....62 C5
Dunmail Raise LA14.....204 D1
Dunmallet Rigg CA2 ....176 C4
Dunnerdale LA17.........151 B5
Dunnerdale Forest Walks★ LA20.....................126 C6
DUNNINGWELL............150 B7
Dunoon St LA14 ....206 F1
Dunvegan St 8 LA14 ....206 F1
DURDAR 30 B1
Durdar Rd CA2 ....30 B3
Durham St LA13 ....207 B3
Durranhill Ind Est CA1...177 D4
Durranhill Rd CA1 ....177 F5
Dyke Hall La LA10 ....159 D8
Dyke Nook CA26............92 D8
Dykes Ave DG12 ....172 D5
DYKESFIELD 18 D2
Dykes La LA5 ....166 F5
Dyke St CA26...............92 D8
Dykes Terr CA3 ....175 F1

E

Eadie St CA14 ....185 A7
EAGLESFIELD 64 A3
Eaglesfield Paddle CE Prim Sch CA13 ....64 B2
Eaglesfield St CA15......182 D6
Eagles Way 2 CA28 ....76 F2
Eaigle Terr CA15 ....183 A6
EALS 34 F7
Eals Bank CA8 ....34 F6
EAMONT BRIDGE.........191 F2
Eamont Cl LA14...........206 B3
Eamont Mews 13 CA11...191 E4
Eamont Pk CA10..........191 E2
Earle Ct LA9...............200 C6
Earle St LA14 ....206 E2
Earl Henry's Dr
Askam CA10...............85 E8
Eamont Bridge CA10 .....191 E1
Penrith CA10 ....71 B2
Earls La CA3..............214 B2
Earl's Rd CA28............186 D2
Earl St
Carlisle CA1..............214 B2
Cleator Moor CA25 ......188 D6
Millom LA18..............202 D5
Earls Way CA6...............19 E2
Easdale Bank CA2 ....176 B3
Easdale Cl LA15 ....205 B3
Easedale Rd LA22........194 A5
East Ave CA14 ....185 B8
EAST CAUSEWAYHEAD.......174 F3
East Cres CA7 ....36 C1
East Croft Terr CA28 .....186 E8
East Ct LA12...............203 A1
East Dale St CA2..........176 F4
East Dr
Swarthmoor LA12 ....203 A1
Ulverston LA12 ....162 F6
EAST END 180 E4
East End Cotts CA7 ....49 F8
Eastern Way CA1 ....177 E4
Eastgate LA9 ....200 E6
East Hecklegirth DG12...172 E2
East La CA14 ....185 B8
East Lakes Bsns Pk CA11 ....191 A5
East Mount 6 LA13......207 B6
East Nelson St CA2 ......214 A1
East Norfolk St CA2......176 F4
EASTON
Burgh by Sands 18 A2
Longtown...................11 B6
East Pk CA5 ....39 B8
East Rd
Egremont CA22 ....189 E7
Lowca CA28...............186 E8
EASTRIGGS 17 E8
East Strand CA28 ....186 C1
East Terr CA7...............50 F8
East Tower La CA3.......214 B3
East Vale Ct CA2 ....176 F4
East View
Kendal LA9...............200 C4
Lindal in F LA12..........162 E6
Oughterside CA7 ....49 F7
East View Cotts CA17....199 C6
East View Ct 8 LA9......200 C4
East View Rd CA14 ......185 C3
Eaves Lea LA6 ....212 B2
ECCLE RIGGS 139 A1
Eccleriggs Ave LA14 .....204 C1
Eccle Riggs La LA20 .....139 A2
Eccleriggs Pl LA22........195 D5
Eccleston Mdw LA11......164 D6

Echo Bank LA9 200 B3
Echo Barn Hill LA9 200 C3
EDDERSIDE 35 E4
Eden Ave LA14 206 B3
Eden Cl
- Cargo CA6 19 D2
- Great Salkeld CA11 57 B3
- Wigton CA7 180 A3

Eden Cres CA3 175 D2
Eden Ct
- Carlisle CA3 175 D1
- Crosby-on-E CA6 20 F2

Eden Dr 1 CA28 76 F2
Edenfold CA16 87 E6
Eden Garth CA10 71 F8
Eden Gr CA10 57 A6
Eden Grange CA4 178 D7
Eden Grove Sch CA16 87 D6
EDENHALL 71 F7
Eden Mdws CA10 72 E1
EDEN MOUNT 208 C5
Eden Mount
- Carlisle CA3 214 A4
- Grange-o-S LA11 208 C5
- Penrith CA11 191 E5
- Ulverston LA12 203 D2
- Wetheral CA4 178 B1

Eden Mount Rd LA11 208 C4
Eden Mount Way LA5 213 E4
Eden Ostrich World* CA11 71 F8
Eden Park Cres CA1 177 E6
Eden Park Rd LA11 208 C5
Eden Pk CA10 57 B8
Eden Pl
- Annan DG12 172 E4
- Appleby-in-W CA16 193 C6
- Carlisle CA3 175 D1

Edenside CA6 19 D2
Eden St
- Carlisle CA3 175 D2
- Silloth CA7 174 C3

Eden Straits CA10 71 F8
EDENTOWN 175 C2
Eden Town Ct CA3 175 D2
Eden Valley Rly* CA16 104 C7
Eden View CA16 73 E2
Edge Brow CA10 86 C1
Edgecombe Ct 5 LA9 200 D5
Edgehill CA28 186 D2
Edgehill Rd CA1 177 F3
Edinboro LA22 195 E6
Edinburgh Ave CA14 184 E3
Edinburgh Rd CA15 182 D3
Edmonson St 3 LA12 203 E5
Ednam St DG12 172 C3
Edward Linton Ct 12 CA13 190 D4
Edward Pl DG12 172 D5
Edward St
- Carlisle CA1 214 C1
- 3 Carnforth LA5 213 C4

Egdale La CA17 120 C1
Egerton Bldgs 2 LA14 206 F1
Egerton Gr CA2 176 B5
Egerton Terr LA15 205 C6
Eggerslack Ho LA11 208 D6
Eggerslack Terr LA11 208 E5
EGREMONT 189 E7
Egremont Castle* CA22 189 D5
Egremont Gdns LA14 204 E1
Egremont Rd
- Hensingham CA28 187 F5
- Hensingham, Mirehouse CA24 91 F5
- St Bees CA27 91 D1

Egremont St LA18 202 D4
Ehen Ave CA28 187 D7
Ehen Court Rd CA22 189 E6
Ehen Ct CA22 189 E6
Ehen Garth CA23 93 A6
Ehen Hall Gdns CA23 188 C3
Ehen Pl CA25 188 F6
Ehen Rd
- Cleator Moor CA25 188 F6
- Thornhill CA22 189 E2

Ehenside Com Sch CA23 188 F6
Eight Acre La LA5 166 F6
Elbra Farm Cl CA15 182 F5
Eldon Dr CA1 177 F4
Eldred Rd CA14 184 E4
Eldred St CA1 177 C6
Elephant Yd 16 LA9 200 C5
Eleventrees CA12 192 E4
ELFHOWE 130 B6
Elim Gr LA23 198 D3
Elim Mews LA23 198 D3
Elizabethan Way LA14 206 F5
Elizabeth Cotts CA10 102 C7
Elizabeth Cres CA28 186 F3
Elizabeth Smyth Bglws LA13 207 C4
Elizabeth St
- 8 Maryport CA15 182 E5
- Workington CA14 184 F5

Elizabeth Terr 11 CA15 182 E5
Ella's Orch LA11 164 D6
ELLENBOROUGH 182 F4
Ellenborough & Ewanrigg Inf Sch CA15 182 E4
Ellenborough Old Rd CA15 182 E5
Ellenborough Pl CA15 182 C4
Ellenborough Rd CA15 182 E5
Ellen Cl CA7 180 B3
Ellenfoot Dr CA15 182 F4
Ellen Garth CA7 50 D8
Ellen Villa 4 CA15 182 F4
Ellen Wharf CA15 182 C5
Elleray Bank LA23 198 E7
Elleray Gdns LA23 198 E6
Elleray Prep Sch LA23 198 E6
Elleray Rd LA23 198 E6
Eller Bank CA14 185 A8
Ellerbeck Brow CA13 64 A5
Ellerbeck Cl CA14 184 F3
Ellerbeck La CA14 184 F3
Eller Beck Raise CA2 176 C2
Ellergreen LA9 130 E2
Ellerigg La LA6 157 F6
Ellerigg Rd LA22 195 D7
Eller Raise LA9 200 E6
Eller Riggs Brow LA12 152 A3
Ellers Brow LA22 113 E2
Ellerside 23 LA12 203 D5
Ellerslie Pk 2 CA20 109 B2
Ellerslie Terr 1 CA20 109 B2
Ellers The LA12 203 D5
Ellerthwaite Rd LA23 198 E5
Ellerthwaite Sq LA23 198 E5
Ellesmere Way CA2 176 B3
Elliot Pk CA12 192 A4
Elliscales Ave LA15 205 B5
Ellis Wood LA12 152 D5
ELLONBY 55 A2
Ellonby Rd CA11 55 B2
Elm Ave CA15 183 C7
Elm Cl
- Endmoor LA8 156 D8
- High Hesket CA4 41 F3

Elm Ct
- Kendal LA9 200 C7
- 1 Keswick CA12 192 A4
- 11 Penrith CA11 191 C5
- Workington CA14 184 E3

Elmfield CA8 179 B4
Elm Garth CA4 178 A3
Elm House Barns CA4 41 F3
Elm Rd
- Annan DG12 172 C2
- Barrow-in-F LA14 206 F6

Elmsfield Park Cotts LA6 156 A3
Elmslack Ct LA5 210 C4
Elmslack La LA5 210 C4
Elm St CA2 214 A1
Elms The CA22 189 B6
Elm Terr
- Penrith CA11 191 C5
- Smithfield CA6 20 E6

Elmvale Sch DG12 172 C3
Elph Howe La LA8 130 B6
Elseghyll Ct CA10 58 B4
ELTERWATER 113 C3
Elterwater Ave CA14 184 D4
Elterwater Cres LA14 204 E1
Ely Cl CA14 184 E3
EMBLETON 65 C5
Embleton Rd CA2 177 B2
Emerald Cl CA14 184 D1
Emesgate La LA5 210 C3
Emlyn St LA14 206 F4
Emmanuel Ct 5 LA14 207 A5
Emperor's Dr
- Hackthorpe CA10 86 A4
- Lowther CA10 85 E5

Empire Ct DG16 173 D2
Empire Rd CA2 176 E5
Empire Way DG16 173 C2
Emplands Cotts LA12 205 F8
Empress Dr LA14 206 D1
Empsom Rd LA9 200 C7
ENDMOOR 156 C7
Engine Lonning CA2 176 C7
Englethwaite Hall Cvn Pk CA4 31 D1
English Damside CA3 214 A2
Englishgate Plaza CA1 214 B2
English St
- Annan DG12 172 C4
- Carlisle CA3 214 B2
- Longtown CA6 10 C3

Ennerdale Ave
- Carlisle CA1 177 D5
- Workington CA14 184 E4

ENNERDALE BRIDGE 93 A7
Ennerdale Cl
- Cockermouth CA13 190 F4
- Dalton-in-F LA15 205 B3
- Millom LA18 202 C4

Ennerdale Dr LA14 204 D1
Ennerdale & Kinniside CE Prim Sch CA23 93 B6
Ennerdale Rd
- Cleator Moor CA25 188 E6
- Maryport CA15 182 E4

Ennerdale Terr CA28 187 B6
Ennerdale View CA14 185 D4
Entrance The CA13 63 E6
Enyeat Rd LA8 156 D7
Epoch Cotts LA6 167 B3
Escott Works CA1 214 B1
Esk Ave CA28 187 D7
Esk Bank CA6 10 B3
Eskdale Ave
- Barrow-in-F LA13 207 B3
- Carlisle CA2 176 D5
- Seascale CA20 123 B8

Eskdale Cl CA25 188 C8
Eskdale Cres CA14 184 D3
Eskdale Dr LA15 205 C3
ESKDALE GREEN 124 F7
Eskdale Green Forest Walks* CA19 124 F7
Eskdale Green Sta* CA19 124 F6
Eskdale Mill* CA19 125 C8
Eskett View CA26 77 E1
Eskin St CA12 192 B3
Esk Pl DG12 172 E4
Esk Rd
- Carlisle CA3 175 C3
- Gretna DG16 173 C2

Eskrigg La LA8 144 C1
Esk St
- Longtown CA6 10 B3
- Silloth CA7 174 C4

Esperanto Way CA16 193 F5
Esplanade The LA11 208 D4
Espland Cl CA11 70 C6
Essex St LA14 207 A5
Esther St CA2 177 B4
Esthwaite Ave LA9 200 F2
Esthwaite Gn LA9 200 F2
Estuary Cl LA18 202 C5
Estuary Pk 2 LA16 162 A8
ETTERBY 175 B1
Etterby Cl
- Carlisle CA3 175 C1
- Cockermouth CA13 190 D3

Etterby Lea Cres CA3 175 D1
Etterby Lea Gr CA3 175 D1
Etterby Lea Rd CA3 175 D1
Etterby Rd CA3 175 B1
Etterby Scaur CA3 175 C1
Etterby St CA3 175 D1
Etterby Terr CA3 175 D1
Europe Way CA13 190 C2
Euryalus St LA14 206 C1
Evening Hill Dr CA13 190 B3
Eveninghill View CA13 190 B3
Everest Mount CA14 184 D2
EVER HOLM 172 C4
Ewan Cl LA13 207 C5
EWANRIGG 182 E4
Ewanrigg Brow CA15 182 F4
Ewanrigg Jun Sch CA15 182 E4
Ewanrigg Rd CA15 182 D4
Ewbank La LA8 144 F5
Ewebank Rd LA8 145 A5
Ewelock La CA5 39 E3
Exchange Ct LA9 200 C5
Exmouth St LA14 206 E4

F

Fairbank LA6 212 B2
Fairfield
- Bowness-on-W LA23 198 C2
- Cark LA11 164 D7

Fairfield Cl
- Cark LA11 164 D7
- Carnforth LA5 213 D3
- Staveley LA8 130 C5

Fairfield Gdns CA2 176 D5
Fairfield Inf & Jun Sch CA13 190 C3
Fairfield La
- Barrow-in-F LA13 207 B5
- Kendal LA9 200 B7

Fairfield Pl DG12 172 C4
Fairfield Rd
- Millom LA18 202 C6
- Windermere LA23 198 F4

Fairfield Row LA10 201 F3
Fairfield View CA13 190 C3
Fairgarth Dr LA6 212 B2
Fair Haven 3 LA23 198 E5
FAIRHILL 47 A2
FAIR HILL 191 C7
Fairhill Cl CA11 191 C7
Fairhill View CA9 181 E3
Fairholme LA10 201 C5
Fairladies CA27 91 D2
Fairmile Rd CA10, LA8 132 F6
Fairthorns Rd LA8 145 B6
Fairview LA6 212 B3
Fair View
- Dalton-in-F LA15 205 B5
- Egremont CA22 189 C6

Fairview Cl CA10 71 C1
Fairview Gdns CA10 71 C1
Fair View Rd LA22 195 D6
Fair View Terr LA22 195 D6
Fairways Dr LA14 206 B2
Fairways The CA20 123 A8
Fairybead La CA11 70 D3
Fairybead Pk CA11 70 D3
Falcon Crag LA8 130 E4
Falcon Dr DG16 173 D3
Falcon Mews CA1 177 D6
Falcon Pl
- Moresby Parks CA28 76 F2
- Workington CA14 184 D6

Falcon St CA14 184 D6
Falkins Hill 9 CA8 179 C5
Fallbarrow Ct LA23 198 C3
Fallbarrow Cvn Pk LA23 198 C3
Fallbarrow Rd LA23 198 C3
Fall Beck Cotts LA8 144 D1
Fall Kirk LA2 167 F1
Fallowfield CA10 86 E8
Fallowfield Ave 3 LA12 203 C5
Fallowfield Ct CA11 191 C4
Fallowfield Rd 24 LA16 162 A8
Fallows The 13 CA13 190 C4
Falls The LA22 195 D6
Falmouth St LA14 206 B1
Fangs Brow CA13 78 E5
Faraday Rd CA17 199 C6
FAR ARNSIDE 210 A5
Farbrow Rd CA1 177 F1
Far Close Dr LA5 165 F8
Far End Cotts LA21 196 A5
Farfield Mill Arts & Heritage Ctr* LA10 146 E6
Farfield Row LA10 146 E6
Farish Cl CA8 179 B5
FARLAM 22 E1
Farlam Dr CA1 177 F5
Farlam House Barn CA8 22 E1
Far Leases La CA17 120 C8
Farleigh Ct CA11 57 A4
FARLETON 156 C3
Farleton Cl LA5 213 B7
Farleton View 4 LA6 156 B1
Farletonview Cvn Pk LA6, LA7 156 B5
Far Moor CA22 188 A3
Far Moss CA14 184 E7
Farm St LA14 206 F1
Farriers Way CA4 41 E5
FAR SAWREY 128 E2
FAUGH 31 F5
Faustin Hill CA4 178 A2
Fawn Cl 35 LA16 162 A8
FEATHERSTONE ROWFOOT 24 F3
Fell Brow 7 LA9 200 C5
Fell Cl
- Grange-o-S LA11 208 C4
- Oxenholme LA9 144 B4
- Sedbergh LA10 201 D5
- Silloth CA7 174 C4
- 11 Ulverston LA12 203 E5

Fell Cotts 2 LA11 208 C4
Fell Croft
- 11 Dalton-in-F LA15 205 C5
- Pooley Bridge CA10 84 F7

Fell Dr LA11 208 C4
FELLDYKE 78 C2
FELL END 134 D5
Fell End Cvn Pk LA5, LA7 166 E8
Fell Foot LA6 156 C4
Fell Foot Brow LA12 141 F2
Fellfoot Cotts LA8 130 B6
Fell Foot Pk* LA12 141 F1
Fellfoot Rd LA6 158 A3
Fellgate La LA10 147 A7
Fell Ho 8 LA14 207 C8
Fell La
- Hallthwaites LA18 150 B8
- Old Town LA6 157 D6
- Penrith CA11 191 D6
- Ravenglass CA18 124 B3
- Waberthwaite LA19 137 C8
- Warcop CA16 104 D7
- Winton CA17 105 B1

Fell Rd LA6 158 B2
Fellside
- Allithwaite LA11 164 F8
- Windermere LA23 141 F6

Fell Side CA12 82 C8
Fellside Ct
- Grange-o-S LA11 208 C4
- Kendal LA9 200 C6

Fellside Gr CA2 176 B5
Fellside Terr CA16 73 F2
Fell St
- Barrow-in-F LA14 206 F3
- Ulverston LA12 203 E5

Fell View
- Anthorn CA7 16 F1
- Branthwaite CA14 77 F7
- Bridgefoot CA14 63 C3
- Cockermouth CA13 190 D3
- Milton CA8 22 E3
- Silloth CA7 174 C4
- Swarthmoor LA12 203 A2
- Welton CA5 39 F3
- Wigton CA7 180 B4

Fell View Ave CA28 187 C5
Fell View Cl CA7 50 D8
Fell View Dr CA22 189 D5
Fell View Pk 5 CA20 109 B2
Fellview Prim Sch CA7 53 C6
Fell View Rd CA20 123 B8
Fell View Trad Pk LA9 131 B1
Fell View Wlk CA14 184 D3
Fenman Cl LA14 207 B3
FENTON 31 F6
Fenton CA12 192 D3
Fenton Gate CA8 31 F8
Fenton La CA8 32 A6
Fenton St LA14 207 A3
Ferguson Pl CA2 176 E4
Ferguson Rd CA2 176 E4
Fergus Way CA2 176 C5
Fern Bank
- Bowness-on-W LA23 198 C2
- Carnforth LA5 213 C3
- Cockermouth CA13 190 C3

Fernbank La CA14 183 B1
Fern Croft LA6 212 E4
Fern Ct CA28 186 F1
Ferney Gn LA9 200 C6
Ferney Green Dr LA23 198 C1
Fern Gr CA28 186 E1
Fernhill Rd LA11 208 C3
Fernlea Cres DG12 172 E5
Fernlea Way CA3 175 C2
Fernleigh Ave LA11 208 D4
Fernleigh Cl
- Seaton CA14 183 C2
- Tallentire CA13 49 E2

Fernleigh Dr CA14 183 C2
Fernleigh Rd LA11 208 C4
Ferns The CA22 189 C6
Fern Way CA28 186 E1
Fernwood Dr LA9 200 B3
Ferry Beach Rd LA14 206 D3
Ferry Ho The LA23 129 A2
Ferry Rd LA14 206 E2
Festival Cres CA15 182 E4
Festival Rd LA18 202 C6
Fiddlergill LA8 131 F2
Fiddler's Cswy LA8 143 D2
Fiddler's La CA10 57 A7
FIELD BROUGHTON 153 F4
Field End LA8 131 E3
Field Foot LA22 194 B4
Field Hall LA18 202 B5
FIELDHEAD 55 D6
Fieldhead Ave LA11 164 D6
Field Head Pl LA11 164 D6
Field House Gdns CA11 191 C6
Fieldside
- Annan DG12 172 D5
- Burnrigg CA8 178 D4

Fieldside Cl CA12 192 E4
Field St LA14 207 A3
Field View CA7 17 D5
Fife St LA13 207 B3
Fifkettle Brow CA14 63 F1
Filbert Cl 4 LA15 205 C4
Finch Cl CA1 177 D6
Finch St LA18 202 C5
Findlay Pl 23 CA14 184 D6
FINGLAND 27 E8
Finglandrigg Wood National Nature Reserve* CA7 28 A7
Finkle St
- Carlisle CA3 214 A3
- Kendal LA9 200 D5
- Pooley Bridge CA10 84 F7
- Sedbergh LA10 201 C5
- St Bees CA27 91 D2
- Workington CA14 184 E6

Finley Cl LA9 200 E7
Finley Dr LA9 200 D7
Finn Ave CA2 176 E6
FINSTHWAITE 141 D2
Finsthwaite La LA12 153 C8
Firbank LA9 200 F5
Fir Ends Prim Sch CA6 20 F8
Fir Garth
- Chapel Stile LA22 113 B4
- Cleator Moor CA25 188 C8

Firlands CA3 175 E2
Firs Cl LA7 211 D3
Firs Flats LA7 211 D3
Firs Rd LA7 211 D3
Firs The CA9 181 D3
First Moss La LA8 143 C5
Firth Dr CA27 91 C2
Firth Ho CA14 183 B2
Firth View CA28 186 E6
Firth View Wlk CA14 184 D3
Fir Tree Cres LA23 198 C1
Firtree La LA8 131 C5
Fir Tree Rise LA13 207 F5
Fish Cross DG12 172 C4
Fisherbeck Pk LA22 195 D4
Fisher Pl CA12 82 B1
Fisher St
- 4 Barrow-in-F LA14 206 F2
- Carlisle CA3 214 A3
- Workington CA14 184 D6

Fisher Street Galleries CA3 214 A3
Fisher's Yd 13 LA14 206 F3
Fitz Rd CA13 190 C3
Fitz Steps LA22 113 B2
Fitz View CA13 190 C3
Five Lane Ends CA10 44 A1
Flag St LA22 197 E5
FLAKEBRIDGE 88 E5
Flakebridge Cotts CA16 88 E5
Flan Cl LA12 203 D6
Flass La LA13 207 D4
Flass Mdws LA13 207 D4
Flat La
- Carlisle CA2 176 C6
- Yealand Conyers LA5 166 F6

Flats Cotts 9 CA11 191 D5
Flatt Walks CA28 187 D8
Fleet St CA14 184 D5
Fleming Dr CA21 108 B5
Fleming Pl CA15 182 D6
Fleming Sq 2 CA15 182 D6
Fleming St CA15 182 D6
Fleswick Ave CA28 187 C5
Fletcher Cl
- 6 Cockermouth CA13 190 C4
- Great Broughton CA13 63 E6

Fletcher Cres CA15 182 E4
Fletcher Hill Pk CA17 199 C5
Fletchers Croft CA13 63 E4
Fletcher St
- Cleator Moor CA25 188 E6
- 7 Cockermouth CA13 190 C4
- 9 Workington CA14 184 D6

FLETCHERTOWN 37 C2
Fletcher Way CA3 175 B6
FLIMBY 183 D8
Flimby Brow CA15 183 D7

Flimby Prim Sch CA15 .. 182 A1
Flimby Sta CA15 .... 183 C8
Flintergill Cl LA10 ....147 B1
FLOOKBURGH 164 E6
Flookburgh CE Prim Sch
LA11.................... 164 D6
Florence Mine Heritage
Ctr* CA22 ....189 F5
Florence St LA14 .... 207 A3
Florence Terr [9] CA15....182 E5
Flosh Cotts CA23 .... 188 D4
Flosh Mdws CA23.......... 188 D4
Flowerden Ct LA7......... 211 D4
Flower St
Carlisle CA1............. 214 C1
Leece LA12 .... 171 C8
Floyd St LA18............. 150 A2
Flusco Wood Cvn Pk
CA11 ....70 A4
Flush Brow LA6.............212 F5
Fold Brow CA13 ....190 E4
Fold The
Cark LA11 .... 164 D7
Old Hutton LA8 .... 144 F3
Folkestone Ave LA14 .... 206 C1
Folly La CA11...............191 E5
Folly The LA10............ 201 C5
Footeran La LA5............166 F6
Force Cotts LA8 ....143 F1
Force Forge Cotts
LA12..................... 141 A5
Force La
Ambleside LA22......... 195 D4
Levens LA8 ....143 F1
Force Mills Forest Wlk*
LA12......................141 B5
Ford La LA5 ....210 E5
Ford Park Cres LA12 .....203 E6
Ford Rd LA11................153 E1
Ford Terr LA9.............. 200 D2
Forelands The CA7........49 F4
Forest Hill CA1 ....177 F2
Forest Houses CA23.......93 A6
Forge Cl LA14 .... 206 D5
Forge Ct CA4................41 E5
Forgeholm [6] DG14.........3 D3
Forge La CA12 .... 192 D4
Forge The
Buckabank CA5 ....40 B7
Coniston LA21 .... 196 A4
Keswick CA12 ....192 E4
Forresters Wlk LA12 .... 153 C7
Fort Putnam CA11 ....70 A5
Foster St
Penrith CA11............ 191 C6
Shap CA10............... 101 C6
FOTHERGILL 182 A1
Fothergills The CA15..... 182 A1
Foulney St LA13 ....171 B3
Foulstep LA22 ....113 E2
Foulyeat Cotts CA24 ......91 F5
Foundary Gdns LA5...... 213 C5
Foundry Rd CA28 ....186 E7
Foundry St LA14.......... 207 B3
Fountain Brow [5] LA9 ... 200 C5
Fountains Ave CA14.......184 E3
Fountain St LA12 .... 203 D5
Four Lane Ends
Burton in L LA2 .... 169 C1
Field Broughton LA11 ..... 154 A5
High Newton LA11....... 154 A4
Leece LA12 .... 171 C7
Fowl Ing La LA9 ....200 E7
FOXFIELD.................. 151 A8
Foxfield Cl [16] LA16 ..... 162 A8
Foxfield Rd
Broughton-in-F LA20 ...... 139 A2
Walney Island LA14...... 206 C5
Foxfield Sta LA20 ....150 F8
Fox Hill CA14.............. 185 C2
Foxhills CA6.................21 E4
Foxhole Rigg La LA10.... 134 A2
Foxhouses Rd CA28........187 E7
Foxhowe [5] LA12 .... 203 D5
Fox La
[10] Whitehaven CA28..... 186 C1
Workington CA14..........184 F6
Fox's Pulpit* LA10........145 E8
Fox St LA12 .... 203 A3
Frances Croft CA14 ....184 F5
Frank Coutts Ct TD9 ....1 B6
Frankland Pk CA10 ...... 118 C6
Franklin St LA14...........206 E4
Fraser Gr CA3 .... 175 C2
Frazer St CA14 .... 184 D5
Frederick St
Barrow-in-F LA13 .... 207 C2
Carlisle CA2..............176 E4
Freer Ct CA2 ....176 F4
Freer St CA2 ....176 F4
Frenchfield Gdns CA11...191 F4
Frenchfield Way CA11....191 F4
French St LA14 .... 206 D2
Freshfield Ct CA1......... 177 D5
Friar Bottom La CA17 ....119 F4
Friargate CA11 .... 191 D5
Friar Row CA7................53 C6
Friars Cl CA11..............191 E5
Friar's Crag Nature Trail*
CA12 .... 192 A1
Friars Ct CA3...............214 B2
Friars Garth
Abbeytown CA7 ....26 C1
Cartmel LA11.............153 F1
Friars La LA13 .... 207 D4
Friars Rd CA11 .... 191 D5
Friars Rise CA11...........191 E5
Friars Terr
Barrow-in-F LA13 .... 207 D4
Penrith CA11..............191 E5
Friars View LA13.......... 207 D4
Friary Cotts CA16 .... 193 C6
Friary Fields CA16 .... 193 C6
Friary Pk CA16............ 193 C6
Frith La CA16................88 C6
FRIZINGTON 92 E8
Frizington Com Prim Sch
CA26 ....92 D8
Frizington Rd
Cleator Moor CA25 ....188 F6
Frizington CA26 ....92 D7
Frome Rd LA14 .... 206 A4
Front Corkickle CA28 ... 187 D8
Front St
Alston CA9............... 181 D3
Armathwaite CA4 ....42 C5
Brampton CA8.............179 B5
Cotehill CA4................31 B1
Mealsgate CA7 ....37 C1
Orton CA10 .... 118 C7
Front The LA18 .... 202 A2
Frostoms Rd CA14 .... 184 D4
Frostrow La LA10......... 201 F3
Fruids Park Ave DG12.... 172 C3
Fulford Wlk [9] CA3 ...... 175 B1
Fulmar Dr LA9..............200 F1
Fulmer Pl CA2............. 176 C7
Furnace Ct CA25.......... 188 D7
Furnace La [1] CA15...... 182 D5
Furnace Pl LA16 .... 162 A7
Furnace Rd CA15 .... 182 D5
Furnace Row CA14.........185 E5
Furness Abbey* LA13.... 207 D8
Furness Bsns Pk LA14....206 E4
Furness Coll LA14 .... 206 D4
Furness General Hospl
LA14..................... 207 C8
Furness Park Rd LA14....207 B6
Furness Rd CA14 ....184 E3
Furness St LA18 .... 202 D4
Furze Ct CA1 .... 177 C6
Furze St CA1 .... 177 C6
Fusehill St CA1........... 214 C1
Fusethwaite La LA23.... 129 C8

G

Gable Ave CA13.............190 F4
Gable Rd CA28..............187 F3
Gable The LA6..............167 B7
Gainsborough Pl LA14 ...206 F6
Gait Barrows Nature
Reserve* LA7............ 166 D8
Gaitle Bridge CA6............9 F3
GAITSGILL 40 C5
Galabank Ave DG12 ...... 172 C5
Galava Roman Fort*
LA22..................... 195 C3
Gale How Pk LA22 .... 195 D5
GALEMIRE 188 A8
Gale Pk LA22 .... 195 D5
Gale Rigg LA22 .... 195 D5
Gale Rigg Ho LA22........ 195 D5
Gale The LA22 .... 195 D5
GALLABERRY................172 F5
Gallansay La CA17 ...... 104 A1
Gallery Ho CA1 .... 177 C3
Galloper Pk CA10..........118 B3
Galloway Cl CA15 ....182 F4
Gallowbarrow
Cockermouth CA13 ...... 190 C3
Kendal LA9............... 200 D1
Gallowber La LA6...........157 B1
GAMBLESBY 58 A6
Gamblesmire La LA8......143 E7
GAMELSBY 27 F3
Gameriggs Rd CA28...... 187 D4
Gandy St LA9...............200 E6
Gap La
Sedbergh LA10 .... 146 D4
Winton CA17 .... 105 A1
Garborough Cl CA15 ....49 B5
Garbridge Ct CA16.........193 E5
Garbridge La CA16.........193 E6
Garburn Rd LA9 ....200 F6
Garden Cl [7] CA11....... 191 C5
Garden Ct LA12........... 162 F7
Gardenia St CA2 .... 177 A4
Garden La CA15 ....35 C1
Garden Lea
[6] Dalton-in-F LA15 ......205 B4
Ulverston LA12 .... 203 D4
Garden Mews LA9 .... 200 D3
Garden Pl LA6 .... 167 C7
Garden Rd LA9 .... 200 D3
Garden St
Carlisle CA1............. 214 C1
Carlisle, Edentown CA3... 175 D1
Kendal LA9............... 200 D3
Gardens The
Barrow-in-F LA14 ....204 E1
Whitehaven CA28 .... 187 D8
Garden Terr
Baycliff LA12 ....163 B3
Dalton-in-F LA15 ....205 B5
Ulverston LA12 .... 203 D6
Garden Village CA2 ....176 B2
Garden Villas CA28.........187 F6
Garden Wlk CA4 ....21 E1
Gardiner Bank LA9........ 200 C6
Gardner Hall CA20 .... 123 A8
Gardner Rd LA5 .... 213 C7
Garfield St
Carlisle CA2............. 214 A1
Garfield St *continued*
Workington CA14..........184 E5
Garland La CA11.............57 A4
GARLANDS....................30 E4
Garlands Rd CA1 ....177 F2
Garlieston Ct CA28....... 187 D7
Garlieston Ho CA28 ...... 187 D7
Garner St CA15 .... 182 C4
Garnet Cres CA14 .... 184 C1
GARNETT BRIDGE 131 B6
Garnett Bridge Rd LA8.. 131 A4
Garnett Croft Yd [15]
LA9...................... 200 C4
GARRIGILL 60 C8
GARSDALE 147 F4
GARSDALE HEAD 148 D7
Garsdale Rd LA10..........201 E4
Garsdale Sta LA10 .... 148 D6
Gars La CA17 .... 119 C3
Garth Bank LA9.............200 B7
Garth Brow LA9 ....200 B7
Garth Heads Rd CA16... 193 D5
Garth Heads Rise
CA16 .... 193 D5
Garth Pk CA4................31 B1
Garth Rd CA14............ 184 C2
GARTH ROW 131 B4
Garth Row La
Kendal LA8................131 B3
Underbarrow LA8 .... 143 C6
Garthside CA7 .... 180 A8
Garth The
Coniston LA21 ....196 B4
Crosby-on-E CA6 ....20 F2
Torver LA21................127 B1
Gaskell Cl LA5............ 210 C3
Gatacre St LA14 .... 206 C2
Gatacre Terr LA14........ 206 C3
GATEBECK 156 D8
Gatebeck Bsns Pk LA8.. 156 D8
Gatebeck Cvn Pk LA8 ... 156 D8
Gatebeck La LA8.......... 156 D8
Gatebeck Rd LA8 .... 156 D8
Gatehead CA14 ....63 A4
Gateheads Brow LA6......212 F3
Gatelands Cvn Site
LA6.......................167 B4
Gatesbield LA23 ....198 E5
GATESGARTH 95 B6
Gateshead St LA13........207 B3
Gatesyde Pl CA19..........124 F7
Gateway LA13 .... 207 D3
Gauber Rd LA6 .... 160 C1
Gavel St CA15 .... 182 D4
Gavels The CA14 ....63 B4
Gawith Pl [4] LA9 .... 200 D5
GAWTHROP 147 A2
GAWTHWAITE.............. 152 A7
Gayle Ave CA10........... 101 C5
Gaythorne Terr CA14 ......63 C3
Geelong Terr CA28....... 187 A2
Gelt Cl CA3................ 175 C3
Gelt Rd CA8 .... 179 C4
Gelt Rise CA8..............179 B4
Geltsdale Ave CA1 ....177 F5
Geltsdale Gdns CA4...... 178 A3
Geltwood Ave CA14 ..... 185 D8
Geneva St [3] LA14...... 207 A2
George Hastwell Sch
LA14......................206 B2
George Moore Ave CA7 ...37 C2
George Moore Ind Est
CA7 ....37 C1
George Romney Jun Sch
LA15..................... 205 C5
George St
Annan DG12............. 172 C4
[21] Keswick CA12..........192 B3
Maryport CA15 .... 182 C5
Newcastleton or Copshaw
Holm TD9 ....1 B6
Whitehaven CA28 .... 186 D1
Wigton CA7 .... 180 D3
George Terr [15] CA15 ......182 E5
Georgian Way CA1,
CA3 ....214 B3
Ghyll Bank
Great Broughton CA13 .....63 E6
Lowca CA28................186 E8
Threlkeld CA12 ....82 C8
Ghyll Cl LA23 ....198 F5
Ghyll Gr CA28 ....186 E8
Ghyll Head Rd LA23.......142 B7
Ghyll Ho [5] LA14 .... 207 C8
Ghyll Rd
Scotby CA4 ....30 F5
Windermere LA23 ....198 F5
Workington CA14......... 184 C2
Ghyllside
Ambleside LA22............195 E5
Dent LA10 ....147 B1
Ghyll Side [10] LA9........ 200 C4
Ghyllside Prim Sch
LA9...................... 200 C4
Ghyll The [8] CA15..........182 F4
Gilbert Rd CA2 .... 176 D1
GILCRUX......................49 F4
GILGARRAN 77 D5
Gilgarran Pk CA14 ....77 D5
Gilgarran View CA14 .... 185 D4
Gillan Way CA11 ....191 B3
Gillbank Cotts CA10.........71 C1
Gillbeck Pk [1] CA15 ......182 F4
Gill Cl CA28 ....187 F7
Gillfoot Ave CA22 .... 189 D7
Gillfoot Rd CA22.......... 189 D7
Gillford Cres CA1 .... 177 D2
Gill Garth LA12 .... 203 C5
Gillhead Brow LA2....... 169 D1
Gillinggate LA9 .... 200 C4
Gillison Cl LA6............ 168 C2
Gillmorend Brow
Aspatria CA7 ....36 F4
Mealsgate CA7 ....37 A4
Gillshaw View DG14..........9 A7
Gill The LA11 .... 154 C3
Gillwood Rd DG12 ....17 D8
Gilmore Cl CA9 .... 181 D4
Gilmour St CA15 .... 182 C4
Gilnockie Tower* DG14 .....3 C5
Gilpin Wlk LA14 .... 206 A4
GILSLAND 14 E1
Gilsland CE Prim Sch
CA8 ....14 D1
Gilsland Rd CA1 ....177 F5
Gilthwaiterigg La LA9.....200 E8
Gilts La CA10 .... 102 C3
GILWILLY 191 B6
Gilwilly Back La [3]
CA11 .... 191 C5
Gilwilly Ind Est CA11......191 B5
Gilwilly La CA11............191 B5
Gilwilly Rd CA11 ....191 B5
Ginns CA28 .... 187 C7
Ginns To Kells Rd
CA28 .... 187 C6
Gladstone St CA14 ...... 184 D6
Gladstone Terr LA14 .... 207 A8
Glaramara Dr CA2 ....176 B3
Glasgow Rd DG16......... 173 D4
Glasgow St LA14......... 207 A3
GLASSON
Maryport 182 C5
Port Carlisle 17 E3
GLASSONBY 57 D5
Glasson Ct CA11.......... 191 D4
Glasson Ind Est CA15 ... 182 C4
Glave Hill CA5...............29 D1
GLEASTON 162 F1
Gleaston Ave LA13 ...... 207 D4
Gleaston Watermill*
LA12......................162 F1
Glebe Cl
Appleby-in-W CA16 ...... 193 C4
[2] Buckabank CA5 ....40 A8
Burton-in-K LA6.......... 167 C7
Keswick CA12 .... 192 A5
Glebe Cres CA16.......... 193 C4
Glebe Ct
Annan DG12............. 172 C3
Kirkby Lonsdale LA6 ......212 B3
Glebe Dr LA23 .... 198 C1
Glebe Fold LA10 ....147 B1
Glebe Gdns LA23 .... 198 C2
Glebe La CA14............ 185 D4
Glebeland Terr CA14 .....185 B7
Glebe Rd
Appleby-in-W CA16 ...... 193 C4
Bowness-on-W LA23 ......198 B1
Distington CA14.......... 185 D4
Kendal LA9............... 200 C3
Glebe Terr CA14 ....185 B8
Glebe The
Castle Carrock CA8 ....32 D6
Chapel Stile LA22......... 113 C4
Great Corby CA4 .... 178 C1
Wetheral CA4 ....178 B1
Glencoe Cl LA18 .... 150 A1
GLENCOYNE PARK.........83 D2
Glendale Cvn Pk CA7 ......17 D3
Glendale Rise CA2.........176 B3
Glenderamackin Terr
CA12 ....82 C7
Glendowlin Lodges
CA10 ....71 A1
Gleneagles Dr CA3........175 B1
Glenedyth LA11.............208 F5
Glenfield Pl CA14...........62 E4
Glenfield Rd [4] LA15......205 B4
Glen Helen Cl CA7.........180 B3
Gleniffer CA10............ 101 C5
Glenn Rd CA14 .... 184 D3
GLENRIDDING 98 C8
Glenridding Dr LA14 .....204 E1
Glenridding Wlk CA28.......91 F7
Glen Terr CA8................31 E5
Glen The LA12 .... 153 C7
Glen View LA12 .... 153 C7
Glenwhelt Bank CA8 ....24 D8
Glen Willie Cotts CA4 .... 178 C2
Globe Ho CA9 .... 181 D3
Globe La
Alston CA9............... 181 D3
Carlisle CA3...............214 B3
Gloucester Rd CA2....... 177 B4
Gloucester Sq [6] LA12 ...203 E5
Gloucester St LA13 ...... 207 C3
Glynt View DG12 .... 172 D2
Glynt Wynd DG12 .... 172 D2
Goad St LA12 .... 203 A3
Go Ape Grizedale*
LA22..................... 128 A1
GOAT 190 C4
Goat Brow CA13 ....190 B6
Golden Lion Ct [16]
CA28 .... 186 C1
Goldsmith Rd CA22 ..... 189 C6
Goldsmith St LA14.........206 F4
Golf Terr CA7...............174 B2
Goodly Dale Cotts
LA23..................... 198 D4
Goodly Dale Prim Sch
LA23..................... 198 D4
Goodman Rd CA14....... 184 C2
Goodmickle La LA6 ....157 B5
Goodwin Cl CA2 ....177 B4
Goodwin Pl CA1 ....177 B4
GOODYHILLS 35 F5
Goosegarth CA4 ....178 A1
Goose Gn [3] LA15 ....205 B4
GOOSE GREEN 156 E7
Gooseland Head CA1 .....177 E1
Gordon St CA14........... 184 D6
Gordon Terr DG12........ 172 C1
Goschen Rd CA2...........176 E4
GOSFORTH.................. 109 A2
Gosforth CE Sch CA20 ...109 B2
Gosforth Gate [7] CA20 .. 109 A2
Gosforth Rd
Carlisle CA2.................29 D6
Seascale CA20.............123 B8
Gosling Dr CA3 .... 175 D3
Gosport St LA14 ....206 F5
Gote Rd CA13.............. 190 C4
Gowan Cl LA8 ....130 B5
Gowan Cres LA8 .... 130 C5
Gowan Lea LA9 ....130 F2
Gowan Terr LA8........... 130 C5
Gowlands Cross LA10 ... 147 A2
Gowrie CA7 ....36 F1
Grace St CA1.............. 177 C6
Gradwell Ct LA13 .... 207 A4
Graham Ave DG12 .... 172 D5
Grahams Croft CA4 ..... 178 A5
Grahams Rigg CA16.......87 D6
Graham St
Carlisle CA2.............. 214 A1
Longtown CA6 ....10 C3
Penrith CA11............. 191 C6
Graigmore Ct [1] CA7 ... 180 D3
Graitney DG16 .... 173 C3
Grammerscroft LA18.... 202 A5
Granary The LA11........ 208 D5
Granby Rd LA11 .... 208 B1
Grandy Cl LA22 .... 194 A5
GRANGE......................96 A8
Grange Ave
Flimby CA15............. 183 C7
Great Broughton CA13 .....63 E6
Grange CE Prim Sch
LA11..................... 208 C4
Grange Cl CA22.............189 E2
Grange Cres [4] LA14.....206 F3
Grange Fell Rd LA11 .....208 B4
Grange Field CA10..........85 E1
Grange Gdns CA7........ 180 C5
Grange La CA13 ....78 F5
Grange Mews LA11 ......208 E5
GRANGE-OVER-
SANDS 208 E4
Grange-Over-Sands Sta
LA11......................208 E5
Grange Pk CA12 .... 192 D3
Grange Rd CA1 .... 177 D3
Grange The
Arnside LA5.............. 210 A8
Ivegill CA5..................40 F1
Whitehaven CA28 ....187 F8
Grange View
Carnforth LA5 .... 213 C5
Wigton CA7 .... 180 C5
Grant Dr CA28 ....186 E3
Grantley Rd LA14 .... 207 A6
Granville Cl CA28 ....187 F7
Granville Rd CA2 .... 176 D6
Granville St LA14 ....206 F5
Grapes La CA3.............214 B2
GRASMERE 194 B4
Grasmere Ave
Whitehaven CA28 ....187 B5
Workington CA14........ 184 D3
Grasmere CE Prim Sch
LA22......................194 B3
Grasmere Cres LA9 ....200 F6
Grasmere Rd
Barrow-in-F LA14 ....207 B6
Ulverston LA12 ....203 E4
Grasmere St CA2 .... 177 A4
Grasmere Terr CA15.......182 E4
Grasmoor Rd CA14....... 184 C1
GRASSGARTH 129 F6
Grassgarth Cotts LA8 ....129 F6
Grasshill Cswy DL13 ....61 F4
Grassiot CA15 .... 182 D4
Grassiot Inf Sch CA15.... 182 C4
Grassiot St CA15......... 182 C4
Grassmoor Ave CA13......190 E4
Graves Mill CA13 .... 190 C4
GRAYRIGG 132 A4
Grayrigg CE Sch LA8..... 132 A4
Grayson Dr CA11 ....57 B3
GRAYSON GREEN..........185 B7
Gray St CA14 ....184 E5
Graythwaite Cl [8]
LA15..................... 205 C4
Graythwaite Ct LA11 .... 208 C3
Graythwaite Hall Gdns*
LA12..................... 141 D6
Grearshill Rd CA3........ 175 C5
GREAT ASBY 103 C3
GREAT BLENCOW 70 A7
GREAT BROUGHTON 63 E6
GREAT CLIFTON 63 B4
GREAT CORBY 178 C1
Great Corby Prim Sch
CA4 .... 178 D2
Greatcross Cotts LA22 ...194 B5
GREAT
CROSTHWAITE........ 192 A5
Great Dockray [18]
CA11 .... 191 D5

Great Heads Rd LA11 208 B3
Greathowe LA8 130 E4
GREAT LANGDALE 113 A5
Great Langdale Camp Site LA22 112 E4
GREAT MUSGRAVE 104 E4
GREAT ORMSIDE 103 E8
GREAT ORTON 28 F5
Great Orton Prim Sch CA5 28 F4
GREAT SALKELD 57 A3
GREAT STRICKLAND 86 C5
GREAT URSWICK 162 F5
Greaves Wood Rd LA11 165 A6
Grecian Ct 15 CA13 190 C4
Grecian Terr CA14 185 A7
Greenacres
Grange-o-S LA11 208 B2
Wetheral CA4 178 A3
Wigton CA7 180 B3
Greenacres Pk CA11 56 C4
GREENBANK 187 C4
GREEN BANK 153 F3
Greenbank LA22 113 B2
Green Bank
Blennerhasset CA7 50 F8
Ulverston LA12 203 D6
Greenbank Ave
Storth LA7 209 E4
Whitehaven CA28 187 D4
Greenbank Cl CA7 49 F7
Greenbank Gdns LA12 162 F4
Greenbank Ho LA22 195 C7
Greenbank La
Cartmel LA11 153 E2
Cockermouth CA13 190 D2
Greenbank Rd LA22 195 C6
Greenber La LA6 212 F5
Greencastle Brow CA13 63 D1
Green Cl
Caldbeck CA7 53 C7
Crosby CA15 49 B5
Lupton LA6 156 E3
Seascale CA20 123 A8
Green Cotts LA21 127 B1
Greencroft CA10 101 C5
Green Croft
Askham CA10 85 D6
Brampton CA8 179 B5
Greencroft Wynd DG12 172 C3
Greendale Dr LA5 213 C5
Greendales LA11 164 F7
Green Dykes CA22 189 D5
Greenfield La CA8 179 B5
Greengarth CA2 177 B2
Green Garth
Great Clifton CA14 63 A4
Holme LA6 156 B1
Greengate
Kendal LA9 200 C3
Levens LA8 143 D1
Seaton CA14 183 B2
Green Gate LA23 114 F1
Greengate Cres LA8 143 D1
Greengate Inf Sch LA13 207 B3
Greengate Jun Sch LA14 207 A3
Greengate La
Crag Bank LA5 213 B2
Kendal LA9 200 C4
Greengate St LA14 207 A3
Greengill La
Penrith CA10 71 B7
Penrith CA11 71 A8
Plumpton CA11 56 D1
Green Haume Cotts LA15 205 A7
GREENHEAD 24 D8
Greenhead Bank CA8 24 C8
Greenhead CE Fst Sch CA8 24 D8
Greenhead Youth Hostel* CA8 24 C8
Greenhill CA8 179 B4
Green Hill LA9 200 C6
Greenhill Cl LA14 206 F8
Green Hollows Cvn Pk CA4 40 F5
GREENHOLME 117 F4
Greenknowe Ave DG12 172 D2
Green La
Allithwaite LA11 164 F7
Bowness-on-W LA23 129 C1
Cark LA11 164 D7
Carlisle CA2 176 A6
Clifton CA10 71 D2
Cowan Bridge LA6 169 B6
Crosby-on-E CA6 20 F2
Dalton-in-F LA15 205 B3
Great Salkeld CA11 57 A3
High Newton LA11 154 A4
Houghton CA3 20 C2
Old Town LA6 157 A7
Penrith CA11 191 C8
South Stainmore CA17 106 B2
Storth LA7 209 E5
Ulverston LA12 162 F6
Greenlands Ave CA28 187 E7
Greenlands Cl CA28 187 F7
Greenlands Rd CA15 49 A2
Green Lane Cotts LA12 162 F6
Greenlea Rd DG12 172 D4
Greenmeadow Gdns DG12 172 B3
Greenmill Rd CA6 9 F3
Green Mkt CA3 214 B2
Green Moor Rd CA22 189 D7
Green Moss LA23 198 E4
Greenmouth La CA8 23 A7
GREENODD 152 E5
Green Rd LA9 200 C6
Green Rd Sta LA18 150 D6
GREENROW 174 C2
Greenrow Mdws CA7 174 C2
GREENSIDE 119 F3
Greenside LA9 200 B4
Green Side LA6 212 C1
Greenside Ct LA7 156 A6
Greenside La CA17 119 F3
Greenside Rd
Carlisle CA2 176 D3
Glenridding CA11 98 C7
Green Sq LA6 212 C1
Green St LA18 150 A1
Greenstile Pk LA23 129 A1
Greens Yd 11 CA13 190 C4
Green The
Ambleside LA22 195 D6
11 Barrow-in-F LA14 207 A3
Bassenthwaite CA12 66 C7
Beck Houses LA8 132 A2
Buckabank CA5 40 A8
Cockermouth CA13 190 E4
Great Broughton CA13 63 E6
Houghton CA3 175 F5
Kendal LA9 200 C4
Kirksanton LA18 149 F3
Levens LA8 143 D1
Lindal in F LA12 162 E6
Natland LA9 144 B4
Penrith CA11 191 E3
Silverdale LA5 210 D2
Staveley LA8 130 B5
Welton CA5 39 F3
Wetheral CA4 178 B1
Whitehaven CA28 186 D2
Greenthwaite CA25 188 D6
Greenvale Ct CA26 92 D8
Green View LA9 200 C6
Greenways Dr LA8 144 C1
GREENWELL 32 C7
Greenwood LA9 200 B4
Greenwood Cl 5 CA5 28 F1
Greenwood Garth 4 CA5 28 F1
Greenwood Terr 1 CA15 182 E4
Gregg's La 2 CA28 186 C1
GRESSINGHAM 168 A1
Greta Ave CA2 176 D5
Greta Ct CA12 192 A3
Greta Grove Ho 3 CA12 192 A4
Greta Hamlet CA12 192 B4
Greta Heath LA6 169 C3
Greta Side CA12 192 B4
Greta Side Ct CA12 192 B4
Greta St CA12 192 B3
Gretenhow DG16 173 B2
GRETNA 173 D2
Gretna Gateway Outlet Village DG16 173 E3
GRETNA GREEN 173 D5
Gretna Ind Est DG16 173 D4
Gretna Loaning DG16 173 D5
Gretna Prim Sch DG16 173 C3
Gretna Sta DG16 173 C4
Greyfriar Cl LA13 207 E5
GREYMOORHILL 175 D6
Greyrigg Ave CA13 190 D2
Greyriggs Ct 7 LA11 208 C4
GREYSOUTHEN 63 E4
Grey St CA1 214 C1
GREYSTOKE 69 E5
Greystoke Cl CA11 191 A5
Greystoke Gdns LA14 204 D1
GREYSTOKE GILL 69 F4
Greystoke Park Ave CA11 191 B4
Greystoke Park Cl CA11 191 B4
Greystoke Park Rd CA11 191 B4
Greystoke Rd
Penrith CA11 70 E4
Penrith, Castletown CA11 191 B4
Greystoke Sch CA11 69 E5
Greystone Ave CA25 188 F6
Greystone Cl CA28 187 E4
Greystone La LA13 162 C2
Greystone Mount LA15 205 C4
Greystone Pl CA25 188 F6
Greystone Rd CA1 177 C6
Greystone Terr CA25 188 F6
Grierson Rd CA2 177 B3
Griffin Cl CA26 92 D8
Griffin St 3 LA20 139 A2
Grigg Hall La LA8 143 B6
Grindal Pl CA27 91 D2
GRINSDALE 19 D1
Grinsdale Ave CA2 176 A7
GRISEDALE 148 C7
Grisedale Cl
Cleator Moor CA25 188 B8
Whitehaven CA28 187 E4
Grisedale La CA9 181 D3
Grisedale Pl CA13 190 F4
Grisedale Rd LA10 148 C7
Grisenthwaite Yd 7 CA11 191 D5
Grisleymires La LA7 211 D4
GRIZEBECK 151 C8
Grizebeck Brow LA17 151 D7
Grizebeck Gdns LA14 206 C5
GRIZEDALE 128 A1
Grizedale Ave LA9 144 C7
Grizedale Cl CA12 192 C3
Grizedale Forest Pk* LA22 128 B1
Grizedale Visitor Ctr* LA22 128 A1
Grizedale Visitor Ctr Forest Walks* LA22 128 A1
Groffa Crag LA12 152 A6
Grosvenor Ct
Carlisle CA3 175 D1
Carnforth LA5 213 B3
Grosvenor Ho
Carlisle CA1 214 C2
Carlisle, Newton CA2 176 C7
Grosvenor Pl
Carlisle CA3 175 D1
Carnforth LA5 213 B3
Grosvenor Rd LA5 213 C3
Grosvenor St LA14 206 E8
Grosvenor Terr LA23 198 C3
Grove Ct CA11 191 C6
Grove Rd CA22 189 D6
Grove St 2 LA15 205 C4
Groves The CA28 187 F5
Grove The
Brampton CA8 179 B4
Crag Bank LA5 213 A3
GRUNE 25 E7
Grune Point Cl CA7 174 F8
Guard Hill La LA7 209 E4
Guard Hos CA7 26 C1
Guards Rd LA12 205 F8
Guard St CA14 184 F5
Guards The
Gleaston LA12 162 E1
Westnewton CA7 36 B2
Guildhall Mus* CA1 214 B2
Guldrey LA10 201 B5
Guldrey Fold LA10 201 B4
Guldrey La LA10 201 B5
Guldrey Terr LA10 201 B5
Gulfs Rd LA9 200 D5
Gulley Flatts CA22 189 D5
Gummers Howe Wlk LA5 213 D2
Gunson Cotts LA20 138 E8
Gurnal Bridge La LA8 131 B4
Guy La LA23 114 F2
Guysgill DG12 172 D5

H

HACKTHORPE 86 A6
Hackthorpe Gdns CA10 86 A6
Hackthorpe Hall Bsns Ctr CA10 86 A5
Hacra La LA10 147 A3
Haddon Ho CA1 214 C2
Hadrians Ave CA7 16 F1
Hadrian's Cres CA8 14 D1
Hadrians Gdns CA3 20 C1
Hadrian's Wall* CA8, NE49 15 D1
Hagget End CA22 189 D6
Hagget End Cl CA22 189 D6
Haggs La
Allithwaite LA11 164 F8
Cartmel LA11 153 F1
Haggy La CA10 71 C1
Haig Ave CA28 186 D3
Haig Colliery Mining Mus* CA28 187 B8
Haig Ent Pk CA28 187 B8
Haig Rd CA1 177 D2
HAILE 108 D7
Haile Pk CA22 108 D7
HALE 155 F1
Hale Green Farm LA7 155 F1
Halfey's La CA1 177 C6
Half Moon La 8 CA7 180 D3
HALFPENNY 144 C2
Halhead Brow LA8 130 D1
Haliburton Rd LA9 200 F1
Halier How La LA12 162 F6
Halla Way CA3 175 C2
Hallbank LA10 146 F6
Hall Bank NE49 24 E3
HALLBANKGATE 23 B2
Hallbankgate Village Sch CA8 23 A2
Hallbeck Pl 5 CA20 109 A2
Hall Brow CA14 184 F6
Hall Ct CA13 49 E2
HALL DUNNERDALE 126 A2
Hallfield LA12 203 C3
Hall Garth
Great Clifton CA14 63 B4
Rampside LA13 171 C5
Hallgarth Circ LA9 200 B7
Hall Garth Gdns LA6 167 B1
Hall Grange CA16 87 D6
Hall House Ind Est LA8 144 E6
Hallin Cres CA2 176 C3
Hallin Croft CA11 191 E6
Hall La
Dent LA10 147 B2
Staveley LA8 130 C7
Hall Lodge La CA14 63 B4
Hallmeadow Pl DG12 172 B3
Hall Moor Ct CA4 178 A2
Hallmore Cvn Pk LA7 166 F8
Hall Pk LA9 130 F2
Hall Rd
Burneside LA9 130 F2
Dent LA10 147 A2
Hallsenna La CA20 123 B8
Hallsenna Rd CA20 123 B8
Halls Mead CA12 192 C3
Hall St
Barrow-in-F LA14 207 A3
Dalton-in-F LA15 205 C5
Hall Terr CA13 64 A3
HALLTHWAITES 150 D8
Hallwood Rd CA14 185 E6
HALTCLIFF BRIDGE 54 A3
HALTON-LEA-GATE 24 B1
Halton Terr CA11 98 C8
Hame's Hall CA13 190 C5
Hamilton La CA28 186 C1
Hamilton Terr
5 Dalton-in-F LA15 205 B4
Whitehaven CA28 187 E8
Hammond Cl CA2 177 B3
Hampsfell Grange 8 LA11 208 D4
Hampsfell Rd
Grange-o-S LA11 208 D5
Ulverston LA12 203 D2
HAMPSFIELD 154 B3
Hampsfield Ho LA11 154 B3
Hampton Ho CA2 176 C7
Hangbridge La LA7 211 F1
Hannahmoor La CA28 91 B5
Hannay Cl 1 LA14 207 A3
Hanover Ct
Carlisle CA2 176 B5
Penrith CA11 191 C5
Harberwain La CA10 102 B5
Harbour Bsns Pk CA15 182 C5
Harbourside 19 CA28 186 C1
Harbour View CA28 186 B1
Harcourt St 11 CA14 184 D6
Hardcragg Way LA11 208 D4
Hardgates Rd CA20 108 D6
Hardingill 1 CA20 109 A2
Hardknott Castle* CA19 126 A8
Hardknott Gdns
Barrow-in-F LA14 204 D1
Kendal LA9 200 F1
Hard Knott Rise LA5 213 D2
Hard Knotts La LA12 171 C8
Hardwicke Cir CA1 214 B3
Hardwick St LA14 206 F5
Hardy St 2 LA14 206 F2
Harecroft Hall Sch CA20 109 B1
Haregate CA16 104 A7
Hare Ghyll
Barrow-in-F LA13 207 C5
Dalton-in-F LA15 205 D5
Hare La
Barrow-in-F LA13 207 C5
Walney Island LA14 170 E2
HARESCEUGH 44 A2
Harewood Cl LA14 206 F8
Hargreaves Ct 11 CA11 191 E4
HARKER 175 D8
Harker Ind Est CA6 175 C8
Harker Pk CA6 175 D8
Harley St 9 LA14 207 A3
Harling Bank LA6 212 B2
Harold St CA2 177 B3
Harpers La CA13 63 D3
Harpur Pl CA22 189 E2
HARRABY 177 F3
Harraby Gdns CA1 177 D3
Harraby Gr CA1 177 D3
HARRABY GREEN 177 C4
Harraby Green Bsns Pk CA1 177 C3
Harraby Green Hall CA1 177 C3
Harraby Green Rd CA1 177 C3
Harraby Grove Ct CA1 177 D3
Harraby St CA1 177 C4
HARRAS MOOR 186 F1
HARRAS PARK 186 E2
Harras Rd CA28 186 E1
Harrel La LA13 207 C5
Harrier Ct 7 CA28 76 F2
Harringdale Rd CA14 185 C7
HARRINGTON 185 A8
Harrington Rd CA14 184 E5
Harrington Sta CA14 76 E8
Harris Brow CA13 63 E6
Harris Cres CA1 177 E2
Harrison St
Barrow-in-F LA14 207 A3
Carlisle CA2 177 B4
7 Penrith CA11 191 C6
Harrison Way CA1 177 C3
Harris St LA16 162 A7
Harriston CA7 50 E8
Harriston Rd CA7 50 D8
Harrogate St LA14 207 A5
Harrot Hill CA13 190 B2
Harrot Rd CA13 190 B3
Harrowbeck Edge CA10 57 A6
Harry Brow LA7 155 F7
HARTBARROW 142 B5
Harthwaite Gdns CA11 71 C4
Hartington Pl CA1 214 C2
Hartington St
Barrow-in-F LA14 206 F4
Carlisle CA1 214 C3
Dalton-in-F LA15 205 C5
Hartington St *continued*
Workington CA14 184 E5
Hartland Rd LA14 207 B7
HARTLEY 199 E6
Hartley Ave CA3 175 B2
Hartley La
Kirkby Stephen, Hartley CA17 199 E6
Kirkby Stephen, Nateby CA17 199 C3
Hartley Rd CA17 199 C6
Hartley St LA12 203 D5
Hartness Rd CA11 191 A6
Hartside Rd LA9 200 C2
HARTSOP 98 F4
Hart St
Carlisle CA1 214 C2
Ulverston LA12 203 D5
Harvest Ind Est CA7 174 C3
Harvey St CA2 176 C7
Hasell St CA2 177 B3
Hastings St LA14 206 C2
Hause The CA10 84 B2
Havelock Rd
Windermere LA23 198 E5
Workington CA14 184 C6
Havera LA10 201 B5
Haverflatts Flats LA7 211 D4
Haverflatts La LA7 211 E5
HAVERIGG 202 A2
Haverigg Gdns LA14 206 C5
Haverigg Ind Est LA18 202 A3
Haverigg Prim Sch LA18 150 A1
Haverigg Rd LA18 202 B3
HAVERTHWAITE 153 A6
Haverthwaite Sta* LA12 153 B7
Haverwood LA7 156 A6
Haw Bank CA11 70 D3
HAWCOAT 204 D1
Hawcoat La LA14 207 B7
Hawes La LA9 144 A4
Hawesmead Ave LA9 200 C3
Hawesmead Dr LA9 200 C2
Hawes St CA2 176 D5
Haweswater Cl CA11 191 B4
Haweswater Rd CA11 191 B4
Hawick St CA2 176 E6
Hawker Marsh CA15 49 A1
Hawke St LA14 206 F3
Hawk Pl 4 CA28 76 F2
Hawkrigg La LA8 144 E6
Hawksgarth LA22 197 E5
HAWKSHEAD 197 D5
Hawkshead Ave CA14 184 F4
Hawkshead Esthwaite Prim Sch LA22 197 E4
Hawkshead Gdns LA14 204 D1
HAWKSHEAD HILL 197 B6
Hawkshead Old Rd LA21 196 A4
Hawksley Terr 12 CA14 184 D6
Hawk St LA5 213 D4
Hawkwood Terr LA15 205 B5
Haws Ave LA5 213 C3
Haws Hill LA5 213 C4
Haws La LA18 150 A1
Haws View Ind Est LA14 204 A1
Hawthorn Ave
Maryport CA15 182 E5
Ulverston LA12 203 D3
Hawthorn Cl CA14 185 D3
Hawthorn Dr
Barrow-in-F LA13 207 F5
Clifton CA11 71 C5
Hawthorne Pl CA2 176 B5
Hawthorn Gdns LA9 200 C8
Hawthorn Gr CA2 176 B5
Hawthorns The
Cleator Moor CA25 188 C8
Gretna DG16 173 B3
Keswick CA12 192 E4
Wigton CA7 180 E1
Hawthwaite La LA14 204 E6
Hayber La CA16 104 C7
Hayclose Cres LA9 200 F1
Hayclose Ct LA9 200 F1
Hayclose La LA8 144 C5
Hayclose Rd LA9 200 F1
Haycock La CA2 176 B3
Hayescastle Rd CA14 185 C1
Hayfell Ave LA9 200 E2
Hayfell Rise LA9 200 E3
Haygarth Ct 3 LA9 200 C4
HAYRAKE 47 F7
HAYTON
Brampton 31 F8
Oughterside 49 E8
Hayton CE Prim Sch CA8 31 F8
Hayton Rd CA1 177 D2
Hazel Bank Gdns CA10 71 A2
Hazel Cl LA14 206 F8
Hazelcroft Gdns 6 LA12 203 C5
Hazel Dene CA1 177 E3
Hazelgarth LA11 164 F7
Hazel Gill LA14 206 F8
Hazelgrove CA14 183 A2
Hazelmount Ave LA5 213 C5
Hazelmount Cres LA5 213 C5
Hazelmount Dr LA5 213 B5
Hazelrigg La LA12 153 E7
HAZELSLACK 209 F2
Hazel St LA23 198 E5

Hazeltree Rd LA12 ...... 203 D2
Hazelwood
Kendal LA9 .... 200 B3
Silverdale LA5 .... 210 C2
Windermere LA23 .... 198 D5
Hazelwood Ct LA11 ...... 208 F6
Hazelwood Hall LA5 ...... 210 D1
Hazelwood Terr LA11 ..... 208 F5
Head House Hill LA11 ... 154 A5
Head La LA8 .... 142 D6
Headland Rise LA14 ..... 170 C6
Headlands Cl 2 CA14 ... 184 D6
Headlands Dr CA28 ...... 187 E8
Headlands The
Glenridding CA11 .... 98 C8
Keswick CA12 .... 192 A3
Headland The 5 LA16 ... 162 A8
Headless Cl LA11 .... 153 E1
HEADLESS CROSS 153 F1
Headmeadow LA13 ..... 207 C4
Heads Dr LA11 .... 208 C3
Heads La
Carlisle CA3 .... 214 B2
6 Keswick CA12 .... 192 A4
Heads Mount CA12 ..... 192 A3
HEADS NOOK 31 E6
Heads Rd CA12 .... 192 A3
Head St CA2 .... 176 E6
Heads The
Grange-o-S LA11 .... 208 C3
Keswick CA12 .... 192 A3
HEANING 129 E6
Heath Cl LA9 .... 200 B3
Heathcliffe Ct LA5 ...... 209 A1
Heathcote Pk CA25 ...... 188 E7
Heather Bank
Barrow-in-F LA13 .... 207 E5
Cleator Moor CA25 .... 188 D7
Swarthmoor LA12 .... 203 A2
Heather Cl CA28 .... 186 E2
Heatherfields CA15 .... 63 C8
Heathfield Cl CA1 .... 177 F5
HEATHWAITE 198 F4
Heathwaite Cl LA7 .... 209 E4
Heatley Ct DG12 .... 172 B3
Hebblethwaite Hall La
LA10 .... 146 F8
Hebden Ave CA2 .... 176 A4
HECKLEGIRTH 172 D3
Hecklegirth Sch DG12 .... 172 D3
Hector St LA13 .... 207 C6
Hector Terr LA13 .... 207 C6
Hedley Ct CA1 .... 177 E2
Heggerscales La CA17 .... 105 E1
HEGGLE LANE 54 A2
Height La LA12 .... 141 E3
Height Rd LA11 .... 154 B7
HELBECK 105 B6
Helbeck Rd CA17 .... 105 B5
Helder St CA14 .... 62 C6
Helena Thompson Mus*
CA14 .... 184 F6
Hellens Ct LA21 .... 196 A4
Hellwell La LA8 .... 115 D3
Helm Cl LA23 .... 198 D2
Helme Chase Gdns
LA9 .... 200 E2
Helme Cl LA9 .... 200 E2
Helme Dr LA9 .... 200 E1
Helme La LA8, LA9 ...... 131 C2
Helm Gr LA12 .... 203 F5
Helm La LA9 .... 144 B3
Helm Rd
Bowness-on-W LA23 ..... 198 D2
Great Ormside CA16 ..... 103 E6
Helm Rigg LA23 .... 198 D2
Helmside Ct LA9 .... 144 C4
Helmside Gdns LA9 ...... 144 C4
Helmside Rd LA9 .... 144 B4
Helmsley Cl CA11 .... 191 F5
Helmsley Dr LA14 .... 206 F7
Helsfell Hall LA9 .... 200 A7
Helsington Laithes
LA9 .... 200 B1
Helsington Rd LA9 ...... 200 C2
HELTON 85 D5
HELTONDALE 85 B3
Helton Rd CA10 .... 85 D6
Helvellyn Cl CA13 .... 190 F4
Helvellyn Ct CA11 .... 191 C3
Helvellyn Rise CA2 ...... 176 B3
Helvellyn St CA12 .... 192 A3
Helvellyn Wlk LA14 ..... 204 D1
Hempland Ave LA13 ..... 207 C5
Henderson Gdns CA2 .... 177 B2
Henderson Rd CA2 ...... 177 A2
Henderson's Croft CA6 .... 20 F2
Hen Parrock La LA12 .... 163 A5
Henry St
Cleator Moor CA25 .... 188 E7
Cockermouth CA13 ...... 190 C3
Newcastleton or Copshaw
Holm TD9 .... 1 B6
Whitehaven CA28 .... 186 D2
HENSINGHAM 187 E6
Hensingham Com Prim Sch
CA28 .... 187 F6
Hensingham Ho CA28 .... 187 F6
Hensingham Rd CA28 .... 187 E7
Herbert Hill 1 CA28 .... 186 D1
Herbert St CA1 .... 177 C3
Herb Gdns The LA6 ..... 168 B3
Herdley Bank Fst Sch
NE49 .... 24 F2
Herdus Rd CA28 .... 187 E4
Heron Cl LA9 .... 200 F2
Heron Corn Mill & Mus of
Paper Making* LA7 .... 155 E2
Heron Dr CA1 .... 177 D6
HERON HILL 200 E2
Heron Hill LA9 .... 200 E2
Heron Hill Prim Sch
LA9 .... 200 E3
Heron's Quay LA7 .... 211 A2
Herons Reach LA5 .... 209 B2
Herschell Terr LA17 ..... 151 C5
Hertford St 2 LA14 ..... 207 A5
Hervey Nature Reserve*
LA11 .... 142 E2
HESKET NEWMARKET 53 D5
Hesket Pl CA4 .... 41 C4
Hespek Raise CA1 .... 177 F5
Hest View Rd LA12 ...... 203 D2
HETHERBANK 11 D1
Hether Dr CA3 .... 175 C3
HETHERSGILL 11 F2
Heughscaur Cl CA10 ...... 84 F7
HEVERSHAM 211 D8
Heversham Cl LA12 ..... 203 D3
Heversham Gdns LA7 .... 211 D7
Heversham St Peter's CE
Prim Sch LA7 .... 155 E7
HEWER HILL 54 B5
Hewetson Ct 7 CA12 .... 192 A4
Hewson's Sq CA15 .... 182 C5
Hewson St CA2 .... 214 B1
Hewson Street Workshops
CA2 .... 214 B1
Hewthwaite La LA10 .... 146 D4
Heysham Park Ave
CA2 .... 176 B6
Hibbert Rd LA14 .... 206 F5
Hicks La 3 CA28 .... 186 C1
Higginson Mill CA2 ...... 176 F4
High Bank LA15 .... 205 C6
Highbank Cl CA1 .... 177 D3
HIGH BANKHILL 43 B1
Highbeck La CA10 .... 118 B4
High Bell Garth CA4 ...... 41 E5
HIGH BIGGINS 212 A1
High Bldgs CA4 .... 178 D6
HIGH BORRANS 129 E8
HIGHBRIDGE 40 D2
High Brigham CA13 .... 63 F5
High Brundrigg LA9 ..... 130 D2
HIGH CARK 153 F5
High Carley Villas
LA12 .... 162 F7
HIGH CASTERTON 212 E3
High Castle Terr CA8 ..... 14 F1
High Cl CA14 .... 185 B6
High Cleater St LA15 .... 205 C5
High Cliff LA14 .... 204 B1
High Close Cvn Pk
CA12 .... 66 D7
Highcote La LA7 .... 155 D1
High Crag Ct LA5 .... 213 D8
Highcroft Cl CA13 .... 49 E2
High Croft Dr LA11 ..... 164 F7
High Cross
Broughton-in-F LA17 .... 139 D1
Hawkshead LA22 .... 197 A6
High Cross Brow LA20 ... 138 F2
High Cross St 1 CA8 .... 179 C5
HIGH CUMMERSDALE ... 176 D1
High Duddon Cl 12
LA16 .... 162 A8
HIGH DYKE 70 C8
High Fell Gate Barns
LA11 .... 208 A4
High Fellside 11 LA9 .... 200 C5
Highfield CA10 .... 118 B3
Highfield Ave CA2 ...... 176 C3
Highfield Cl CA20 .... 123 B8
Highfield Ct CA7 .... 180 B5
Highfield Gdns CA7 ..... 180 B5
Highfield Hall LA9 ...... 144 B3
Highfield Ho
Hawkshead LA22 .... 197 D6
Sedbergh LA10 .... 201 C5
Highfield Pk CA7 .... 180 C4
Highfield Rd
Barrow-in-F LA14 ...... 207 A6
Carnforth LA5 .... 213 D2
Cleator Moor CA25 ...... 188 D6
Cockermouth CA13 ...... 190 F4
Grange-o-S LA11 .... 208 C4
Sedbergh LA10 .... 201 C5
Highfields CA28 .... 187 F8
Highfields Ct CA28 ...... 187 E8
Highfieldside LA22 ...... 194 A5
Highfields Rd DG12 ..... 172 E5
Highfield Villas LA10 .... 201 C5
High Gale LA22 .... 195 D5
High Garth
Kendal LA9 .... 200 B8
Penny Bridge LA12 ..... 152 E5
Highgarth Ct CA2 .... 177 B1
High Garth Mdws CA5 .... 40 F2
Highgate LA9 .... 200 C4
High Gate LA12 .... 153 C6
Highgate La LA9 .... 144 E3
High Gr
Whitehaven CA28 .... 187 F8
Workington CA14 .... 184 F4
HIGH GREEN 114 F2
High Greenbank LA22 ... 195 C7
High Green Croft CA1 .... 177 F1
HIGH HARRINGTON 185 D7
High Hasket CE Sch
CA4 .... 41 F3
HIGH HESKET 41 F3
High Hill CA12 .... 192 A4
High House Rd CA27 ...... 91 D3
HIGH IREBY 51 F4
High Kepplewray LA20 .. 139 A2
High Kingate LA23 ...... 114 F4
High Knott Rd LA5 ...... 209 B1
High La
Kentmere LA8 .... 115 E3
Newbiggin-on-L CA17 ... 119 E4
Highlands Ave LA13 ..... 207 D6
Highlands Gr LA13 ...... 207 D6
Highland View CA28 ..... 186 D2
HIGHLAWS 36 C8
High Lea CA22 .... 189 D6
High Leases La CA17 .... 120 C8
High Lea Wlk LA14 ..... 204 B1
High Longthwaite CA11 ... 84 B6
HIGH LORTON 79 E8
High Mdw CA2 .... 176 B6
High Mead LA9 .... 200 C7
High Midgeholme CA8 .... 24 B1
HIGHMOOR 180 E2
Highmoor CA7 .... 180 E2
Highmoor Bglws CA7 .... 180 E2
Highmoor Gdns CA7 ..... 180 E2
Highmoor La CA16 .... 88 C5
High Moor La CA24 ..... 188 A5
Highmoor Mans CA7 ..... 180 E2
Highmoor Pk CA7 .... 180 E1
High Moor Rd 11 CA28 .... 76 F2
HIGH NEWTON 154 B5
HIGH NIBTHWAITE 140 C4
High Park Cvn Pk LA8 .. 144 C5
High Park Ho LA8 ...... 144 C5
Highpark Wood Forest
Trail* CA12 .... 97 B7
High Portinscale CA12 .... 81 A6
High Rd
Blennerhasset CA7 .... 50 F8
Carlisle CA1 .... 177 D3
Middleton LA6 .... 157 F7
Thornhill CA22 .... 189 E2
Whitehaven CA28 ...... 187 B5
High Ridge LA9 .... 200 B7
High Ridley NE49 .... 24 F2
High Rigg CA13 .... 63 F5
HIGH ROW
Dockray 83 B4
Hesket Newmarket 53 F2
High Row LA12 .... 153 C7
High Sand La 1 CA13 ... 190 D4
HIGH SCALES 37 A4
High School Ho LA9 ..... 200 E5
High Seat Hill CA10 ...... 57 A6
HIGH SEATON 183 C3
HIGH SELLAFIELD 108 B3
High Sparrowmire LA9 .. 200 B8
High St
Annan DG12 .... 172 C4
Barrow-in-F LA14 ...... 206 F4
Bigrigg CA22 .... 188 A3
Brough CA17 .... 105 B5
Burton in L LA6 .... 169 C3
Cleator Moor CA25 ..... 188 D7
Keswick CA12 .... 192 B3
Kirkby Stephen CA17 ... 199 C5
Longtown CA6 .... 10 B3
Maryport CA15 .... 182 D6
Morland CA10 .... 86 F5
Pooley Bridge CA10 ...... 84 F7
Whitehaven CA28 ...... 186 D1
Wigton CA7 .... 180 D3
Windermere LA23 ...... 198 E6
Workington CA14 ...... 184 F5
High Style Cl CA28 .... 77 A1
High Tenterfell LA9 ..... 200 C5
HIGH WHINNOW 28 D2
High White Cl LA14 ..... 206 F8
High Wiend CA16 .... 193 C5
High Winder La CA22,
CA23 .... 92 E2
High Woodbank CA4 ...... 30 C3
Highwood Cres CA1 ..... 177 E2
HIGH WRAY 128 E6
Hilden Rd CA23 .... 188 D4
Hilderstone La LA5 ..... 167 A7
HILL 123 E6
Hillary Cl CA14 .... 184 C1
Hillary Gr CA1 .... 177 E2
Hill Cl
Kendal LA9 .... 200 C4
Sedgwick LA8 .... 144 A1
Hill Cotts CA14 .... 185 D4
Hill Cres CA13 .... 63 F5
Hillcrest
Milnthorpe LA7 .... 211 D4
Ousby CA10 .... 58 C1
Workington CA14 ...... 184 E8
Hill Crest
Distington CA14 .... 185 C2
Workington CA14 ...... 184 E7
Hillcrest Ave
Carlisle CA1 .... 177 D3
Whitehaven CA28 ...... 187 E8
Hillcrest Cl CA1 .... 177 D4
Hillcrest Ct CA1 .... 177 D3
Hillcrest Dr LA7 .... 155 E1
Hillcrest Ho CA1 .... 177 D3
Hillcroft Cvn Pk CA10 .... 84 F7
Hillend Gdns DG12 ...... 172 B2
Hillend Rd DG12 .... 172 C2
Hillersdon Terr CA9 ...... 47 A2
Hill Fall LA12 .... 203 E5
Hillgarth LA8 .... 143 B7
Hill Head CA4 .... 30 F6
Hill House La CA9 ...... 181 E3
Hill La LA10 .... 147 A3
Hill Pl LA9 .... 144 C4
Hill Rd LA14 .... 207 B7
Hill Rise LA15 .... 205 C6
Hillside
Holme LA6 .... 156 B2
Hillside continued
Laversdale CA6 .... 21 C5
St Bees CA27 .... 91 D2
Temple Sowerby CA10 .... 72 E2
Hillside Cl 6 CA15 ..... 182 F4
Hillside Cotts LA11 ..... 154 C3
Hillside Rd LA12 .... 203 D3
Hill St
Carnforth LA5 .... 213 C3
Cockermouth CA13 ..... 190 C3
Hillswood Ave LA9 ..... 200 B3
Hill Terr CA19 .... 123 E6
Hill The
Brigham CA13 .... 63 F5
Eaglesfield CA13 .... 64 A1
Hill Top* LA22 .... 128 D2
Hill Top
Milnthorpe LA7 .... 211 D5
Windermere LA23 ...... 198 E3
Hill Top Cl LA5 .... 166 F6
Hilltop Cotts CA9 .... 47 A2
Hilltop Ho 1 LA14 ..... 207 A6
Hilltop Rd CA28 .... 187 B7
Hill Top Rd LA22 .... 195 D6
Hillview Cres DG12 ..... 172 E4
Hillview Ct DG16 .... 173 E5
HILTON 89 B3
Hilton Terr CA28 .... 186 D2
Himalaya Ave LA14 ..... 170 C6
HINCASTER 155 F7
HINDPOOL 206 F4
Hindpool Rd LA14 ...... 206 F3
Hinnings Rd CA14 ...... 185 C3
Historic Resources Ctr
DG12 .... 172 C4
Hoad La LA12 .... 203 F6
Hoad Terr 2 LA12 ...... 203 D6
Hoad View LA12 .... 163 D8
Hobsons La CA17 ...... 199 C7
Hobson's La LA6 .... 167 C2
Hodbarrow Lake Nature
Reserve* LA18 .... 202 C2
Hodden Ct CA7 .... 53 C6
Hodgehowe LA23 .... 198 C8
Hodgson Brow LA8 ..... 115 D3
Hodgson Cl CA9 .... 181 E3
Hodgson Gdns LA18 .... 202 B4
Hodgsons Cl 2 CA7 .... 180 D3
Hodgsons Ct CA3 ...... 214 B3
Hodgson Terr LA18 ..... 150 C6
HOFF 103 B8
Hoggs La CA10 .... 87 C4
Hog House La
Cartmell Fell LA11 ..... 142 C1
Hawkshead LA22 ...... 128 D6
Hogue St LA14 .... 206 D1
Holbeck Cl LA23 .... 129 A8
HOLBECK GHYLL 114 D1
Holbeck La LA23 .... 129 A8
Holbeck Park Ave
LA13 .... 207 F5
Holborn Hill LA18 ...... 202 B5
Holcroft Hill LA13 ..... 207 C3
Holden Pl CA25 .... 188 E6
Holden Rd CA14 .... 185 A8
Holebeck Rd LA13 ..... 207 E4
Holehird Gdns* LA23 .. 129 B7
Holesmire La CA17 .... 104 D1
Holgates Cvn Pk LA5 .. 210 B5
HOLKER 164 D8
Holker Cl LA15 .... 205 D4
Holker Hall* LA11 ..... 164 C8
Holker St LA14 .... 206 F5
Holliday Cres CA7 ..... 174 C3
Hollies The
Egremont CA22 .... 189 C6
18 Keswick CA12 ...... 192 B3
Hollin Bank Hill LA8 .. 143 A6
Hollin La LA8 .... 115 D3
Hollinrigg La LA8 ..... 115 D2
Hollins Cl
High Harrington CA14 .. 185 B7
Whitehaven CA28 ..... 187 F4
Hollins La
Arnside LA5 .... 209 C1
Burneside LA9 .... 130 E2
Silverdale LA5 .... 210 D1
Hollins Pk CA24 .... 188 A5
Hollins Row LA9 ...... 130 F2
Hollins The CA28 ..... 187 F4
Hollowgate Rd LA16 ... 162 B8
Hollow La
Barrow-in-F LA13 ..... 207 B6
Dent LA10 .... 147 A3
Lindale LA11 .... 154 B3
Hollowrane LA6 .... 167 C7
HOLLOWS 3 B5
Hollows DG14 .... 3 C5
Hollow W LA21 .... 140 A8
Holly Bank
Ulverston LA12 .... 203 E3
Warton LA5 .... 213 C7
Whitehaven CA28 .... 186 E1
Holly Cl LA7 .... 211 D7
Holly Dr CA3 .... 175 E2
Holly Gate Rd LA15 .. 205 B4
Holly La CA1 .... 30 E4
Holly Rd LA23 .... 198 E5
Holly Terr CA28 ..... 187 F6
Holmacres Dr CA1 .... 177 D2
Holm Cultram Abbey CE
Sch CA7 .... 26 C1
HOLME 156 B2
Holme Cl CA4 .... 30 E6
Holme Cres CA14 ..... 185 B8
Holmecroft CA5 .... 29 A2
Holme Ct CA16 .... 193 C5
Holme Eden Gdns CA4 .. 178 C6
Holme Eden Hall CA4 ... 178 C7
Holme Farm Ct CA4 ...... 30 F3
Holme Fauld CA4 .... 30 E6
Holmefield 3 LA6 ...... 156 B1
Holme Ground Cotts
LA21 .... 127 E8
Holme Head Way CA2 .. 176 E3
Holme Houses LA9 .... 130 F2
Holme La
Allithwaite LA11 ...... 164 F7
Carlisle CA2 .... 176 C8
Kirkandrews-on-E CA5 ... 19 C1
Scotby CA4 .... 30 E7
Holme Lo LA9 .... 200 E1
Holme Mdw CA4 .... 30 F3
HOLME MILLS 167 A8
Holme Mills LA6 ...... 156 B1
Holme Mills Ind Est
LA6 .... 167 B8
Holme Open Farm*
LA10 .... 146 A5
Holme Park Sch LA8 ... 144 D6
Holme Prim Sch LA6 ... 156 B1
Holme Rd LA11 .... 154 C6
Holme Riggs Ave CA11 .. 191 C3
HOLME ST CUTHBERT 35 E6
Holme St Cuthbert Sch
CA15 .... 35 E6
Holmes Ave CA2 ...... 177 A2
Holmes Rd LA8 .... 143 B4
Holme St CA16 .... 193 C5
Holme Terr CA2 ...... 214 A2
Holmewood Ave CA13 .. 190 B3
Holmewood Paddock
CA13 .... 190 C3
Holmfoot TD9 .... 1 B6
Holm Garth CA6 .... 19 D2
HOLMROOK 123 E6
Holmrook Rd CA2 ..... 176 A5
HOLMSFOOT 46 F3
HOLMWRANGLE 42 D7
Holy Family RC Prim Sch
LA13 .... 207 C6
Holyoake Ave LA13 ... 207 C6
Holyoake Terr
Beckermet CA21 ...... 108 C5
Penrith CA11 .... 191 B5
Holywell Cres CA1 ... 177 E5
Holy Well La LA11 ... 164 F5
Home Farm Cl CA15 .... 49 B3
Homefield CA11 .... 98 C7
Homethwaite Ho CA12 .. 192 C3
Homewood Dr CA28 ... 187 F4
Homewood Hill CA28 .. 187 F4
Homewood Rd CA28 ... 187 F5
Honister Dr
Cockermouth CA13 .... 190 B3
Kendal LA9 .... 200 F2
Workington CA14 ..... 184 D4
Honister Pass CA13 ..... 95 B5
Honister Rd CA28 .... 187 F4
Honister Slate Mine*
CA12 .... 95 E4
Hood St LA14 .... 206 E4
Hooks La LA12 .... 162 F5
Hoo La The LA23 .... 198 D7
HOPEBECK 79 E6
Hopedene CA25 ...... 188 C8
Hopes Hill Dr CA1 ... 177 E2
Hope St
6 Barrow-in-F LA14 .... 207 A2
Carlisle CA2 .... 176 F4
1 Dalton-in-F LA15 .... 205 C5
Millom LA18 .... 202 D4
Hophouse La LA6 .... 157 C3
Hopper Hill CA10 .... 102 C6
Hopping Ho CA3 ..... 214 A3
Horland Ct 4 LA14 ... 207 A2
Hornbeam Cres LA13 .. 207 F4
Horncop La LA9 ..... 200 C7
Hornedale Ave LA13 .. 207 B5
Horn Hill LA18 ...... 202 C5
HORNSBY 32 A1
HORNSBY GATE 32 A1
Horse Close La LA12 .. 162 F6
Horse Market LA6 ... 212 C2
Horsfield Cl CA28 ... 187 F7
Horsley Terr CA11 ... 191 E6
Horsman Ct 5 CA13 .. 190 C4
Horsman St CA13 .... 190 C4
Hospital Rd DG12 ... 172 E6
Hosticle La LA6 ..... 168 C7
Hotchberry Brow CA13 ... 63 F4
Hotchberry Rd CA13 .... 63 F4
Hothfield Ct CA16 ... 193 D6
Hothfield Dr CA16 ... 193 D5
HOUGHTON 175 F6
Houghton CE Sch CA3 .. 175 F5
Houghton Pk TD9 .... 1 B6
Houghton Rd CA3 .... 20 C1
Houghton Rd N CA3 ... 175 F6
Housesteads Rd CA2 .... 29 D6
HOW 31 F7
Howard Arms La CA8 .. 179 B5
Howard Ct CA2 ...... 176 D6
Howard Gdns CA8 ... 179 B5
Howard Mews LA5 ... 213 B3
Howard Pk CA11 .... 69 F6
Howard Pl CA1 ...... 214 C2
Howard Rd CA8 ..... 179 B6
Howard St
Carlisle CA2 .... 176 D6
Kendal LA9 .... 200 D2
Penrith CA11 .... 191 B5
Howard View CA8 ...... 23 C2

Howbank Rd CA22 ...... 189 D7
Howe Bank Cl LA9 ......144 B5
Howe Bank View LA22 ....113 B4
Howe Ct LA9 ....144 B5
Howe Gdns LA9 ....144 B5
Howe La
Portinscale CA12 ....81 A6
Row LA8 ....143 A3
How End Cotts CA13 ......65 C5
HOWES 172 B4
Howe St
Barrow-in-F LA14 ....206 F4
Carlisle CA1 ....214 C1
HOWGATE 76 F4
Howgate Foot CA16 ..... 193 D5
HOWGILL 133 A3
Howgill Brae DG12 ....172 F4
Howgillbridge DG12 .....172 F3
Howgill Cl
Bolton Low Houses CA7 ....37 F3
Burneside LA9 ....130 F2
Howgill Houses LA9 .....130 F2
Howgill La
Beck Foot LA10 ....133 A2
Sedbergh LA10 ....201 B5
Howgill St CA28 ....187 C8
HOW HILL 54 D2
How La
Heads Nook CA8 ....31 F7
Portinscale CA12 ....81 A7
Howrahs Ct CA12 .... 192 A4
Howrigg Bank CA7 ....180 E4
How St
Hayton CA8 ....31 F8
Hayton, Townhead CA8 .....32 B8
Howthorne Fields
CA23 ....188 D4
HOWTOWN 84 C2
HUBBERSTY HEAD 142 D6
Hub of the North Pennines Mus The★ CA9 ....181 D4
Huddleston Rd LA18 .... 202 C6
Hugh Little Garth CA2 .. 177 C2
Hugh St CA28 ....186 D2
Humber Terr LA14 ...... 206 A4
Hummer La LA21 ....139 F8
Hunday Ct CA14 ....184 F4
Hundith Hill Rd
Cockermouth CA13 ....64 F3
Embleton CA13 ....65 A4
Hundreds Rd LA23 ...... 114 D1
Hunriggs La CA16 ...... 193 D7
HUNSONBY 57 E2
Hunter Bank CA14 ....63 B4
Hunter Hall Sch CA11 ......71 C4
Hunter Ho LA23 ....198 D5
Hunter Rise CA21 ....108 B5
Hunter's Cl CA14 ....183 B3
Hunters Cres CA1 ....177 F3
Hunters Croft LA9 ....200 E8
Hunter's Dr CA14 ....183 B3
Hunter's La 2 CA11 .... 191 D5
Hunter St
Carnforth LA5 ....213 C4
Workington CA14 ....184 E5
Hunting Hill Cvn Pk
LA5 ....213 B3
Hunting Hill Rd LA5 ..... 213 A3
Hunting Lodge Cl CA7 ....51 A5
Huntington Pl CA14 ......183 B2
Huntley Ave CA11 .... 191 D3
Huntley Ct CA11 .... 191 C3
Huntsman La CA1 ....30 E5
Hurley Rd CA4 ....178 D7
HURST 54 F7
HUTTON 69 E1
Hutton Cl LA6 .... 167 C7
Hutton Ct 8 CA11 ...... 191 D5
HUTTON END 55 C5
Hutton Gdns
Penrith CA11 ....191 E6
Warton LA5 ....213 B6
Hutton Hill CA11 ....191 E5
Hutton-in-the-Forest★
CA11 ....55 E2
Hutton Pl CA15 .... 182 C5
HUTTON ROOF 157 A1
Hutton Way CA2 .... 176 A5
HYCEMOOR 137 A4
Hycemoor Way LA19 .....136 F4
Hyde St CA14 .... 184 D6
Hylton Terr CA7 .... 174 C4
Hyndburn Cl LA5 ....213 E4
Hyning LA8 ....143 E1
Hyning Brow LA8 ....142 F5
Hyning Ct LA8 .... 143 D1
Hyning Rd LA5 ....166 F4
HYTON 137 A2
Hyton Cvn Pk CA7 ...... 174 C3

I

ICKENTHWAITE 140 F4
Icold Rd CA11 ....69 F5
Ilkley Rd LA14 ....207 B6
Infield Cres LA13 .... 207 C7
Infield Gdns LA13 .... 207 C7
Infield Pk LA13 .... 207 C7
Infirmary Rd CA14 ....184 E5
Infirmary St CA2 .... 176 D7
Ing La
Beck Foot LA10 .... 133 A1
Troutbeck LA23 ....114 F3
Ingleborough View
LA5 .... 213 D2
Ingleby Terr CA15 ...... 182 D6
Inglemere Cl LA5 ....209 B1
Inglemere Dr LA5 ....209 B2
Inglemere Gdns LA5 .....209 B1
Inglenook Cvn Site
CA14 ....78 C3
INGLETON 169 F3
Ingle View LA6 .... 169 C3
Inglewood
Barrow-in-F LA13 .... 207 C7
Waverton CA7 ....37 E6
Inglewood Cl CA14 ..... 185 D8
Inglewood Cres CA2 .... 176 C5
Inglewood Ct
Arnside LA5 ....209 B2
Calthwaite CA11 ....55 D5
Carlisle CA2 .... 176 C5
Inglewood Inf Sch CA1 ...177 E3
Inglewood Jun Sch
CA1 ....177 E3
Inglewood Rd
Carlisle CA2 .... 176 C5
Penrith CA11 ....70 F7
Inglewood Terr
Broughton-in-F LA20 .....150 F8
Calthwaite CA11 ....55 F7
Inglis Ct CA15 ....182 E4
Ingman Lodge Rd
BD24 .... 160 C1
Ingmire Back La LA10 ... 146 A6
INGS 129 F5
Ings Hall LA8 ....129 F5
Ings Mill Cvn Pk LA8 .....129 F6
Ingwell Dr CA24 ....91 F5
Inkerman Terr CA28 ......187 E7
Inmoor Rd CA10 ....86 C5
Inner Ling Rd CA14 ......183 B2
IREBY 51 F6
Ireby CE Sch CA7 ....51 F5
Ireby Rd LA6 .... 169 C3
Iredale Cres CA14 ...... 184 D4
IRELETH 162 B8
Ireleth Brow LA16 ....162 B8
Ireleth Court Rd 11
LA16 .... 162 A8
Ireleth Rd LA16 .... 162 A8
Ireleth St Peter's CE Prim Sch LA16 ....162 B8
Irene Ct 17 CA13 .... 190 C4
IRESHOPE MOOR 61 F3
Irish St
Maryport CA15 .... 182 C5
Whitehaven CA28 .... 187 C8
Ironworks Rd LA14 ..... 206 D4
Irt Ave CA28 .... 187 D7
Irthing Bsns Ctr CA8 .....179 B5
Irthing Ct CA6 ....21 E4
Irthing Pk
Brampton CA8 ....179 B5
Gilsland CA8 ....14 D1
Irthing St CA1 .... 177 C6
IRTHINGTON 21 F4
Irthington Village Sch
CA6 ....21 E4
Irthing Vale Cvn Pk
CA8 .... 179 A5
Irthing View CA4 ....21 E1
Irthing Wlk 4 CA8 ....179 B4
Irton Cross★ CA19 ...... 124 A7
Irton Pl CA2 .... 176 C3
Irton Road Sta★ CA19 ...124 E6
Irving Ct 12 CA11 ....191 E4
Irvings Pl CA2 .... 176 C2
Irving St CA14 ....184 E5
Irvings Terr CA15 ....63 C8
Irving Vale CA14 ....63 B4
Irwell Rd LA14 ....206 B4
Isabella Rd CA14 ....184 B7
Isabella St CA2 .... 176 D6
ISEL 65 B8
Isel Rd CA13 ....190 E5
Island Rd LA14 ....206 F1
Island The CA7 ....16 E1
Islay Pl CA14 .... 184 D4
Ismay Cl CA15 ....182 F4
Ismay Wharf CA15 ...... 182 C5
IVEGILL 40 F2
Ivegill CE Sch CA4 ....41 A2
Ivison La 8 CA14 ....184 E6
Ivory Cl CA2 .... 176 C6
Ivy Ave LA14 ....206 E2
Ivy Cl CA6 ....19 D2
Ivy Cres LA9 ....130 F2
Ivy Garth LA9 ....200 E5

J

Jack Hill LA11 ....164 F7
Jackson Croft
Morland CA10 ....86 F5
Shap CA10 .... 101 C6
Jackson Rd CA14 .... 185 A8
Jackson's La CA10 ..... 101 C6
Jackson St
Carlisle CA1 .... 177 C6
Seaton CA14 ....183 B1
Jackson Terr LA5 .... 213 C5
Jacktrees Cres CA25 .... 188 D6
Jacktrees Rd CA25 ..... 188 D6
James Dr CA28 .... 187 D8
James Freel Cl LA14 .... 206 D4
James Pit Rd CA28 ..... 186 D2
James Rennie Sch
CA3 .... 175 D5
James St E LA16 .... 162 A8
James St W 7 LA16 .... 162 A8
James St
8 Askam in F LA16 ..... 162 A8
Barrow-in-F LA14 .... 207 A3
Carlisle CA2 ....214 B1
Cleator Moor CA25 ....188 E7
10 Maryport CA15 ....182 E5
Penrith CA11 .... 191 C5
Whitehaven CA28 .... 187 C8
Workington CA14 ....184 E6
James Street Workshops
CA2 ....214 B1
James Terr 4 LA15 ..... 205 C5
James Watt Terr LA14 ... 170 D6
Jane St
Carlisle CA2 ....176 E7
13 Maryport CA15 ....182 E5
Workington CA14 ....184 E6
Jarrow St LA13 ....207 B3
Jasmine Cl CA11 ....71 C5
Jason St LA14 .... 170 C6
Jaysmith Cl CA3 .... 175 D3
Jefferson Dr LA12 ...... 203 C2
Jefferson Garth CA11 .....69 E5
Jenkin Gap CA13 ....79 C4
Jenkin Rise LA9 ....200 F6
Jennet Croft CA4 .... 178 A1
Jennings Brewery★
CA13 .... 190 D4
Jennings Terr LA9 ...... 200 D4
Jericho Prim Sch
CA28 ....187 F7
Jericho Rd CA28 ....187 F7
Jesmond Ave LA13 ....207 B5
Jesmond St CA1 .... 177 C6
Jesson Way LA5 ....213 B3
Jingling Ct LA6 .... 212 C2
Jingling La LA6 .... 212 C2
Jinny Hill LA8 ....143 B7
Jocks Hill CA8 .... 179 C5
Joe McBain Ave CA28 .....76 F1
JOHNBY 69 E8
John Colligan Dr CA25 .. 188 C8
John Colligan Wlk
CA25 .... 188 C8
John Gaskell Ct CA28 ....187 F5
John Johnston Ct CA1 .. 177 D2
John Roberts Gdns
CA2 ....176 E6
John Ruskin Sch LA21 .. 196 A3
John's La 11 CA28 ..... 186 C1
Johnson Cl LA5 ....213 B3
Johnson Mill CA2 ....176 F4
John's Pl CA2 .... 214 A2
John St
26 Askam in F LA16 ..... 162 A8
Carlisle CA2 ....176 E6
4 Carnforth LA5 .... 213 C4
Cockermouth CA13 ...... 190 D3
Maryport CA15 .... 182 D6
Moor Row CA24 ....188 B5
Workington CA14 ....184 E5
Johnstone St DG12 ..... 172 C4
Johnston St 19 CA14 ... 184 D6
Johny Bulldogs Lonning
CA1 ....177 F7
Jollybeard Gate CA9 .....181 E3
Jollybeard La CA9 ....181 E3
Jones's Yd LA6 .... 167 B7
Jordan La LA10 .... 146 A4
Joseph Noble Rd CA14 ....77 C8
Joseph Wilson Meml
Homes CA8 ....22 E3
Joss La LA10 .... 201 C5
Jubilee Cl CA11 ....191 E4
Jubilee Cotts CA14 ..... 184 C3
Jubilee Ctr LA18 .... 202 D4
Jubilee Gdns CA22 ..... 188 A3
Jubilee La LA6 ....156 E3
Jubilee Rd
Carlisle CA2 .... 177 A3
High Harrington CA14 ....185 F7
Whitehaven CA28 ....187 F8
Jubilee Ret Pk CA15 .... 182 C6
Jubilee Terr CA15 ...... 182 D4
Junction St CA2 .... 214 A2
Juniper Cl 8 LA15 ...... 205 B4
Juniper Gr CA28 ....186 E1
Juniper Way CA11 ....191 F5
Juno St LA14 .... 206 D1
Jutland Ave LA11 ...... 164 D6

K

KABER 105 B2
Kaber Cross CA17 ....105 B2
Kates La CA9 .... 181 D3
Katherine St LA18 ...... 202 D5
Kavean Ct CA7 .... 180 D4
Kaye Cl CA2 .... 176 C4
KEARSTWICK 212 B4
Keasdale Ave LA7 ....209 E3
Keasdale Rd LA7 ....209 E3
Keats Ave CA14 ....184 F4
Keats Cl LA13 .... 207 D6
Keats Dr CA22 .... 189 D6
Keekle Flats CA25 ....188 B8
Keekle Terr CA25 ....92 A7
Keer Holme La LA6 ....167 E4
Keir Hardie Ave CA25 ....188 F6
KEISLEY 88 F6
Keith St LA14 ....206 F3
Keld Cl CA10 ....70 D3
Keld Head CA11 ....70 D3
Keld La CA10 ....101 B5
Keld Rd CA2 ....29 D6
Keldwyth Dr LA23 ...... 198 D8
Keldwyth Pk LA23 ...... 198 D8
KELLETH 119 A4
Kellet La LA6 ....167 B3
Kellet Rd
Carnforth LA5 ....213 E3
Over Kellet LA6 .... 167 A1
Kellet Road Ind Est
LA5 ....213 E3
KELLS 187 B6
Kells Inf Sch CA28 ....187 B6
Kell's Pl CA3 ....175 E1
Kellybark La CA16 ...... 103 C4
Kelly St CA14 ....184 E5
Kelsick Cotts LA22 ..... 195 D6
Kelsick La 4 CA28 ..... 186 C1
Kelsick Pk CA14 ....183 B1
Kelsick Rd LA22 .... 195 D5
Kelton Croft CA26 ....78 B1
Kelvin Gr CA2 .... 176 D4
Kempas Ave LA13 ....207 F4
Kemplay Bank CA10 ......191 E2
Kemplay Foot CA10 ......191 E2
KENDAL 200 E5
Kendal Bsns Pk LA9 ......200 E6
Kendal Coll LA9 .... 200 C3
Kendal Coll Allen Bldg
LA9 .... 200 D6
Kendal Gn LA9 .... 200 C7
Kendall Croft LA13 ..... 207 C5
Kendal Mus★ LA9 ...... 200 D6
Kendal Parks Cres LA9 ...200 F1
Kendal Parks Rd LA9 .....200 F1
Kendal Rd
Bowness-on-W LA23 ..... 198 C1
Kirkby Lonsdale LA6 ......212 B2
Staveley LA8 .... 130 C4
Kendal St
Barrow-in-F LA14 .... 207 A5
Carlisle CA2 ....176 E6
Kendal Sta LA9 .... 200 D6
Kendal Village Her Ctr★
LA9 .... 200 D3
Kenmount Pl CA2 ....176 E5
Kennedy Rd CA14 ....183 B3
Kennedy St LA12 .... 163 D8
Kennels Rd DG12 .... 172 D5
Kennet Rd LA14 .... 206 A3
Kent Cl LA8 ....130 E3
Kent Ct LA9 .... 200 D3
Kentdale Rd LA9 ....200 F6
Kent Dr LA8 .... 130 C5
Kent Lea
Kendal LA9 .... 131 A1
Kendal LA9 .... 200 C8
KENTMERE 115 D2
Kentmere Brow LA9 ......200 F6
Kentmere Cres LA14 .... 204 D1
Kentmere Gr CA2 .... 176 D3
Kent Park Ave LA9 ...... 200 C1
Kent Pl LA9 .... 200 D4
KENTRIGG 200 C8
Kentrigg LA9 .... 200 C8
Kentrigg Wlk LA9 .... 200 C8
KENTS BANK 208 A1
Kents Bank Ho LA11 .... 165 A6
Kents Bank Rd LA11 .... 208 C3
Kents Bank Sta LA11 .... 165 A6
Kents Ford Ho LA11 ......208 B1
Kentsford Rd LA11 ....208 B1
Kentsford Terr LA11 .... 165 A6
Kent Sq 8 LA12 ....203 E5
Kent St
Barrow-in-F LA13 ....207 B3
Kendal LA9 .... 200 D5
Kent View 10 LA9 ...... 200 D5
Kentwood Rd LA9 ....200 B1
Keppel St LA14 ....206 E4
Kepplewray Dr LA14 .... 204 C1
Kepplewray Hill LA20 ... 139 A2
Kerry Park Trad Est
CA14 .... 184 C3
Kersey Rd CA22 .... 189 D2
KERSHOPEFOOT 1 A2
Kershopefoot TD9 ....1 A1
Kershope Rd CA3 .... 175 C3
Kestrel Dr LA15 .... 205 C4
Kestrel Gr 5 CA28 ....76 F2
Kestrel Hill DG16 ...... 173 D3
KESWICK 192 A3
Keswick Art Gal & Mus★
CA12 ....192 B4
Keswick Ave LA14 ...... 204 D1
Keswick Bridge CA12 ... 192 C4
Keswick Mining Mus★
CA12 ....192 B4
Keswick Pl DG12 ....172 F3
Keswick Sch CA12 ...... 192 A5
Kettlewell Rd LA9 ....200 B8
Keyes St LA14 ....206 F4
Keyhow CA19 ....124 E7
Key's Brow CA14 ....185 B6
Kidside Cotts LA7 ....156 B5
Kilbride Pl CA26 ....92 D8
Killhope Lead Mining Ctr★
CA9 ....47 E1
KILLINGTON 145 E4
Killington Dr LA9 ....200 E2
Kilmidyke Dr LA11 ....208 B1
Kilmidyke Mans LA11 ....208 B2
Kilmidyke Rd LA11 ....208 B1
Kiln Bank Cross LA20 ... 139 A8
Kiln Brow CA23 .... 188 D3
Kiln Croft LA9 .... 131 C2
Kilner Cl LA9 ....200 F5
Kiln Green Ave CA14 .... 185 C7
KILNHILL 66 A7
Kiln Hill CA15 .... 183 C8
Kiln La LA12 .... 171 C8
Kilnside CA14 .... 185 D4
Kilnside Pl CA14 .... 185 D4
Kimmeter Pl DG12 ....172 E4
Kimmeter Sq DG12 ....172 E5
Kimmeter Wynd DG12 ....172 F4
King Alfred St LA14 .... 206 C1
King Arthur's Round Table Henge★ CA10 ....191 E1
King Edwards Fauld
CA5 ....18 F2
Kingfisher La DG16 ..... 173 D3
King Garth CA6 ....19 D2
King George's Cl CA25 ...188 E7
Kingmoor Bsns Pk
CA6 .... 175 A7
Kingmoor Ind Est CA3 ...175 B2
Kingmoor Inf Sch CA3 .. 175 C3
Kingmoor Jun Sch
CA3 .... 175 C4
Kingmoor Nature Reserve★
CA3 ....175 B3
Kingmoor Park Central
CA6 .... 175 A5
Kingmoor Park Harker Est
CA6 ....175 B8
Kingmoor Park Heathlands
Est CA6 ....19 E4
Kingmoor Park Rd CA6 ...19 E2
Kingmoor Park Rockcliffe
Est CA6 ....19 D3
Kingmoor Park South
CA6 .... 175 A4
Kingmoor Rd CA3 ....175 B3
Kingmoor Sidings Nature Reserve★ CA3 ....175 B2
Kingmoor Terr CA3 ......175 B2
Kingrigg CA2 .... 176 C3
Kings Arms Croft LA9 ... 200 C5
King's Arms La CA9 .... 181 D4
King's Arms Yd CA7 .... 180 C3
King's Ave CA14 ....62 E4
Kings Cl LA5 ....209 B1
Kings Ct
Kirkby Lonsdale LA6 ..... 212 C2
Sedbergh LA10 .... 201 C5
Kings Dr
Carlisle CA6 .... 175 A4
Egremont CA22 .... 189 C5
King's Dr
Carnforth LA5 .... 213 D3
Dalton-in-F LA15 ....205 B5
Kingsgarth CA7 ....180 B8
Kingsland Rd LA18 ....202 B5
Kingsley Ave LA12 ...... 203 A3
KING'S MEABURN 87 C4
Kingsmoor Park North
CA6 .... 175 A7
Kings Mount LA15 ....205 B5
King's Rd LA12 .... 203 D5
King St
Ambleside LA22 .... 195 D5
Aspatria CA7 ....50 C8
Carlisle CA1 .... 214 C1
Carnforth LA5 .... 213 C3
Cleator Moor CA23 ....188 F6
Dalton-in-F LA15 .... 205 C5
Great Broughton CA13 .....63 E6
Maryport CA15 .... 182 C6
Millom LA18 .... 202 D5
Penrith CA11 .... 191 D5
Ulverston LA12 .... 203 D5
Whitehaven CA28 .... 186 C1
Wigton CA7 ....180 E4
Workington CA14 ....184 F5
KINGSTOWN 175 D5
Kingstown Broadway
CA3 ....175 B5
Kingstown Ind Est CA3 ...175 B5
Kingstown Rd CA3 ..... 175 D4
Kingsway
Carlisle CA6 .... 175 A5
Ulverston LA12 ....203 E5
Kings Yd LA22 ....197 E5
Kingwater Cl CA8 ....179 B4
Kinn Barns LA8 ....144 F8
Kinniside Ave CA28 .... 187 D4
Kinniside Pl CA25 ....188 E6
Kinn Rd LA8 ....144 F8
Kipling Ave CA14 .... 185 D8
Kirkandrews Moat CA6 ....10 E8
KIRKANDREWS-ON-EDEN 19 C1
KIRKBAMPTON 28 D7
Kirkbampton CE Sch
CA5 ....28 E7
Kirkbank CA13 .... 190 D3
Kirkbank La
Kirkby Stephen CA17 .... 199 D8
Winton CA17 .... 105 A1
KIRKBARROW 200 C3
Kirkbarrow LA9 .... 200 D3
Kirkbarrow La LA9 ..... 200 D4
Kirkbeck Cl CA3 ....175 B2
Kirkbeck Dr CA21 ....108 B5
Kirkbie Gn LA9 ....200 E5
Kirkbie Kendal Sch
LA9 .... 200 D3
Kirkbrae CA3 .... 175 C2
KIRKBRIDE 27 C7
Kirkbride Prim Sch CA7 ...27 C7
Kirkby Cl 17 LA16 ..... 162 A8
Kirkby Ct 6 CA15 ...... 182 D6
Kirkby Gdns LA14 ...... 206 C5
KIRKBY-IN-FURNESS 151 B5
Kirkby-in-Furness Sta
LA17 ....151 B5
KIRKBY LONSDALE 212 B2

Kirkby Lonsdale Rd LA6 167 B1
Kirkby Slate Rd LA12 151 F5
Kirkby St CA15 182 D6
KIRKBY STEPHEN 199 B6
Kirkby Stephen Gram Sch Sports Coll CA17 199 C6
Kirkby Stephen Ind Est CA17 199 C7
Kirkby Stephen Prim Sch CA17 199 D5
Kirkby Stephen Sta CA17 199 A2
KIRKBY THORE 87 D8
Kirkby Thore Sch CA10 73 A1
KIRKCAMBECK 12 F3
Kirkcroft CA8 31 F3
Kirkfell Ave CA13 190 E3
Kirkfield LA22 195 D6
Kirkfield Rise LA22 195 D6
Kirk Flatt LA12 162 F5
Kirkgate
Bolton CA16 87 D7
Cockermouth CA13 190 D4
Milnthorpe LA7 211 D5
Kirkgate Ctr CA13 190 D4
Kirkgate La
Milnthorpe LA7 211 E5
Priest Hutton LA6 167 B4
KIRKHAUGH 45 D8
Kirkhaugh Sta CA9 45 D8
Kirkhead LA7 211 D4
Kirkhead Cotts LA11 165 A6
Kirkhead Rd LA11 165 A6
Kirk Hey LA11 165 A6
KIRKHOUSE 22 F2
Kirk La LA23 129 A8
KIRKLAND
Blencarn 73 B7
Ennerdale Bridge 78 B1
Wigton 38 D7
Kirkland LA9 200 D4
Kirkland Ave CA7 180 E4
Kirkland Cl CA7 180 E4
KIRKLAND GUARDS 51 A7
Kirkland Mdws CA7 180 E4
Kirkland Rd
Ennerdale Bridge CA23 93 B7
Wigton CA7 180 E4
Kirklands
Camerton CA14 183 F3
Cockermouth CA13 190 C3
Kirklands Rd CA2 177 B2
Kirklea CA13 63 E6
KIRKLINTON 11 B2
KIRKOSWALD 57 B8
Kirkoswald CE Sch CA10 57 B8
KIRKSANTON 149 E3
Kirkside CA11 70 D3
Kirkstall Cl LA13 207 C6
Kirkstead Cl CA2 29 D6
Kirkstead Rd CA2 29 D7
Kirkstone Ave CA13 190 B3
Kirkstone Cl
Ambleside LA22 195 D6
Kendal LA9 200 E1
Kirkstone Cotts CA11 69 B3
Kirkstone Cres
Barrow-in-F LA14 204 C1
Carlisle CA2 176 D5
Kirkstone Mews LA9 200 E1
Kirkstone Pass
Ambleside LA22 114 D5
Hartsop CA11 98 E1
Kirkstone Rd
Ambleside LA22 195 E6
Whitehaven CA28 187 F4
Kirk The 4 CA28 186 D1
Kirriemuir Way 10 CA3 175 B1
Kirtle Pl DG16 173 C3
Kitchener St LA14 206 C3
Kitchen Syke LA21 127 B1
Kittygill La LA6 212 A1
Kittyson Ho CA13 190 D4
Kittyson La CA13 190 D3
KNARSDALE 34 E5
Knights Dr CA6 175 A5
KNIPE FOLD 197 C8
KNOCK 73 E1
Knoll The
Thornhill CA22 189 E2
Ulverston LA12 203 C5
Knott La
Arnside LA5 210 A8
Broughton-in-F LA20 139 A2
Orton CA10 118 D7
Knotts Hill Cvn Site CA11 84 B4
Knott St LA22 195 D5
KNOWEFIELD 175 E2
Knowefield Ave CA3 175 E2
Knowefield Cl CA3 175 E2
Knowe Park Ave CA3 175 E1
Knowe Rd CA3 175 E1
Knowe Terr 1 CA3 175 E1
Knowe The CA7 36 F1
Knox St LA14 206 D2
Kylbarrow La LA5 166 F5

L

Laburnum Cres LA14 206 F6
Laburnum Ct CA3 175 E2
Laburnum Gr CA15 182 F5
Laburnum Pk LA5 213 B2
Laburnum Way CA11 191 F5
Ladies Walk Brewery 10 CA14 184 E6
Ladies' Wlk CA14 184 E6
Ladstock Hall CA12 80 E7
Ladybank CA6 175 A7
Lady Ct CA14 184 E3
Lady Hall La LA18 138 E1
Lady Ing La CA17 105 A2
Ladylands La CA5 19 C1
Ladypit Terr CA28 186 D2
Ladyseat CA6 10 C3
Ladyseat Gdns CA6 10 C3
Lady St DG12 172 C4
Ladysteps CA4 30 F5
Lady's Well DG12 172 C4
LAITHES 70 B8
Laithwaite Cl CA13 190 C3
Lake District Bsns Pk LA9 200 D8
Lake District Coast Aquarium★ CA15 182 C6
Lake District Visitor Ctr (Brockhole)★ LA23 129 A7
Lake Gdns LA23 198 C1
Lakehead Ct CA12 192 A3
Lakeland Ave
Barrow-in-F LA13 207 D4
Whitehaven CA28 187 B6
Lakeland Bird of Prey Ctr★ CA10 85 F6
Lakeland Bsns Pk CA13 190 B2
Lakeland Ct CA12 82 C8
Lakeland Heavy Horse Ctr★ CA15 49 A1
Lakeland Pk CA12 192 D2
Lakeland Sheep & Wool Ctr★ CA13 190 C1
Lakelands The LA22 195 D5
Lakeland View
Cleator Moor CA25 188 F5
Egremont CA22 107 E6
Workington CA14 184 E3
Lakeland Wildlife Oasis★ LA7 166 F8
Lakeland Workshops LA21 196 B3
Lake Rd
Ambleside LA22 195 D4
Coniston LA21 196 B3
Keswick CA12 192 A2
Keswick CA12 192 B3
Windermere LA23 198 D4
Lakes Coll-West Cumbria CA14 185 E6
Lakes Glass Ctr The★ LA12 203 F6
LAKESIDE 141 E2
Lakeside Cvn Pk CA12 192 A3
Lakeside & Haverthwaite Railway★ LA12 153 C7
Lakeside Sta★ LA12 141 E2
Lakes Par LA14 207 B8
Lakes Rd CA14 184 B4
Lakes Sch The LA23 129 B7
Lake View
Coniston LA21 196 A2
Kirkland CA26 93 A8
Lakeview Ave CA2 177 C1
Lake View Dr LA22 194 B3
Lamb Croft LA13 207 C4
LAMBFOOT 65 B5
Lambfoot Rake CA13 65 B5
Lambgill Bank CA11 84 B5
Lambhowe Cvn Pk LA8 142 D6
Lamb La CA22 189 E6
Lamb Lea CA10 57 A6
LAMBLEY 24 E1
Lamb St CA2 177 C1
Lamley Gdns CA11 191 C6
LAMONBY 54 F2
LAMPLUGH 78 C3
Lamplugh CE Sch CA26 78 A1
Lamplugh Rd CA13 190 C3
Lamplugh St CA1 214 B1
Lamport St CA14 184 E5
Lancashire Rd LA18 202 C5
Lancaster Pl CA13 190 B3
Lancaster Rd LA5 213 B2
Lancaster Sq 9 LA12 203 E5
Lancaster St
Barrow-in-F LA14 207 A5
Carlisle CA1 214 B1
2 Dalton-in-F LA15 205 C5
Landing Cl LA12 141 E2
Landing How LA12 141 E2
Lands Cl LA12 171 E8
Landsdown Cl LA9 200 F3
LANE END 137 B8
Lane Ends LA11 164 F7
Lanefoot CA23 93 A6
Lane Head
Coanwood NE49 24 F2
Spark Bridge LA12 152 D7
Windermere LA23 198 F4
LANERCOST 22 E6
Lanercost CE Prim Sch CA8 22 E6
Lanercost Priory★ CA8 22 E6
Laneside Rd LA11 208 B1
Lanes The CA3 214 B3
Lane Terr CA8 24 C1
Langber End La LA6 169 F1
Langdale CA7 180 B3
Langdale Ave CA2 176 E5
Langdale CE Sch LA22 113 C4
Langdale Cl
Millom LA18 202 C4
Whitehaven CA28 187 D4
Langdale Cres
Dalton-in-F LA15 205 B3
Kendal LA9 200 F6
Windermere LA23 198 E3
Langdale Crest LA7 209 E5
Langdale Dr CA13 190 F4
Langdale Gr 2 LA13 207 B3
Langdale Rd
Carlisle CA2 176 E5
Carnforth LA5 213 D2
Workington CA14 184 D4
Langholm St TD9 1 B6
Langley Gdns CA4 178 E7
LANGRIGG 104 F5
Langrigge Ct LA23 198 D2
Langrigge Dr LA23 198 D2
Langrigge Howe LA23 198 C2
Langrigge Pk LA23 198 C2
Langrigg Rd CA2 176 D4
LANGTON 88 F2
Langton Ct 3 CA11 191 D4
Langton St 2 CA11 191 D4
LANGWATHBY 71 F8
Langwathby CE Prim Sch CA10 71 F8
Langwathby Sta CA10 72 A8
Laning LA10 147 B2
LANKABER 87 C1
LANRIGG 36 E5
Lansbury Pl CA25 188 F6
Lansdowne Cl CA3 175 E3
Lansdowne Cres CA3 175 D2
Lansdowne Ct CA3 175 E3
Lansdowne Gr CA28 187 F8
Lantern Moss Cvn Pk CA21 108 A4
Lanty Cl CA13 63 F5
Lapstone Rd LA18 202 C5
Larch Cl CA11 191 F5
Larch Ct CA24 188 A5
Larch Dr CA3 175 E2
Larches The CA22 189 C6
Larch Gr
Kendal LA9 200 F4
Keswick CA12 192 E4
Ulverston LA12 203 E2
Larch Rise LA13 207 E5
Larkfield CA11 191 B6
Larkin View CA11 55 E7
Lark La CA11 191 C6
Latimer Rd DG12 172 D4
Latona St LA14 206 C3
Latrigg Cl CA12 192 D4
Latrigg Rd CA28 187 E4
Latrigg St CA7 174 C4
Launchy Gill Forest Trail★ CA12 97 A6
Laundry Hill 5 LA11 208 D4
Laundry St 7 LA14 206 F3
Laurel Bank
Seascale CA20 123 A8
Whitehaven CA28 186 E1
Laurel Ct CA28 186 E1
Laurel Dr LA13 207 F5
Laurel Gdns LA9 200 C8
Laurel & Hardy Mus The★ LA12 203 D5
Laurels The
Egremont CA22 189 B6
20 Ulverston LA12 203 D5
Laurel Terr CA7 180 D3
Laurence Ave LA13 207 C5
Laver Holme Ct 5 LA14 207 A2
Laverock Hill LA8 131 C2
Laverock Terr CA14 184 D4
LAVERSDALE 21 C5
Lawn Terr CA7 174 B4
Lawrance St CA14 184 C6
Lawrence Dr LA5 209 A1
Lawrence St CA14 184 C6
Lawson Cl CA28 187 B6
Lawson Garth CA13 63 F5
Lawson St
Aspatria CA7 36 D1
Barrow-in-F LA14 206 F3
Carlisle CA2 176 D7
Maryport CA15 182 D5
Workington CA14 184 C7
Laybourn Ct CA14 184 F3
Laybourn Ho CA14 184 F3
Layfield La CA25 188 D8
LAZONBY 57 B6
Lazonby CE Sch CA10 57 B6
Lazonby Hall CA10 57 A7
Lazonby Hall Cotts CA10 56 F7
Lazonby Row CA7 17 E3
Lazonby Sta CA10 57 A6
Lazonby Terr CA1 177 C4
Leabank Rd CA3 175 C5
Leabourne Rd CA2 177 A2
Leacett La CA17 105 B4
LEADGATE 45 E2
Leagarth La CA16 89 B3
Leagate Brow CA20 109 C3
LEASGILL 211 D8
Leasgill Cotts LA7 211 D8
Leaside CA8 24 C1
Leatham St CA2 176 E6
Lea The CA11 70 B8
Leather La 1 LA12 203 D5
Leathwaite CA28 187 E8
Lea Yeat Brow LA10 148 B2
LECK 169 B7
Leck St Peter's CE Prim Sch LA6 169 B7
Leconfield Ind Est CA25 188 D7
Leconfield St CA25 188 D7
Lediard Ave CA2 177 A3
LEECE 171 C8
Leece Dr LA15 205 B3
Leece La LA13 207 F4
Leeches Terr CA15 183 A6
Leeds Ave LA14 206 F7
Leeming La LA6 169 C3
Lees Hill CE Sch CA8 13 B2
Lees The CA7 27 B7
LEGBURTHWAITE 82 C2
Leicester St
Barrow-in-F LA13 207 B3
Carlisle CA2 176 F4
Leighton Cl LA7 155 D1
Leighton Dr
Slack Head LA7 155 D1
Walney Island LA14 206 C4
Leighton Hall★ LA5 166 E5
Leighton Moss Nature Reserve★ LA5 166 D6
Leighton Moss Visitor Ctr★ LA5 210 F2
Leith Beck Fold CA10 86 B8
Leith Cl CA10 86 E7
Leith Flat Brow LA13 207 C8
LENACRE 146 D4
Leonards Pl 9 CA12 192 B3
Leonard St CA12 192 B3
Leopard St LA14 206 C3
Lesh La LA13 207 C5
Lesketh How LA22 195 C7
Leskew Cotts 3 CA20 109 B2
LESSONHALL 27 B1
Level The
Cockermouth CA13 190 C3
High Newton LA11 154 A4
LEVENS 143 E1
Levens CE Sch LA8 155 D8
Levens Cl
Dalton-in-F LA15 205 D4
Kendal LA9 200 D2
Levens Dr CA2 176 D3
Levensgarth LA12 153 B6
Levens Hall★ LA8 155 E8
Levens La LA8 155 E8
Levens Terr 10 LA14 207 B2
Levens Way LA5 210 C3
Leven Valley CE Prim Sch LA12 153 C7
Lewis Ct CA2 214 A1
Leyfield Cl LA18 202 C5
Leyfield Ct LA6 212 C1
LEYS 78 A1
Leythey La LA12 163 B3
Leywell Dr CA1 177 F3
Library Rd LA9 200 C5
Lichen Gr CA2 176 C5
Lichfield Cl LA14 207 A6
Lickbarrow Cl LA23 198 F3
Lickbarrow Rd
Bowness-on-W LA23 198 F3
Windermere LA23 198 E4
Lidalia Cvn Pk TD9 1 B6
Liddel Bank DG14 3 F4
Liddel Rd CA6 10 C4
Liddesdale Heritage Ctr★ TD9 1 B6
Liddle Cl
Barrow-in-F LA13 207 E2
Carlisle CA3 175 C4
Lightburn Ave LA12 203 D4
Lightburn Ind Est LA12 203 C4
Lightburn Rd LA12 203 D5
Lightfoot Dr CA1 177 D2
Lilac Sq CA4 30 E6
Lilacs The CA22 189 B6
Lillyhall Bsns Ctr CA14 185 F8
Lillyhall Bsns Pk CA14 185 F7
Lillyhall Ind Est CA14 77 C8
Lime Gr
Carlisle CA2 176 B5
Maryport CA15 182 F5
Lime House Sch CA5 40 B6
Limekiln La CA22 92 E1
Lime Kiln Wlk LA14 206 F8
Lime La CA16 88 C5
Limepots Rd CA12 192 A5
Lime Rd CA14 185 A7
Lime St
Barrow-in-F LA14 206 F6
Carlisle CA2 214 A1
Shap CA10 101 C5
Limes The CA22 189 B6
Limethwaite Rd LA23 198 F4
Limetree Cres CA13 190 E5
Lime Tree Gr CA7 180 C5
Lime Tree Rd LA12 203 D3
Lincoln Rd CA28 187 F6
Lincoln St
Barrow-in-F LA14 207 A5
Millom LA18 202 D4
Lindal Bsns Pk LA12 162 E6
Lindal Cl LA15 205 B3
LINDALE 154 D3
Lindale Brow LA11 154 C4
Lindale CE Prim Sch LA11 154 C3
Lindale Cl LA5 209 B2
Lindale Rd LA11 208 F6
LINDAL IN FURNESS 205 F8
Lindal & Marton Prim Sch LA12 162 D7
Lindal St 4 LA14 207 A3
Linden Fold LA11 208 C2
Linden Pk CA10 72 E2
Linden Terr CA1 177 E3
Linden Wlk CA14 62 F3
Lindeth Cl LA5 210 C2
Lindeth Coll of F Ed LA23 129 B2
Lindeth La LA23 129 C2
Lindeth Rd LA5 210 C2
Lindisfarne Ct CA1 177 C5
Lindisfarne St CA1 177 C5
Lindow St CA26 92 D8
Lingarth LA11 154 C3
Ling Beck Cres CA14 183 A2
Ling Beck Pk CA14 183 A2
Ling Beck View CA14 183 A2
Ling Cl CA14 184 E8
Lingfell Ave CA13 190 E4
Ling La CA5 39 E4
Lingla Bank CA26 92 C7
Lingley Fields CA26 92 D8
Lingley Rd CA26 92 D8
Lingmell Cl CA28 187 D3
Lingmell Cres CA20 123 B8
Lingmell Ctyd CA20 123 B8
Lingmell Wood CA20 123 B8
Lingmoor Rise LA9 200 F3
Lingmoor View LA22 113 B4
Lingmoor Way CA1 177 D3
Ling Rd
Egremont CA22 189 C5
Seaton CA14 183 B2
Lingside Cres CA1 177 D2
Lingy Cl CA5 29 E3
LINGY CLOSE 29 E3
Link Rd CA28 187 E3
Links Cl CA7 174 B3
Links Cres CA20 123 A8
Linnet Gr LA9 200 F1
Linns View DG14 4 B5
LINSTOCK 20 D1
Linstock Ave CA13 190 D2
Linsty Gn LA12 153 C8
Linton St CA1 177 C5
Lismore Pl
Carlisle CA1 214 C3
3 Workington CA14 184 E6
Lismore St CA1 214 C2
Lister Ct CA2 176 C6
Listers Cotts CA13 63 E6
Litchmead Gr LA13 207 B6
LITTLE ASBY 119 D8
Little Aynam LA9 200 D5
LITTLE BAMPTON 27 F6
LITTLEBECK 87 C2
Littlebeck La CA10 87 C3
LITTLE BLENCOW 70 A8
LITTLE BROUGHTON 63 F7
Little Brow CA13 63 F6
Little Camp St 1 CA15 182 D6
LITTLE CLIFTON 63 C3
LITTLE CORBY 178 E7
Little Corby Rd CA4 178 D7
Little Croft
Barrow-in-F LA13 207 D4
Cleator Moor CA25 188 C7
High Harrington CA14 185 B7
Littledale LA9 200 F3
Little Dockray 10 CA11 191 C5
Little Fields LA15 205 B4
Little Heads LA11 208 C3
Little Hills 17 CA12 192 B3
LITTLE LANGDALE 113 B2
Little Mill CA22 189 E5
Little Mill Cl CA13 190 E3
Little Moss LA21 196 A4
Little Moss Cl LA21 196 A4
LITTLE MUSGRAVE 104 D4
LITTLE ORMSIDE 103 F7
LITTLE ORTON 29 C6
LITTLE SALKELD 57 C3
Little Salkeld Watermill★ CA10 57 C3
Little Sandhill CA10 57 B8
LITTLE STRICKLAND 86 C2
LITTLE TOWN 80 F2
LITTLE URSWICK 162 F4
Litt Pl CA25 188 D8
Liverpool Lodge LA18 202 C5
Liverpool St 3 LA14 206 C1
Loaning The CA9 181 E5
Loanthwaite La LA22 197 F7
Loanwath Rd DG16 173 C2
Lochinvar Cl CA6 10 C3
Lochinvar Sch CA6 10 C3
Locka La LA6 167 F3
Locker La LA11 164 F7
Lockhart Gdns DG12 172 D6
LOCKHILLS 42 D6
Lodge Cl
Cockermouth CA13 190 D3
Great Clifton CA14 63 B4
Holme LA6 156 B1
Lodge La LA2, LA6 168 D1
Lodge Terr 7 LA20 139 A2
Lodore Dr CA2 29 D6
Lodore Falls★ CA12 81 C1
Lofts The CA10 57 A6
Loftus Hill LA10 201 C4
Loftus Manor LA10 201 C4
Logan Rd DG16 173 C2
London Rd
Carlisle CA1 177 D3
Lindal in F LA12 162 E6

London Road Ret Pk
CA1 177 C4
London Road Terr CA1 177 C4
Long Acre Cl LA5 213 B2
Long Bank LA14 170 C6
Longbarrow CA25 188 D6
Longber La LA6 169 B3
LONGBURGH 18 E1
Longburgh Fauld CA5 18 E1
Long Cl LA9 200 C3
LONGCROFT 17 A1
Longcroft
Braithwaite CA12 80 F6
Cockermouth CA13 190 E3
Long Croft
Barrow-in-F LA14 204 B1
Egremont CA22 189 D7
Long Cswy DL11, CA17 122 E7
LONGDALES 42 E3
Longdyke Dr CA1 177 F2
Longfield Dr LA5 213 B2
Longholme Rd CA1 177 F2
Long Island Pk CA2 214 B1
Long La
Blawith LA12 140 A2
Carlisle CA3 214 A3
Newbiggin LA12 171 D7
Sedbergh LA10 201 D5
Stainton w A LA13 205 D2
Longlands Ave LA13 207 D5
Longlands Cl
Carlisle CA3 175 F1
Egremont CA22 189 D7
Longlands Lake Nature Reserve* CA23, CA25 188 C2
Longlands Rd
Bowness-on-W LA23 198 C3
Carlisle CA3 175 F1
Longlands View LA9 200 E7
Long Level LA6 168 F8
Longmans Cl CA1 177 F2
LONG MARTON 88 A7
Long Marton Rd CA16 193 C7
Long Marton Sch CA16 88 A7
Longmeadow Ave
DG12 172 B2
Longmeadow La LA9 144 B4
Long Meg Cotts CA10 57 C3
Longmere Cres LA5 213 B2
Longmire Rd
Troutbeck Bridge LA23 129 C8
Troutbeck LA23 114 F1
Longmynd Ave LA14 206 F5
Longpool LA9 200 E6
Longreins Rd LA14 207 A4
Long Row
Kirkby-in-F LA17 151 C6
Swarthmoor LA12 203 A2
LONGSOWERBY 176 E4
Longsowerby Rd CA2 176 D4
Longtail Brow LA8 132 A4
Longtail Hill LA23 129 B2
LONGTHWAITE 84 B5
Longthwaite Cres CA7 180 C2
Longthwaite Farm Ct
CA4 178 D6
Longthwaite Gr CA7 180 D2
Longthwaite Rd CA7 180 C2
Longtom Rigg CA5 39 F2
Longton's Cotts LA6 167 B1
LONGTOWN 10 C3
Longtown Ind Est CA6 10 C3
Longtown Prim Sch
CA6 10 C3
Longtown Rd CA8 179 B5
Longway LA13 207 D2
Longwood LA8 156 D8
Lonning Foot CA6 19 D4
Lonning Head CA8 179 B4
Lonscale View CA12 192 E4
Lonsdale Cl CA15 49 D5
Lonsdale Ct
6 Penrith CA11 191 E4
Whitehaven CA28 186 E3
Lonsdale Ho
Carlisle CA2 176 C7
2 Keswick CA12 192 A4
Lonsdale Pk CA4 31 B2
Lonsdale Pl CA28 186 E3
Lonsdale Rd LA18 202 D5
Lonsdale Rise LA6 212 C2
Lonsdale St
Barrow-in-F LA14 207 A2
Carlisle CA1 214 B2
Whitehaven CA28 186 D2
Workington CA14 184 D6
Lonsdale Terr
Cockermouth CA13 190 B3
Cotehill CA4 31 B2
Crosby Villa CA15 49 D6
Dearham CA15 49 A2
Millom LA18 202 D5
3 Penrith CA11 191 D5
St Bees CA27 91 D2
Lonsdale View CA15 49 A2
Lonsties CA12 192 D3
Loop Rd N CA28 186 E3
Loop Rd S CA28 186 D1
LOPPERGARTH 162 E8
Lord Roberts St LA14 206 C2
Lord's Lot Rd
Capernwray LA6 167 D1
Over Kellet LA6 167 C1
Lord's Plain Cswy LA8 143 D1
Lord St
22 Askam in F LA16 162 A8
Barrow-in-F LA14 207 A3
Carlisle CA1 214 C1
Dalton-in-F LA15 205 D5
Millom LA18 202 D5
Lords Way CA6 175 A7
Loreburn Ct DG12 172 E4
Lorne Cres CA2 214 A1
Lorne Rd LA13 207 B4
Lorne St CA2 214 A1
Lorne Terr 7 CA8 179 B5
Lorne Villas CA14 184 F5
Lorton Ave CA14 184 F4
Lorton Cl CA28 187 D4
Lorton Rd CA13 190 D3
Lorton Sch CA13 79 D8
Lorton St CA13 190 D3
Lostrigg Cl CA14 63 C3
Lots Rd LA16 162 A7
Loughrigg Ave
Ambleside LA22 195 D4
Kendal LA9 200 E2
Loughrigg Brow LA22 195 B5
Loughrigg Mdw LA22 195 C4
Loughrigg Pk LA22 195 C4
Loughrigg Terr CA2 176 C3
Loughrigg View LA22 195 D5
Lound Rd LA9 200 D3
Lound Sq LA9 200 D3
Lound St LA9 200 D3
Lovers La CA6 10 C4
Lovers' La CA8 179 C5
Lovers' Wlk DG12 172 C2
LOW BIGGINS 212 B1
LOW BORROWBRIDGE 132 E8
LOW BRAITHWAITE 41 A1
LOW BRIGHAM 192 C4
Low Brow Edge LA12 153 C7
Lowbyer Pk CA9 181 D5
LOWCA 186 E8
Lowca Com Sch CA28 76 E5
Lowca La CA14 183 A3
Low Castle Terr CA8 14 F1
Low Cliff LA14 206 F8
Low Corkickle CA28 187 D8
LOW COTEHILL 31 C1
Low Cotts LA8 156 D7
Low Croft CA20 108 E4
LOW CROSBY 20 F2
Low Cross St 1 CA8 179 B5
Lower Abbotsgate LA6 212 B2
Lower Brook St 13
LA12 203 D5
Lower Castle Pk LA9 200 E5
Lower Gale LA22 195 D5
Lower Gate CA10 87 A5
Lower Haverflatts LA7 211 E6
LOWER HAWTHWAITE 139 A3
Lower Stonecroft
LA22 195 D4
LOWER WESTHOUSE 169 D4
LOWESWATER 79 C3
Loweswater Ave
Whitehaven CA28 187 C5
Workington CA14 184 E4
Loweswater Cl CA13 190 F3
Loweswater Rd CA15 182 E3
Loweswater Terr LA15 205 B4
Low Farm CA10 71 F8
Low Farm Cl LA12 162 E6
Low Fellside LA9 200 C5
Lowfield LA22 195 D5
Lowfield La LA8 115 D2
Lowfields La LA6 212 D7
Low Fold LA23 198 C2
Low Furness CE Prim Sch
LA12 162 F5
Low Gale LA22 195 D5
Low Garth LA9 200 B8
Lowgate LA8 143 D1
Low Gate LA12 153 C6
LOWGILL 132 F3
Low Glenridding CA11 98 C7
LOW HARKER 175 B8
LOW HESKET 41 E5
Low House Farm Barns
CA11 56 B1
Low House Gdns LA12 162 F4
Low Ibbotsholme LA23 129 B7
LOWICK 140 B1
LOWICK BRIDGE 140 C1
LOWICK GREEN 152 C8
Low Kepplewray 11
LA20 139 A2
Low Kiln Ct CA12 66 A7
Lowkirkbarrow La LA9 200 D4
LOW KNIPE 85 E2
Low La
Leck LA6 169 B7
Levens LA8 143 C4
Middleton LA6 157 E8
Ravenstonedale CA17 120 B2
Tebay CA10 118 B3
Lowland View CA15 63 C8
Low Langstaffe LA10 201 C5
Low Leases La CA17 120 C8
Low Lonnin CA20 109 D2
LOW LORTON 79 D8
Low Mdw
Carlisle CA2 176 B6
Old Hutton LA8 144 F3
Low Mead LA9 200 C8
Low Mill
Langwathby CA10 71 F8
Thornhill CA22 189 D2
Low Mill Bsns Pk LA12 203 F4
Low Moor Ave CA2 30 B3
Low Moorlands CA5 29 D1
Lowmoor Rd CA7 180 E2
Lowmoor Row CA10 72 F1
Low Moor Terr LA14 206 F8
LOW MORESBY 76 F3
LOW NEWTON 154 B5
Low Padstow CA25 92 A7
Low Park La LA8 144 D1
Low Plains Ct CA11 56 B8
Low Portinscale CA12 81 A6
Low Rd
Brigham CA13 63 F5
Cockermouth CA13 190 B4
Whitehaven CA28 187 D6
Lowrey Cl CA21 108 B5
Low Road Cl CA13 190 B4
LOW ROW
Aspatria 37 B3
Brampton 23 B6
Low Row
Backbarrow LA12 153 C7
Cark LA11 164 D7
Lowry Cl CA3 175 C4
Lowry Gdns CA3 175 C4
Lowry Hill Rd CA3 175 B4
Lowry St CA2 177 A1
Low Sand La CA13 190 C4
Lowscales Dr CA13 190 E2
LOW SEATON 183 C1
Lowside Cres LA12 141 D2
Low Sleights Rd LA6 160 A1
Low St
Burton in L LA6 169 C3
Milburn CA10 73 C4
LOWTHER 85 F6
Lowther Arc CA3 214 B2
Lowther Browns Lonning
CA2 176 C4
Lowther Cres LA14 206 C4
Lowther Ct 4 CA11 191 C6
Lowther Endowed Sch
CA10 85 F6
Lowther Gdns 1 LA11 208 D4
Lowther Glen CA10 191 E2
Lowther Leisure & Wildlife Pk* CA10 85 F5
Lowther Pk LA9 200 F4
Lowther Rd
Millom LA18 202 C4
Workington CA14 184 C5
Lowther St
Carlisle CA3 214 B2
Flimby CA15 183 C8
Great Clifton CA14 63 A4
Kendal LA9 200 D5
Penrith CA11 191 D6
Waberthwaite LA19 137 C8
Whitehaven CA28 186 C1
Lowther View CA10 71 C1
Lowther Village CA10 85 F6
Lowther Went 10 CA13 190 D4
LOW WHINNOW 28 D1
Low White Cl LA14 206 F8
Low Wiend CA16 193 C5
Low Winder La CA22 92 D2
Low Wood Water Sport & Activity Ctr* LA23 128 F8
Loyne Pk LA6 168 D7
LUDDERBURN 142 B6
Ludgate Hill CA5 18 F1
Ludgate Terr CA7 180 C4
Lumley Rd LA9 200 B2
Lumley St 1 LA14 207 B2
Lund Cres CA2 176 F3
Lund Hall LA12 203 F5
Lund Rd LA12 203 E5
LUNDS 135 E1
Lund Terr LA12 203 E5
Lune Cl LA6 212 C2
Lunefield Dr LA6 212 C1
Lunefield Gdns LA6 212 C2
Lune Valley Cotts
CA10 118 B2
Lune Valley Ct CA10 118 B2
LUPTON 156 E4
Lupton Ct 4 LA23 198 E5
Lyalls' Pl 5 CA15 182 E5
Lydia's Cotts CA12 192 D4
Lynchetts The CA10 101 C6
Lyndale Ave LA13 207 B5
Lyndene Dr LA11 208 F8
Lyndhurst Gdns CA2 176 B3
Lyndhurst Pk LA12 203 D4
Lyne Cl
Carlisle CA3 175 C4
Walney Island LA14 206 B3
Lyne Riggs Est LA5 213 C3
Lyngarth CA1 177 F4
Lynngarth Dr LA9 200 C4
Lynslack Terr LA5 210 B8
Lynter Ct 1 LA14 207 B6
Lyon St LA14 206 E4
Lytham Cl CA2 176 B5

M

MacAdam Gdns CA11 191 C6
MacAdam St LA14 207 B2
MacAdam Way CA11 191 C6
Macan St CA15 182 D7
MCcarron Cl CA15 182 F4
McClintock St LA14 206 E4
McGowan St CA14 62 D6
Machell Cl 4 LA12 203 C5
McImoyle Way CA2 214 A1
McIver Cl LA22 195 D3
McIver La LA22 195 D3
McKeating Croft CA14 184 C3
Mackies Dr DG16 173 C3
Mackreth Row 8
CA13 190 D4
McLean Cl 2 LA14 207 A3
MCmurdo Rd DG12 172 C3
MacNeish Dr DG12 172 D5
Madam Banks Rd 5
CA5 40 A8
Mafeking Pl DG12 172 D4
Maidenhill Rd CA11 71 C7
Maidenlands Cres
LA15 205 C6
Maiden Way CA10 73 B2
Main Rd
Baycliff LA12 163 B3
Flimby CA15 183 B7
Great Clifton CA14 63 B4
High Harrington CA14 185 C7
Maryport CA15 182 C4
Seaton CA14 183 B1
Swarthmoor LA12 203 A2
Ulverston LA12 162 F7
Windermere LA23 198 E5
Mains Brow LA18 150 C8
Mains Fauld CA5 29 A5
Mainsgate Rd LA18 202 C4
Main St
Abbeytown CA7 26 C1
Allonby CA15 35 C1
Baycliff LA12 163 B3
Bootle LA19 137 B3
Brampton CA8 179 C5
Brough CA17 105 B5
Burton-in-K LA6 167 B7
Cleator CA23 188 D4
Cockermouth CA13 190 D4
Dearham CA15 49 B3
Dent LA10 147 B1
Distington CA14 185 C2
Egremont CA22 189 E6
Elterwater LA22 113 C3
Endmoor LA8 156 C7
Flimby CA15 183 C8
Flookburgh LA11 164 D6
Frizington CA26 92 D8
Grange-o-S LA11 208 D5
Great Broughton CA13 63 E6
Gretna DG16 173 E5
Greysouthen CA13 63 E4
Haverigg LA18 150 A1
Hawkshead LA22 197 E5
Hensingham CA28 187 F6
Keswick CA12 192 A4
Kirkby Lonsdale LA6 212 C2
Kirkby Thore CA10 87 D8
Levens LA8 143 D1
Maryport CA15 182 F4
Milnthorpe LA7 211 D4
Newbiggin-on-L CA17 119 E4
Parton CA28 186 D5
Pennington LA12 162 E8
Penny Bridge LA12 152 E5
Ravenglass CA18 123 F3
Sandwith CA28 187 A2
Sedbergh LA10 201 C5
Shap CA10 101 C5
Silecroft LA18 149 E4
Staveley LA8 130 C5
St Bees CA27 91 D2
Warton LA5 213 C7
Whittington LA6 168 D7
Mains The
Beetham LA7 155 E2
Stainton CA11 70 D3
Maitland St CA2 177 A3
Mallard Dr LA14 206 B1
Mallard Pl DG16 173 D3
Mallsknowe CA6 10 B3
Mall The 10 LA14 206 F3
Mallyclose Dr CA1 177 E1
Malor Pk DG16 173 B3
Maltings The
10 Ulverston LA12 203 D6
Whittington LA6 168 D7
Malt Kiln Rd LA12 171 E8
Maltmill Ho CA3 214 A3
Malton Cres 5 LA14 207 B6
Manchester St LA14 206 F4
Mandle Terr
Crosby Villa CA15 49 D6
7 Maryport CA15 182 E5
Manesty Rise CA28 76 F3
Manesty View CA12 192 C3
Manor Cl LA6 169 C3
Manor Croft CA4 30 F7
Manor Ct
Cockermouth CA13 190 C4
Kirkby Stephen CA17 199 C5
Wigton CA7 180 C3
Manor Farm LA6 168 D7
Manor Gdns
Brampton CA8 179 B5
Whitehaven CA28 187 F4
Manor House Wynd
CA17 105 A1
Manor Pk
Barrow-in-F LA13 207 C7
Keswick CA12 192 C3
Manor Pl CA2 177 C2
Manor Rd
Barrow-in-F LA13 207 D8
Carlisle CA2 177 C2
Manorside LA11 164 D6
MANSERGH 157 D5
Mansergh High La LA6 157 D6
Mansfield Ho DG16 173 C3
Mansion Gdns CA22 189 D7
MANSRIGGS 152 B3
Manx View 4 LA16 162 A8
Maple Ave LA12 203 D2
Maple Cl
Greystoke CA11 69 F5
Maryport CA15 182 F5
Sedbergh LA10 201 B5
Workington CA14 184 C1
Maple Ct LA23 198 E6
Maple Dr
Kendal LA9 200 B3
Penrith CA11 191 F4
Maple Gr
Carlisle CA3 175 E2
Whitehaven CA28 187 E7
Maple St LA14 206 F6
Marconi Rd CA2 176 B7
Mardale CA7 180 B3
Mardale Cl CA11 191 B4
Mardale Gr LA13 207 B3
Mardale Rd
Carlisle CA2 176 D6
Penrith CA11 191 B4
Margaret Creighton Gdns
CA1 177 C5
Margaret St CA15 183 C8
Margaret's Way CA16 193 B4
Margate St LA14 206 C2
Margery St CA1 177 C6
Margery Terr CA2 176 D1
Margrats Croft CA10 86 F4
Marina Cres CA2 177 A2
Marina The LA23 129 A2
Marine Rd CA15 182 C5
Mariners Way CA28 187 F5
Marine Terr
Roa Island LA13 171 B3
Silloth CA7 174 C4
Whitehaven CA28 186 D2
Marine View LA18 202 A2
Market Arc CA3 214 B3
Market Cross LA22 195 D6
Market Ct 12 CA11 191 D5
Market Hill CA7 180 D4
Market Pl
Alston CA9 181 D3
Ambleside LA22 195 D5
3 Brampton CA8 179 C5
Cleator Moor CA25 188 D7
Cockermouth CA13 190 D4
2 Dalton-in-F LA15 205 B4
Egremont CA22 189 E6
1 Kendal LA9 200 D5
3 Keswick CA12 192 B3
Ulverston LA12 203 D5
17 Whitehaven CA28 186 C1
Wigton CA7 180 C3
Workington CA14 184 F6
Market Sq
Aspatria CA7 50 C8
Cleator Moor CA25 188 D7
4 Keswick CA12 192 B3
Kirkby Lonsdale LA6 212 C2
Kirkby Stephen CA17 199 D6
Millom LA18 202 C5
15 Penrith CA11 191 D5
Market St
Barrow-in-F LA14 206 F3
6 Broughton-in-F LA20 139 A2
Carlisle CA3 214 A3
Carnforth LA5 213 C4
Cleator Moor CA25 188 D7
Cockermouth CA13 190 D4
Dalton-in-F LA15 205 B5
Egremont CA22 189 E6
Flookburgh LA11 164 D6
Kirkby Lonsdale LA6 212 C2
Kirkby Stephen CA17 199 D6
Millom LA18 202 D5
Ulverston LA12 203 D5
Marks Ave CA2 176 B6
Marlborough Ave
CA14 185 D7
Marlborough Gdns
CA3 214 A4
Marlborough St CA28 186 C1
Marl Bsns Pk LA12 203 E4
Marmaduke Cotts LA6 168 D4
Marne Ave LA11 164 D6
Marron La CA14 63 D4
Marsden St LA14 207 B3
Marshall Terr CA10 101 C5
Marsh Garth LA17 151 C6
Marsh Gdns LA11 164 D6
Marsh House Gdns CA5 18 F1
Marsh La
6 Askam in F LA16 162 A8
Cautley LA10 134 A1
Marsh Rd LA7 211 B5
Marsh Side LA17 151 C6
Marsh St
1 Askam in F LA16 162 A8
Barrow-in-F LA14 207 A3
Barrow-in-F, Salthouse
LA14 207 B3
Workington CA14 184 C6
Marsh Terr 2 CA15 182 F4
Mart Cl CA7 50 C8
MARTHWAITE 201 A5
Martinagap La CA10 118 B6
MARTINDALE 84 B2
Martindale Cl CA28 91 F7
Martindale View CA16 104 C6
MARTON 162 C8
Marton Cl LA15 205 C2
Marvejols Pk CA13 190 B2

Mar–MOS 229

Marvic Yard The [2] LA9 200 C4
Maryfell LA10 201 D4
Mary Hannah Cotts [4] CA3 175 B1
Mary Hewetson Cottage Hospl CA12 192 A5
Maryland Cl LA5 210 D2
Mary Langley Way CA11 191 E4
MARYPORT 182 B5
Maryport Ave LA14 206 B2
Maryport CE Jun Sch CA15 182 E7
Maryport Cotts CA2 176 F3
Maryport Ct CA2 176 F3
Maryport Inf Sch CA15 182 D7
Maryport Maritime Mus* CA15 182 C6
Maryport Rd CA15 49 A2
Maryport Sta CA15 182 D5
Mary St
Carlisle CA1 214 B2
Carnforth LA5 213 C5
Longtown CA6 10 C3
Silloth CA7 174 C4
Mask Rd
Crosby Garrett CA16, CA17 104 B3
Great Asby CA16 103 F5
MASONGILL 169 D6
Masongill Fell Lane LA6 169 E7
Mason St CA14 184 E4
Mason Terr CA15 183 C8
Matheson Terr DG12 172 D5
Matlock Rd [6] LA14 207 A6
MATTERDALE END 83 D6
Matty Lonning CA5 28 F1
Maude St LA9 200 C6
Maudy Lonning CA10 86 B5
MAULDS MEABURN 102 C7
MAWBRAY 35 C5
Mawflat La LA14 170 D3
Mayburgh Ave CA11 191 D3
Mayburgh Cl CA10 191 E1
Mayburgh Henge* CA10 191 D1
Maychells Orch LA11 164 F7
Mayfair Ave LA13 207 B5
Mayfield CA2 30 B3
Mayfield Ave
Carlisle CA1 177 D3
Holme LA6 156 B1
Mayfield Rd
Kendal LA9 200 F2
Ulverston LA12 203 C4
Mayfield Sch CA28 91 F8
Mayfield Terr LA11 208 C3
Maylands Ave LA13 207 D6
Maylands Gr LA13 207 D6
Mayo Pk CA13 190 B3
Mayor's Dr CA3 214 A4
Mayo St CA13 190 B3
Mayson St CA2 177 A3
Meade Rd CA1 177 D2
Meadley Pl CA25 188 E6
Meadow Bank
Arnside LA5 209 B1
Beetham LA7 155 E2
Oughterside CA7 49 F7
Meadow Bank Bsns Pk LA9 131 B1
Meadow Bank Cl CA13 190 E3
Meadowbank Fold LA11 208 B4
Meadowbank La LA11 208 B4
Meadow Cl
Appleby-in-W CA16 193 D6
Aspatria CA7 50 C8
Bowston LA8 130 E3
[6] Gosforth CA20 109 A2
Maryport CA15 182 F5
Meadowcroft
Bowness-on-W LA23 129 A2
Holme LA6 156 B2
Meadow Croft
Penrith CA11 191 E5
Thursby CA5 28 F1
Meadowcroft Cotts
Bowness-on-W LA23 129 A2
Windermere LA8 129 F5
Meadow Croft La LA23 129 A2
Meadowcroft Rd CA26 92 D7
Meadow Ct
Appleby-in-W CA16 193 D6
Langwathby CA10 57 C1
Meadow Edge CA14 62 E4
Meadowfield
Carlisle CA6 19 E4
Gosforth CA20 109 B2
Meadowfield Gr [4] CA20 109 A2
Meadow Gr
Cockermouth CA13 190 D3
Dalton-in-F LA15 205 C5
Grange-o-S LA11 208 B1
Meadow Ho CA27 91 D3
Meadow La LA12 171 D6
Meadowlands Ave LA13 207 D6
Meadow Rd
Kendal LA9 200 C2
Whitehaven CA28 187 D4
Wigton CA7 180 B3
Windermere LA23 198 E3
Meadows Cl LA5 166 F6
Meadowside
Chapel Stile LA22 113 C4
Swarthmoor LA12 203 A2
Meadowside Cl LA8 144 C1
Meadows The
Arnside LA5 210 C8
Cliburn CA10 86 E8
Kirkby Lonsdale LA6 168 F8
Langwathby CA10 57 C1
Southwaite CA4 41 C4
Yealand Redmayne LA5 166 F6
Meadow Vale CA14 183 A2
Meadow View
Cark LA11 164 D7
Carlisle CA1 177 F3
Egremont CA22 189 D6
Lowca CA28 186 F8
Whitehaven CA28 187 C7
Meadow View Pk CA7 174 D5
Meadow Way
Arkholme LA6 168 B3
Maryport CA15 182 E5
MEAL BANK 131 C2
Meal Bank LA8 131 D2
Mealbank Mill Trad Est LA8 131 D2
Mealbank Rd LA9 131 C1
Mealo House Cvn Site CA15 49 C8
MEALRIGG 36 B4
Mealrigg La LA6 168 A7
MEALSGATE 37 D1
Means Brow CA11 83 D5
Mearness Dr LA12 203 D2
MEATHOP 154 E3
Meathop Grange LA11 154 E3
Meathop Rd
Grange-o-S LA11 208 F5
Lindale LA11 154 E2
Medway Rd LA14 206 B2
Meetinghouse La CA7 180 C3
Meeting House La
Great Broughton CA13 63 E6
Penrith CA11 191 D5
Sockbridge CA10 70 F1
Ulverston LA12 203 C2
Meeting Ind Est LA14 204 A1
Meetings View LA14 204 B1
Meggy Loaning CA8 32 D1
Melampus St LA14 206 C3
Melbourne Ave DG12 17 D8
Melbourne Rd CA1 177 C5
Melbourne St LA14 206 E4
Melbourne Terr CA14 185 B7
Melbreak Ave
Cleator Moor CA25 188 D6
Cockermouth CA13 190 E4
[4] Maryport CA15 182 E4
Melbreak Cl CA28 187 E3
MELKINTHORPE 86 C8
Mellbecks CA17 199 D6
Mellbutts CA12 82 C8
Mell Fell View CA11 69 D2
MELLING 168 C1
Melling Brow LA6 168 C2
Melling St Wilfrid CE Prim Sch LA6 168 D2
Mell Wood CA17 199 C5
MELMERBY 58 B4
Melrose Terr CA1 177 C5
Mendip Gdns LA14 206 F5
Mercer St LA14 207 A3
Merchant's Dr CA3 175 B6
Merewood Lodge LA23 129 A8
Merith Ave CA1 177 E5
Merle Bank CA12 82 B8
Merlin Dr
Dalton-in-F LA15 205 C4
Moresby Parks CA28 76 F2
Mersey Rd LA14 206 B3
Metcalfe St CA2 214 A1
Methuen St LA14 206 C2
Methven Cl LA11 208 C3
Methven Rd LA11 208 C3
Mews Cotts CA16 193 D5
Mews The
Bampton CA10 85 D1
Ulverston LA12 203 C5
Michaelson Rd
Barrow-in-F LA14 206 F2
Kendal LA9 200 B2
Michael St CA28 186 D1
Micklam Cotts CA14 76 E5
MICKLEWAITE 28 B1
Middle Barrow La LA12 162 E5
Middle Cl CA16 193 D6
Middle Cliff LA14 204 B1
Middle Entrance Dr LA23 129 A1
Middlefield LA14 204 B1
Middlegate
Great Clifton CA14 63 B4
Penrith CA11 191 C5
Middle Hill LA13 207 C4
Middle La
Haverigg LA18 149 F1
Kendal LA9 200 C5
Middle Pk CA9 181 C3
Middle Rigg CA2 176 C3
MIDDLESCEUGH 54 E8
MIDDLESHAW 144 E4
Middleshaw Cres LA8 144 E4
MIDDLETON 145 F1
Middleton Ave LA13 207 C5
Middleton Gr CA13 49 E2
MIDDLETOWN 189 A2
Middle White Cl LA14 206 F8
Midfield Mews CA16 193 D6
MIDGEHOLME 24 A1
Midland Row CA10 57 A6
Midland Terr LA5 213 C5
Midland Units LA5 213 D5
Mid Liddle St TD9 1 B6
Mid St CA28 187 B6
Midtown CA5 28 F5
Midtown Cl CA14 185 D4
Mid Town Cott CA14 185 B7
Mikasa St LA14 206 D1
Milbourne Cres CA2 214 A2
Milbourne St CA2 214 A2
MILBURN 73 C4
Milburn Croft CA14 183 B1
Milburn Ct [6] CA8 179 B5
Milburn Dr DG16 173 B3
Milburn Rd CA10 72 F3
Milburn Sch CA10 73 C4
Milburn St CA14 184 D6
Mile La CA11 70 E4
Miles MacInnes Ct CA3 214 B4
Milestone Ho LA6 212 C1
Millans Ct LA22 195 D6
Millans Pk LA22 195 D6
Millans Terr LA22 195 C5
Mill Bank
Barrow-in-F LA14 206 F8
Low Hesket CA4 41 E5
Mill Bank Cotts CA12 192 B4
Millbank Ct CA2 177 B3
Millbanks Ct CA14 63 C4
MILLBECK 66 E1
Millbeck
Carlisle CA2 176 C2
Kendal LA8 144 F5
Mill Beck Cl LA23 129 D4
Millbeck Cotts CA12 66 E1
Millbecks CA12 80 E6
Millbeckstock LA23 198 C4
Mill Brook CA8 178 F3
Millbrook Cvn Pk LA8 156 D8
Millbrook Rd CA3 175 C5
Mill Brow
Armathwaite CA4 42 C4
Kirkby Lonsdale LA6 212 C2
Windermere LA23 198 F5
Mill Brow Ho LA6 212 C2
Millburn Terr CA8 24 C8
Mill Cl LA11 164 D7
Mill Cott LA8 144 A5
Mill Cotts LA8 130 E4
Millcroft CA3 30 C8
Mill Ct
Carlisle CA1 177 C3
Egremont CA22 189 E5
[6] Wigton CA7 180 D3
Mill Dam [4] LA12 203 D6
Milldikes La CA5 19 B2
Miller Bridge Ho LA22 195 C5
Miller Cl LA13 162 C2
Miller Ct [9] LA9 200 D5
Miller Pk CA7 180 C4
Millerstone Rise CA10 87 E8
Millers Wlk CA23 188 D3
Millfield
Brampton CA8 179 C4
[3] Ulverston LA12 203 D6
Millfield Gdns CA12 192 C3
Mill Fields The CA21 108 B5
Millfield Terr LA8 130 C5
Mill Gate CA10, CA11 57 B4
Mill Gdns CA17 199 D6
MILLGILLHEAD 78 C3
Mill Gr CA13 190 D3
MILLHEAD 213 B5
MILL HILL 9 E2
Mill Hill
Appleby-in-W CA16 193 D4
Cleator Moor CA25 188 C8
Mill Hill Sch LA10 147 B1
Millholme Ave CA2 177 A3
MILLHOUSE 54 A4
Millicent Cl CA14 185 D8
Mill La
Beckermet CA21 108 C6
Beetham LA7 155 E2
Carnforth LA5 213 C6
Crosthwaite LA8 142 F5
Glasson CA7 17 E3
Great Asby CA16 103 B6
Great Ormside CA16 103 D7
Hutton Roof LA6 157 A1
Kirkby Stephen CA17 199 D6
Milburn CA10 73 B4
Sedbergh LA10 146 E7
Sedbergh, Lenacre LA10 146 C4
Soulby CA17 104 C1
Underbarrow LA8 143 B7
Walney Island LA14 206 B3
MILLNESS 156 C5
Millness Hill Holiday Pk LA7 156 C5
Millness La LA7 156 C5
MILLOM 202 E5
Millom Ct LA5 209 B1
Millom Folk Mus* LA18 202 C5
Millom Hospl LA18 202 C4
Millom Inf Sch LA18 202 C4
Millom Rd LA18 202 D5
Millom Sch LA18 202 C5
Millom Sta LA18 202 C5
Millpark Cres DG12 172 C4
Millpark Terr DG12 172 D4
Mill Pk LA18 150 C7
Millrace Cl [4] CA7 180 D3
Mill Race Dr CA10 191 D1
Millrace Rd CA2 176 E7
Mill Race View CA2 176 F3
Mill Rd CA7 17 E3
Millriggs CA4 178 D7
Millrigg St CA14 184 E4
Mill Rise LA23 198 F5
Mill Row LA22 113 C3
Mill St N [2] CA15 182 D5
MILL SIDE 154 F7
Mill St
Barrow-in-F LA14 207 A4
Bootle LA19 137 B3
Cleator CA23 188 D4
Frizington CA26 92 D8
Longtown CA6 10 C3
Maryport CA15 182 D5
Penrith CA11 191 C5
Ravenstonedale CA17 120 A3
Ulverston LA12 203 D5
Whitehaven CA28 187 C8
Millstone Ave LA14 206 F8
Millstream Ct LA11 164 D7
Mill Terr CA11 191 C5
MILLTHROP 201 D3
Millview Terr DG12 172 E5
Millwood La LA14 204 F2
Mill Yd
Harrington CA14 185 A7
Kendal LA9 200 D1
Milner Mount CA11 191 E5
MILNTHORPE 211 E3
Milnthorpe Prim Sch LA7 211 D3
Milnthorpe Rd
Holme LA6 156 B1
Kendal LA9 200 C2
MILTON 22 E3
Milton Dr CA14 184 F4
Milton La
Burgh by S CA5 18 F2
Milness LA7 156 C6
Milton Rd CA22 189 C7
Milton St
Barrow-in-F LA14 206 F4
Penrith CA11 191 C6
Milton Terr
[3] Grange-o-S LA11 208 C4
Milton CA8 22 E3
Minster Cl CA14 184 E3
Minster La LA13 207 D4
Mint Bridge Rd LA9 200 E8
Mint Cl LA9 200 D7
Mint Dale LA9 200 D7
MINTSFEET 200 D7
Mintsfeet Rd LA9 200 D7
Mintsfeet Rd N LA9 200 D7
Mintsfeet Rd S LA9 200 D7
Mint St LA9 200 E7
Miramar LA11 208 C3
MIREHOUSE 187 D5
Mirehouse* CA12 66 C3
Mirehouse Rd CA28 187 E3
Mirk La CA13 64 D1
Mislet Brow LA23 129 E6
Mitchelgate LA6 212 B2
Mitchell Ave CA14 184 E8
MITE HOUSES 123 E4
Miterdale Cl CA28 187 F8
MOAT 10 F8
Moat CA6 10 F8
Moat Rd DG12 172 C4
Moatside [7] CA8 179 C5
Moat St CA8 179 C5
MOCKERKIN 78 D6
Moffat Terr CA26 92 D8
Mona Rd
Whitehaven CA28 186 D3
Workington CA14 184 C1
Mona St CA26 77 F1
Monk Castle Bglws CA4 41 A4
MONKHILL 19 B1
Monkhill Rd CA5 29 A7
Monkhouse Rd CA14 184 C2
Monk Moors LA19 137 A7
Monks Brow LA13 207 C3
Monks Cl CA11 191 C7
Monks Close Rd CA2 176 E6
Monks Croft Ave LA14 207 C8
Monks Hill CA27 91 C3
Monk St LA14 206 F4
Monksvale Gr LA13 207 C6
Monkwray Brow CA28 187 C7
Monkwray Cotts CA28 187 C7
Monkwray Ct CA28 187 B6
Monkwray Jun Sch CA28 187 C7
Monkwray Rd CA28 187 B6
Monkwray Villas CA28 187 C6
Monnington Way CA11 191 C7
Montague St [2] LA14 206 F3
Montagu St TD9 1 B6
Montgomery Ct CA1 177 F6
Montgomery Way CA1 177 F6
Montreal Ave CA25 188 D6
Montreal CE Prim Sch CA25 188 E6
Montreal Cl CA25 188 D6
Montreal Pl CA24 188 B6
Montreal St
Carlisle CA2 177 A3
Cleator Moor CA25 188 D7
Monument Ho [18] LA9 200 C4
Monument Way LA12 203 F5
Moorbanks Rd CA14 184 D4
Moor Cl
Great Orton CA5 28 F4
Moor Cl *continued*
Millom LA18 202 B4
MOORCLOSE 184 F3
Moorclose Croft CA14 184 D3
Moor Close La LA6 167 B1
Moorclose Rd
Harrington CA14 185 A8
Workington CA14 184 D2
Moorcock Cotts LA10 148 E7
Moor Cres CA6 10 C3
Moordale Cvn Pk CA7 25 B2
Moore Field Cl LA9 200 B8
MOOR END 28 F1
Moore Way CA14 185 D7
Moorfield Ave CA14 184 F4
Moorfield Bank CA13 63 E6
Moorfield Cotts [12] LA14 207 B2
Moorfields CA15 63 C8
Moorfield St LA13 207 C3
Moorgarth LA12 203 A3
Moor Ho [9] LA14 207 C8
MOORHOUSE
Carlisle 29 A7
Wigton 27 F2
Moorhouse Courtyards CA5 28 F7
Moor House National Nature Reserve* CA9 74 D8
Moorhouse Rd CA2 176 A7
Moorhowe Rd LA23 129 D7
Moor La
Beetham LA7 211 F1
Clifton CA10 71 D3
Flookburgh LA11 164 D6
Melkinthorpe CA10 86 A8
Satterthwaite LA12 141 A7
Moorlands Dr CA14 62 E3
MOOR PARK 49 A5
Moor Park Ave CA2 176 A7
Moor Pk LA18 202 B5
Moor Pl
Carlisle CA3 175 B2
Frizington CA26 92 D8
Longtown CA6 10 C3
Moor Rd
Askam in F LA12 151 C1
Great Broughton CA13 63 E6
Great Clifton CA14 63 B4
Longtown CA6 10 C4
Millom LA18 202 B5
Stainburn CA14 62 F3
MOOR ROW
Abbeytown 37 D8
Cleator Moor 188 A5
Moor Row Com Prim Sch CA24 188 A5
Moorside
Flookburgh LA11 164 D6
Hunsonby CA10 57 E2
Melling LA6 168 D2
Oughterside CA7 49 F7
Yanwath CA10 71 A2
Moorside Cl LA6 168 D2
Moorside Dr
Carlisle CA1 30 E5
Maryport CA15 182 F4
Moorside Rd LA8 144 C1
Moor Tarn La LA14 206 B2
Moor Terr LA18 202 B4
Moorthwaite La LA6 157 F5
Moorview Cl CA14 185 C8
MOORVILLE 175 C3
Moorville Dr CA3 175 D3
Moorville Dr N CA3 175 D3
Moorville Dr S CA3 175 D3
Moorville Way CA3 175 D4
Moorwood Cl CA1 177 F5
Morass Rd CA21, CA22 108 B6
Morecambe Bank LA11 208 D4
Morecambe Bay Nature Reserve* LA5 165 F6
Morecambe Cres LA14 206 F8
Morecambe Rd LA12 203 E4
MORESBY PARKS 76 F1
Moresby Parks Rd CA28 76 F2
Moresby Prim Sch CA28 76 F2
Moresby Rd CA28 91 F8
Moresby Terr CA28 186 E6
Morewood Dr LA6 167 C7
Moricambe Cres CA7 16 F1
Moricambe Pk CA7 174 E8
MORLAND 86 F5
Morland Area CE Prim Sch CA10 86 F5
MORLAND MOOR 87 A4
Morland Pl CA13 190 C3
Morley St
Carlisle CA2 214 A1
Workington CA14 184 C5
Morningside CA7 50 C5
Morningside Rd DG12 172 E5
Morpeth Cl CA8 179 C6
MORTON
Calthwaite 55 C6
Carlisle 176 C4
Morton Cl LA13 207 D4
Morton Ct CA2 176 C4
Morton Park Prim Sch CA2 176 C3
Mortonrigg CA2 176 C4
Morton Sch The CA2 176 B4
Morton St CA2 176 E6
MOSEDALE 68 C7

Mosedale Cres CA15 .... 182 D4
Mosedale Rd CA14 .... 184 E4
Moser Hill Brow LA10 ... 201 C1
Mosley St LA14 .... 207 B3
MOSSBAY 184 C4
Mossbay Rd CA14 .... 184 C3
MOSSEDGE 11 F3
Moss End La LA7 .... 156 C5
MOSSER 78 F7
Mosser Ave CA13 .... 190 E3
MOSSER MAINS 78 F8
Moss Force★ CA13 .... 95 B8
Moss Ghyll LA9 .... 200 C8
Moss Gr CA10 .... 101 C5
Mossknowe Pl DG16 .... 173 D3
Moss La
Allonby CA15 .... 35 C2
Holme LA6 .... 156 A1
Holme Mills LA5 .... 167 A8
Leece LA12 .... 171 C7
Silverdale LA5 .... 210 F5
Moss Lea LA8 .... 144 D1
Moss Lonning CA7 .... 37 A7
Moss Pl
Gretna DG16 .... 173 C2
Newcastleton or Copshaw Holm TD9 .... 1 B6
Moss Rd
Cliburn CA10 .... 86 E8
Newcastleton or Copshaw Holm TD9 .... 1 B6
Mossrigg CA2 .... 176 C3
MOSS SIDE 26 E3
Moss Side CA15 .... 35 C2
Moss Side Rd LA7 .... 211 B7
Mosswell Terr CA28 ..... 186 D2
MOTHERBY 69 E3
Mothercroft CA10 .... 86 F5
Mountain Ash Ct LA23 .. 198 D6
Mountain View
Carlisle CA3 .... 175 D3
Cockermouth CA13 ...... 190 C3
Harrington CA14 .... 185 A8
High Hesket CA4 .... 41 F3
Kendal LA9 .... 200 C6
Moresby Parks CA28 .... 76 F2
Sedbergh LA10 .... 201 C4
Mount Barnard View LA12 .... 203 D2
Mountbarrow Rd LA12 .. 203 C2
Mountbarrow Way LA12 .... 203 D2
Mountbatten Way LA18 .... 202 A5
Mountjoy Brow LA8 ...... 143 B7
Mount Pleasant
Arnside LA5 .... 210 C8
12 Barrow-in-F LA14 ..... 207 A3
6 Holme LA6 .... 156 B1
13 Kendal LA9 .... 200 C5
Lindal in F LA12 .... 162 E7
Mount Pleasant Gdns CA7 .... 180 D2
Mount Pleasant La LA5 .... 213 B1
Mount Pleasant Rd CA2 .... 177 A2
Mounts Meadow Cl LA12 .... 162 E1
Mount St 6 LA9 .... 200 C4
Mount The
Camerton CA14 .... 183 F3
Cockermouth CA13 .... 190 B5
Mouzell Bank LA15 ...... 205 D6
Mowbray Dr LA6 .... 167 C7
Mowing's La LA12 .... 203 C6
Muirbeck Rd DG12 ...... 172 A1
Muirfield Cl 7 CA3 ...... 175 B1
Muirfield Gdns DG12 ..... 172 E4
Mulberry Way LA13 ...... 207 F5
Mulcaster Cres CA3 ...... 175 E1
Mulgrew Cl CA15 .... 182 F4
Muncaster Castle★ CA18 .... 124 B3
Muncaster Cl CA28 .... 91 F7
Muncaster Halt★ CA18 .... 124 A4
Muncaster Rd
Walney Island LA14 ..... 206 C5
Whitehaven CA28 .... 91 F7
MUNGRISDALE 68 D5
Munroe Ave LA18 .... 202 C6
Murley Moss LA9 .... 200 E1
Murley Moss Bsns Pk LA9 .... 200 E1
Murley Moss La LA9 ..... 200 E2
Murray Ct DG12 .... 172 C3
Murraydale Terr 1 CA14 .... 184 E6
Murrayfield Cotts DG12 .... 172 D3
Murrayfield Terr CA18 .... 123 F3
Murray Rd CA14 .... 184 E6
Murray St DG12 .... 172 D4
Murrell Hill LA11 .... 208 C4
MURTON 89 B4
Murton Cl CA16 .... 193 C4
Murton Ct CA26 .... 77 E2
Murton Pk CA26 .... 77 E2
Murton View CA16 ...... 193 C5
Museum Sq CA12 .... 192 A3
Museum Villas CA14 ..... 185 C2
Musgrave La
Brough CA16 .... 104 F7
Brough CA17 .... 105 A5
Musgrave St CA11 .... 191 B5
Muslins The CA7 .... 50 C5
Mus of Lakeland Life★ LA9 .... 200 D4
Mus of the Old Grammar School★ LA22 .... 197 E5
Myddleton St CA1 ...... 214 C2
Myddleton Terr CA1 .... 214 C2
Myerscough St 6 LA14 .... 207 B2
Myerscroft LA12 .... 163 B3
Myers La CA11 .... 191 C4
Myers St 23 CA12 .... 192 B3
Mylnbeck Ct LA23 .... 198 D3
Mylnegarth Gdns LA23 .. 198 E5
Myrtle Gr LA15 .... 205 B5
Myrtle Terr LA15 .... 205 B5
Myrtle Villas CA12 ...... 192 B4

N

Nabs Rd LA8 .... 143 B3
Naddle Gate CA10 .... 100 D7
Naiad St LA14 .... 206 D1
Nairn St CA15 .... 183 C8
Nairn Way CA2 .... 176 C5
Nannycatch Rd CA23 ...... 92 D5
Nannypie La LA8 .... 143 F2
Napier St
Barrow-in-F LA14 .... 206 F4
Dalton-in-F LA15 .... 205 C5
Workington CA14 .... 184 D5
Natal Rd LA14 .... 206 D1
NATEBY 199 D2
Nateby Rd CA17 .... 199 C4
NATLAND 144 A4
Natland Mill Beck La LA9 .... 200 D1
Natland Rd LA9 .... 200 D1
Naworth Castle★ CA8 ..... 22 E5
Naworth Dr CA3 .... 175 C4
NEALHOUSE 29 A2
Neals Row LA12 .... 162 F5
Near Field Wlk LA14 .... 204 B1
Near Pk CA4 .... 30 E6
NEAR SAWREY 128 E2
Neaum Crag Cvn Chalet & Camping Site LA22 ..... 113 E2
Neddy Hill LA6 .... 167 B7
Needham Dr CA14 .... 184 D2
Nelson Bridge CA2 ...... 214 A1
Nelson Bridge Ct CA2 ... 214 A1
Nelson Rd LA23 .... 198 F4
Nelson Sq
Egremont CA22 .... 189 D6
Levens LA8 .... 155 D8
Nelson St
Barrow-in-F LA14 .... 206 F4
Carlisle CA2 .... 214 A1
Dalton-in-F LA15 .... 205 B5
Maryport CA15 .... 182 C6
Maryport CA15 .... 182 D7
Millom LA18 .... 202 D4
Nelson Thomlinson Sch The CA7 .... 180 D3
Nent Ct CA9 .... 47 A2
NENTHALL 46 D4
NENTHEAD 47 A2
Nenthead Mines Heritage Ctr★ CA9 .... 47 A2
Nenthead Prim Sch CA9 .. 46 F2
NENTSBERRY 46 E4
NEPGILL 63 D4
Nepgill CA14 .... 63 D4
NER Cottage Homes CA4 .... 178 C2
Ness Way CA2 .... 176 B4
Nest Brow CA12 .... 192 F2
Nether Beck LA6 .... 213 F5
NETHER BURROW 168 E6
Netherby Dr
Barrow-in-F LA14 .... 206 F8
Carlisle CA3 .... 175 C4
Netherby Rd CA6 .... 10 C4
Netherby St CA6 .... 10 B3
Nethercroft LA8 .... 143 D1
Netherend Rd CA11 ..... 191 D3
Netherfield CA6 .... 11 E1
Netherfield Cl
Hensingham CA28 .... 188 A8
Walney Island LA14 ..... 170 C6
Netherhall Sch CA15 .... 182 E6
Netherleigh Dr LA11 .... 208 C4
NETHER ROW 53 C4
Nether St LA9 .... 200 D3
NETHERTON 182 D5
Netherton Inf Sch CA15 .... 182 E5
NETHERTOWN 107 F6
Nethertown Rd CA27 ...... 91 D2
Nethertown Sta CA22 .... 107 E6
Nether View
Maryport CA15 .... 182 F5
Wennington LA2 .... 168 E1
NETHER WASDALE 110 A3
Netherwood Gdns LA11 .... 208 E5
Neville Ave CA11 .... 191 C4
Neville Ct 25 LA12 ...... 203 D5
Neville St LA12 .... 203 D5
Neville Terr 24 LA12 .... 203 D5
New Acres LA5 .... 213 E4
Newark Terr CA1 .... 214 B3
NEWBARNS 207 C6
New Barns Cl LA5 ...... 165 F8
Newbarns Ct 3 LA13 ... 207 C5
Newbarns Prim Sch LA13 .... 207 C5
Newbarns Rd LA13 ..... 207 C3
New Barns Rd LA5 ...... 154 F1
NEWBIE 172 A1
Newbiebarns DG12 .... 16 C7
NEWBIGGIN
Barrow-in-Furness 171 E8
Castle Carrock 43 B8
Kirkby Lonsdale 156 E2
Penrith 70 B4
Temple Sowerby 72 F3
Newbiggin LA9 .... 200 C8
Newbiggin Cotts LA19 .. 124 A1
Newbiggin La LA6 ...... 156 E2
NEWBIGGIN-ON-LUNE 119 F4
Newbiggin Rd CA4, CA5 ... 30 C2
New Bldgs 6 CA11 ..... 191 C6
New Bridge Rd CA14 .... 184 D7
New Bridge St CA15 .... 182 D4
NEWBY 86 F4
NEWBY BRIDGE 141 E1
Newby Bridge Halt★ LA12 .... 141 D1
Newby Ct CA10 .... 86 F4
NEWBY EAST 21 C1
NEWBY HEAD 86 E4
Newby Terr LA14 .... 207 A6
Newcastle St
6 Barrow-in-F LA13 ..... 207 B3
Carlisle CA2 .... 176 E6
NEWCASTLETON OR COPSHAW HOLM 1 C6
Newcastleton Prim Sch TD9 .... 1 B6
New Church La 7 LA12 .... 203 C5
New Cl
Eskdale Green CA19 ..... 124 F7
Newbiggin LA12 .... 171 E8
Newclose La CA16, CA17 .... 119 F8
New Cotts LA11 .... 154 C3
NEW COWPER 36 A4
Newcroft LA5 .... 213 D8
New Croft CA7 .... 180 C3
New England Cvn Pk LA6 .... 167 B3
Newfield LA20 .... 126 B2
Newfield Dr CA3 .... 175 D4
Newfield Pk CA3 .... 175 D4
New Gr CA14 .... 184 E5
NEW HUTTON 144 F6
Newington Ave DG12 ... 172 D4
Newington Prim Sch DG12 .... 172 E5
Newington Rd DG12 .... 172 D5
New La
Burton-in-K LA6 .... 167 B7
Carlisle CA3 .... 214 B2
Newlaithes Ave CA2 .... 176 C3
Newlaithes Inf Sch CA2 .... 176 C4
Newlaithes Jun Sch CA2 .... 176 C4
NEWLAND 203 F8
NEWLAND BOTTOM 152 C3
Newland Rd LA12 .... 203 F6
NEWLANDS
Hesket Newmarket 53 E6
Keswick 80 F3
Newlands Ave CA28 ..... 187 D4
Newlands Gdns CA14 ... 184 E4
Newlands La CA14 ...... 184 E4
Newlands La S CA14 .... 184 D3
Newlands Pk
Dearham CA15 .... 49 A2
Workington CA14 .... 184 F5
Newlands Pl CA11 ...... 191 B4
Newlands Rd
Carlisle CA2 .... 177 B3
Cockermouth CA13 ...... 190 C3
Crosby Garrett CA17 ..... 104 A2
Newlands Rise DG12 .... 172 E5
Newlands Terr 6 CA11 .... 191 C5
New Leys LA13 .... 207 C4
New Lowther St CA28 ... 186 C1
Newman RC Sch CA1 .... 214 C3
Newmarket Rd CA1 ..... 214 B3
New Market St 18 LA12 .... 203 D5
New Midland Cotts CA17 .... 199 A2
NEW MILL 108 F3
New Path DG12 .... 172 D5
Newport St LA14 .... 206 F6
New Prom CA15 .... 182 D8
New Rd
Askam in F LA16 .... 162 A7
Askham CA10 .... 85 F7
Beck Foot LA10 .... 133 A1
Brough CA17 .... 105 B5
Burneside LA9 .... 130 F2
Cockermouth CA13 ...... 190 D3
Great Asby CA16 .... 103 F5
Ingleton LA6 .... 169 F4
Kendal LA9 .... 200 D5
Kirkby Lonsdale LA6 ..... 212 C2
Matterdale End CA11 ...... 83 C6
Shap CA10 .... 101 A8
Silverdale LA5 .... 210 F1
Thornhill CA22 .... 189 E2
Whitehaven CA28 .... 186 D2
Windermere LA23 .... 198 E5
NEW RENT 55 D3
New Row CA7 .... 49 F7
Newry St LA14 .... 206 E2
New Shambles 3 LA9 .. 200 D5
New South Watt St CA14 .... 184 D6
New St
Barrow-in-F LA14 .... 207 B2
Bigrigg CA22 .... 188 A3
Bolton Low Houses CA7 .... 37 F3
Broughton-in-F LA20 .... 139 A2
Burneside LA9 .... 130 F2
Carnforth LA5 .... 213 C4
Cockermouth CA13 ...... 190 C4
6 Keswick CA12 .... 192 B3
Sedbergh LA10 .... 201 C5
Silloth CA7 .... 174 C3
Whitehaven CA28 .... 186 C1
Wigton CA7 .... 180 D4
NEWTON
Dalton-in-Furness 162 C2
Whittington 168 C5
NEWTON ARLOSH 26 F6
Newton Brow LA13 ..... 207 D3
Newton Com Prim Sch CA2 .... 176 C6
Newton Cross Rd
Dalton-in-F LA13 .... 205 D1
Newton LA13 .... 162 C2
Newton Hall Barn LA11 .... 154 B5
Newton Mdws CA11 .... 70 C6
Newton Prim Sch LA13 .... 162 C2
Newton Rd
Barrow-in-F LA13 .... 207 F8
Dalton-in-F LA13, LA15 .. 205 B2
Penrith CA11 .... 70 E5
NEWTON REIGNY 70 C6
NEWTON RIGG 70 E6
Newtonrigg CA2 .... 176 C4
Newton Sq DG16 .... 173 D5
Newton St
Millom LA18 .... 202 D4
Ulverston LA12 .... 203 E5
Newton Terr LA18 ...... 202 B5
NEWTOWN
Askham 85 E7
Brampton 21 F5
Carlisle 176 C6
Silloth 35 D7
Newtown CA26 .... 92 D8
New Town CA28 .... 187 C8
Newtown Cl CA2 .... 176 C6
Newtown Ind Est CA2 ... 176 C7
Newtown Rd CA2 .... 176 C6
New Villas CA14 .... 62 D6
New Yd CA14 .... 184 C4
Next Ness Cotts LA12 ... 152 D1
Next Ness La LA12 ...... 203 F6
Nichol Hill 8 CA11 ...... 191 C6
Nicholson Cl LA18 ...... 202 B4
Nicholson La CA11 ...... 191 D6
Nicholson Pl DG12 ...... 172 B3
Nicholson St
Annan DG12 .... 172 B3
Carlisle CA2 .... 177 B4
Niger St LA14 .... 206 D1
Nightingale Ct CA4 .... 30 F5
Nilsson Dr CA14 .... 184 D2
Nine Rigg CA5 .... 29 D1
Nineteen Acre La LA5 ... 166 F6
Niobe St LA14 .... 206 C3
Nittyholm DG14 .... 3 B6
Nixon Terr CA15 .... 63 C8
Noble Croft CA7 .... 50 D8
Noble Knott Forest Wlks★ CA12 .... 80 E7
Noble's Rest LA9 .... 200 C5
NOOK 156 D5
Nookdales Cotts LA6 .... 169 F1
Nook La
Ambleside LA22 .... 195 D7
Buckabank CA5 .... 40 A8
Farleton LA6 .... 156 D4
Underbarrow LA8 .... 143 B7
Nook Lane Cl 1 CA5 ...... 40 A8
Nook St
Carlisle CA1 .... 177 C6
Frizington CA26 .... 92 D8
Workington CA14 .... 184 F5
Nook The
Brampton CA8 .... 179 C5
Carlisle CA3 .... 175 D2
Finsthwaite LA12 .... 141 D2
Great Broughton CA13 ..... 63 E6
Silecroft LA18 .... 149 E4
Wigton CA7 .... 28 A4
Norbeck Pk CA25 .... 188 C7
Norfolk Ct CA2 .... 176 F4
Norfolk Pl CA11 .... 191 B4
Norfolk Rd
Carlisle CA2 .... 176 E4
Penrith CA11 .... 191 B5
Norfolk St
Barrow-in-F LA14 .... 207 A6
Carlisle CA2 .... 176 F4
Norfolk Terr CA2 .... 176 F4
Norham Cl LA13 .... 207 D4
Norland Ave LA14 ...... 207 B8
Norman St CA1 .... 177 C6
Norman Street Prim Sch CA1 .... 177 C6
North Cl CA13 .... 190 B3
Northcote St CA14 ...... 184 C3
North Cotts LA23 .... 198 D3
North Craig LA23 .... 198 D3
North Cumbria Tech Coll CA1 .... 177 F3
North Dr CA20 .... 108 D4
NORTH DYKES 57 A4
North End CA16 .... 87 D6
Northern Terr LA5 ...... 210 F5
Northfield Ave CA14 .... 185 C8
Northfield Park Ave DG12 .... 172 D6
Northfield Park Gdns DG12 .... 172 D6
Northfield Pk DG12 ..... 172 D6
Northgate
Annan DG12 .... 172 C5
Kendal LA9 .... 200 E6
North Gn LA12 .... 162 F7
North Hermitage Sq TD9 ... 1 B6
North Hermitage St TD9 ... 1 B6
NORTH HOWES 172 B5
North La LA18 .... 150 A2
North Lakes Bsns Pk CA11 .... 70 A3
North Lakes Sch CA11 .. 191 D3
North Liddle St TD9 .... 1 B6
North Lodge CA15 .... 35 C2
North Lonsdale Rd LA12 .... 203 F5
North Lonsdale Terr LA12 .... 203 E5
North Park Cotts CA4 ..... 30 D2
North Quay CA15 .... 182 C6
North Range The CA10 .... 86 A5
North Rd
Ambleside LA22 .... 195 D6
Aspatria CA7 .... 36 C1
Barrow-in-F LA14 .... 206 E3
Carnforth LA5 .... 213 D4
Egremont CA22 .... 189 D7
Holme LA6 .... 156 B2
Kirkby Stephen CA17 .... 199 C6
Whitehaven CA28 .... 186 D3
North Road Prim Sch LA5 .... 213 C3
NORTH ROW 66 B7
North Row
Barrow-in-F LA13 .... 207 E3
Whitehaven CA28 .... 187 B7
NORTH SCALE 206 B5
North Scale LA14 .... 206 C4
North Shore Rd CA28 ... 186 C2
North Shore St CA14 .... 185 A7
NORTH SIDE 184 E8
Northside Prim Sch CA14 .... 184 D8
Northside Rd CA14 ..... 184 E7
North St
Annan DG12 .... 172 C5
Barrow-in-F LA13 .... 207 C2
Carlisle CA2 .... 176 F4
Cleator Moor CA25 ...... 188 D7
Maryport CA15 .... 182 D6
Mealsgate CA7 .... 37 C2
NORTH STAINMORE 105 F6
North Terr
Bowness-on-W LA23 .... 198 D3
Tebay CA10 .... 118 B2
Northumberland St
Carlisle CA2 .... 214 A1
Workington CA14 .... 184 E5
Northview CA16 .... 103 B3
North View
Aspatria CA7 .... 36 C1
Carlisle CA3 .... 175 E1
Crosby CA15 .... 49 B5
NORTH WALNEY 206 B4
North Walney Nature Reserve★ LA14 .... 161 C3
North Walney Prim Sch LA14 .... 206 B3
North Watt St 3 CA14 .. 184 D6
Northwood Cres CA3 .... 175 E2
Norwood Dr CA13 ...... 190 D3
NUNCLOSE 42 B4
Nunnery Hill Way CA9 ... 46 F2
Nuns Ave LA7 .... 209 E3
Nurseries The CA6 .... 20 D1
Nursery Fold LA11 ...... 164 E6
Nursery Gdns LA15 ..... 205 C5
Nursery Pl
Annan DG12 .... 172 C4
Hensingham CA28 .... 187 F6
Nursery Rd
Beckermet CA21 .... 108 C5
Carlisle CA2 .... 177 B2
Nutberry Pl DG16 ...... 173 C2
Nutting Hall La LA7 ..... 156 C7
Nutwood Cres LA11 ..... 208 E5
Nutwood Manor LA11 ... 208 E5

O

Oakbank
Kendal LA8 .... 131 A3
Whitehaven CA28 .... 186 D2
Oak Bank
Houghton CA3 .... 175 F5
Newbiggin CA11 .... 70 B4
Oakbank Ave CA28 ...... 186 D3
Oak Cres CA28 .... 186 E4
Oak Dr CA6 .... 21 E5
Oakfield Ct CA28 .... 187 F8
Oakfield Ho CA12 .... 66 E1
Oak Head Rd LA14 ...... 170 C6
Oak Hill LA23 .... 198 D4
Oak La
Carlisle CA1 .... 30 E4
Crosthwaite LA8 .... 142 F6
Oakland LA23 .... 198 D7
Oakland Ave CA15 ...... 182 F4
Oakland Dr LA23 .... 198 D7

Oaklands
Ambleside LA22 .... 195 C6
Beckermet CA22 .... 108 B6
Oaklands Cvn Site CA10 ... 86 B5
Oaklands Dr CA2 .... 177 B1
Oakland View CA6 .... 20 F5
Oak Lea Rd LA14 .... 204 D5
Oakleigh Way CA1 .... 177 E5
Oakley Ave CA14 .... 185 D8
Oakmoss LA12 .... 153 B6
Oak Pk CA8 .... 179 D4
Oak Rd
Barrow-in-F LA14 .... 206 F6
Penrith CA11 .... 191 E5
Oakroyd Cl LA5 .... 209 B2
Oaks Field LA22 .... 195 D6
Oakshaw Cl CA3 .... 175 B3
OAKSHAW FORD 5 D3
Oaks La CA5 .... 28 D7
Oak St LA23 .... 198 E5
Oaks The CA22 .... 189 C6
Oakthwaite Rd LA23 .... 198 E4
Oak Tree Cl CA10 .... 101 C5
Oaktree Cres CA13 .... 190 E5
Oak Tree Rd LA9 .... 200 F5
Oak Vale LA12 .... 152 D5
Oakwell Ct CA8 .... 179 D4
Oakwood LA9 .... 200 B4
Oakwood Cl LA8 .... 143 D1
Oakwood Crest LA12 .... 203 D2
Oakwood Dr
Barrow-in-F LA13 .... 207 F4
Ulverston LA12 .... 203 D2
Oakwrea Bank CA15 .... 49 D6
Oasis Whinfell Holiday Village CA10 .... 72 A1
Ocean Rd LA14 .... 170 C6
Oddfellows Terr CA22 .... 189 D7
Oglanby's Terr CA7 .... 37 C2
Old Arrowthwaite CA28 .... 187 C7
Old Auction Mart LA6 .... 212 C2
Old Bakery The DG16 .... 173 C2
Old Barn The LA12 .... 152 E1
Old Brewery Yard CA8 .... 179 C4
Old Bridge CA22 .... 189 E5
Old Chapel La LA8 .... 143 D1
Old Chapel The CA4 .... 178 B6
Old Church La CA8 .... 22 A4
Old College La LA23 .... 198 E5
Old College Pk LA23 .... 198 D6
Old Corn Mill The CA13 .... 190 C5
Old Farm Cl LA14 .... 207 A8
Old Farmhouse Mews The CA12 .... 80 F6
Oldfield Ct LA23 .... 198 E5
Oldfield Rd LA23 .... 198 E4
Old Fire Station The 8 LA9 .... 200 D5
Old Furness Rd LA21 .... 196 A3
Old Graitney Rd DG16 .... 173 B2
Old Hall CA23 .... 188 C3
Old Hall Dr LA12 .... 203 D7
Old Hall Pk Cvn Site LA6 .... 167 C1
Old Hall Rd
Troutbeck Bridge LA23 .... 198 C8
Ulverston LA12 .... 203 C7
Old Hall Went 6 CA13 .... 190 D4
Oldham St 8 LA14 .... 207 A3
Old Harker Cotts CA6 .... 175 B8
OLD HUTTON 144 F3
Old Hutton CE Sch LA8 .... 144 E3
Old Kells CA28 .... 187 B6
Old Lake Rd LA22 .... 195 D4
Old London Rd CA11 .... 191 D4
Old Lound LA9 .... 200 D3
Old Midland Cotts CA17 .... 199 A2
Old Mill Cres LA23 .... 129 A1
Old Mill Ct DG12 .... 172 B3
Old Moor Gdns LA18 .... 202 D4
Old Myse The LA7 .... 209 F5
Old Nurseries The LA11 .... 208 C2
Old Orch The CA15 .... 49 C3
Old Park La LA14 .... 170 E1
Old Police Station The LA22 .... 197 E5
Old Powleys CA10 .... 71 F8
Old Raffles Par CA2 .... 176 C5
Old Rake LA21 .... 139 F8
Old Rampside Rd LA13 .... 207 E3
Old Rd
Crosby CA15 .... 49 B5
Garsdale Head LA10 .... 148 C6
Kendal LA8 .... 131 B5
Levens LA8 .... 155 C8
Longtown CA6 .... 10 C3
OLD ROOSE 207 E4
Old Roose LA13 .... 207 E4
Old Row
Greenhead CA8 .... 24 D7
Sedgwick LA8 .... 144 A2
Old Scotch Rd
Beck Foot LA8 .... 132 D3
Killington LA8 .... 145 C4
Old Town LA6 .... 157 C7
Old Shambles LA9 .... 200 C5
Old Shore Rd CA19 .... 123 D6
Old Smithy Visitor Ctr★ DG16 .... 173 D5
Old Station The LA6 .... 168 F8
Old Tannery The
Kirkby Lonsdale LA6 .... 212 C2
Scotby CA4 .... 30 E6
OLD TEBAY 118 C4
OLD TOWN
High Hesket 41 F2
Kirkby Lonsdale 157 C6
Old Town Hill LA11 .... 154 A4
Old Town Lodge CA4 .... 41 F2
Old Warehouse CA2 .... 214 A1
Old Woodyard The 15 LA9 .... 200 C5
Olive Cl 7 LA15 .... 205 B4
Oliver Pl
Carnforth LA5 .... 213 D4
Newcastleton or Copshaw Holm TD9 .... 1 B6
Onchan View LA14 .... 206 B1
Orange Grange Cvn Pk CA5 .... 29 C2
Orcades Gn LA14 .... 170 C6
Orchard Ave LA13 .... 207 B6
Orchard Cl
Bardsea LA12 .... 163 C5
Burgh by S CA5 .... 18 F1
Cartmel LA11 .... 153 F1
Long Marton CA16 .... 88 A7
Seaton CA14 .... 183 B2
Sedgwick LA8 .... 144 A2
Silverdale LA5 .... 210 B2
Orchard Cres LA5 .... 209 B2
Orchard Ct CA28 .... 187 E5
Orchard Dr CA11 .... 69 E5
Orchard Garth CA4 .... 30 E1
Orchard Gdns CA3 .... 175 F5
Orchard Gr CA11 .... 70 C6
Orchard Ho LA9 .... 200 E5
Orchard La CA3 .... 175 F5
Orchard Paddock CA7 .... 49 C6
Orchard Pl CA25 .... 188 E6
Orchard Rd
Arnside LA5 .... 209 B2
Bardsea LA12 .... 163 C5
Wigton CA7 .... 180 E4
Orchard St CA1 .... 214 C1
Orchard The
Armathwaite CA4 .... 42 C4
Bassenthwaite CA12 .... 66 B7
Grange-o-S LA11 .... 208 C2
Great Corby CA4 .... 178 C1
Lindale LA11 .... 154 C3
Linstock CA6 .... 20 D1
Milnthorpe LA7 .... 211 E4
Orepit Cotts CA22 .... 188 A2
Oreton Villas 5 LA11 .... 208 C4
Orfeur St CA1 .... 214 C2
Orgill Prim Sch CA22 .... 189 C6
Oriana Mews LA14 .... 206 C2
Orion Terr LA14 .... 170 C6
ORMATHWAITE 192 C7
ORMSGILL 206 F8
Ormsgill La
Barrow-in-F LA14 .... 206 E7
Barrow-in-F, Ormsgill LA14 .... 206 F8
Ormsgill Prim Sch LA14 .... 206 F8
Oronsay Gdns LA14 .... 170 C6
Orontes Ave LA14 .... 170 C6
Orrest Dr LA23 .... 198 E5
Orrest Drive Flats LA23 .... 198 E6
Orsova Gdns LA14 .... 170 C6
ORTON 118 C7
Orton CE Sch CA10 .... 118 C7
Orton Pl CA2 .... 176 B5
Orton Rd
Carlisle CA2 .... 176 B5
Tebay CA10 .... 118 B3
Osborne Ave CA2 .... 176 E6
Osborne Pl CA7 .... 49 F7
Osborne St LA14 .... 206 F5
Osprey Dr LA14 .... 206 B1
Osprey Gdns CA28 .... 76 F2
Ostley Bank LA13 .... 207 C6
Ostley Gdns LA13 .... 207 B7
Oswald St CA1 .... 177 C5
Otley Rd CA12 .... 192 B4
Otters Holt CA10 .... 72 D4
OUBUS HILL 203 F6
OUGHTERBY 28 C6
OUGHTERSIDE 49 F7
Oughterside Prim Sch CA7 .... 49 F7
OULTON 180 B8
Oulton Terr CA8 .... 179 C4
Our Lady of Lourdes RC Prim Sch LA5 .... 213 D3
Our Lady of the Rosary RC Prim Sch LA15 .... 205 D5
Our Lady & St Patrick's RC Prim Sch CA15 .... 182 D4
OUSBY 58 B1
OUTCAST 203 F4
Outfield Lonning CA7 .... 37 A7
Outgang Rd CA7 .... 36 C1
OUTGATE 197 F8
OUTHGILL 135 D8
Out Rigg CA27 .... 91 D2
Oval Ct CA1 .... 30 E4
Oval The
High Cummersdale CA2 .... 176 D1
Whitehaven CA28 .... 187 E3
Overbeck Dr LA13 .... 207 F3
Overburn CA9 .... 181 E3
OVER BURROW 168 E7
Overdale Cl LA9 .... 200 B8
Overend Rd
Greysouthen CA13 .... 63 E4
Whitehaven CA28 .... 91 F7
OVER KELLET 167 B1
Oversands 7 LA11 .... 208 D4
OVERTOWN 168 F7
Overwater CA9 .... 46 F2
Overwood Pl CA16 .... 193 B4
Owlet Ash Fields LA7 .... 211 E4
Oxen Croft LA13 .... 207 C4
OXENHOLME 144 C4
Oxenholme La LA9 .... 144 B4
Oxenholme Rd LA9 .... 200 F1
OXEN PARK 140 E2
Oxford Cl CA28 .... 187 F5
Oxford Pl 2 LA14 .... 207 B6
Oxford Rd LA14 .... 207 B6
Oxford St
Barrow-in-F LA14 .... 207 A6
Carnforth LA5 .... 213 C3
Millom LA18 .... 202 D4
Ulverston LA12 .... 203 D5
Workington CA14 .... 184 E6
Oxlands LA6 .... 156 B1

P

Pack Horse Ct 5 CA12 .... 192 B3
Pack The CA5 .... 18 F2
Paddock Cl CA7 .... 36 D1
Paddocks The
Great Broughton CA13 .... 63 E6
Thursby CA5 .... 28 F1
Paddock The
Keswick CA12 .... 192 C3
Sedbergh LA10 .... 201 D5
Threlkeld CA12 .... 82 C8
Paddock Way LA7 .... 209 F4
Paddy La LA9 .... 144 D7
Page Bank La LA13 .... 171 C6
Palace La LA11, LA12 .... 153 E6
Palmer Rd CA2 .... 176 A7
Palmer's Ct CA23 .... 188 D3
Palmers Hill LA10 .... 201 C5
Palmers La LA18 .... 202 B5
PANNATT HILL 202 B6
Pannatt Hill LA18 .... 202 B5
PAPCASTLE 190 A5
Papcastle Rd CA13 .... 190 C5
Parade St LA14 .... 206 F3
Parade The LA5 .... 213 A3
Paradise LA16 .... 151 B1
Paradise La LA7 .... 211 E2
Paradise St LA14 .... 207 A3
PARDSHAW 78 D7
PARDSHAW HALL 78 E8
Parham Dr CA2 .... 176 B6
Parham Gr CA2 .... 176 B6
Park Ave
27 Askam in F LA16 .... 162 A8
Barrow-in-F LA13 .... 207 A4
Kendal LA9 .... 200 D3
Seaton CA14 .... 183 B1
Swarthmoor LA12 .... 203 A2
Swarthmoor LA12 .... 203 A3
Windermere LA23 .... 198 E4
PARK BROOM 20 E1
Park Brow CA11 .... 83 D3
Park Cl
Natland LA9 .... 144 A4
Penrith CA11 .... 191 E5
Scotby CA4 .... 30 E6
Windermere LA23 .... 198 E4
Park Cotts LA9 .... 144 A4
Park Dr
Barrow-in-F LA13 .... 207 B4
Stainburn CA14 .... 62 E3
Ulverston LA12 .... 203 E4
Whitehaven CA28 .... 187 D8
Parkend La LA8 .... 143 D3
Park End Rd CA14 .... 184 F5
Parkers Croft CA10 .... 101 C6
Parker St LA14 .... 206 F4
Parkett Hill CA4 .... 30 E6
Park Field LA12 .... 203 A2
Parkfields Rd CA28 .... 76 F2
Park Foot Cvn Site CA10 .... 84 F6
Parkfoot Lodges LA6 .... 169 E3
Park Garth LA12 .... 162 F4
PARKGATE 37 D5
PARKHEAD 53 D7
PARK HEAD 57 E8
Park Head
Brampton CA8 .... 179 B6
1 Workington CA14 .... 184 D6
Parkhead Rd
Brampton CA8 .... 179 B5
Ulverston LA12 .... 203 D1
Parkhill Rd CA3 .... 175 C5
Park Holme CA12 .... 192 B5
PARKHOUSE 175 B6
Park House Animal Farm★ LA13 .... 207 E7
Park House Dr LA7 .... 211 D7
Parkhouse Rd
Barrow-in-F LA13 .... 207 E7
Carlisle CA3 .... 175 C6
Dalton-in-F LA13 .... 205 B1
Parkin Hill CA16 .... 193 C4
Park La
Alston CA9 .... 181 C3
Holme LA6 .... 156 B2
Orton CA10 .... 118 B7
Walney Island LA14 .... 206 C2
Workington CA14 .... 184 D6
Parkland Ave CA1 .... 30 E5
Parkland Dr CA1 .... 30 E4
Parkland Mews CA1 .... 30 E4
Parklands Cres CA11 .... 191 F5
Parklands Dr
Askam in F LA16 .... 162 A8
Egremont CA22 .... 189 D5
Parklands The
Cockermouth CA13 .... 190 B3
Penrith CA11 .... 191 F5
Parklands View CA11 .... 191 F5
Parklands Way CA11 .... 191 F5
Park Links CA26 .... 92 D7
Park Rd
Aspatria CA7 .... 36 D1
Barrow-in-F LA14 .... 204 B3
Bothel CA7 .... 51 A5
Carlisle CA2 .... 176 D4
Grange-o-S LA11 .... 208 D3
Greystoke CA11 .... 69 E5
Millom LA18 .... 202 D4
Milnthorpe LA7 .... 211 B3
Scotby CA4 .... 30 E6
Silverdale LA5 .... 210 D4
Storth LA7 .... 209 E4
Swarthmoor LA12 .... 203 A2
Wigton CA7 .... 180 B3
Windermere LA23 .... 198 F4
Park Road Est CA7 .... 51 A5
Park Road Ind Est LA14 .... 204 B2
Parkside
Carlisle CA3 .... 175 C2
Crosby CA15 .... 49 B5
Park Side LA12 .... 203 A2
Parkside Ave CA13 .... 190 C3
Parkside Bsns Pk LA9 .... 200 E3
Parkside Cl LA12 .... 162 D7
Parkside Dr LA5 .... 209 A1
Parkside Mdw LA9 .... 200 E4
Parkside Rd
Cleator Moor CA25 .... 92 D6
Kendal LA9 .... 200 E3
Park Side Rd LA9 .... 200 F4
Park Sq CA7 .... 180 C3
Park St
Ambleside LA22 .... 195 D6
Frizington CA26 .... 92 D7
Kendal LA9 .... 200 D3
Park Terr
Hallbankgate CA8 .... 23 B2
Kirkby Stephen CA17 .... 199 C4
Leece LA12 .... 171 C8
5 Maryport CA15 .... 182 D6
Silloth CA7 .... 174 C4
Workington CA14 .... 184 F6
Park The
Old Hutton LA8 .... 144 E3
1 Thursby CA5 .... 28 F1
Park View
Arnside LA5 .... 209 B1
Askham CA10 .... 85 D6
Bassenthwaite CA12 .... 66 B7
Carlisle CA1 .... 177 F4
Carnforth LA5 .... 213 C5
Cartmel LA11 .... 153 E1
Egremont CA22 .... 189 D6
Great Asby CA16 .... 103 C4
Whitehaven CA28 .... 186 D2
Park View La CA9 .... 181 E3
Parkview Sch LA13 .... 207 B5
PARK VILLAGE 24 F4
Parrock Gn LA14 .... 204 B1
Parrock Mews LA22 .... 194 B4
Parr St LA9 .... 200 D4
Parry St LA14 .... 206 F4
Parsonage Fold LA7 .... 155 E2
PARSONBY 50 C5
Parsonby Brow CA7 .... 50 C5
Parson's Way LA7 .... 155 F7
PARTON
Whitehaven 186 E5
Wigton 28 A1
Parton Brow CA28 .... 186 D5
Parton Sta CA28 .... 186 D6
Partridge Pl CA2 .... 176 C5
Pascway Terr LA14 .... 204 B1
Pass Of Dunmail Raise CA12, LA22 .... 97 C2
Pasture Houses CA9 .... 60 D8
Pasture La CA7 .... 53 E4
Pasture Rd CA26 .... 77 F1
Pasture The LA7 .... 209 E5
Pasture Wlk CA1 .... 177 F5
PATEGILL 191 F4
Pategill Ct 3 CA11 .... 191 E4
Pategill Farm 2 CA11 .... 191 E4
Pategill Hamlet 4 CA11 .... 191 E4
Pategill Pk CA11 .... 191 E3
Pategill Rd CA11 .... 191 E4
Pategill Sq 9 CA11 .... 191 E4
Pategill Wlk CA11 .... 191 E3
Paternoster Row CA3 .... 214 A2
Patten Garth CA7 .... 49 F8
PATTERDALE 98 D6
Patterdale Ave CA28 .... 91 F7
Patterdale CE Sch CA11 .... 98 D7
Patterdale Cl CA28 .... 91 F7
Patterdale Dr LA14 .... 204 D1
Patterdale Rd LA23 .... 198 D8
Pattinson Cl CA10 .... 85 F6
PATTON BRIDGE 131 E4
Pavilion The CA11 .... 70 D3
Paving Brow CA8 .... 179 C3
Paxton St LA14 .... 206 F3
Pearl Rd CA14 .... 184 C1
Pearson Cl CA24 .... 188 B5
Pearson Ct CA11 .... 191 C3
Pearson La CA16 .... 88 B6
Pearson St CA14 .... 184 D5
Peart Rd
Maryport CA15 .... 182 D4
Workington CA14 .... 184 B4
Peartree Bank LA13 .... 207 E5
Pear Tree Gdns CA13 .... 63 E6
Pear Tree Pk LA6 .... 156 B2
Pear Tree Way CA11 .... 71 C5
Peascod La CA3 .... 214 B3
Pease Close La LA11 .... 153 F5
Peasholmes La LA13 .... 171 C6
Peat Bank LA9 .... 200 B8
Peatfield Rd CA14 .... 183 B3
Peat La LA9 .... 200 F6
Pebbles Rise CA22 .... 107 F6
Pecklewell La CA15 .... 182 F4
Pecklewell Terr 2 CA15 .... 182 E4
Peckmill CA27 .... 91 C2
Peddar Cotts LA11 .... 164 D7
Peel Gdns CA22 .... 188 A3
Peel St CA2 .... 176 D6
Peel Tower (Clifton Hall)★ CA10 .... 71 C2
Pegbank La LA6 .... 168 A8
Peggy Hill LA22 .... 195 D6
Peggy Nut Croft CA10 .... 101 C6
Pegwell La CA14 .... 78 A7
Pelham Dr CA20 .... 108 E4
PELUTHO 36 A8
Pembroke Cl LA13 .... 207 D4
Pembroke Ct LA9 .... 200 C2
Pembroke Pl CA11 .... 191 C7
Pembroke St CA16 .... 193 D6
Penarth St 9 LA14 .... 207 A2
Pendle Dr CA28 .... 187 D8
Pendragon Castle★ CA17 .... 121 A1
Pennine Cl
Hackthorpe CA10 .... 85 F6
Silloth CA7 .... 174 C4
Pennine Gdns
Barrow-in-F LA14 .... 206 F5
Carlisle CA1 .... 177 E4
Pennine Rd CA6 .... 24 C1
Pennine Terr CA10 .... 57 E2
Pennine View
Appleby-in-W CA16 .... 193 C1
Armathwaite CA4 .... 42 C5
Blencarn CA10 .... 73 A6
Carlisle CA1 .... 30 E5
Newbiggin CA11 .... 70 B4
Silloth CA7 .... 174 C4
Skelton CA11 .... 55 B2
Pennine View Cl CA1 .... 30 E5
Pennine Way
Calthwaite CA11 .... 55 E7
Carlisle CA1 .... 177 F4
Penrith CA11 .... 191 E5
Pennine Way Prim Sch CA1 .... 177 F4
PENNINGTON 162 F8
Pennington CE Sch LA12 .... 162 F8
Pennington Cl LA15 .... 205 B2
Pennington Dr CA3 .... 175 E3
Pennington La LA12 .... 162 E7
PENNY BRIDGE 152 D5
Penny Bridge CE Sch LA12 .... 152 E5
Pennygill Rd CA15 .... 183 D8
Pennyhill Pk CA11 .... 191 B7
PENRITH 191 E6
Penrith Campus Univ of Cumbria CA11 .... 70 E6
Penrith Castle★ CA11 .... 191 C4
Penrith Hospl CA11 .... 191 E3
Penrith Ind Est CA11 .... 191 B4
Penrith Mus★ CA11 .... 191 C5
Penrith North Lakes Sta CA11 .... 191 C4
Penrith Pl LA14 .... 207 A3
Penrith Rd CA12 .... 192 C4
Penrith St 13 LA14 .... 207 A3
PENRUDDOCK 69 E2
Penruddock Prim Sch CA11 .... 69 D2
PENTON 4 D4
Penton Cl CA3 .... 175 C3
Penzance St CA24 .... 188 A5
Peppercoats Brow CA13 .... 78 D8
Peppercorn La LA9 .... 200 D4
Pepper Hall Wlk LA18 .... 202 A2
Percy Rd CA2 .... 176 E4
Peregrine Cl 3 CA28 .... 76 F2
Peterfield Rd CA3 .... 175 C5
Peter Gate CA4 .... 31 A2
Peter Green Way LA14 .... 206 E4
Peter La
Carlisle CA2 .... 176 B1
Yealand Conyers LA5 .... 166 E5
Peter's Dr LA18 .... 202 B6
Peter St
Carlisle CA3 .... 214 B3
Whitehaven CA28 .... 186 D1
Workington CA14 .... 184 E5
Petrel Bank LA14 .... 170 C6
Petteril Bank Rd CA1 .... 177 D2
Petteril Bank Sch CA1 .... 177 D1
Petteril Rd CA11 .... 191 C6
Petteril St
Carlisle CA1 .... 177 C6
Silloth CA7 .... 174 C4
Petteril Terr
Carlisle CA1 .... 177 D4

Petteril Terr *continued*
Plumpton CA11 56 A3
Silloth CA7 174 C4
Petton Pl 3 CA20 109 A2
Pheasants Rise CA26 77 F1
Philpin La LA6 159 F1
Phoenix Ct LA14 206 D5
Phoenix Pk CA11 55 B2
Phoenix Rd LA14 206 D5
Phoenix Way LA23 198 E6
PICA 77 C5
Pickles Fold LA7 211 D4
Picture Ho The CA1 214 C1
Piel Castle* LA13 171 B2
PIEL ISLAND 171 B2
Piel St LA13 171 B3
Piel View Gr LA13 207 D3
Pier La LA5 209 B2
Pig La LA11 208 D4
Pikeingthorne LA19 137 B3
Pikestone La CA10 118 A3
Pilgrim St CA14 184 D5
Pillar Rd CA28 187 E4
Pinders La LA6 156 B1
Pine Cl
Grange-o-S LA11 208 C3
Kendal LA9 200 F2
Pinecroft CA3 175 D5
Pine Gr CA10 57 A6
Pine Lake Resort*
LA6 213 F7
Pine Rd LA14 206 F7
Pine Terr CA7 174 C5
Pinetree Rd LA12 203 D3
Pine Vale Cotts CA12 80 E8
Pinewood Dr CA15 182 F5
Pinewoods CA14 77 D6
Pinfold Cl CA13 190 E4
Pinfold Cvn Site LA10 201 E4
Pinfold St CA14 184 F5
Piper La CA10 87 D8
Pipers Cl LA7 209 E4
Pipers Ct 3 CA28 186 D1
Piper's La
Clawthorpe LA6 167 C8
Holme LA6 156 C1
Pitcairn Cres 3 CA15 182 E4
Pit La
Kirkby Lonsdale LA6 157 C1
Lindal in F LA12 162 D7
Pitt Garth LA11 153 F1
Pittwood Rd CA14 185 F6
Plains Rd CA4 178 A3
Plantation Ave LA5 210 C8
PLANTATION BRIDGE 130 C3
Plantation Gr LA5 210 C8
Plaskett's La CA7 180 D4
Players Ct 14 CA11 191 C5
Pleasant View
Hunsonby CA10 57 D2
Wetheral CA4 178 A2
Pleaslands Lonning
CA7 37 A6
Plimsoll Cl 2 CA11 191 C6
Ploughlands La CA17 104 D4
Plover Cl LA16 161 F8
PLUMBLAND 50 D5
Plumbland CE Sch CA7 50 C6
Plumdon Park Ave
DG12 172 D2
PLUMPTON 56 C3
PLUMPTONFOOT 56 A6
Plumpton Sch CA11 56 B4
Plymouth St LA14 206 C1
Police Court Yd 2
CA12 192 B3
Police Sq LA7 211 D4
Pond St LA5 213 C4
Pond Terr LA5 213 C4
PONSONBY 108 F4
Pool Darkin La LA7 211 E1
Poole Rd CA14 184 C2
Pooles Cl CA28 188 A8
Poole St LA14 206 F5
POOLEY BRIDGE 84 F7
Poolside LA18 202 A2
Poplar Bank LA13 207 F5
Poplar Gr LA12 203 E6
Poplar Pl 1 CA11 191 C6
Poplar St CA12 192 B3
Popping La CA17 105 B2
Popplemire La LA8 144 E3
PORT CARLISLE 17 D5
Porter St 9 LA15 205 C5
Port Haverigg Holiday Village LA18 202 B2
Porthouse Rd CA11 191 C3
PORTINSCALE 81 A6
Portland Cres LA14 207 B8
Portland Pl
Carlisle CA1 214 B2
Penrith CA11 191 C5
Portland Sq
Carlisle CA1 214 C2
Workington CA14 184 F6
Portland St CA14 184 F6
Portland Wlk LA14 206 F3
Port Rd CA2 176 E6
Port Road Ind Est CA2 176 D7
Portsmouth St LA14 206 C1
Port St DG12 172 B3
Post Office Row
Gleaston LA12 162 E1
Tunstall LA6 168 D4
Westhouse LA6 169 E4
Post Office Terr CA8 23 E2
Potter Fell Rd
Bowston LA8 130 F4
Kendal LA8 131 A5
Potters' Bank
Kirkoswald CA10 57 B8
Staffield CA10 43 B1
Potters' La CA9 181 F2
Potter's Pl CA2 176 E6
Pottery La CA15 49 A2
Pottery Rd CA28 187 C7
Pottery St 5 LA14 207 B2
Pound Farm Cvn Pk
LA8 130 C2
Pow Ave CA28 187 D7
Pow Beck Ct CA28 187 E4
Powdrake Cres CA6 10 C4
Powerful St LA14 206 C3
POWFOOT 16 A8
POWHILL 27 C6
Pow La CA10 101 C6
Powleys Garth CA10 72 A8
Pow St CA14 184 E6
Powsy Sike CA4 42 F5
Preedy Rd CA14 184 D5
Premier Bsns Pk LA14 206 D2
Prescott Rd CA2 176 E4
Prestonfield Rd
Annan DG12 172 D5
Annan DG12 172 E6
Preston Gdns DG12 172 E6
Preston Pk DG12 172 E6
Preston St
Barrow-in-F LA14 206 F3
Carnforth LA5 213 C4
Whitehaven CA28 187 C8
Priestclose La CA10 86 B5
Priest Hill Forest Trail*
TD9 1 D7
PRIEST HUTTON 167 C4
Priest La
Cartmel LA11 153 F1
Milburn CA10 73 A1
Temple Sowerby CA10 72 F1
Priests Mill* CA7 53 C6
Primrose Bank
Crosby-on-E CA6 20 F2
1 Holme LA6 156 B1
Wigton CA7 180 D1
Primrose Cres CA14 185 A8
Prince Ave LA5 213 D3
Prince Charles Cl
CA11 191 E4
Princes Ave DG12 172 D4
Princes Ct 19 CA11 191 D5
Prince's Ct CA1 177 D2
Prince's Ct CA11 70 D3
Princes Rd CA13 190 C3
Prince's Rd LA23 198 E4
Princess Ave CA14 62 E4
Princess Dr CA15 182 D3
Princess Park Way CA6 19 E2
Princess St
5 Barrow-in-F LA14 207 A6
Carlisle CA1 214 C1
Workington CA14 184 D5
Princes St
Cleator Moor CA23 188 F6
Penrith CA11 191 D4
Prince's St
8 Broughton-in-F LA20 139 A2
Ulverston LA12 203 D5
Prince St LA15 205 C5
Princes Way LA7 211 D7
Prince's Way CA14 184 B5
Princewood Dr LA13 207 F5
Pringle CA7 50 C8
Pringle Bank LA5 213 C8
Printing House Mus The*
CA13 190 C4
Prior Ave 8 DG14 3 D3
Priors Lea LA13 207 C8
Priors Path LA13 207 C4
Priorwood Cl CA2 29 D6
Priory Cl CA26 92 D8
Priory Cotts LA23 198 C7
Priory Cres LA11 165 A6
Priory Ct LA12 203 E4
Priory Dr CA25 188 E6
Priory Gdns LA23 198 D7
Priory Grange LA23 198 D7
Priory La LA11 165 A6
Priory Manor LA23 198 D7
Priory Rd
Carlisle CA2 176 E6
St Bees CA27 91 C2
Ulverston LA12 203 E2
Priory The CA14 78 B8
Proctor's Row CA7 180 D3
Proctor's Sq 13 CA7 180 D3
Promenade
Bowness-on-W LA23 198 C2
Walney Island LA14 206 C3
Walney Island, Vickerstown LA14 206 D1
Promenade The
Arnside LA5 209 B2
Maryport CA15 182 D7
PROSPECT 49 F7
Prospect Ave LA13 207 B6
Prospect Pl CA7 174 B2
Prospect Rd LA13 207 B6
Prospect Row CA23 188 C4
Prospect View CA14 185 D3
Provincial St LA13 207 C3
Pryors Wlk 13 LA16 162 A8
Puddlemire La LA6 156 D3
Pugin St CA2 176 E5
Pump Sq CA17 105 B5
Punton Rd CA3 175 E1
Purser Rd CA14 185 A8
Pye La LA22 194 B5
Pye's Bridge La
Beetham LA7 155 F1
Holme LA6, LA7 156 A2
Pypers Croft LA13 207 C4

Q

Quaggs Rd LA8 143 D2
Quaker Fold LA12 203 C3
Quakers Cl CA10 70 E1
Quakers La CA10 70 F1
Quality Cnr CA14 183 B2
QUALITY CORNER 186 F4
Quantock Gn LA14 206 F5
Quarry Brow
Barrow-in-F LA14 207 A8
Bowness-on-W LA23 198 C3
Quarry Cl CA17 199 C4
Quarry La
Allithwaite LA11 164 F7
Bolton CA16 87 D4
Quarry Rd CA25 188 E7
Quarry Rigg LA23 198 C3
Quarry St CA7 37 C1
Quaysiders LA22 195 D3
Quay St
Harrington CA14 76 E8
Ulverston LA12 203 E5
Whitehaven CA28 186 C1
Quebec Ave CA2 177 A3
Quebec St LA12 203 E5
Queen Elizabeth Gram Sch
CA11 191 C4
Queen Elizabeth Sch
LA6 212 B2
Queen Katherines Ave
LA9 200 E8
Queen Katherine Sch The
LA9 200 E7
Queen Katherine St
LA9 200 D4
Queens Ave CA15 182 D3
Queen's Ave CA14 62 E4
Queensberry Ct LA12 162 E6
Queensberry St DG12 172 C4
Queens Cl CA28 91 F8
Queens Cres CA26 92 D8
Queens Ct 14 LA12 203 D5
Queens Dr
Arnside LA5 209 B1
Carlisle CA3, CA6 175 A4
Egremont CA22 189 C4
Queen's Dr
Carnforth LA5 213 D3
Sedbergh LA10 201 B4
Windermere LA23 198 E4
Queens Lo 16 LA9 200 C4
Queens Pk CA7 36 D1
Queen's Pk LA18 202 B5
Queens Rd CA14 185 C7
Queen's Rd LA9 200 C5
Queen's Sq
Bowness-on-W LA23 198 C2
Kirkby Lonsdale LA6 212 C2
Queen St
Aspatria CA7 50 C8
Barrow-in-F LA14 207 A6
Carlisle CA2 176 E6
Carnforth LA5 213 C3
Cleator Moor CA25 188 D7
Dalton-in-F LA15 205 C5
5 Kendal LA9 200 C4
Maryport CA15 182 D5
Millom LA18 202 D5
5 Penrith CA11 191 D5
Ulverston LA12 203 D5
Whitehaven CA28 186 C1
Whitehaven CA28 187 C8
Workington CA14 184 D5
Queen's Terr LA15 205 C5
Queen's Terr LA6 156 B2
Queensway
Annan DG12 172 D4
Carlisle CA2 176 B4
Quillet The LA5 210 F3
Quintin Pl DG16 173 D5

R

RABY 26 E2
Race Gr LA18 150 C7
Rachael's Ct 21 LA12 203 D5
Raeburn Cres DG16 173 C2
Raefield CA6 10 C3
RAFFLES 176 C6
Raffles Ave CA2 176 C6
RAF Millom Mus*
LA18 149 F2
Raglan Ct 8 LA14 207 B2
Raglan's Ct CA7 174 C4
Raglan St 7 LA14 207 B2
Railton Gdns CA2 176 A4
Railton Yd LA10 201 C5
Railway Cotts
Crosby Garrett CA17 120 A8
Dalston CA5 29 D1
Langwathby CA10 72 A8
Long Marton CA16 88 A7
Newby Bridge LA12 141 E1
Railway Terr
Beck Foot LA8 132 F4
Railway Terr *continued*
Blennerhasset CA7 50 F8
Cockermouth CA13 190 D3
6 Dalton-in-F LA15 205 C4
Garsdale Head LA10 148 D6
Lindal in F LA12 162 E6
1 Maryport CA15 182 E5
Moor Row CA24 188 B6
Seascale CA20 123 A7
RAISBECK 118 E6
Raise Bank CA9 181 C3
Raise Hamlets CA9 181 C3
Raiselands Croft CA11 191 B7
Raiselands Rd CA2 176 D3
Raisthwaite La LA12 140 B2
Rakehead Cl LA12 203 C3
Rake La
Leece LA12 171 C7
Ulverston LA12 203 D3
Rakes La
Marton LA15 162 C7
Walney Island LA14 170 D4
Rakesmoor La LA14 204 D3
Rake The
Bassenthwaite CA12 66 B7
Penny Bridge LA12 152 D5
Raleigh St LA14 206 F4
Ralfland View CA10 101 C5
Rampkin Ho CA16 193 C4
Rampkin Pastures
CA16 193 C4
RAMPSIDE 171 C5
Rampside Rd
Barrow-in-F LA13 207 E2
Roosebeck LA13 171 B7
RAMPSON 106 B4
Ramsay Brow CA14 184 F6
Ramsden Dock Rd
LA14 170 D6
Ramsden Inf Sch LA13 207 A4
Ramsden Sq LA14 206 F3
Ramsden St
Barrow-in-F LA14 207 A3
Carnforth LA5 213 C4
Ramsey Dr CA28 186 E5
Ramsey Pk LA13 207 A4
Ramsgate Cres LA14 206 C2
Randall St CA2 214 A1
Randlaw La CA4, CA8 31 E3
Range Ho LA19 137 A7
Rannerdale Dr CA28 186 E4
Rashdall Rd CA2 176 D3
Ratcliffe Pl 22 CA12 192 B3
RATHER HEATH 130 C3
Ratherheath La LA9 130 D2
Ratherheath Lane Camping & Cvn Site LA8 130 C2
Rating La LA13 207 D7
RATTEN ROW 53 B7
Rattlingate La
Kirkandrews-on-E CA5 19 C1
Moorhouse CA5 29 C8
RAUGHTON HEAD 40 B4
Raughton Head CE Sch
CA5 40 B4
Ravelands Brow CA16 104 B5
Ravencragg CA10 84 D4
Raven Garth LA8 130 B5
Ravenghyll CA10 57 B8
RAVENGLASS 123 F3
Ravenglass & Eskdale Rly*
CA19 124 C6
Ravenglass Railway Mus*
CA18 123 F3
Ravenglass Rd LA14 204 D1
Ravenglass Roman Bath
Ho* CA18 123 F2
Ravenglass Sta CA18 123 F3
Ravenhill La CA28 187 B7
Ravenhill Rd CA28 187 B7
Raven La CA12 192 A8
Raven Nook CA1 177 C5
Raven Pl DG16 173 D3
Ravens Close Brow
LA2 168 F1
Ravenscourt LA11 208 F5
RAVENSEAT 122 C2
Raven St CA1 177 C5
RAVENSTONEDALE 120 A2
Ravenstonedale Endowed
Sch CA17 120 A3
Ravenstone Way CA2 176 A5
RAVENSTOWN 164 C6
Rawes Garth LA8 130 B5
Rawlinson Pl LA15 205 B5
Rawlinson St
Barrow-in-F LA14 207 A3
Dalton-in-F LA15 205 B5
Rawthey Gdns LA10 201 B4
Rayend La LA18 149 D4
Raygarth LA6 212 B3
Raygarth Gdns LA6 212 B3
Raygarth La LA6 212 A3
Rayrigg Gdns LA23 198 E5
Rayrigg Rd LA23 198 C5
Rayrigg Rise LA23 198 C3
Read Dr CA28 186 E3
Reading Rooms The
CA22 188 A3
REAGILL 102 A8
Rectory Cl CA14 185 A8
Rectory Dene CA10 86 E7
Rectory Pl CA14 185 D4
Rectory Rd
Bowness-on-W LA23 198 C1
Castle Carrock CA8 32 D6
Rectory Sq CA14 185 D4
Red Bank LA22 113 D4
Red Bank Rd LA22 194 B3
Red Bank Sq CA2 177 A4
Red Bank Terr CA2 177 A4
Red Beck Pk CA25 188 F6
Red Bridge La LA5 210 F4
Red Court Cvn Pk LA5 213 C3
RED DIAL 38 B5
Red Dial Cotts CA7 38 B5
Redding Brow LA11 164 E7
Red Gables CA1 214 C2
Redgate La CA17 105 D2
Red Gate La LA11 154 D4
RED HILLS 191 A1
Red Hills Bsns Pk
CA11 191 A2
Red Hills Rd LA5 209 A1
Red La
Bardsea LA12 163 D6
Ulverston LA12 163 C6
Red Ley La LA14 206 B5
Red Lion Yd LA22 197 E5
Red Lonning CA28 91 F8
Red Lonning Ind Est
CA28 186 F1
Redmayne Ave LA14 207 B8
Redmayne Cl CA7 180 D4
Redmayne Ct CA7 180 D4
Redmayne Dr LA5 213 E4
Redmayne Rd CA17 199 C6
Redoak Ave LA13 207 E4
Red Peth NE49 24 F6
Red Pike Cl CA28 76 F1
Red River Wlk LA13 207 D4
Redruth Dr LA5 213 B3
Redshaw Ave LA13 207 E2
Red Tarn Rd LA9 200 F1
Red Terr CA7 50 F8
Redwater Gdns LA13 207 D4
Redwood Dr CA3 175 E2
Reedlands Rd CA14 184 C4
Reeds Gdns LA12 162 F4
Reed's La 3 CA7 180 D3
Reeth Rd CA2 176 A5
Regent Ho CA2 176 C7
Regent St CA2 177 B4
Regent The 6 LA11 208 D4
Reiver Ct CA3 175 D3
Reiver Pl CA3 175 D3
RENWICK 43 F2
Rescue Station Cotts
CA14 62 F1
Reservoir Rd LA8 145 B5
Reservoir St 1 LA14 207 A5
RESTON 130 A5
Reston Cotts LA8 130 A5
Retreat The CA28 187 E7
Reynolds Pl LA14 206 F6
Rheda Cl CA26 92 C7
Rheda Pk CA26 92 C7
Rheda Terr CA25 92 C7
Rheged Exhibition &
Discovery Ctr* CA11 70 E3
Ribble Gdns LA14 206 B3
RIBBLEHEAD 160 C2
Ribblehead Sta LA6 160 B1
Ribblehead Viaduct*
LA6 160 A2
Ribton Moor Side
CA28 187 E6
Richardson St CA2 176 E3
Richard Thornton's CE
Prim Sch LA6 169 B3
Richmond Cl CA14 62 E2
Richmond Cres CA27 91 C2
Richmond Croft CA14 184 C2
Richmond Gdns LA18 150 A1
Richmond Gn CA2 176 B5
Richmond Hill Rd CA28 91 F7
Richmond Rd CA14 184 D2
Richmond St LA18 202 D4
Richmond Terr
Barrow-in-F LA14 207 B6
Ulverston LA12 203 D4
Whitehaven CA28 187 C8
RICKERBY 177 D8
Rickerby Ct CA1 177 C8
Rickerby Ho CA3 30 C8
Rickerby La CA12 81 A6
Rickergate CA3 214 B3
Rickettrae LA8 142 D7
Riddings La LA12 162 F1
Ride The CA16 88 D8
Ridgemount 7 CA15 182 D6
Ridgemount Rd CA1 177 D2
Ridge The DG12 17 D8
Ridgevale Terr CA8 179 D5
Ridgeway LA11 164 F7
Ridley Gdns 5 CA8 179 C5
Ridley Pl CA2 177 A3
Ridley Rd CA2 177 A3
Rifle Terr CA21 108 C5
Riggs Cl LA11 208 E5
Riggside CA11 191 E4
Riggside Mews CA11 70 D5
Rigg St CA2 176 E6
Rigmaden Ct LA6 157 E8
Rigney Bank LA7 211 D3
Rimington Way CA11 191 F4
Rinkfield LA9 200 D2
Risedale Fold LA11 208 B2
Risedale Ho 3 LA14 207 C8
Risedale Rd LA13 207 B3
RISEHOW 182 B2
Risehow Ind Est CA15 182 B1
Rise The CA28 187 C7
Risingside LA13 207 C5
Risman Pl 7 CA14 184 E6
Ritson Cl CA3 175 D4

Ritson Row CA7 49 D6
Ritson St CA14 184 E5
Ritson Wharf CA15 182 C5
Ritz Sh Ctr CA14 184 E6
Riverbank Ct 11 CA3 175 B1
River Bank Rd LA9 200 C1
Riverdale Ct LA9 200 D2
Riverdale Dr CA13 190 D2
River Pk DG12 172 B4
Riversdale CA8 14 D1
Riverside
Buckabank CA5 40 B8
Caldbeck CA7 53 C6
Great Clifton CA14 63 A4
Kirkby Stephen CA17 199 D6
Riverside Bsns Pk LA9 200 D2
Riverside Cotts
Ambleside LA22 195 C4
Skelwith Bridge LA22 113 E2
Riverside Ct
Appleby-in-W CA16 193 C6
Keswick CA12 192 A4
Riverside Dr CA22 189 E8
Riverside Flats CA12 192 B4
Riverside Gdns LA13 207 D3
Riverside Lodge CA12 192 B4
Riverside Pk 9 DG14 3 D3
Riverside Terr 2 CA13 190 C4
Riverside View CA16 103 B4
Riverside Way CA1 177 D6
Riverside Wlk DG12 172 B3
River St CA1 177 C6
River View
Carlisle CA2 176 F3
Stainburn CA14 62 E4
Rivington Pk CA16 193 D6
Roachburn Cotts CA8 23 E2
Roadend DG14 4 A5
ROADHEAD 5 D1
ROA ISLAND 171 B3
Roa Island Rd LA13 171 B4
Roanhead La LA14 207 A8
Roanlands Brow LA18 150 D8
Roatary Way CA1 177 F7
Robby Lea Dr LA9 144 B4
Robert Chance Gdns
CA2 176 C3
Robert Ferguson Prim Sch
CA2 176 F4
Robertlands La CA10 58 A7
Robert Owen Ave CA25 188 F6
Robert Owen Pl CA25 188 F6
Roberts Ct LA5 213 C8
Robert St
Barrow-in-F LA14 207 A3
Carlisle CA2 214 B1
Robin Croft LA2 168 A1
Robin La LA23 114 E1
Robinson Ave CA2 177 B3
Robinson Pl LA23 198 C2
Robinson Row LA18 202 B5
Robinson St
Carlisle CA2 177 B4
3 Penrith CA11 191 C6
Workington CA14 184 D5
Robinson's Terr 3
CA15 182 F4
Robinson Yd CA11 191 C4
Robins Wood CA3 175 E2
Robraine LA6 212 C1
Robson Ct CA11 70 C4
Rochester Pl 4 LA13 207 C3
ROCKCLIFFE 19 D4
Rockcliffe CE Sch CA6 19 C4
ROCKCLIFFE CROSS 19 B5
Rockery Terr 6 LA11 208 C4
Rock Farm Cl CA13 49 E2
Rockland Rd LA11 208 C4
Rock Terr LA5 209 B2
Rock View LA9 200 C4
Rockwell Gdns LA11 208 C5
Rockwood 8 LA11 208 C4
Roddan Terr CA7 174 B3
Roding Gn LA14 206 B3
Rodney St LA14 206 F4
Rogerfield CA12 192 C2
ROGER GROUND 197 E3
Roger Row LA9 130 F2
Romanby Cl CA3 175 E1
Roman Rd
Appleby-in-W CA16 193 E5
Penrith CA11 191 E5
Roman Way 3 CA3 175 E1
Romany Way CA16 193 C7
Romely Pl CA13 190 C3
Rome St CA2 214 B1
Romney Ave
Dalton-in-F LA15 205 A5
Kendal LA9 200 D2
Romney Ct LA9 200 D3
Romney Gdns LA9 200 D3
Romney Grange LA22 195 D3
Romney Pk LA15 205 A5
Romney Rd
Barrow-in-F LA14 206 F6
Dalton-in-F LA15 205 C4
Kendal LA9 200 D3
Roods Ct CA10 57 B8
Roods Dr CA10 57 B8
Roods Pl CA10 57 B8
Roods The LA5 213 D8
ROOKBY 105 C1
ROOKING 98 E7
ROOSE 207 F3
ROOSEBECK 171 D6
ROOSECOTE 207 F2
Roosecote Terr LA13 207 E3
Roose Cotts LA13 207 E3
Roose Farm La LA13 207 E3
ROOSE GATE 207 D2
Roose Rd LA13 207 D3
Roose Sch LA13 207 E3
Roose Sta LA13 207 E3
Roper Ct CA28 187 C8
Roper St
Cleator Moor CA23 188 F5
Maryport CA15 182 C4
Penrith CA11 191 D4
Whitehaven CA28 186 C1
Workington CA14 184 E6
Roper Terr CA14 185 A8
Ropery St CA15 182 C4
Rose Acre La LA5 166 F5
Rosebank
Hensingham CA28 187 F6
Stainton CA11 70 D3
Rosebank Cl CA4 178 D7
Rosebank Cotts CA5 40 A5
Rosebank Ct DG16 173 D4
Rosebank Terr DG12 172 C4
Roseberry St CA14 184 E5
Rosebery Rd CA3 175 D1
Rose Cswy CA5 40 B5
Rose Ct CA1 214 C1
Rose Garth CA13 190 E3
Rose Gate CA4 30 F7
Rose Gdns CA14 77 D5
Rosehill CA8 14 D1
Rose Hill
Gilsland CA8 14 D1
Harrington CA14 76 E8
Rosehill Dr CA2 176 D3
Rose Hill Gr LA7 209 F6
Rosehill Ind Est CA1 177 F6
Rose La CA13 190 E2
Rosemary Cl CA28 186 F3
Rosemary La
Carlisle CA3 214 B3
Great Clifton CA14 63 B4
4 Kendal LA9 200 C5
Whitehaven CA28 186 C1
Workington CA14 184 F5
Rosemede Ave LA9 200 D7
Rosemount Cres DG12 172 E5
Roseneath CA28 76 F4
Rose Paddock CA8 31 E6
Rose St
Annan DG12 172 D4
Carlisle CA2 177 B4
Rose Terr CA12 192 C4
Rosetrees La CA6 9 E2
Rosevale CA1 177 F4
Rosevine Terr DG12 172 C1
ROSLEY 39 C4
Rosley CE Sch CA7 39 B6
Rosomond Ct DG16 173 D2
Rosse Field LA13 207 D3
ROSSGILL 100 F7
ROSSIDE 203 A6
Rosside LA12 203 A6
Ross View CA28 186 E6
ROSTHWAITE
Broughton in Furness 139 D5
Keswick 96 C5
Rothay Rd LA22 195 C5
Rothay Road Ind Est
LA22 195 C5
Rother Gn LA14 206 B4
Rotherwood LA23 198 E4
Rothesay St LA14 206 F1
ROTTINGTON 91 B4
Rottington Rd
Millom LA18 202 D4
Sandwith CA28 187 A1
ROUGHSIKE 5 E2
Round Cl 6 CA28 76 F2
Round Close Pk CA28 76 F2
ROUNDTHWAITE 118 A2
ROW
Kendal 143 A4
Melmerby 58 C1
Rowan Ave LA12 203 D3
ROWANBURN 3 F3
Rowan Cl CA14 184 E3
Rowan Ct
Ambleside LA22 195 C5
Penrith CA11 191 E5
Rowan Dr LA13 207 E4
Rowan Garth LA6 212 C2
Rowan Side LA11 208 B2
Rowans The CA22 189 C6
Rowantree Cl CA28 186 E4
Rowan Tree Cres LA9 144 C7
ROW BROW 49 C3
Row Brow Pk CA15 49 B3
Rowcliffe La 21 CA11 191 D5
ROWE HEAD 162 F8
Rowe Head Ct LA12 162 F8
Rowell La LA7 156 A5
ROW END 104 D1
Rowe Terr CA14 184 C3
Rowgate CA17 199 C4
Row La LA8 143 A4
Rowntree Cres 8 CA28 76 F2
Rowntree Gdns CA22 189 E7
ROWRAH 77 F1
Rowrah Rd CA26 77 F1
Row Rd LA8 143 A4
Row The
Crosby-on-E CA6 20 F2
Silverdale LA5 210 E3
Spark Bridge LA12 152 D7
Royal Arc CA17 199 D6
Royal Dr CA22 189 D4
Royal Ho LA6 212 C2
Royal Oak 7 CA12 192 B3
Rubbybanks Rd CA13 190 D3
Ruby Rd CA14 184 D1
RUCKCROFT 42 F3
Rudchester Cl CA2 176 A6
Rudds Ct 15 CA28 186 C1
Rueberry Dr CA20 123 B7
Rufford Dr LA11 208 C4
Rufus Ho CA3 214 A3
Rufus La LA12 203 A3
Rum Story The (Mus)*
CA28 186 C1
Rupert St LA5 213 C5
Ruskin Ave
Coniston LA21 196 A4
Dalton-in-F LA15 205 B3
Ruskin Cl
High Harrington CA14 185 D8
Kendal LA9 200 E2
Millom LA18 202 B4
Ruskin Dr
Kirkby Lonsdale LA6 212 C2
Whitehaven CA28 187 F8
Workington CA14 184 F4
Ruskin Mus* LA21 196 A4
Ruskin Pl CA25 188 B8
Ruskin Terr 14 LA14 207 B2
Rusland Ave LA14 207 A7
Rusland Cres LA12 203 C2
Rusland Dr LA15 205 C4
Rusland Pk LA9 200 F5
Russell Rd LA5 213 D3
Ruthella St CA2 176 D7
Ruth Lancaster James
Cottage Hospl CA9 181 D3
RUTHWAITE 51 F3
Rutland Ave CA28 187 F4
Rutland St LA14 206 F5
Rutter Force* CA16 103 C6
RYDAL 114 A5
Rydal Ave
Barrow-in-F LA14 204 D1
Maryport CA15 182 E5
Whitehaven CA28 187 B6
Rydal Cl
Dalton-in-F LA15 205 B4
Millom LA18 202 C4
Wigton CA7 180 A3
Rydal Cres CA11 191 D3
Rydal Ct CA11 191 D3
Rydal Dr CA13 190 F4
Rydal Mount LA9 200 C6
Rydal Mount & Gardens*
LA22 114 A5
Rydal Pl CA1 214 C1
Rydal Rd
Ambleside LA22 195 C6
Kendal LA9 200 F6
Ulverston LA12 203 E4
Rydal St
Carlisle CA1 214 C1
Frizington CA26 92 D8
Workington CA14 184 D6
Rydal View LA22 195 C6
Rye Cl CA2 30 B3
Rye Hill Cres CA15 183 C8
Ryehill Pk CA6 20 F8
Rye Hill Rd CA15 183 C8
Ryehills Rd CA7 174 E8
Ryley Field Rd LA7 211 D4

S

Sacred Heart RC Prim Sch
LA14 207 B2
Saddleback View CA12 82 C7
Saddler Nook La LA6 168 C8
SADGILL 116 A4
St Aidan's High Sch
Specialist Sports Coll
CA1 214 C2
St Aidan's Rd CA1 177 C7
St Albans Row CA3 214 B2
St Andrew's Churchyard 14
CA11 191 D5
St Andrews Cl CA1 177 E6
St Andrew's Pl
Gretna DG16 173 C2
16 Penrith CA11 191 D5
St Andrews Rd CA14 62 F3
St Andrew's St 5 LA14 206 F1
St Andrew's View 13
CA11 191 D5
St Anne's Cl LA22 195 D6
St Annes Ct 5 CA3 175 B1
St Anne's Ct LA22 195 D6
St Anne's Hospl CA16 193 C5
St Anne's Sch LA23 129 B7
St Ann's Cres CA3 175 C2
St Ann's Rd CA3 175 B1
St Anthony's Cl LA7 211 D4
St Anthony's Hill LA7 211 D4
St Augusta View CA3 175 B1
St Austell Pl LA5 213 B2
St Bede's RC Prim Sch
CA2 176 D5
ST BEES 91 D3
St Bees Dr LA14 204 D1
St Bees Head Nature
Reserve* CA28 91 A4
St Bees Rd CA28 187 D3
St Bees Sch CA27 91 D3
St Bees Sch (Abbots Ct)
CA27 91 C3
St Bee's Sta CA27 91 D2
St Bees Vill Prim Sch
CA27 91 D2
St Bega's CE Prim Sch
CA19 124 E7
St Begh's RC Jun Sch
CA28 187 D8
St Benedict's RC High Sch
CA28 91 F8
St Bernard's RC High Sch
LA13 207 D7
St Bridget's CE Sch
CA13 63 E5
St Bridget's CE Sch
CA28 186 D5
St Bridgets Ct CA20 108 E5
St Bridget's La CA22 189 D6
St Bridget's RC Prim Sch
CA22 189 D6
St Catherine's RC Prim Sch
CA11 191 C6
St Catherin's Ct 11
CA11 191 C6
St Columba's RC Prim Sch
LA14 206 C2
St Columba's RC Sch
DG12 172 E4
St Cuthbert's Ct CA1 214 C2
St Cuthbert's La CA3 214 B2
St Cuthberts Pl CA11 71 F7
St Cuthbert's RC Prim Sch
CA7 180 D4
St Cuthbert's RC Prim Sch
LA23 198 E4
St Cuthbert's RC Sch
CA1 177 E6
St David's Rd LA12 203 D6
St Edmunds Pk CA2 176 A4
St Francis Gdns LA14 206 F7
St Gabrel's Ct CA1 214 C3
St George's CE Sch
LA14 207 A2
St George's Cres CA3 214 A4
St George's Rd LA18 202 C5
St George's Sq 8
LA14 207 A2
St George's Terr
Millom LA18 202 C5
Whitehaven CA28 186 D2
St George's Wlk LA9 200 D5
St Gregory & St Patrick's
RC Com Sch CA28 187 E6
St Gregory's RC Prim Sch
CA14 184 E3
ST HELENS 183 B6
St Helen's LA14, LA15 204 F6
St Helens Ave CA15 183 C8
St Helen's Bsns Pk
CA14 62 C5
St Helens Cl CA13 190 E4
St Helens La CA15 183 A6
St Helens St CA13 190 E4
St Herbert's CE Prim Sch
CA12 192 C4
St Herbert St CA12 192 C3
St James' Ave CA2 176 E5
St James' CE Inf Sch
CA28 186 D1
St James' CE Jun Sch
Barrow-in-F LA14 206 E4
Whitehaven CA28 186 D1
St James RC Prim Sch
LA18 202 D5
St James' Rd CA2 176 E5
St James's Ct 2 CA28 186 D1
St James's Dr LA6 167 B7
St John's Ave LA5 210 C3
St Johns Cl CA4 31 B1
St John's Cl
Carlisle CA2 177 B2
Cleator Moor CA25 188 D7
St John's Cres CA11 70 D3
St John's Ct CA1 214 C1
St John's Ct CA28 187 F6
St John's Ct CA11 70 D3
St John's Ct CA14 184 E6
St John's Gdns LA23 198 D4
St John's Gr LA5 210 C3
ST JOHN'S IN THE
VALE 82 B5
St John's Rd
Annan DG12 172 C3
Stainton CA11 70 D3
Thornhill CA22 189 E2
St John's St CA12 192 B3
St John's Terr CA24 91 F4
St John's View LA8 144 E3
St Josephs Ct CA1 177 E6
St Joseph's Gdns CA1 177 D6
St Joseph's RC High Sch,
Bsns & Enterprise Coll
CA14 184 E5
St Joseph's RC Prim Sch
Cockermouth CA13 190 C3
Frizington CA26 92 D8
St Kentigerns Cl CA12 192 A5
St Kentigerns Ct CA7 50 C8
St Kentigerns Way CA7 50 C8
St Lawrence La CA5 18 F1
St Leonard's Cl CA13 190 C4
St Leonard's La CA13 190 C5
St Luke's Ave LA13 207 C2
St Luke's Rd LA18 150 A1
St Luke's St LA13 207 C3
St Margaret Mary's RC
Prim Sch CA2 177 B2
St Mark's CE Prim Sch
LA9 144 B4
St Marks Cl CA3 175 D2
St Marks Fold LA9 144 B3
St Martin's Cl 3 CA8 179 B4
St Martins Ct LA21 196 A4
St Martin's Ct 1 CA8 179 B4
St Martin's Dr CA8 179 B4
St Martin's Par LA23 198 C2
St Martin's Pl LA23 198 C2
St Mary's CE Inf Sch
LA23 198 E4
St Marys CE Prim Sch
LA6 212 B2
St Mary's Ct CA14 184 D3
St Mary's Garth LA12 162 F5
St Mary's Gate CA3 214 A2
St Mary's Gn LA8 142 F6
St Mary's La LA22 195 D5
St Mary's Mews 8
LA12 203 D6
St Mary's Pk LA23 198 D6
St Mary's RC Prim Sch
CA14 185 A8
St Mary's RC Prim Sch
LA12 203 D4
St Mary's RC Prim Sch
CA28 187 B6
St Mary's Rd LA13 207 D5
St Matthew's CE Sch
CA7 36 B3
St Matthew's Mews 3
LA14 207 A5
St Mellion Cl 2 CA3 175 B1
St Michael's CE Prim Sch
CA7 51 A6
St Michael's CE Prim Sch
CA5 29 E1
St Michael's Inf Sch
CA14 184 D6
St Michaels La CA16 193 D5
St Michaels Rd LA13 171 B5
St Michael's Rd CA14 184 E5
St Monica's Prep Sch Ltd
CA3 175 C1
St Mungo's Pk CA7 36 C1
St Nicholas Ave CA15 183 C8
St Nicholas Bridges
CA2 177 B4
St Nicholas Gate Trad Est
CA1 214 C1
St Nicholas St CA1 214 C1
St Ninian's Ave CA2 177 C1
St Ninian's Ct CA2 177 C2
St Ninian's Rd CA2 177 C2
St Oswalds CE Prim Sch
LA9 130 F2
St Oswald's View LA9 130 F2
St Patrick's CE Sch
LA8 156 D8
St Patricks RC Prim Sch
CA14 184 E7
St Patrick's RC Prim Sch
CA25 188 E5
St Patrick's Rd LA14 206 E2
St Paul's Ave CA26 92 D7
St Paul's Ave CA14 183 B2
St Paul's CE Jun Sch
LA14 207 B7
St Pauls Mews 3
LA14 207 B6
St Paul's Sq CA1 214 B2
St Peters Cl CA3 175 D4
St Peters Dr CA3 175 C4
St Pierre Ave CA3 175 B1
St Pius X RC Prim Sch
LA14 206 E7
St Quintin Ave LA13 207 C5
St Stephen's St CA2 214 B1
St Thomas's CE Prim Sch
LA9 200 C7
St Thomas's Cross
CA22 189 F5
St Ursula's Convent High
Sch CA7 180 D4
St Vincent St 9 LA14 206 F3
Salford Terr CA22 189 E6
Salisbury Ct CA14 184 C3
Salisbury Pl 5 LA23 198 E5
Salisbury Rd CA2 177 B4
Salisbury St CA14 184 C3
SALKELD DYKES 57 A3
Salkeld Rd
Great Salkeld CA11 57 A3
Langwathby CA10 71 F8
Penrith CA11 191 D8
Plumpton CA11 56 F2
Sally Scot's Cnr CA5 28 F1
Salmoor Way CA15 182 C5
SALTA 35 C4
SALT COATES 26 D4
SALTCOATS 123 E4
Saltcoats Cvn Pk CA19 123 E4
SALTERBECK 184 C1
Salterbeck Dr CA14 185 A8
Salterbeck Rd CA14 184 C1
Salterbeck Terr CA14 184 B1
Salterbeck Trad Est
CA14 184 D1
Salter Lonning CA7 54 A4
Salterwath Cl CA7 49 F7
SALTHOUSE 207 B2
Salthouse Gdns LA13 207 D3
Salthouse Mills Bsns Ctr
LA13 207 D2
Salthouse Rd
Barrow-in-F LA13 207 C2
Barrow-in-F, Salthouse
LA14 207 B2
Millom LA18 202 C6

Salt Lake Cotts LA6 160 C1
Salt Marsh Cvn Pk
LA14 170 C6
Saltom Rd CA28 187 B7
Saltpie La CA10 118 B6
Salt Pie La LA6 212 C2
Sampool La LA8 155 D7
Samuel King's Sch
CA9 181 D3
Sand Aire Ho 12 LA9 200 D5
SANDALE 52 B7
Sandalwood Cl LA13 207 F4
Sand Croft CA11 191 D6
Sanderling La LA15 205 C4
Sanderson Cl CA3 175 C4
Sanderson Pk CA25 188 D8
Sandersons Croft CA10 87 E8
Sandes Ave LA9 200 D6
Sandes Ct LA9 200 D6
Sandes' Hospital Cotts 12
LA9 200 C5
SANDFORD 104 A7
Sandford Fold CA16 104 B7
SAND GATE 164 C6
Sandgate
Kendal LA9 200 E6
11 Penrith CA11 191 D5
Sandgate Ct
Long Marton CA16 88 A7
6 Penrith CA11 191 D5
Sandgate Sch LA9 200 E6
Sandhall LA12 163 D8
Sandhall Cotts LA12 163 D7
Sandham La LA18 150 A1
Sandhill CA10 57 B8
Sandhills Ct 8 CA28 186 C1
Sandhills La 9 CA28 186 D1
Sandhurst Dr CA28 187 F8
Sand La
Flimby CA15 183 C8
Warton LA5 213 B6
Sandpiper Cl 34 LA16 162 A8
Sandringham Ave CA28 91 F8
Sandringham Cl LA14 207 A6
Sandscale Cotts LA14 204 B8
Sandscale Haws Nature
Reserve* LA14 161 D6
Sandscale Terr LA14 204 B1
Sands Cl LA12 203 D2
Sands Cotts CA8 179 C5
Sandsfield Rd CA2 29 D6
SANDSIDE 211 A2
SAND SIDE 151 B5
Sandside LA12 163 D8
Sandside Lodge Sch
LA12 163 D8
Sandside Rd LA5, LA7 209 D3
Sands Rd LA12 203 E2
Sands The CA16 193 D5
SANDWITH 187 A2
Sandy Gap La LA14 206 B1
Sandy Gr CA22 189 D6
Sandy La
23 Askam in F LA16 162 A8
Broadwath CA8 178 D3
Great Corby CA4 178 D2
Shap CA10 101 C6
Sandylands La LA13 207 C6
Sandylands Rd LA9 200 E6
Sandy Lonning CA15 182 D4
SANDYSIKE 20 A8
SANTON 124 B8
Santon CA19 124 A8
SANTON BRIDGE 124 C8
Santon Way CA20 123 B8
Sark Cl CA3 175 C4
Sarkfoot Cl DG16 173 D3
Sarkfoot Rd DG16 173 D3
Sarkside Pl DG16 173 D5
Sarsfield Rd CA14 184 C2
SATTERTHWAITE 141 B7
Sattery La LA21 140 B8
Saul's Dr LA5 210 A8
Saunders Cl LA14 206 C3
Saves La LA16 162 A8
Savinhill Rd
Row LA8 143 A4
Row LA8 143 B3
Savoy Gdns LA12 203 C2
Sawmill Cl LA9 200 F5
Sawmill La
Brampton CA8 179 C5
Kendal LA9 200 E5
Sawrey Ct 2 LA20 139 A2
Sayle La CA16 103 B3
Scafell Cl
Cockermouth CA13 190 F4
Whitehaven CA28 187 E6
Scafell Dr LA9 200 F2
Scalebarrow CA27, CA22 91 C3
Scalebeck Ct CA14 184 E5
Scaleber La LA6 212 D8
SCALEBY 20 F6
Scaleby Cl CA2 177 B1
Scale Force* CA13 94 D8
Scalegate Rd CA2 177 B2
Scalegill Pl CA24 91 F5
Scalegill Rd CA24 188 A5
Scale Hill CA2 176 C2
SCALES
Kirkoswald 43 C1
Ulverston 163 A3
Scalesceugh Gdns CA4 41 C8
Scales Cl LA15 205 B2
Scales View LA18 202 A5
Scale Villas CA20 123 A8
Scarbarrow La LA12 171 C8
Scar Foot LA8 131 C2
Scar House La LA22 197 F6
SCARNESS 66 B5
SCARROWHILL 32 A1
Scarrows La CA10 57 A7
Scarth Rd LA14 204 C3
Scar View Rd LA9 144 B4
Scattergate CA16 193 C4
Scattergate Cl CA16 193 C4
Scattergate Cres CA16 193 C4
Scattergate Gn CA16 193 C4
Scaurbank Rd CA3 175 B1
Scaurbank Terr 6
CA3 175 B1
Scaur Cl CA10 57 A6
Scaur La CA10 57 A6
Scaur Terr CA10 118 B3
Scaur The CA6 10 B3
Scawfell Ave CA14 184 E4
Scawfell Cres CA20 123 B8
Scawfell Rd CA2 176 E5
Scawfield CA14 185 C8
Scaw Rd CA14 185 D8
SCAWS 191 E6
Scaws Dr CA11 191 E6
SCEUGH 85 B2
Schneider Rd LA14 206 F7
Schneider Sq 11 LA14 206 F3
Scholars Gn CA7 180 E2
School Brow
Appleby-in-W CA16 193 D6
Brigham CA13 63 F5
Moresby Parks CA28 76 F2
School Cl
Broughton Moor CA15 63 C8
Maryport CA15 182 D4
School Dr CA15 182 A1
School Hill LA11 154 C3
School Hos LA7 156 C6
Schoolhouse Ct 8
CA28 186 D1
Schoolhouse La 9
CA28 186 C1
Schoolhouse The 8
CA12 192 A4
School Knott Cl LA23 198 F4
School Knott Dr LA23 198 F4
School La
Bothel CA7 51 A6
Kirkby Stephen CA17 120 C6
Rockcliffe CA6 19 C4
Silloth CA7 174 C5
Staveley LA8 130 B5
School Rd
Carlisle CA1 177 E3
2 Thursby CA5 28 F1
School St
25 Askam in F LA16 162 A8
10 Barrow-in-F LA14 207 A3
Carlisle CA1 177 C5
Moor Row CA24 188 A5
School Terr
Alston CA9 181 D4
Lindal in F LA12 162 D7
Millom LA18 202 C4
Parton CA28 186 D6
Schoolwaters LA15 205 B3
Schooner St LA14 206 F1
Schoose Cotts CA14 62 E2
Scot Brow LA23 114 F2
SCOTBY 30 F5
Scotby CE Prim Sch
CA4 30 E6
Scotby Cl CA1 177 F5
Scotby Gdns CA1 177 E5
Scotby Grange CA4 30 E6
Scotby Green Steading
CA4 30 F6
SCOTBY HOLMES 30 E8
Scotby Rd CA4 30 F6
Scotch Jeans LA10 145 E6
Scotch St
Carlisle CA3 214 B3
Port Carlisle CA7 17 D5
Whitehaven CA28 187 C8
Scotgate Cvn Pk CA12 80 F6
Scotland Rd
Carlisle CA3 175 D2
Carnforth LA5 213 D5
Penrith CA11 191 C6
Scotraby Brow CA7 36 C4
Scots Croft CA14 63 C4
SCOTSDIKE 10 C8
Scott's St DG12 172 D3
Scott St
Barrow-in-F LA14 206 F3
Newcastleton or Copshaw
Holm TD9 1 B6
SCOUT GREEN 117 F6
Screel View CA28 186 D5
Scroggie Mdw DG12 172 C2
Scroggs Cl LA8 130 B5
Scroggs La LA9 200 C1
SCUGGATE 4 C1
Sculpture Valley* CA4 40 E2
SCURGILL 189 F4
Scurgill Terr CA22 189 F4
Seacote Cvn Pk CA7 174 E7
Seacroft CA20 123 A7
Seacroft Cvn Pk LA13 171 F8
Seacroft Dr CA27 91 D2
Seadown Dr CA14 185 D8
Seafield Rd DG12 172 F2
Seaforth Ave DG12 172 D3
Seaforth Pk DG12 172 D3
Sea La CA22 107 E7
Sealford La
Hutton Roof LA6 157 A2
Lupton LA6 156 F2
Sea Mill La CA27 91 D2
Seams The 15 CA12 192 B3
SEASCALE 123 B8
Seascale Pk CA20 123 B8
Seascale Prim Sch
CA20 123 B8
Seascale Sta CA20 123 A8
Seat Hill CA10 57 A6
SEATHWAITE
Coniston 126 C2
Keswick 95 F3
Seathwaite Ave CA28 187 D4
Seathwaite Cl LA18 202 C4
Seathwaite La LA22 195 E6
Seathwaite Rd LA14 204 D1
SEATLE 153 E6
Seatle La LA11 153 E6
SEATOLLER 96 A4
Seatoller Cl CA2 176 C3
Seatoller Pl LA14 204 D1
SEATON 183 C2
Seaton CE Jun Sch
CA14 183 A1
Seaton Inf Sch CA14 183 B2
Seaton Pk CA14 183 A1
Seaton Rd
Broughton Moor CA15 63 B8
Seaton CA14 62 E4
Sea View
Haverigg LA18 202 A2
Millom LA18 202 B5
Oughterside CA7 49 F7
7 Ulverston LA12 203 D6
Workington CA14 184 C7
Seaview Dr CA28 187 F8
Sea View Pl CA25 188 E6
Sea View Rd CA28 186 D2
Sea View Terr CA27 91 D2
SEAVILLE 26 B4
SEBERGHAM 53 F8
Second Moss La LA8 143 C5
SEDBERGH 201 A5
Sedbergh Dr LA9 200 F5
Sedbergh Prim Sch
LA10 201 D4
Sedbergh Rd LA9 200 E5
Sedbergh Sch LA10 201 C4
Sedgefield Rd LA13 207 E4
SEDGWICK 144 A2
Sedgwick Ct
Grange-o-S LA11 208 C2
Kendal LA9 200 C2
Sedgwick Ho LA8 144 A2
Sedgwick Mews LA8 144 A1
Seedfield LA8 130 C4
Seed Howe LA8 130 B5
Seg La LA12 162 F7
Selby Terr
Hensingham CA28 187 F6
Maryport CA15 182 D5
Seldom Seen CA11 83 B1
Selina Terr 5 CA15 182 F4
Sella Brow LA20 138 E7
Sellafield Sta CA20 108 C2
SELSIDE 131 C6
Selside CE Prim Sch
LA8 131 C5
Semple Rd CA1 177 E2
Senhouse Cl 20 CA14 184 D6
Senhouse Roman Mus*
CA15 182 D7
Senhouse St
Maryport CA15 182 D5
5 Whitehaven CA28 186 C1
Workington CA14 184 D6
Workington, Siddick CA14 62 D6
Senhouse Terr 7
CA14 184 D6
Senhouse Wlk 22
CA14 184 D6
Senset Well La LA5 213 D7
Sentinal St LA14 206 C3
Sepulchre La
Endmoor LA8 144 C1
Kendal LA9 200 C5
Serpentine Rd LA9 200 C5
Settlebeck LA10 201 D5
Settlebeck High Sch
LA10 201 D4
Settle St
Barrow-in-F LA14 207 A5
Millom LA18 202 C5
Seven Acres CA28 186 D5
Seven Acres Cvn Pk
CA19 123 E8
Sevenoaks Terr CA7 180 B5
Severn Rd LA14 206 A3
Sewell Pl CA2 177 A2
Sewell Rd CA2 177 A2
Seymour Ct LA14 206 F4
Shacklabank La LA10 145 F6
Shaddongate CA2 176 E6
Shaddon Mill CA2 214 A2
Shady Grove La CA2 176 C6
Shady Grove Rd CA2 176 C6
Shakespeare Ave CA22 189 C6
Shakespeare St 1
LA14 206 F4
Shankhill CE Prim Sch
CA6 11 F6
Shankly Rd CA2 176 F4
Shanny La LA9 144 B4
SHAP 101 C6
Shap Abbey (rems of)*
CA10 101 A6
Shap CE Prim Sch
CA10 101 C6
Shap Gr CA2 176 D4
Shap Rd LA9 200 E7
Sharps La LA9 130 E2
Sharp St LA16 162 A8
Shawbank Brow CA14 78 B8
Shawfield Rd LA12 163 B3
Shaw Gn LA7 209 F5
Shawhill Ct DG12 172 F5
Shawhill Rd DG12 172 E4
Shawk Cres 3 CA5 28 F1
Shaw La LA7 209 F5
Shaw's Hill CA6 4 E1
Shaw St
Maryport CA15 182 E5
Workington CA14 184 D5
Shaw's Wiend CA16 193 C4
Shearwater Cres LA14 206 B1
Sheehan Cres CA2 176 B5
Sheenan Gdns CA2 176 B5
Sheepbarrow Cl LA11 154 C3
Sheeplands Gr LA13 207 D6
Sheernest 5 LA6 156 B1
Sheernest La LA6 156 B1
Sheffield St CA2 214 A1
Sheila Fell Cl CA7 36 D1
Shelley Ct CA14 184 C1
Shelley Dr LA13 207 D6
Shepherd Cl CA2 176 E4
Sherborne Ave LA13 207 D4
Sheriff Bank LA12 152 E5
Sheriff's Gate CA26 93 A8
Sheriff Well Cl LA12 152 E5
Sherwen's Terr CA22 189 F5
Sherwin St LA13 207 C2
Ship St LA14 206 F1
SHIRE 58 B2
SHOPFORD 6 C1
Shore Cl LA5 210 B2
Shore Cotts LA5 210 B3
Shoregill CA16 104 C6
Shore Gn LA5 210 B2
Shoreline Bsns Pk LA7 211 A3
Shore Rd
Drigg CA19 123 C5
Silverdale LA5 210 B2
Workington CA14 184 B2
Shore Side CA14 62 C6
Shore St LA14 207 A2
Shore Terr CA14 184 C2
Shorley La CA12 192 B3
Short Acres CA15 182 E5
Shortbutts La LA6 157 A1
Short St CA1 177 C6
Shovel La LA7 211 D4
Showfield CA8 179 B4
Shu-le-Crow Gdns 11
CA12 192 B3
Shuts La CA10 86 B8
Shuttle St LA20 139 B5
Shyreakes LA8 144 B2
Shyreakes La LA8 144 B2
SIDDICK 62 D6
Side Gates LA22 112 F2
Sidings Ind Est The
CA10 118 B2
Sidney St LA14 206 F3
Sids Field CA8 32 D6
Siemen's St 3 LA14 206 F1
Sikemeadow LA14 204 B1
Sikeside La CA17 104 C2
SILECROFT 149 D4
Silecroft CA13 63 E3
Silecroft Gdns LA14 206 C5
Silecroft Sta LA18 149 D5
SILLOTH 174 B4
Silloth Cres LA14 206 B4
Silloth Ind Est CA7 174 D4
Silloth Prim Sch CA7 174 C4
Silloth St CA2 176 E6
Silver Band Villas CA16 73 E2
SILVERDALE 210 C3
Silverdale Dr LA9 200 F5
SILVERDALE GREEN 210 D3
Silverdale Moss Rd
LA5 210 D7
Silverdale Rd
Arnside LA5 209 B1
Carlisle CA1 177 F4
Holme Mills LA5 166 E7
Silverdale St John's CE
Prim Sch LA5 210 C3
Silverdale St
5 Barrow-in-F LA14 207 A3
Haverigg LA18 150 A1
Silverdale Sta LA5 210 F3
Silverhill DG12 172 D5
Silverhill Pl DG16 173 C2
Silver Howe Cl LA9 200 E2
Silver La LA12 152 C7
Silverlaw DG12 172 D5
Silverlaw Cres DG12 172 D5
Silverlaw Ind Est DG12 172 D5
Silvermount DG12 172 C5
Silver Ridge Cvn Pk
LA7 155 F1
Silver St
Bolton CA16 87 D6
Crosby Ravensworth
CA10 102 C5
Kirkby Stephen CA17 199 C6
Marton LA12 162 D7
Staveley LA8 130 C5
Silverwalk DG12 172 D5
Sim Court Ho 8 CA11 191 E4
Sim Ct 10 CA11 191 E4
Simmerson Dr CA1 177 F2
Simonscales La CA13 190 D2
SIMPSON GROUND 142 B1
Simpson Ground Rd
LA11 154 B8
Simpson St CA14 185 A7
Sinclair Ct CA1 177 E6
Singleton Park Rd LA9 144 C6
Singleton Pk LA8 144 D6
Sipling CA4 41 E5
Sir John Barrow Sch
LA12 203 E5
Sir John Barrow Way
LA12 203 F5
Siskin Ave 7 LA15 205 C4
Sizergh Castle and
Garden* LA8 143 E2
Skeldene Cl LA15 205 B5
Skelgate LA15 205 B5
Skelghyll La
Ambleside LA22 195 D3
Ambleside, Waterhead
LA23 195 E1
Troutbeck Bridge LA23 129 A8
Skelgillside Workshops
CA9 181 F3
Skellands Ride CA10 85 E7
Skelsceugh Rd
Arlecdon CA26 77 E1
Frizington CA26 92 E8
SKELTON 55 B2
Skelton Sch CA11 55 B2
SKELTON WOOD END 54 E5
SKELWITH BRIDGE 113 E2
Skelwith Cl CA2 176 B5
Skelwith Dr
Barrow-in-F LA14 204 E1
Dalton-in-F LA15 205 C3
SKELWITH FOLD 113 F1
Skelwith Force* LA22 113 E2
Skiddaw Ave CA15 182 D7
Skiddaw Cl CA7 174 C4
Skiddaw Cres CA14 185 D5
Skiddaw Gdns LA14 204 D1
Skiddaw Rd
Carlisle CA2 176 D5
Whitehaven CA28 187 E3
Skiddaw St
Keswick CA12 192 C3
Silloth CA7 174 C3
Skiddaw Terr CA7 37 C1
Skiddaw View
Cockermouth CA13 190 C3
Penrith CA11 191 A5
Wigton CA7 180 B3
Skiddaw View Cvn Pk
CA7 50 F4
SKINBURNESS 174 F8
SKINBURNESSBANK 25 D7
Skinburness Cres CA7 174 D6
Skinburness Dr CA7 174 D6
Skinburness Rd CA7 174 D7
Skinner How La LA22 197 C7
Skinner St CA13 190 D3
Skipton Gate LA6 169 C2
SKIRSGILL 191 B2
Skirsgill Bsns Pk CA11 191 B2
Skirsgill Cl CA11 191 C3
Skirsgill Gdns CA11 191 C3
Skirsgill La CA10 191 D2
SKIRWITH 72 E7
Skitby Rd CA6 20 F8
Skye The 6 LA9 200 C5
Slackbury La LA8 143 A7
Slackgap La CA17 199 E8
SLACK HEAD 155 E1
Slack Randy CA10 102 B4
Slacks La LA10 146 A7
Slack The LA22 195 D5
Slackwood La LA5 210 E2
SLAGGYFORD 34 E3
Slape La LA6 167 C8
Slapestones CA11 70 E3
Slatefell CA13 190 F3
Slatefell Dr CA13 190 E4
Slater St
Barrow-in-F LA14 206 F3
Dalton-in-F LA15 205 C5
SLEAGILL 86 F2
Sleastonhow La CA10 87 E8
SLEETBECK 5 C3
Sleetbeck Rd CA6 5 C3
Slipway 21 CA28 186 C1
Sloan Cl CA14 185 D7
Sloop St LA14 206 F1
Slop La LA13 205 F2
Smailes Ct 3 CA13 190 D4
SMARDALE 120 C7
Smardale Gill Nature
Reserve* CA17 120 B6
Smeaton Pl CA9 46 F2
Smeaton St LA14 207 A2
SMITHFIELD 20 F8
Smithfield
Dalston CA5 29 D1
Egremont CA22 189 D7
Smithfield Pk CA22 189 C7
Smithfield Rd CA22 189 D7
Smith Rd CA14 184 C2
Smith's Ct 11 LA12 203 D5
Smithy Banks CA19 123 E6
Smithy Brow
Ambleside LA22 195 D6
Coniston LA21 127 F8
Smithybrow La CA19 124 F7
Smithy Cl LA9 144 A4
Smithy Cotts LA9 144 A4
Smithy Croft CA3 175 F5
Smithy Ct CA11 69 E5

Smithy Garth CA7 26 F6
Smithy Hill LA11 154 C3
Smithy How LA6 212 E3
Smithy La
Bowland Bridge LA11 142 C4
Bowness-on-W LA23 198 C1
Broughton-in-F LA20 138 E3
Caldbeck CA7 53 C6
Clifton CA10 71 C1
Westhouse LA6 169 E4
Snaefell View LA14 206 B1
Snape La LA5 166 F5
Snape Rd CA14 184 C5
Snebro Rd CA28 187 E6
Sneckyeat Ct CA28 187 F5
Sneckyeat Gr CA28 91 F7
Sneckyeat Rd
Hensingham CA28 187 F5
Whitehaven CA28 91 F7
Sneckyeat Road Ind Est CA28 91 F7
Snowdon Ave CA25 188 C8
SOCKBRIDGE 70 E1
Sockbridge Dr CA10 70 F1
Solomon Ct CA28 186 D1
Solway Ave CA15 183 C7
Solway Aviation Museum* CA6 21 D4
Solway Bsns Ctr CA6 175 B7
Solway Com Tech Coll CA7 174 C4
Solway Cres DG12 172 D3
Solway Ct 3 CA15 182 D6
Solway Dr
Anthorn CA7 16 E1
Walney Island LA14 206 B4
Solway Est CA15 182 C4
Solway Holiday Village CA7 174 D5
Solway Pk
Annan DG12 172 D2
Carlisle CA2 176 B5
Solway Rd
Gretna DG16 173 C2
Lowca CA28 186 E8
9 Moresby Parks CA28 76 F2
Whitehaven CA28 187 B7
Workington CA14 184 C4
Solway Rise CA27 91 C2
Solway St
Annan DG12 172 D3
Silloth CA7 174 C4
Workington CA14 184 C7
Solway Terr CA15 182 D6
Solway View
Bolton Low Houses CA7 37 F3
Kirkbampton CA5 28 E7
Whitehaven CA28 186 D2
Somerwood Cl CA16 88 A7
Somme Ave LA11 164 D6
SOSGILL 78 E6
SOULBY
Kirkby Stephen 104 C1
Pooley Bridge 84 E8
SOUTERGATE 151 C4
Soutergate LA12 203 D6
Soutersykes CA13 65 A4
Southampton St LA14 206 C2
South Bank Cl CA7 180 D1
South Craig LA23 198 D3
South Cres LA23 198 D5
South Croft CA3 175 F5
Southdale St CA2 177 B3
South End
Bolton CA16 87 E5
Wigton CA7 180 D2
South End Cvn Site LA14 170 E1
Southend Rd CA11 191 D4
SOUTHERNBY 54 A6
Southesk CA10 72 D4
Southey Ave CA22 189 C6
Southey Hill Trad Pk CA12 192 A4
Southey St CA12 192 B3
Southey Wlk CA22 189 C6
Southfield CA5 18 F1
Southfield Rd LA10 201 B4
Southfield Tech Coll CA14 184 D2
South George St CA2 214 B1
South Gn LA12 162 F6
South Henry St
Carlisle CA1 214 C1
Carlisle CA1 214 C2
South Hermitage Sq TD9 1 B6
South Hermitage St TD9 1 B6
South John St CA2 214 B1
South John Street Workshops CA2 214 B1
South Lakes Wild Animal Pk* LA15 205 D7
South Liddle St TD9 1 B6
South Lodge CA13 190 D2
SOUTH NEWBARNS 207 C4
South Par CA20 123 A7
Southport Dr LA14 206 B2
South Quay CA15 182 C6
South Range The CA10 86 A5
South Rd
Kendal LA9 200 D3
Kirkby Stephen CA17 199 C4
South Row
Barrow-in-F LA13 207 E3
Whitehaven CA28 187 B6
South St
Carlisle CA1 214 C1
Cockermouth CA13 190 D4
South St *continued*
Egremont CA22 189 E5
Mealsgate CA7 37 C2
SOUTH STAINMORE 106 A3
South Terr
Bowness-on-W LA23 198 D3
Great Broughton CA13 63 D6
Tebay CA10 118 B2
South Tynedale Rly* CA9 181 C6
SOUTH ULVERSTON 163 D8
South Vale Ct CA2 176 F4
South View
Aspatria CA7 50 C8
Barrow-in-F LA14 207 A6
Mealsgate CA7 37 A1
South View La LA9 200 C6
South View Rd
Distington CA14 185 C3
Whitehaven CA28 186 D3
South View Terr
Carlisle CA1 214 C1
Wigton CA7 180 B4
SOUTHWAITE
High Hesket 41 D3
Kirkby Stephen 121 A2
Southwaite Barns CA4 41 D4
Southwaitegreen Mill CA10 191 D1
Southwaite Rd CA4 41 E4
South Wakefield Cl CA3 175 C3
South Walney Inf Sch LA14 206 C1
South Walney Jun Sch LA14 206 C1
South Walney Nature Reserve* LA14 171 A1
South Walney Nature Trails* LA14 170 F1
South Watt St 6 CA14 184 D6
South Western Terr CA2 177 A4
South William St CA14 184 E6
Sowerby Ave LA14 204 B1
Sowerby Ct CA2 176 E4
SOWERBY ROW 54 D7
Sowerby Wood Rd CA5 29 E3
Sowerby Woods Bsns Pk LA14 204 C3
Sow How La LA11 142 A2
SPARK BRIDGE 152 D7
SPARKET 84 B8
Sparrowmire La LA9 200 C7
Spedding Cl CA22 189 E7
Speedwell La CA14 184 E6
Spencer Ho CA1 214 B2
Spencer St CA1 214 B2
Spenser Cl CA22 189 C6
Spicka La LA22 128 C7
Spindrift Cl 3 LA16 162 A8
Spinners Yd CA3 214 A3
Spinney La LA5 210 C8
Spinney The
Arnside LA5 210 C8
Bowness-on-W LA23 198 C1
Spital Ing La CA13 190 C5
Spital Pk LA9 200 E7
Spital View 3 LA9 200 C5
Spittal Farm CA7 180 E5
Spooner Vale LA23 198 D6
Spoonygreen La CA12 192 B5
Spout Force Forest Wlk* CA13 80 A8
Spout Force (waterfall)* CA13 65 D1
Spout Ho CA28 187 A2
Spout La
Ulverston LA12 203 E6
Wennington LA2 168 F1
Spring Bank
Silverdale LA5 210 C3
Whitehaven CA28 187 E7
Spring Bank Rd LA11 208 B5
Springbells DG12 172 E5
Springbells Rd DG12 172 E5
Springbells Workshops DG12 172 E5
Spring Croft Cl CA13 63 F5
SPRINGFIELD 173 E5
Springfield
Arnside LA5 209 B2
Hensingham CA24 91 F4
Heversham LA7 211 D7
Holme LA6 156 B1
Springfield Ave
High Harrington CA14 185 C7
Ulverston LA12 203 D4
Whitehaven CA28 187 E7
Springfield Cl LA14 206 C5
Springfield Farm Ct DG16 173 E5
Springfield Gdns CA22 188 A3
Springfield Gr CA28 187 F7
Springfield Mans LA12 203 D4
Springfield Park Rd LA12 203 D3
Springfield Prim Sch DG16 173 D6
Springfield Rd
Bigrigg CA22 188 A3
Carlisle CA1 177 F4
Ulverston LA12 203 D4
Windermere LA23 198 E4
Spring Field Rd 16 CA15 182 E5
Springfields CA7 180 D1
Spring Gardens La CA3 214 B3
Spring Gdns
1 Kendal LA9 200 C5
Kirkby-in-F LA17 151 C8
Spring Gr LA14 207 B6
Springkell CA7 36 D1
Springs Garth CA12 192 C2
Springs Rd CA12 192 C2
Spring St 1 LA14 207 A2
Spring Vale LA12 203 A2
Spring Wood LA22 197 E4
Sprint Holme LA9 130 F2
Spruce Gr CA28 186 F1
Spruce Rise LA13 207 F4
Square The
Allithwaite LA11 164 F7
Allonby CA15 35 C2
Bouth LA12 152 F8
Brough CA17 105 B5
5 Broughton-in-F LA20 139 A2
Burton-in-K LA6 167 B7
Cartmel LA11 153 E1
Dalston CA5 29 D1
2 Gosforth CA20 109 A2
Hawkshead LA22 197 E5
High Cummersdale CA2 176 E1
Kirkoswald CA10 57 B8
Longtown CA6 10 C4
Milnthorpe LA7 211 D3
Orton CA10 118 C7
Parton CA28 186 D6
Sandford CA16 104 A7
Storth LA7 209 F5
Whitehaven CA28 186 D2
Stables Ct 9 CA13 190 C4
Stable Yd 13 CA12 192 B3
Stackbraes Rd CA6 10 C4
Stackwood Ave LA13 207 C5
Stack Yd The CA16 88 A5
STAFFIELD 43 A1
Staffield Cotts CA10 43 A1
Stafford Ct CA25 188 D6
Stafford St
Askam in F LA16 162 A7
Barrow-in-F LA14 207 A5
Dalton-in-F LA15 205 C6
Stagshaw Gdns* LA22 195 D2
Stagstones Farm CA11 71 C6
Stagstones Rd CA11 71 C6
Stainbank Rd LA9 200 B3
STAINBURN 62 F3
Stainburn Rd CA14 62 E4
Stainburn Sch CA14 62 E3
Stainmore Rly Co* CA17 199 B4
STAINTON
Carlisle 176 B8
Kendal 156 B8
Penrith 70 D3
Stainton CE Prim Sch CA11 70 D3
Stainton Cross LA8 156 B8
Stainton Ct LA8 156 B8
Stainton Dr LA15 205 B3
Stainton La LA13 162 E3
Stainton Rd CA3 175 A1
Stainton St LA5 213 C5
STAINTON WITH ADGARLEY 205 F2
STAIR 80 F4
STAITH 179 D5
Stalker Rd CA11 191 B5
Stamford Hill Ave CA28 186 F8
Stampery The CA7 180 D4
Stanah Cotts CA12 82 B2
Stanah La CA12 82 B1
Stanbeck Mdws CA14 184 F5
Standalane DG12 172 D4
Standalane Ct DG12 172 E4
Standings Rise CA28 187 E8
STANDINGSTONE 180 D5
Standingstone Hts CA7 180 C5
Standish St CA12 192 B3
Stanegate CA6 21 E4
Stanegate Way CA8 23 B6
Stanger St CA12 192 B4
Stanhope Rd CA2 176 E6
STANK 162 C1
Stankelt Ho LA5 210 C2
Stankelt Rd LA5 210 C2
Stank La LA13 162 C1
Stanley Cres CA8 14 D1
Stanley Rd
Barrow-in-F LA14 206 E2
Brampton CA8 179 C6
Stanley St
Beetham LA7 155 E2
Carnforth LA5 213 C3
Ulverston LA12 203 D6
Workington CA14 184 C6
Stanley View CA28 187 E3
Stan Lonning CA13 63 F5
STANWIX 175 D1
Stanwix Bank CA3 214 A4
Stanwix Pk Holiday Ctr CA7 174 B2
Stanwix Prim Sch CA3 175 E1
Stanyan Lodge LA12 203 E6
STAPLETON 12 C6
Stapleton Rd DG12 172 F4
Stapleton Road Ind Est DG12 172 E4
Stark St LA14 207 A2
Starnthwaite Ghyll LA8 142 E7
Starnthwaite Ghyll Cotts LA8 142 E7
Star St LA12 203 C6
Station App
Cark LA11 164 D7
Dalton-in-F LA15 205 C4
Station Ave CA12 192 B4
Station Bldgs
Carnforth LA5 213 C4
Kendal LA8 144 C5
Station Bsns Pk CA2 214 B1
Station Cl
3 Dalton-in-F LA15 205 C4
Egremont CA22 189 E7
Station Cotts
Greenhead CA8 24 C8
Melling LA6 168 D2
Station Cres CA21 108 B5
STATION HILL 180 B5
Station Hill
Ravenglass CA18 123 F3
Wigton CA7 180 B4
Station La
Burton-in-K LA6 167 B7
Staveley LA8 130 B5
Station Rd
Alston CA9 181 D4
Annan DG12 172 C3
Appleby-in-W CA16 193 D6
Armathwaite CA4 42 C5
Arnside LA5 209 C2
Aspatria CA7 50 C8
Brampton CA8 179 D5
9 Broughton-in-F LA20 139 A2
Burgh by S CA5 18 F1
Cark LA11 164 D7
Cockermouth CA13 190 D3
Coniston LA21 196 A4
Crosby Garrett CA17 120 A8
Culgaith CA10 72 E4
Dalston CA5 29 D1
Dalton-in-F LA15 205 C4
Drigg CA19 123 D5
Flimby CA15 183 C8
Holme LA6 156 B1
Holme Mills LA6 167 B8
Kendal LA9 200 D6
Keswick CA12 192 B4
Kirkby Stephen CA17 199 C4
Millom LA18 202 C5
Penruddock CA11 69 D3
Sedbergh LA10 201 B4
Shap CA10 101 C5
Silloth CA7 174 B3
Staveley LA8 130 B5
St Bees CA27 91 C2
Temple Sowerby CA10 72 F3
Threlkeld CA12 82 B7
Whitehaven CA28 187 D8
Wigton CA7 180 C4
Workington CA14 184 D6
Station Road Ind Est CA7 174 B3
Station St
Cockermouth CA13 190 D4
Keswick CA12 192 B3
Maryport CA15 182 D5
Station Terr
Bridgefoot CA14 63 C4
1 Dalton-in-F LA15 205 C4
Embleton CA13 65 B5
Lindal in F LA12 162 E6
Station View CA15 49 D5
Station Yard CA7 180 C4
Station Yard Ind Est LA11 208 E5
Station Yd 10 LA16 162 A8
STAVELEY 130 B5
Staveley CE Sch LA8 130 B5
STAVELEY-IN-CARTMEL 141 F1
Staveley Mill Yard Ind Est LA8 130 C5
Staveley Sta LA8 130 B5
Steamer St LA14 206 F1
Steel Brow CA26 77 C2
Steele's Bank CA4 178 B1
Steele's Row LA9 130 F2
STEEL GREEN 202 B3
Steelmen Wlk 6 CA14 184 E6
Steel St
Askam in F LA16 162 A8
Barrow-in-F LA14 206 E4
Ulverston LA12 163 D8
Steeple Cl CA28 187 E5
Steer Ave CA15 182 D4
Stephenson Croft CA16 87 D6
Stephenson Ind Est CA2 176 D8
Stephenson Rd CA1 177 D4
Stephensons La 6 CA8 179 C5
Stephen St LA14 206 F3
Stevenson Pl DG12 172 B3
Stewart Cl LA5 210 B8
Stewart St LA14 206 E2
Stile Brow LA23 129 D1
Stileman Wlk LA14 207 A3
Stockbeck LA9 200 E6
STOCKBRIDGE 137 A8
Stockbridge Ct LA12 203 C5
Stockbridge La LA12 203 C6
Stockdale Farm LA11 164 D6
STOCKDALEWATH 40 C3
Stockgate LA9 200 E6
Stockghyll Brow LA22 195 D5
Stockghyll Ct LA22 195 E5
Stockghyll Force* LA22 195 E6
Stockghyll La LA22 195 E6
Stock Hill Kennels CA7 50 E8
Stock La LA22 194 B3
Stocks Hill Cl CA14 185 B7
Stocks Hill Rise CA14 185 B7
Stockwell Rd CA2 30 B3
Stokoe Ct CA2 176 F4
Stonebank Gn LA9 200 A3
Stone Barrow La LA15, LA13 162 E4
Stonebeck Cotts LA11 154 C3
Stone Cl LA13 205 F2
Stone Croft LA22 195 D5
Stonecroft Gdns CA4 41 F3
Stonecross Gdns
Kendal LA9 200 C2
Ulverston LA12 203 C5
Stonecross Gn LA9 200 C2
Stonecross Rd LA9 200 B2
Stone Dike La LA12 162 F5
Stonedross La LA6 212 E8
Stone Dyke LA13 207 F4
Stonedyke La LA13 207 F4
Stonegarth
Carlisle CA2 176 C4
Greystoke CA11 69 E5
Stonehall La LA10 201 F6
Stoneham Cl LA13 207 E3
Stonehill Mews CA17 199 D6
STONE HOUSE 148 B1
Stonehouse Pk CA5 29 A1
Stone How Lonning CA7 37 A7
Stone Lands LA8 155 D8
Stoneleigh Cl LA13 207 C6
Stoneleigh Ct LA5 210 C3
Stoneraise Sch CA5 40 E8
Stone Rigg Outrake LA10 146 F1
Stonesdale La DL11 122 E1
Stoneshot CA17 199 D6
Stones La LA22 128 E2
Stone Terr 1 LA11 208 C4
STONETHWAITE 96 C4
Stoneycroft CA14 63 B4
Stoneycroft Dr LA5 209 B1
Stoney Croft Dr LA5 213 D8
Stoney La
Ambleside LA22 195 C6
2 Kendal LA9 200 C5
Stony Banks CA7 180 D3
Stonydale LA12 203 D2
Stonyhurst Dr CA28 187 D8
Stopford St TD9 1 B6
Storey Bank CA10 72 A8
Storey Sq
Barrow-in-F LA14 207 A3
15 Dalton-in-F LA15 205 C5
Stormont Cres DG16 173 D2
STORRS 129 A1
Storrs La LA5 166 D6
STORTH 209 F5
Storth Brow CA7 37 A5
Storth CE Sch LA7 209 F5
Storth Rd LA7 209 F3
Stott Park Bobbin Mill* LA12 141 E3
Strait Loaning CA10 43 A1
Straits 10 CA7 180 D3
Stramongate LA9 200 D5
Stramongate Prim Sch LA9 200 D5
Strand LA14 207 A2
Strand Ct 3 LA11 208 D4
Strand Rd CA1 214 C3
STRANDS 150 D7
Strand St
Maryport CA15 182 C6
Whitehaven CA28 186 C1
Strands The
Milnthorpe LA7 211 C3
Milnthorpe LA7 211 D3
Strand Terr CA7 180 D4
Strand The CA4 30 F7
Strathaird Ave LA14 206 C1
Strathclyde Ave CA2 176 C6
Strathmore Ave LA14 206 C1
Strathnaver Ave LA14 206 C1
STRAWBERRY BANK 142 C4
Strawberry How CA13 190 E2
Strawberry How Bsns Ctr CA13 190 E2
Strawberry Howe Rd CA13 190 F1
Strawberry Terr CA3 175 C1
Street CA10 86 D6
Street La CA10 118 D8
Street The CA7 53 C5
Strickland Ct LA9 200 C6
Stricklandgate
Kendal LA9 200 C5
Penrith CA11 191 C6
Strickland Terr 10 CA11 191 C6
Stripes La CA16 104 C6
STUBBLE GREEN 123 C6
Stubshead La CA19, CA20 109 B1
Studio Ho LA22 195 D5
Stybarrow Terr CA11 98 C7
Sty Gate CA14 78 C4
Stylecroft CA7 180 C8
Suffolk Cl CA28 187 F5

Suffolk St LA13 207 B3
Sullart St
  Cockermouth CA13 190 C3
  16 Cockermouth CA13 190 C4
Summerfields CA5 29 D1
Summergate Cres DG12 172 D3
Summergate Rd DG12 172 D2
Summergrove Pk CA28 188 A8
Summerhill LA9 200 C4
Summer Hill
  Bootle LA19 137 B3
  Carlisle CA1 177 C4
Summer Hill Cvn Pk LA23 142 A6
Summerhill Gdns LA14 207 B8
Summerhow LA9 131 B1
SUMMERLANDS 144 C1
Summerlands Trad Est LA8 144 C1
Summersty Bank LA23 142 A6
Summervale Ave DG12 172 D2
Summervale Pl DG12 172 D2
Summerville Rd LA7 211 D4
Summit Ave LA13 207 B6
SUNBRICK 163 B4
Sunbrick La LA12 163 B4
Suncroft CA15 49 B5
Sun Croft CA7 51 F5
SUNDERLAND 50 F2
Sunderland Terr LA12 203 E5
Sunningdale Cl CA3 175 B1
Sunningdale Gdns 8 CA3 175 B1
Sunnybank CA12 82 B8
Sunny Bank
  Cark LA11 164 D7
  Lindal in F LA12 162 D7
  Stainton CA11 70 D3
  Stainton w A LA13 205 F2
Sunny Bank Rd LA23 198 E4
Sunny Brae 9 LA11 208 C4
Sunnymeade CA2 177 C1
Sunnyside
  9 Cockermouth CA13 190 D4
  Egremont CA22 189 D6
  Kendal LA9 200 D4
  Seaton CA14 183 C3
Sunray Terr CA10 57 A6
Sunscales Ave CA13 190 E2
Sunset View CA9 181 D4
Sun St
  Askam in F LA16 162 B8
  Ulverston LA12 203 C6
Surgery La 4 CA8 179 C5
Surrey St LA18 202 D4
Surrone Ct DG16 173 C3
Surrone Gdns DG16 173 C3
Surrone Rd DG16 173 C3
Sutcliffe Ho CA4 21 E1
Sutherland St LA14 207 A3
Sutherland Terr DG12 172 C1
Suttle Cl CA2 176 B4
Sutton Ct CA4 30 F5
Swallow Cl LA9 200 F2
SWALLOWHURST 137 B6
Swan Ave CA17 105 B5
Swan La LA22 194 B5
Swan St
  Longtown CA6 10 C3
  Ulverston LA12 203 E5
Swarthdale Ave LA12 203 D3
SWARTHMOOR 203 B3
Swarthmoor Hall★ LA12 203 C3
Swarthmoor Hall La LA12 203 B3
Swartle The CA8 179 D6
Sweden Bridge La LA22 195 D7
Sweden Pk LA22 195 D6
Swillings La CA17 104 E4
Swinate Rd LA5 209 C1
Swinburn Dr CA3 175 C3
Swindale La CA10 100 D4
Swine Market LA6 212 C2
Swinestead La LA12 163 C3
Swingpump La 18 CA28 186 C1
SWIN HOPE 47 F6
SWINSIDE 81 A4
Swinside Cl CA13 190 F3
Sybil St CA1 177 C5
Sycamore Ave
  Sedbergh LA10 201 B5
  Ulverston LA12 203 D3
Sycamore Cl
  Endmoor LA8 156 D8
  Whitehaven CA28 186 E3
Sycamore Ct CA14 184 E3
Sycamore Dr CA11 191 F5
Sycamore Garth CA14 63 C3
Sycamore Gr
  Barrow-in-F LA14 206 F6
  Milnthorpe LA7 211 E4
Sycamore La CA1 30 E4
Sycamore Rd CA15 182 E5
Syke Bsns Pk CA7 180 E1
Syke Pk CA7 180 E1
Syke Rd CA7 180 E1

T

Tail Bank Lonning LA20 138 E3
Tait St CA1 214 C2
Talbot Rd CA2 176 E5
Talisman Cl 4 LA14 207 B3
TALKIN 32 D8
Talkin Cl CA1 177 F5
Talkin Gdns CA1 177 F5
Talkin Tarn Ctry Pk★ CA8 179 F1
TALLENTIRE 49 E2
Tallow Whins CA10 57 A6
Tamar Gdns LA14 206 A4
Tamworth Dr LA13 207 D4
Tangier Bldgs 1 CA28 186 C1
Tangier St CA28 186 C1
Tannery Court Flats CA1 177 C3
Tannery Ct
  Carlisle CA1 177 C3
  12 Wigton CA7 180 D3
Tanpits La LA6 167 B7
Tantabank LA15 205 C4
Tarnbrook Cl LA5 213 B3
Tarn Cl
  Kendal LA9 200 E2
  Storth LA7 209 F5
  Ulverston LA12 203 B6
Tarn Flatt LA12 162 C7
Tarn Green Rd LA11 154 C7
Tarnhead LA18 150 A2
Tarnhead La LA18 150 A2
Tarn Ho 6 LA14 207 C8
Tarn How La CA20 109 A1
Tarn Hows★ LA21 196 F8
Tarn La
  Burton-in-K LA6 167 B6
  Crosby Garrett CA17 120 B8
Tarn Rd CA8 179 D3
TARNSIDE 142 E5
Tarnside CA2 177 B1
Tarn Side LA12 203 D5
Tarnside Cvn Pk CA21 108 A5
Tarn St CA14 184 E5
TARRABY 175 F3
Tarraby La CA3 175 E1
Tarraby Mews CA3 175 F3
Tay Ct LA14 206 E4
Teal Beck LA9 200 F2
Teal Cl LA16 161 F8
Teasdale Rd
  Carlisle CA3 175 C3
  Walney Island LA14 206 C5
TEBAY 118 B3
Tebay Com Prim Sch CA10 118 B3
Tebay La LA12 203 F7
Tees Gdns LA14 206 B2
Telford Rd CA1 177 D4
Telford St 2 LA14 207 B2
TEMPLAND 164 E7
Templand Garth LA11 164 F7
Templand Gate LA11 164 F7
Templand Pk LA11 164 F7
Temple Ct LA5 166 E7
TEMPLE SOWERBY 72 E2
Temple Sowerby CE Prim Sch CA10 72 E2
Temple Terr
  Aspatria CA7 50 D8
  Whitehaven CA28 186 D1
Tennyson Ave LA13 207 D6
Tennyson Dr CA22 189 C6
Tenterfell Ct 14 LA9 200 C5
Tenters CA7 180 D3
Terrace The
  Dearham CA15 49 B3
  Windermere LA23 198 E6
Tewfittmire La CA10 86 A8
TEWITFIELD 167 A4
Tewthwaite Hill Rd CA16, CA17 104 A3
Thacka La CA11 191 B6
THACKTHWAITE 79 C6
Thames Rd LA14 206 B3
Thanet Terr CA16 193 D6
Theatre St 15 LA12 203 D5
THE GREEN 150 C7
THE HILL 150 D5
THE HOWE 143 A3
THE LOUND 200 E3
Third Moss La LA8 143 C5
Thirlemere Rd CA15 182 E4
Thirlmere Ave
  Cockermouth CA13 190 E3
  Workington CA14 184 F4
Thirlmere Cl
  Dalton-in-F LA15 205 C3
  Millom LA18 202 C4
Thirlmere Pk CA11 191 C3
Thirlmere Rd LA9 200 F6
Thirlmere St CA2 177 A4
Thirlwall View CA8 24 C8
Thirlwell Ave CA1 177 D6
Thirlwell Gdns CA1 177 D6
Thirnby Ct LA6 212 C2
Thistle Cl CA28 186 E1
THOMAS CLOSE 55 B7
Thomas La CA2 176 B7
Thomas Rd CA14 184 C2
Thomas St
  Annan DG12 172 C4
  Carlisle CA2 214 A1
Thomlinson Ave CA2 176 C6
Thomlinson Jun Sch CA7 180 D3
Thompson Cl CA25 188 D7
Thompson Ct CA11 191 C6
Thompson St 7 LA14 207 A3
Thompsons Terr CA15 183 C8
Thompson's Yd CA14 63 B4
Thomson St CA1 177 C5
Thorburn Cres DG12 172 D5
Thornbarrow Rd LA23 198 E4
THORNBY 28 C3
Thorncliffe Rd LA14 207 A7
Thorncliffe Sch LA14 207 A7
Thorncroft Ct CA14 184 F5
Thorncroft Gdns CA14 184 F5
Thornfield Cl CA25 188 D6
Thornfield Pk LA14 207 A7
Thornfield Pl LA11 208 C3
Thornfield Rd LA11 208 C3
THORNHILL 189 E2
Thornhill LA23 198 E4
Thornhill Prim Sch CA22 189 E2
Thornleigh Dr LA6 167 C7
Thornleigh Rd LA9 200 C2
Thornsbank LA10 201 D5
Thornship La CA10 101 B5
Thorns La
  Sedbergh LA10 201 D5
  Underbarrow LA8 143 C6
THORNTHWAITE 80 E8
Thornthwaite Forest Walks★ CA12 66 C3
Thornthwaite Rd LA23 198 F4
THORNTON IN LONSDALE 169 F4
Thornton La
  Dent LA6, LA10 159 C3
  Ingleton LA6 169 F5
Thornton Pk LA15 205 B3
Thornton Rd
  Carlisle CA3 175 D1
  Whitehaven CA28 187 F7
Thorntrees Dr CA22 189 E2
Thorny Hills LA9 200 E5
Thorny La
  Newbiggin-on-L CA17 119 E4
  Thornhill CA22 189 E3
Thorny Nook La LA14 170 C5
Thorny Rd CA22 189 E2
Thoroughfare The LA5 213 C7
THORPE 70 E1
Thorpe Field CA10 70 E1
Thorpe The CA11 69 F6
Thrang Brow LA22 113 B4
Thrang Brow La LA5 166 E7
Threagill La LA5 213 E7
THREAPLAND 50 E6
Threaplands CA25 188 C8
Threave Ct CA1 177 D6
Three Bridges LA12 203 B4
Three Trees Rd DG12 16 C7
THRELKELD 82 B8
Threlkeld CE Prim Sch CA12 82 B8
Threlkeld Gdns LA14 204 E1
Threlkeld Quarry and Mining Mus★ CA12 82 C7
THRIMBY 86 C3
Throstle Ave CA7 180 B3
Throughs La LA7 209 F5
Thrums St LA13 207 D3
THRUSHWOOD 192 A6
Thurland Mill Cotts LA6 168 D3
Thurlow Way LA14 207 A6
THURSBY 28 F1
Thursby Prim Sch CA5 28 F1
Thurston Bank LA21 127 C4
THURSTONFIELD 28 E7
Thwaite Bank CA14 184 E8
Thwaite Brow La LA5 213 A1
THWAITE FLAT 204 E5
Thwaite Flat Cotts LA14 204 F5
Thwaite Flat Rd LA14 204 F5
Thwaites Holme LA23 198 D3
Thwaites La LA23 198 F5
Thwaites Lee LA23 198 F4
Thwaites Sch LA18 150 C8
Thwaite St LA14 207 A4
Thwaiteville CA28 187 B8
Tideway Dr LA14 170 C6
Tiffin La 9 CA14 184 E6
Tilberthwaite Ave LA21 196 A4
Tilbury Rd CA1 177 E6
Timber Hill 13 LA20 139 A2
Timber Wood Cl LA18 150 A1
TINDALE 23 E2
Tindale Dr CA1 177 F4
Tindale Terr CA8 23 E2
Tinkler's La
  Askham CA10 85 F8
  Clifton CA10 71 C1
Tippin's La LA16, LA17 151 B2
TIRRIL 70 F1
Titchfield St LA14 206 F5
Tithebarn Cotts 9 LA9 200 C4
Tithebarn Ct 4 CA12 192 A4
Tithebarn Hill CA4 178 A6
Tithebarn St
  Carlisle CA2 177 B4
  5 Keswick CA12 192 A4
Tivoli Cotts CA28 76 F3
TODHILLS 19 E6
Todholes Rd CA25 188 E6
Toll Bar Ct LA6 167 C7
Toll Bar Est LA10 201 A4
Tollbar Hos CA14 185 E5
Tom Fold LA22 195 D6
Tomlin Ave CA28 187 E5
Tommy Rd CA17 120 E2
Topaz Terr CA14 184 C1
Torduff Rd DG16 173 C3
Toronto St CA2 177 B3
TORPENHOW 51 C6
Torridge Dr LA14 206 A4
TORVER 127 B1
Totter Bank LA8 142 E6
TOTTLEBANK 152 E7
TOWCETT 86 D1
Tower Cotts CA12 81 B6
Tower Ct
  Carlisle CA3 214 A3
  Warcop CA16 104 C6
Tower Hill CA28 187 E7
Towers La CA13 190 E2
Towerson St CA23 188 F6
Towers St LA12 203 E5
Tower St LA13 171 B3
Tower View CA22 189 D6
Town Bank Rd LA12 203 D7
Town Bank Terr 1 LA12 203 D6
Towncroft CA15 49 B3
Town Cross CA12 82 C8
TOWNEND 114 E1
TOWN END
  Grange-over-Sands 154 F6
  Grasmere 194 C3
  Kirkby Lonsdale 157 F5
  Kirkby Thore 87 D8
Townend★ LA23 114 E1
Town End Cl LA11 154 F6
Town End Croft CA10 71 C1
Town End Ct LA8 144 B4
Town End Farm CA7 28 C4
Town End Fold LA5 213 B7
Town End Mdw LA11 153 F1
Townfield Cl CA18 123 F3
TOWNFOOT 181 D3
Town Foot CA11 55 B2
Townfoot Ct CA8 179 A4
Townfoot Farm House CA8 179 A4
Townfoot Ind Est CA8 179 A5
Townfoot Pk CA8 179 A5
TOWNGATE 42 E5
Towngate CA17 120 B7
TOWNHEAD
  Alston 181 D3
  Dearham 49 B2
  Hayton 32 A8
  Lazonby 57 A6
  Ousby 58 D1
  Penrith 191 B6
TOWN HEAD
  Ambleside 114 F2
  Cliburn 86 E8
  Crosby Ravensworth 102 B5
  Dufton 88 D7
  Grasmere 194 A8
  Great Asby 103 C3
  Kirkby Thore 87 E8
  Morland 87 A5
Town Head
  Haverigg LA18 150 A1
  Sleagill CA10 86 E1
Townhead Brow LA23 114 F2
Town Head Cl CA10 86 B5
Townhead Ct
  Cumwhinton CA4 31 A3
  Melmerby CA10 58 B4
Townhead Farm Ctyd CA4 30 F5
Town Head Fold LA6 156 B2
Town Head Garth CA10 87 E8
Townhead La
  Cliburn CA10 86 E8
  Ravenstonedale CA17 120 B2
Townhead Rd
  Cotehill CA4 31 B1
  Dalston CA5 29 D1
Town Quay CA14 184 C7
Townsfield LA5 210 C4
Town St LA12 203 D6
Town View LA9 200 C6
Town View Rd LA12 203 D6
Towpath Wlk 2 LA5 213 C3
Tows Bank NE49 34 F7
Tow Scar Rd LA6 169 F6
Tow Top Rd LA11 154 B6
Trafalgar Ct LA15 205 B5
Trafalgar Sq CA26 92 D8
Trafalgar St CA2 214 A1
Tram La LA6 212 C2
Tram The LA9 200 C5
Tranthwaite La LA8 143 C7
Tree Gdns CA8 179 D4
Tree Rd
  Brampton CA8 179 D4
  Carlisle CA1 177 C4
Tree Terr CA8 179 D4
Treetops CA22 188 A3
Trent Vale LA14 206 B2
Trevor St CA1 177 C4
Tribune Dr CA3 20 C2
Trinity Ct
  5 Ulverston LA12 203 C5
  Whitehaven CA28 187 C8
Trinity Dr
  Holme LA6 156 B1
  Workington CA14 184 E8
Trinity Drive Ct CA14 184 E8
Trinity Ent Ctr LA14 206 D4
Trinity Gdns 8 LA12 203 C5
Trinity Rd LA18 202 C6
Trinity Sch CA1 214 B3
Trinity St LA14 206 F1
Trinity Terr LA13 171 B3
Trinity Way CA12 192 D4
Trinkeld Ave LA12 203 A2
Troon Cl CA3 175 C3
Trotter's World of Animals★ CA12 65 F7
TROUTBECK 114 E2
TROUTBECK BRIDGE 129 B7
Troutbeck Cotts CA11 69 B3
Troutbeck Dr CA2 176 A5
Troutbeck Gdns LA14 204 D1
Troy Gdns LA13 207 C6
Trumpet Rd CA23 188 F5
Trumpet Terr CA23 188 E5
Tubal Cnr CA7 36 F8
Tuchwud LA23 198 E6
Tudor Ct CA11 191 C5
Tudor Sq 12 LA15 205 C5
Tullie House Mus & Art Gall★ CA3 214 A3
Tullie St CA1 177 C6
Tullythwaite Garth LA8 143 C6
Tun Ho CA3 214 A3
TUNSTALL 168 E4
Turbary Rd LA6 169 E7
Turnberry Cres DG12 172 F5
Turnberry Rd DG12 172 E5
Turnberry Way CA3 175 D3
Turners Cl LA6 156 B2
Turning Course Lonning CA8 179 E6
Turnmuir Dell DG12 172 F4
Turnside Dr CA2 176 C7
Turnstone Cres LA16 161 F8
Tweedie Terr DG12 172 D5
Tweed Mill La CA13 190 D3
Tweed Rise LA14 206 B2
Twentyman Ct 10 CA12 192 B3
Twickenham Ct CA1 30 E4
Twine Walk LA7 211 D4
Twine Wlk LA6 169 C3
Twinter Bank LA6 156 B2
Tymparon Cl CA11 70 B4
Tyne Close Ave CA11 191 C4
Tyne Close Terr CA11 191 C4
Tynefield Ct CA11 191 D4
Tynefield Dr CA11 191 E3
Tyne Rd LA14 206 B2
Tyne St CA1 177 C4
Tyson Sq 10 LA12 203 E5

U

Udale Ct CA14 184 F3
Udale St CA14 184 E6
ULCAT ROW 83 E5
ULDALE 52 B3
Uldale Rd
  Carlisle CA2 177 B2
  Stainburn CA14 62 E3
  Whitehaven CA28 187 D5
Uldale View CA22 189 D4
Ullcoats Ind Est CA22 92 C1
ULLERBANK 32 E8
ULLOCK 78 B7
Ullswater Ave
  Whitehaven CA28 91 F7
  Workington CA14 184 E4
Ullswater Cl
  Dalton-in-F LA15 205 C3
  Ulverston LA12 203 E4
Ullswater Com Coll CA11 191 D4
Ullswater Cres LA5 213 D2
Ullswater Ct CA11 98 C8
Ullswater Cvn & Camping Site The CA11 84 B5
Ullswater Dr CA13 190 F3
Ullswater Rd
  Carlisle CA2 176 D5
  Kendal LA9 144 C8
  Maryport CA15 182 D4
  Penrith CA11 191 C4
ULPHA 138 E8
ULVERSTON 203 C6
Ulverston CE Inf Sch LA12 203 D6
Ulverston Hospl LA12 203 C6
Ulverston Rd
  Dalton-in-F LA15 205 D5
  Gleaston LA12 162 E2
  Lindal in F LA12 205 E7
  Swarthmoor LA12 203 A3
Ulverston Sta LA12 203 C4
Ulverston Victoria High Sch LA12 203 D4
UNDERBARROW 143 B6
Underbarrow Rd
  Kendal LA9 200 A4
  Underbarrow LA8 143 E7
Undercliff Rd LA9 200 B5
Underfell LA11 164 F8
Undergreens Rd LA14 207 A8
Underhill LA8 143 D1
Underley Ave LA9 200 C7
Underley Hall Sch LA6 212 C5
Underley Hill LA9 200 B7
Underley Rd LA9 200 B7
UNDERWOOD 78 E7
Underwood LA9 200 B3
Underwood Rd LA12 203 D3

Und–Wes 237

Underwood Terr LA15 . . . 205 A4
Union Ct [2] CA8 . . . . 179 C5
Union La
Brampton CA8 . . . . 179 C5
Penrith CA11 . . . . 191 B5
Ulverston LA12 . . . . 203 C6
Union Pl [7] LA12 . . . . 203 D5
Union Rd DG16 . . . . 173 C3
Union St
Cleator Moor CA25 . . . . 188 E7
Dalton-in-F LA15 . . . . 205 C5
Kendal LA9. . . . . 200 C6
Newcastleton or Copshaw Holm TD9 . . . . 1 B6
Ulverston LA12 . . . . 203 D5
Wigton CA7 . . . . 180 C3
Union Terr CA11 . . . . 191 B5
University of Cumbria (Ambleside Campus) LA22. . . . . 195 D6
University of Cumbria (Kelsick site) LA22 . . . . . 195 E5
Univ of Cumbria
Carlisle CA1. . . . . 214 C2
Carlisle, Stanwix CA3 . . . . . 175 E1
UNTHANK
Melmerby. 58 B7
Skelton. 55 C3
UNTHANK END 55 D2
Unwin Pk DG16 . . . . 173 D3
Upfront Gallery* CA11. . . . . 55 D2
Uplin Cres LA11 . . . . 164 F7
Upper Brook St LA12. . . . . . 203 D5
UPPERBY 177 B2
Upperby Ct CA2 . . . . 177 C2
Upperby Prim Sch CA2. . . 177 B2
Upperby Rd CA2 . . . . 177 B2
Upperby Way CA2. . . . . 177 B3
UPPER DENTON. 23 E8
Upper Oak St LA23. . . . . . . 198 E5
Upphall La LA6 . . . . 167 C4
UPTON 53 B6
Upton Cotts CA7. . . . . 53 C6
Upton St [4] CA14 . . . . 184 E6
Urswick Gn LA13 . . . . 207 D3
Urswick Rd
Dalton-in-F LA15 . . . . 205 E5
Ulverston LA12 . . . . 203 C2

V

Vale Cl CA13. . . . . 190 B2
Vale Cotts CA13. . . . . 79 D8
Vale Side Gdns LA13 . . . . 207 C4
Vale View
Camerton CA14 . . . . 183 F3
Coniston LA21 . . . . 196 A3
Frizington CA26 . . . . 92 D8
Lowca CA28. . . . . 186 F8
St Bees CA27. . . . . 91 D2
Valley Dr
Barrow-in-F LA13 . . . . 207 B6
Carlisle CA1. . . . . 30 E5
Kendal LA9. . . . . 200 F2
Valley Pk CA28. . . . . 187 E7
Valley Prim Sch CA28 . . . . 187 E4
Valley View CA14. . . . . 63 C3
Valley View Rd CA28 . . . . 187 C4
Vallum Cl CA3 . . . . 175 F1
Vallum Pl CA5 . . . . 19 B1
Vancouver Dr DG12 . . . . 17 E8
Vancouver Pl DG12 . . . . 17 D8
Vancouver Rd DG12. . . . . . . 17 E8
Vasey Cres CA1 . . . . 177 C6
Vengeance St LA14 . . . . . . 206 C1
Verdun Ave LA14. . . . . 206 C1
Vernon St LA14 . . . . 206 F4
Vestaneum CA6. . . . . 20 F2
Viaduct CA14 . . . . 184 D6
Viaduct Estate Rd CA2, CA3 . . . . 214 A2
Vicarage Cl
Burton-in-K LA6. . . . . 167 C7
Grange-o-S LA11 . . . . 208 C4
Vicarage Dr
Brough CA17 . . . . 105 B4
Kendal LA9. . . . . 200 C3
Vicarage Hill
Frizington CA26. . . . . 92 D7
Keswick CA12 . . . . 192 A5
Vicarage La
Allithwaite LA11 . . . . 164 F7
Burton-in-K LA6. . . . . 167 C7
Cockermouth CA13 . . . . . . 190 E3
Ennerdale Bridge CA23 . . . . . 93 A6
Hawkshead LA22. . . . . 197 D5
Kirkby Lonsdale LA6 . . . . . 212 C2
Sedbergh LA10 . . . . 201 D5
Temple Sowerby CA10. . . . . . 72 E1
Vicarage Mount LA14 . . . 206 D2
Vicarage Park CE Prim Sch LA9. . . . . 200 C3
Vicarage Rd
Ambleside LA22. . . . . 195 C5
Levens LA8 . . . . 143 D1
Vicarage Terr
Nenthead CA9 . . . . 47 A2
Tebay CA10. . . . . 118 B3
Vicar La LA6. . . . . 168 C2
Vicars Fields LA9 . . . . 200 C3
Vicars Garth LA9. . . . . 200 C3
Vicars Hill LA9. . . . . 200 C3
Vicars Wlk LA9 . . . . 200 C3
VICKERSTOWN 206 C1
Vickerstown Sch LA14. . . 206 C3
Victoria Ave
Annan DG12. . . . . 172 C3
Victoria Ave *continued*
Barrow-in-F LA14 . . . . 207 A6
Victoria Cnr CA17. . . . . . . 199 D5
Victoria Cottage Hospl CA15 . . . . 182 D4
Victoria Ct [2] CA13 . . . . . 190 D4
Victoria Inf Sch
Barrow-in-F LA14 . . . . 207 A6
Workington CA14. . . . . 184 D4
Victoria Jun Sch
Barrow-in-F LA14 . . . . 207 A6
Workington CA14. . . . . 184 D5
Victoria Mews [4] LA14 . . 207 A5
Victoria Pk LA12. . . . . 203 D6
Victoria Pl
Carlisle CA1. . . . . 214 C3
Whitehaven CA28 . . . . 186 D2
Workington CA14. . . . . 184 E5
Victoria Rd
Annan DG12. . . . . 172 C3
Barrow-in-F LA14 . . . . 207 A6
Carlisle CA1. . . . . 177 E6
Cockermouth CA13 . . . . . . 190 D3
Penrith CA11 . . . . 191 D4
Ulverston LA12 . . . . 203 D4
Whitehaven CA28 . . . . 186 E3
Windermere LA23 . . . . 198 F4
Workington CA14. . . . . 184 D5
Victoria Rd N LA23. . . . . . . 198 F4
Victoria Sq
Alston CA9. . . . . 181 D3
Kirkby Stephen CA17. . . . . 199 D5
Victoria St
Askam in F LA16 . . . . 162 A7
Carnforth LA5 . . . . 213 C3
Cleator Moor CA25 . . . . 188 E7
Dalton-in-F LA15 . . . . 205 C5
Frizington CA26. . . . . 92 D7
Hawkshead LA22. . . . . 197 E5
Keswick CA12 . . . . 192 B4
Millom LA18. . . . . 202 C5
Windermere LA23 . . . . 198 E6
Victoria Terr
[14] Dalton-in-F LA15 . . . . . 205 C5
[2] Maryport CA15. . . . . 182 E5
Victoria Viaduct CA3 . . . . 214 B2
Victoria Villas CA28 . . . . . 187 F6
Victory Ave DG16 . . . . 173 C3
Victory Cres CA15. . . . . . . 182 E5
Villas The CA22 . . . . 189 E5
Vine Rd LA9 . . . . 200 E6
Violet Bank CA13 . . . . 190 E1
Viver La LA7, LA8. . . . . 156 A7
Vulcan Cl [29] LA16. . . . . . . 162 A8
Vulcan Rd LA14. . . . . 207 B2
Vulcan's La CA14 . . . . 184 E6

W

WABERTHWAITE 137 C8
Waberthwaite CE Sch LA19. . . . . 137 B8
Wadsworth Pk CA14 . . . . . . 77 F7
Wadsworth Rd CA2 . . . . . . 176 F4
Waingap La CA10 . . . . 118 F4
Wain Gate CA11 . . . . 57 A4
Waingatebridge Cotts LA18. . . . . 150 A2
WAITBY 120 D7
Waitholme La LA5 . . . . 167 A7
Wakefield Mdw LA8. . . . . . 144 A2
Wakefield Rd
Carlisle CA3. . . . . 175 D4
Cockermouth CA13 . . . . . . 190 C4
Wakefield St [33] LA16. . . . . 162 A8
WALBY 20 E3
Walby Garth CA10 . . . . 72 A8
Waldegrave Rd CA2. . . . . . . 176 E4
Walden Gr CA3 . . . . 175 D2
Walker Brow CA14 . . . . . . 185 A8
Walker Croft CA13 . . . . 190 C3
Walker Rd CA14 . . . . 184 C2
Walker Rise CA11. . . . . 191 C7
Walker St
[9] Askam in F LA16 . . . . . . 162 A8
Cockermouth CA13 . . . . . . 190 C3
Walk Mill CA5 . . . . 40 B8
Walkmill Cl [12] CA28 . . . . . . 76 F2
Walk Mill Community Woodland* CA28. . . . . 77 A1
Walkmill Cres CA1. . . . . . . 177 D6
Walkmill Cl CA28 . . . . 91 F8
Walkmill Gdns [4] CA20 . . . . 109 B2
Wallace Cres DG12. . . . . . . 172 C5
Wallace Gdns CA1 . . . . 177 D6
Wallace La
Kirkandrews-on-E CA5. . . . . . 19 B3
Maryport CA15 . . . . 182 C6
Wallace St [3] LA14 . . . . . . 206 F3
Walled Gdn The LA8 . . . . . 144 A1
WALL END 151 C6
Waller St CA1 . . . . 177 D6
Walling's La LA5. . . . . 210 B4
Walls Cotts CA18 . . . . 123 F3
Walls Cvn Pk CA18. . . . . . . 123 F3
Walls Dr CA18 . . . . 123 F3
Walls Rd CA14 . . . . 184 C1
Wall St [13] CA14. . . . . 184 D6
Walltown Quarry Trail* CA8 . . . . 24 D8
Walna Scar Rd LA20 . . . . . 126 C3
WALNEY ISLAND 206 B4
Walney Rd LA14 . . . . 206 E6
Walney Road Ind Est LA14. . . . . 206 E4
Walney Sch LA14 . . . . 206 B1
Walnut Hill LA13. . . . . 207 E4
Walter St TD9 . . . . 1 B6
Walthwaite Terr LA22 . . . 113 C4
WALTON 22 B7
Walton La LA13. . . . . 207 C3
WAMPOOL. 27 D5
Wampool Pl CA7. . . . . 180 B3
Wampool St CA7. . . . . 174 C4
Wandales La
High Casterton LA6 . . . . . . 212 F2
Natland LA9. . . . . 144 B4
Wandsworth Gdns CA10 . . . . 101 C5
Wansfell Ave CA2 . . . . 176 D4
Wansfell Bank LA22. . . . . . 195 D4
Wansfell Dr LA9 . . . . 200 E2
Wansfell Holme LA23 . . . . 195 E2
Wansfell Rd LA22 . . . . 195 D5
Wansfell Terr LA22. . . . . . 195 D4
Wansfell Tower Ct LA22. . . . . 195 D5
WARCOP. 104 C6
Warcop CE Prim Sch CA16 . . . . 104 C6
Warcop Sta* CA16. . . . . . . 104 D6
WARDHALL COMMON 50 C4
Wardhall Cotts CA7 . . . . 50 A5
Ward St
Longtown CA6 . . . . 10 C3
[4] Maryport CA15. . . . . 182 E5
Wardway The CA9. . . . . 181 C3
Warnell Dr CA1 . . . . 177 E3
Warren Hill CA8 . . . . 31 F6
Warren St LA14. . . . . 206 D3
Wart Barrow La LA11 . . . . 164 F8
Warth La LA6. . . . . 169 F2
WARTON. 213 C7
Warton Archbishop Hutton's Prim Sch LA5. . . . . 213 C7
Warton Crag Nature Reserve* LA5. . . . . 213 B8
Warton Old Rectory* LA5. . . . . 213 C7
Warton Rd LA5 . . . . 213 C4
Wartonwood View [1] LA5. . . . . 213 C3
WARWICK BRIDGE. 178 C7
Warwick Bridge Sch CA4 . . . . 178 C6
Warwick Dr LA8 . . . . 144 C1
Warwick Farm CA4 . . . . . . 178 A5
Warwick Mill Bsns Village CA4 . . . . 178 D6
WARWICK-ON-EDEN 178 A6
Warwick Pl
Penrith CA11. . . . . 191 C4
Workington CA14. . . . . 184 E6
Warwick Rd CA1. . . . . 177 D6
WARWICKSLAND 4 C3
Warwick Sq CA1. . . . . 214 C2
Warwick St
Barrow-in-F LA14 . . . . 207 A5
Carlisle CA3. . . . . 214 B3
Wasdale
Shap CA10. . . . . 101 C6
Wigton CA7 . . . . 180 B3
Wasdale Cl
Cockermouth CA13 . . . . . . 190 F4
Kendal LA9. . . . . 200 E3
Whitehaven CA28 . . . . 187 E4
Wasdale Gr LA13 . . . . 207 B3
WASDALE HEAD. 111 A7
Wasdale Pk CA20 . . . . 123 A7
Wasdale Rd
Gosforth CA20. . . . . 109 B2
Millom LA18. . . . . 202 D4
Washington Dr LA5 . . . . . 213 D8
Washington St CA14 . . . . . 184 E6
Waste La CA13. . . . . 190 E4
Wastwater Ave CA14 . . . . 184 D3
Wastwater Cl
Carlisle CA2. . . . . 176 D5
Cleator Moor CA25 . . . . 188 C8
Wastwater Rd CA28 . . . . . . 187 C5
Wastwater Rise CA20 . . . . 123 B8
WATCHGATE 131 C6
WATCHHILL
Annan 172 F3
Aspatria. 37 B1
Watchhill Pk [1] DG14 . . . . . . 3 D3
Watchhill Rd [2] DG14 . . . . . . 3 D3
WATENDLATH 96 D7
Water Bank CA7 . . . . 52 B2
Water Cl LA12 . . . . 153 C8
Watercrook Farm LA9. . . . 200 C1
WATEREND 78 F5
Waterfalls Rd CA10 . . . . 86 B7
WATERFOOT 84 E7
Waterfoot Cvn Pk CA11 . . . 84 E7
Waterfoot Rd DG12 . . . . . . 172 B2
Watergap La CA17 . . . . 199 D2
Water Garth LA14. . . . . 170 C6
Watergates Lonning CA7 . . . . 37 D7
WATERHEAD 195 D3
Waterhead Cotts LA22 . . . 195 D3
Waterhouse Mill* LA7 . . . 155 E2
Waterloo St CA13. . . . . 190 D4
Waterloo Terr CA26 . . . . 77 E1
Watermans Wlk CA1 . . . . . . 177 F3
WATERMILLOCK. 84 C5
Waters Edge
Milnthorpe LA7 . . . . 211 A3
Seaton CA14 . . . . 62 E4
Waters Edge Cvn Pk LA7. . . . . 156 C6
WATERSIDE. 37 E4
Waterside
[19] Askam in F LA16 . . . . . . 162 A8
Kendal LA9. . . . . 200 D4
Waterside Ho CA2 . . . . 176 F3
Waterside Pottery LA6 . . . 169 C2
WATERSLACK 210 E6
Waterslack Rd LA5. . . . . . . 210 E6
Waters Meet CA4 . . . . 178 D6
Water St
[4] Barrow-in-F LA14. . . . . . 207 A6
Carlisle CA2. . . . . 214 B1
Glasson CA7 . . . . 17 E3
Morland CA10 . . . . 86 F5
Wigton CA7 . . . . 180 D3
WATER YEAT 140 B4
Watery La
Crosthwaite LA8 . . . . 142 E5
Endmoor LA8. . . . . 156 F8
Millness LA6, LA7 . . . . 156 B4
Ulverston LA12 . . . . 203 E4
WATH
Newbiggin-on-Lune 119 C4
Silloth 25 E5
Wath La CA17. . . . . 119 C4
Watson St CA1 . . . . 177 C5
Watsons Terr CA7. . . . . 49 F7
Watson Terr CA11. . . . . 191 C5
Wattsfield Ave LA9. . . . . . . 200 D2
Wattsfield La LA9. . . . . 200 D2
Wattsfield Rd LA9. . . . . 200 D2
Wavell Dr CA1 . . . . 177 F6
WAVERBRIDGE. 37 E8
Waver Ct
Rampside LA13 . . . . 171 B5
Silloth CA7. . . . . 174 C4
Waver La CA7 . . . . 180 B3
Waverley Gdns CA3 . . . . . . 175 D2
Waverley Rd CA3 . . . . 175 D2
Waver Rd CA7 . . . . 16 F1
Waver St CA7. . . . . 174 C4
Waver Terr CA7 . . . . 26 C1
WAVERTON 37 E6
Wayside Terr CA11 . . . . 55 E6
Weardale Rd CA2 . . . . 176 E5
WEASDALE 119 D3
Weathercock La LA10. . . . . 146 A6
Weaver Gn LA14. . . . . 206 A4
Weavers Bank CA3. . . . . . . 214 A3
Weavers Ct LA9. . . . . 200 D4
Weavers Yd LA10 . . . . 201 C5
Webster Cres CA2 . . . . 177 A3
Websters Yd [1] LA9. . . . . . 200 C4
Webstray Cl LA14 . . . . 170 C6
Weddicar Gdns CA25. . . . . 188 C8
Wedgwood Rd CA15 . . . . . 183 C8
Weint La LA12. . . . . 163 A6
Weint Little Union St [9] LA12. . . . . 203 D5
Well Bank CA2. . . . . 176 E4
Well Bank Pl CA2 . . . . 176 E4
Well Beck Cl LA13 . . . . 207 C6
Wellgate CA4 . . . . 30 F5
WELLGILL. 46 F3
Wellhead [2] LA12. . . . . 203 D5
Wellhead Cotts CA7. . . . . . . 50 D6
Wellheads La LA8. . . . . 144 A1
Well Heads La LA7, LA8. . . 156 A8
Well House Rd CA16 . . . . . 193 F5
Well Ings LA9. . . . . 200 C3
WELLINGTON 109 B3
Wellington Ct LA6 . . . . 212 B2
Wellington Pl LA15 . . . . . . 205 B5
Wellington Row CA28 . . . . 186 D1
Wellington St
Annan DG12. . . . . 172 C4
Dalton-in-F LA15 . . . . 205 B5
Millom LA18. . . . . 202 D5
Well La
Barrow-in-F LA13 . . . . 207 D3
Carlisle CA3. . . . . 175 E1
Egremont CA22 . . . . 107 E7
High Casterton LA6 . . . . . . 212 F2
Hutton Roof LA6 . . . . 157 B2
Maryport CA15 . . . . 182 C6
Morland CA10. . . . . 87 A5
Ulverston LA12 . . . . 203 E4
Warton LA5 . . . . 213 D7
Yealand Redmayne LA5. . . . 166 F6
Well Lonning Cl CA8 . . . . . 179 B4
Wellmeadow [8] CA8 . . . . . 179 C5
Wells Cl CA14 . . . . 184 E3
Wells Cotts CA10 . . . . 71 F8
Wellside LA12 . . . . 163 A3
Wellside Wlk CA1. . . . . 30 E5
Well St [10] LA12. . . . . 203 D5
Welltree Brow CA10. . . . . . . 87 B4
Welsh Rd CA1 . . . . 177 E2
WELTON. 39 F3
Welton Sch CA5 . . . . 39 F2
WENNINGTON. 168 E1
Wennington Hall Sch LA2. . . . . 168 E1
Wensum Lea LA14 . . . . 206 B3
Went House Ct CA13 . . . . . . 63 E4
Went Mdws CA13 . . . . 63 D4
Went The CA15 . . . . 49 A2
Wentworth Dr CA3. . . . . . . 175 D3
Wentworth Pk CA14. . . . . . . 62 F3
Wesleyan Ct [22] LA12. . . . . 203 D5
Wesley Ct
Ambleside LA22. . . . . 195 D6
[7] Dalton-in-F LA15 . . . . . . 205 C5
Harrington CA14 . . . . 185 A7
Workington CA14. . . . . 184 C6
Wesley Pl LA14 . . . . 206 F3
Wesley St CA14 . . . . 184 C6
West Ave
Barrow-in-F LA13 . . . . 207 B5
West Ave *continued*
Wigton CA7 . . . . 180 D2
Westbourne Cres LA13 . . . 207 B5
Westbourne Rd LA5. . . . . . 213 B6
Westbrook Fields CA17 . . . . 199 C5
WEST CAUSEWAYHEAD. 174 D2
West Cl CA10 . . . . 101 C6
Westcliffe Gdns LA11 . . . . 208 C4
West Cres LA23 . . . . 198 D5
West Croft CA14 . . . . 183 B1
West Croft Terr CA28. . . . . 186 E8
West Ct CA7. . . . . 50 F8
West Cumberland Hospl CA28 . . . . 187 F5
WEST CURTHWAITE 39 C8
West End
Allonby CA15 . . . . 35 C1
Great Broughton CA13 . . . . . 63 E6
West End Cl
Flimby CA15. . . . . 183 C7
Oulton CA7. . . . . 180 B8
West End Croft CA5. . . . . . . 18 E1
West End La LA12. . . . . 203 F3
West End Rd CA10 . . . . 118 B7
WESTERN BANK. 180 B3
Western Bank Ind Est CA7 . . . . 180 A3
WESTFIELD 184 C3
Westfield Bridge Ct CA14 . . . . 184 D3
Westfield Dr
Egremont CA22 . . . . 189 D5
Workington CA14. . . . . 184 D2
Westfield Nature Trail* LA13. . . . . 171 B5
Westfield Prim Sch CA14 . . . . 184 D2
Westfield Terr [13] LA14 . . . 207 B2
Westfield View CA15 . . . . . 183 C8
Westgarth Ave CA17 . . . . . 199 C5
Westgarth Ct CA17. . . . . . . 199 C5
Westgarth Gate CA17 . . . . . 199 C5
Westgarth Gr CA17. . . . . . . 199 C5
Westgarth Rd CA17 . . . . . . 199 C5
Westgate LA9. . . . . 200 E6
Westgate La LA6. . . . . 169 E5
West Gate Rd LA14 . . . . . . 206 F5
West Ghyll Pl CA14 . . . . . . 185 B6
Westgill Rd DG16 . . . . 173 D5
Westgill Sq DG12 . . . . 172 E5
West Gn LA12. . . . . 162 F6
West Gr
Kendal LA9. . . . . 200 C6
Workington CA14. . . . . 184 E5
West Hall La LA6 . . . . 168 C7
Westhaven CA5. . . . . 28 F1
West Hill Ho [2] CA8 . . . . . 179 B4
Westhill Pl DG16. . . . . 173 C2
West Hills Dr LA12. . . . . . . 203 C1
WESTHOUSE. 169 E5
West Ing LA22 . . . . 195 D4
West La
Flimby CA15. . . . . 183 C7
Kirkbride CA7 . . . . 27 B7
Penrith CA11 . . . . 191 C4
Shap CA10. . . . . 101 C6
Westlakes Science Pk CA24 . . . . 91 F5
WESTLINTON 20 A7
Westminster Ave LA14 . . 170 C6
WESTMOOR END. 49 E6
Westmoor Rd CA3 . . . . 175 B4
Westmore Cl LA12 . . . . 171 E8
Westmorland Bsns Pk LA9. . . . . 131 A1
Westmorland Ct CA2. . . . . 214 A1
Westmorland General Hospl LA8. . . . . 144 B5
Westmorland Pl CA16 . . . 193 C6
Westmorland Rd
Appleby-in-W CA16 . . . . . . 193 D6
Hensingham CA28 . . . . 187 F5
Westmorland Rise CA16 . . . . 193 C7
Westmorland Sh Ctr The [6] LA9. . . . . 200 D5
Westmorland St
Barrow-in-F LA14 . . . . 206 F5
Carlisle CA2. . . . . 214 A1
West Mount LA14 . . . . 207 B
WESTNEWTON 36
Weston Ave LA12 20
Weston Hos LA8 1
Westover Ave LA5 . . . . . .
Westover Gr LA5. . . . . .
Westover Rd LA5 . . . .
West Pk CA5 . . . . . .
West Rd
Kirkland CA26 . . .
Wigton CA7 . . .
Westrigg Rd C
West Row
Barrow-in-F
Whitehav
West Sh
West S
WEST
We
W

West St continued
  Wigton CA7 . . . . 180 C3
WEST STONESDALE 122 E1
West Strand CA28 . . . . . 186 B1
West Terr CA7 . . . . 50 F8
West Tower St CA3 . . . . . 214 B3
Westvale Ct CA2 . . . . . . 176 F4
West View
  Allithwaite LA11 . . . . . . 164 F7
  Brampton CA8 . . . . 179 C3
  Carnforth LA5 . . . . 213 C5
  Cumwhinton CA4 . . . . . . 31 A3
  Hensingham CA28 . . . . . 187 F6
  Kirkby-in-F LA17 . . . . . 151 B5
  Whitehaven CA28 . . . . . 186 D2
West View Rd
  Barrow-in-F LA14 . . . . . 207 A5
  Distington CA14 . . . . . . 185 C3
West View Wlk CA14 . . . . 184 C3
Westville CA1 . . . . 177 E4
West Walls CA3 . . . . 214 A2
Westway LA13 . . . . 207 D3
Westwood CA2 . . . . 176 B3
Westwood Ave LA9 . . . . . 200 C3
WETHERAL 178 A2
Wetheral Pasture CA4 . . . 31 B4
WETHERAL PLAIN 178 B3
Wetheral Priory
Gatehouse*
  CA4 . . . . 178 B1
Wetheral St CA2 . . . . . . 176 E6
Wetheral Station CA4 . . . 178 B2
WETHERIGGS 191 D3
Wetheriggs La CA11 . . . . 191 D3
Wetheriggs Pottery*
  CA10 . . . . 71 E1
Wetheriggs Rise CA11 . . 191 C4
Wether Riggs Rd CA14 . . 184 C1
Wetheral St LA14 . . . . . 206 B2
WHALE 85 E4
Whalley Dr CA28 . . . . . . 187 E8
Wharton La CA17 . . . . . 120 E4
WHASSET 211 F3
Wheatclose Rd LA14 . . . 207 B7
Wheatlands CA2 . . . . . . 176 D5
Wheatsheaf Ct CA7 . . . . . 26 C1
Wheatsheaf Gdns CA4 . . 178 A1
Wheatsheaf La CA7 . . . . 180 C3
Wheelbarrow Ct CA14 . . . 30 E7
Whelpdale Ho 5 CA11 . 191 D4
WHELPO 53 A6
Whernside CA2 . . . . 176 A5
Whernside Gr LA5 . . . . . 213 E4
Whetstone La LA8 . . . . . 143 E4
WHICHAM 149 E5
Whicham Terr LA14 . . . . 149 E4
Whimbrel Dr CA1 . . . . . . 177 D6
Whinbarrow Cl CA7 . . . . . 36 C1
Whinbarrow La CA7 . . . . . 36 C1
Whinfell Ave CA13 . . . . . 190 E4
Whinfell Dr LA7 . . . . 200 F6
Whinfell Rd CA16 . . . . . . 87 D5
Whinfell Terr CA10 . . . . 118 B2
Whinfield Pl 10 LA16 . . . 162 A8
Whinfield Rd
  Ulverston LA12 . . . . . . 203 D6
  Windermere LA23 . . . . . 198 E4
Whinlatter Cl LA18 . . . . . 202 B4
Whinlatter Dr
  Barrow-in-F LA14 . . . . . 204 D1
  Kendal LA9 . . . . 200 F1
Whinlatter Forest Pk*
  CA12 . . . . 80 D8
Whinlatter Forest Wlk*
  CA12 . . . . 80 D7
Whinlatter Pass CA12,
  CA13 . . . . 80 C7
Whinlatter Rd CA28 . . . . 187 E5
Whinlatter Visitor Ctr*
  CA25 . . . . 80 C7
Whinlatter Visitor Ctr
  Forest Wlk* CA12 . . . . . 80 C7
Whinlatter Way CA2 . . . . 176 E5
Whinney Ends LA13 . . . . 207 C4
Whinney Fold LA5 . . . . . 210 B2
Whinnie House Pk
. . .use Rd 176 B5
. . . 176 F1
. . . E3

WHITECLOSEGATE 30 C8
Whiteclosegate
  Carlisle CA3 . . . . 30 C8
  Houghton CA3 . . . . 20 C1
Whitecroft CA20 . . . . . 109 B2
White Croft CA15 . . . . . 182 C4
White Croft Ct CA15 . . . 182 C3
White Cross Bay Holiday Pk
  LA23 . . . . 129 A7
Whitegate
  Egremont CA22 . . . . . . 189 D6
  Levens LA8 . . . . 143 D1
  Wetheral CA4 . . . . 178 A2
Whitegate Ct CA22 . . . . 189 D6
White Gill Cl LA12 . . . . . 163 C5
White Gill La LA12 . . . . . 163 B5
WHITEHALL 47 A3
White Hall Cvn Pk LA12,
  LA13 . . . . 171 D6
White Hart Yd 9 CA11 . 191 C5
WHITEHAVEN 187 E5
Whitehaven Castle
  CA28 . . . . 187 D8
Whitehaven Commercial
  Pk CA28 . . . . 76 F1
Whitehaven Rd CA25 . . . 188 C8
Whitehaven Sch CA28 . . . 91 F8
Whitehaven Sta CA28 . . 186 C2
Whitehead Cl LA14 . . . . 207 A4
Whitehead St LA14 . . . . 207 A4
White Ho CA16 . . . . 193 C5
Whitehouse CA8 . . . . 22 B7
White House Gdns 6
  CA11 . . . . 191 C5
White La LA7 . . . . 156 A6
White Moss Ct LA9 . . . . 200 B8
White Ox Way CA11 . . . 191 C7
White Pk CA28 . . . . 186 D1
White Row CA5 . . . . 18 F2
White School Cl CA28 . . 187 B6
Whiteside Ave CA13 . . . 190 E3
Whiteside Cotts LA12 . . 153 C7
White St LA14 . . . . 206 D3
White Star Way CA15 . . 182 C5
Whitestiles CA14 . . . . . 183 C3
White Stiles LA9 . . . . . 200 D7
Whites Yd CA15 . . . . . . 183 D7
Whitewater Ave CA2 . . . 176 B3
Whitfield Ct 8 CA14 . . 184 D6
WHITRIGG
  Bothel 51 C5
  Kirkbride 27 B8
WHITRIGGLEES 27 D8
Whitriggs Cl LA18 . . . . . 202 A3
Whittaker St 1 LA14 . . 206 F3
WHITTINGTON 168 D7
Whitton Terr LA9 . . . . . 200 D4
Whole House Rd CA20 . . 123 B8
Whooff Ho CA4 . . . . 30 F7
Whyber La CA16 . . . . 87 D4
WIGGONBY 28 C4
Wiggonby CE Sch CA7 . . 28 C4
WIGTON 180 D3
Wigton Hospl CA7 . . . . . 180 B5
Wigton Inf Sch CA7 . . . . 180 C2
Wigton Rd
  Allonby CA15 . . . . 35 C1
  Carlisle CA2 . . . . 176 C5
  Silloth CA7 . . . . 174 C4
Wigton Sta CA7 . . . . 180 C4
Wiiow Tree Cvn Pk
  LA11 . . . . 164 D6
Wildman St LA9 . . . . . . 200 D6
Wild Rose Cvn Pk
  CA16 . . . . 103 D7
Wilfred St CA1 . . . . 214 B2
Wilkie Rd LA14 . . . . 206 E5
William Cl LA15 . . . . . . 205 C6
William Fletcher Ct CA7 . 37 C1
William Howard Sch
  CA8 . . . . 179 B5
William Morris Ave
  CA25 . . . . 188 C6
William Pitt Ind Est
  CA28 . . . . 186 C3
Williamson La CA28 . . . 187 F6
Williamson's La CA28 . . 187 F6
William St
  6 Barrow-in-F LA14 . . 206 F3
  Carlisle CA1 . . . . 214 C3
  Carnforth LA5 . . . . 213 C5
  Cotehill CA4 . . . . 31 B1
  Great Clifton CA14 . . . . 63 A4
  Haverigg LA18 . . . . . . 150 A1
  4 Maryport CA15 . . . . 182 D6
  4 Penrith CA11 . . . . . 191 D5
  Ulverston LA12 . . . . . . 203 E5
  Wigton CA7 . . . . 180 D3
  Workington CA14 . . . . 184 D7
Willie Horne Way LA14 . 206 E4
Willow Bank CA2 . . . . . 176 E7
. . .low Ct CA11 . . . . 191 F4
. . .ow Ct
  . . .arrow La 153 C7
  . . .moor LA12 . . . . . . 203 A3
  . . .on CA4 . . . . 184 E3
. . .e Gdns
  . . . . 203 C7
  . . . . 200 F4
  . . . . 187 E2
  . . . . 176 E7

Willowholme Gdns
  CA2 . . . . 176 E7
Willow Holme Ind Est
  CA2 . . . . 176 E7
Willow Holme Rd CA2 . . 176 E7
Willow La
  Cockermouth CA13 . . . 190 E2
  Flookburgh LA11 . . . . . 164 E6
Willow Pk CA1 . . . . 177 D6
Willow Pl CA1 . . . . 30 E5
Willow Rd LA14 . . . . . . 206 F7
Willowside Pk LA18 . . . 202 A3
Willows The
  Durdar CA2 . . . . 30 B2
  Egremont CA22 . . . . . 189 B6
  Milnthorpe LA7 . . . . . . 211 D3
Willow Tree Cl LA12 . . . 203 E6
Wilson Ave LA18 . . . . . 150 A2
Wilson Homes
  Milton CA8 . . . . 22 B8
  Walton CA8 . . . . 22 B7
Wilson Memorial Homes
  CA8 . . . . 179 D5
Wilson Pit Rd CA28 . . . 187 C3
Wilson Pl LA8 . . . . 143 F2
Wilson St
  Carlisle CA2 . . . . 176 C7
  Carlisle CA2 . . . . 200 D3
  Workington CA14 . . . . 184 F6
Wilson's Terr CA15 . . . . 63 C8
WILTON 92 D2
Winchester Dr CA28 . . . 91 F8
Winchester St LA13 . . . 207 C3
Winderbowe Ave CA12 . 192 C3
WINDER 92 E8
Winder Farm Ct CA15 . . 49 B3
Winder Garth LA6 . . . . 167 B1
Winder Gate CA28 . . . . 92 E8
Winder La LA11 . . . . . . 164 C6
Winder Lonning LA13 . . 63 E6
WINDERMERE 198 F6
Windermere Ave
  Barrow-in-F LA14 . . . . 204 D1
  Maryport CA15 . . . . . . 182 D4
Windermere Bsns Ctr
  LA23 . . . . 198 E5
Windermere CE Jun Sch
  LA23 . . . . 198 E4
Windermere Cl LA15 . . 205 B3
Windermere Gdns
  LA18 . . . . 202 C4
Windermere Marina Village
  LA23 . . . . 129 A2
Windermere Pk LA23 . . 198 E3
Windermere Rd
  Burneside LA9 . . . . . . 130 E1
  Carlisle CA2 . . . . 176 D5
  Carnforth LA5 . . . . . . 213 D2
  Grange-o-S LA11 . . . . . 208 E7
  Kendal LA9 . . . . 200 B7
  Staveley LA8 . . . . 130 B5
  Whitehaven CA28 . . . . 187 C6
Windermere Sta LA23 . . 198 F6
Winderwath Gardens*
  CA10 . . . . 72 C4
Windmill Brow 5
  CA28 . . . . 186 D1
Windmill Cl CA13 . . . . 190 E3
Windmill La LA13 . . . . 190 E3
Windrigg Cl CA22 . . . . 189 E7
Windrush Cres LA14 . . 206 A4
Windsor Cres LA12 . . . 203 C2
Windsor Ct
  7 Penrith CA11 . . . . . 191 E4
  Workington CA14 . . . . 187 F7
Windsor Dr CA11 . . . . . 191 B4
Windsor Ho CA14 . . . . . 176 C7
Windsor Rd CA14 . . . . . 184 C2
Windsor St
  Barrow-in-F LA14 . . . . 207 A5
  Millom LA18 . . . . 202 D4
Windsor Terr CA28 . . . . 186 F1
Windsor Way CA3 . . . . . 175 D3
Windward Way LA23 . . 129 A2
Windy Hall Rd LA23 . . . 129 B2
Windy Hill LA7 . . . . 211 D4
Winfield Rd LA10 . . . . . 201 C5
Wingate Rd CA1 . . . . . . 177 F6
Wings Sch LA6 . . . . . . 156 A3
Winifred St CA14 . . . . . 184 E6
WINSCALES 62 F1
Winscales Ave CA14 . . 185 E5
Winscales Rd CA14 . . . . 63 A1
Winscale Way CA2 . . . . 176 D3
WINSKILL 57 E1
Winstanley Pl LA8 . . . . 130 E3
WINSTER 142 C8
Winston Dr CA28 . . . . . 187 F7
Winterhope Rd DG12 . . 172 E5
Winter La LA8 . . . . 130 E3
Winter's Pk CA11 . . . . 191 F4
WINTON 105 A1
Winton Cres CA1 . . . . . 177 E3
Winton Manor Ct CA1 . 105 A1
WITHERSLACK 154 E6
Witherslack Hall Sch
  LA11 . . . . 142 E1
Wiza Ave CA7 . . . . 180 B3
Woburn Ct 3 CA6 . . . . 175 B1
Wodow Rd CA22 . . . . . 189 D2
WOLSTY 25 B1
Wolsty Cl CA3 . . . . 175 E3

Wood Ave DG12 . . . . . . 172 C3
Woodbank
  Egremont CA22 . . . . . 189 E5
  Endmoor LA8 . . . . 156 D8
Wood Broughton LA11 . 153 F4
Wood Close Cvn Pk
  LA6 . . . . 212 D1
Wood Close Gdns LA5 . 209 B2
WOODEND 188 B2
Woodend Dr CA2 . . . . . 176 D4
Woodend Terr CA10 . . . 118 B3
Woodgate LA10 . . . . . . 200 E6
Woodhall Brow CA14 . . . 78 B8
WOODHALL PARK 190 D7
Woodhayes CA2 . . . . . . 30 B2
Woodhead Terr 4
  LA11 . . . . 208 C4
Woodhill Cres LA13 . . . 171 B5
WOODHOUSE
  Milnthorpe 156 A6
  Whitehaven 187 C5
Woodhouse La LA7 . . . . 211 D7
Woodhouse Rd CA28 . . 187 C5
WOODHOUSES 28 F3
Wood La
  Appleby-in-W CA16 . . . 88 C7
  St Bees CA27 . . . . 91 D3
WOODLAND 139 D4
Woodland Cl LA23 . . . . 198 E5
Woodland Pk LA14 . . . 207 A6
Woodland Rd
  Ulverston LA12 . . . . . 203 C4
  Windermere LA23 . . . . 198 E5
Woodlands
  Gosforth CA20 . . . . . . 109 A2
  Great Corby CA4 . . . . . 178 C2
  Penrith CA11 . . . . 191 D3
  Whitehaven CA28 . . . . 187 F8
Woodlands Cl
  Carlisle CA3 . . . . 175 E2
  Endmoor LA8 . . . . 156 D7
  Hackthorpe CA10 . . . . . 85 F6
  Lakeside LA12 . . . . . . 141 E2
  Storth LA7 . . . . 209 F4
Woodlands Dr
  Allithwaite LA11 . . . . . 164 F7
  Maryport CA15 . . . . . . 182 E5
  Silverdale LA5 . . . . . . 210 C4
Woodlands Grange
  CA13 . . . . 64 A8
Woodland Vale LA12 . . 141 E2
Woodland Way CA14 . . . 72 D4
Woodlands Gr CA25 . . . 188 A8
Woodleigh CA8 . . . . 22 B7
Woodman Ave DG12 . . 172 E3
Woodman La LA6 . . . . . 168 F6
Woodrouffe Terr LA14 . 214 C1
WOODROW 37 E4
Woodsghyll Dr CA1 . . . 177 D1
WOODSIDE 182 F1
Woodside
  Broughton Moor CA15 . . 63 C8
  Endmoor LA8 . . . . 156 D8
  Longtown CA6 . . . . 10 B1
  Workington CA14 . . . . 184 D4
Woodside Ave
  Cockermouth CA13 . . . 190 E3
  Sedbergh LA10 . . . . . . 201 B5
Woodside Cl
  Endmoor LA8 . . . . 156 D8
  Whitehaven CA28 . . . . 187 F8
Woodside Cotts LA12 . . 153 C8
Woodside Cres LA8 . . . 156 D7
Woodside Cvn Pk CA11 . 69 F6
Woodside N CA12 . . . . 177 C1
Woodside Rd
  Bowland Bridge LA11 . . 142 D4
  Endmoor LA8 . . . . 156 D8
  Gretna DG16 . . . . 173 C3
Wood St
  Carlisle CA1 . . . . 177 E6
  Carlisle, Newton CA2 . . 176 D6
  Maryport CA15 . . . . . . 182 D6
Woodstock La CA28 . . . 187 C8
Wood View LA6 . . . . . . 169 C3
Woodville Terr CA10 . . . 101 C5
Woodville Way CA14 . . 185 D8
Woodward Ave LA13 . . 207 C5
Woodwell La LA5 . . . . . 210 C1
Woollencroft CA14 . . . . 62 E3
Wootton Way CA2 . . . . 176 B4
Worcester St LA13 . . . . 207 C3
Wordsworth Cl CA28 . . 189 C6
Wordsworth Ct
  Bowness-on-W LA23 . . 198 C2
  14 Cockermouth CA13 . 190 C4
Wordsworth House Mus*
  CA13 . . . . 190 C4
Wordsworth Rd CA28 . . 187 E2
Wordsworth St
  Barrow-in-F LA14 . . . . 206 F4
  Hawkshead LA22 . . . . 192 C3
  Keswick CA12 . . . . . . 197 C4
  Penrith CA11 . . . . 191 D6
  Workington CA14 . . . . 184 D5
Wordsworth Terr
  1 Cockermouth CA13 . 190 D3
  Penrith CA11 . . . . 191 D6
Wordsworth View
  CA14 . . . . 184 C1
WORKINGTON 184 B6

Workington Bridge
  CA14 . . . . 184 F7
Workington Com Hospl
  CA14 . . . . 184 D6
Workington Hall*
  CA14 . . . . 184 F6
Workington Rd CA15 . . 183 A6
Workington Sixth Form Ctr
  CA14 . . . . 184 E2
Workington Sta CA14 . . 184 C6
World of Beatrix Potter
  Visitor Ctr* LA23 . . . . 198 C3
Worthington Pl CA1 . . . . 30 E5
Wrae Pl DG14 . . . . 9 B8
Wray Cres LA9 . . . . . . 200 F2
Wray Head CA19 . . . . . 123 D6
Wraysholme La LA11 . . 164 F6
WRAYTON 168 E3
WREAKS END 139 B1
WREAY
  Carlisle 41 B8
  Pooley Bridge 84 C6
Wreay CE Prim Sch CA4 . 41 B7
Wreay Gdns CA4 . . . . . . 41 B7
Wreay Mans CA10 . . . . . 84 C6
Wulstan Hall 12 LA14 . 184 E6
Wybrow Terr LA14 . . . . 184 E6
Wykeham Ho CA1 . . . . 214 C2
Wyndam Terr CA22 . . . 189 E7
Wyndham Row
  Broughton Moor CA15 . . 63 C8
  5 Cockermouth CA13 . 190 D4
Wyndham Sch CA22 . . . 189 D6
Wyndham St CA25 . . . . 188 E7
Wyndham Way CA22 . . 189 E6
Wyndsore Ave LA7 . . . . 211 D4
Wynd The 4 DG14 . . . . . 3 D3
Wynlass Pk LA23 . . . . . 198 D7
Wyre Gn LA14 . . . . 197 C4
WYTHBURN 97 C4
Wythburn Cl CA28 . . . . 91 F7
Wythburn Rd CA28 . . . . 91 F7
WYTHOP MILL 65 C4
Wyvern Cl CA2 . . . . . . 176 C5

Y

Yans La LA7 . . . . 209 F5
YANWATH 71 A2
Yanwath Prim Sch
  CA10 . . . . 71 A2
Yarl Mdw LA13 . . . . . . 207 D3
YARLSIDE 207 F4
Yarlside Cres LA13 . . . 207 E5
Yarlside Prim Sch
  LA13 . . . . 207 E5
Yarlside Rd LA13 . . . . . 207 E5
Yarl Well LA15 . . . . . . 205 D5
Yealand CE Prim Sch
  LA5 . . . . 166 F6
YEALAND CONYERS . . . 166 F5
Yealand Dr
  Barrow-in-F LA14 . . . . 207 B8
  Kendal LA9 . . . . 200 F3
  Ulverston LA12 . . . . . 203 D3
Yealand Gr LA5 . . . . . . 213 D4
Yealand Rd LA5 . . . . . . 166 F5
YEALAND REDMAYNE . . 166 E6
YEALAND STORRS 166 E7
Yearl Rise CA14 . . . . . . 62 E4
Yeathouse Rd CA26 . . . . 92 D8
Yeats Cl LA9 . . . . 200 C2
Yeorton Brow CA22 . . . 108 C6
Yew Tree La LA6 . . . . . 157 F5
Yetlands CA1 . . . . 29 C1
Yewbank La CA28 . . . . 187 F7
Yewbarrow Cl CA28 . . . 187 F4
Yewbarrow Est LA11 . . 208 D5
Yewbarrow Lodge
  LA11 . . . . 208 D5
Yewbarrow Rd LA12 . . 203 D2
Yewbarrow Terr LA11 . 208 E5
Yew Cl CA2 . . . . 176 C4
YEWDALE 196 C2
Yewdale Ave LA14 . . . 204 E1
Yewdale Rd
  Carlisle CA2 . . . . 176 A5
  Coniston LA21 . . . . . . 196 A4
Yewdale Sch CA2 . . . . 176 A5
Yew Tree La LA6 . . . . . 157 F5
Yew Tree Cl LA6 . . . . . 156 B2
Yew Tree Ct CA2 . . . . . 176 C5
Yew Tree Gdns
  Barrow-in-F LA13 . . . . 207 C5
  Silverdale LA5 . . . . . . 210 C2
Yew Tree Rd LA11 . . . . 208 C2
Yew Tree Wlk 1 LA5 . . 207 C5
York Ct CA2 . . . . 177 B3
York Gdns CA2 . . . . . . 177 B3
York Rd
  Whitehaven CA28 . . . . 187 B7
York Sq 9 LA12 . . . . . 203 E5
York St
  Barrow-in-F LA14 . . . . 207 A5
  Carlisle CA2 . . . . 176 E6
  Penrith CA11 . . . . 191 C5
York Terr CA28 . . . . . . 186 D2
YOTTENFEWS 108 D4